STUART M. BERGER, M.D.

TWO COMPLETE BOOKS

Forever Young

How To Be Your Own Nutritionist

STUART M. BERGER, M.D.

TWO COMPLETE BOOKS

Forever Young

How To Be Your Own Nutritionist

WINGS BOOKS

New York • Avenel, New Jersey

This omnibus was originally published in separate volumes under the titles:

Forever Young, copyright © 1989 by Stuart M. Berger, M.D.
Illustrations copyright © 1989 by Arlene Goldberg
How To Be Your Own Nutritionist, copyright © 1987
by Stuart M. Berger, M.D.

This 1993 edition is published by Wings Books,
distributed by Outlet Book Company, Inc., a Random House Company,
40 Engelhard Avenue, Avenel, New Jersey 07001,
by arrangement with William Morrow & Company, Inc.

Random House
New York • Toronto • London • Sydney • Auckland

Printed and bound in the United States of America

Library of Congress Cataloging-in-Publication Data
Berger, Stuart.
  [Forever young]
  Two complete books / Stuart M. Berger.
      p.   cm.
  Both works originally published: New York: Avon Books, 1989.
  Includes bibliographical references and index.
  Contents: Forever young—How to be your own nutritionist.
  ISBN 0-517-09279-4
  1. Nutrition.   2. Health.   3. Longevity.   I. Berger, Stuart. How to be your
own nutritionist.   1993.   II. Title.   III. Title: Forever young.   IV. Title: How
to be your own nutritionist.
RA784.B385   1993
613—dc20   93-814
                                                                                     CIP

8 7 6 5 4 3 2 1

Contents

FOREVER YOUNG

20 YEARS YOUNGER
IN 20 WEEKS

For Marlaine, my best friend,
whose support is always
invaluable.

Acknowledgments

I want to express my gratitude to Pat Golbitz, Howard Kaminsky, Larry Hughes, Allen Marchioni, Lori Ames, and Carolyn Reidy, who represent the best in publishing.

To Lorna Darmour, Arthur Klebanoff, David Nimmons, and Marilyn O'Reilly for their knowledge, expertise, and dedication in completing this project.

A special thanks to Sally Jessy Raphael and Karl Soderlund for coming to me with this exciting idea.

And most of all to my parents, Otto and Rachel, who taught me the healing nature of laughter, and who are always there with love and support.

Contents

1.

Looking Forward to Getting Younger

The sixteenth century was a dozen years old or so when a Spanish galleon appeared off the coast of the Florida peninsula. On its decks, the famed Spanish explorer Juan Ponce de León sensed that he was within days of completing his sacred mission. As the ship rolled gently beneath his feet, he scanned the horizon. On those shores, he had heard tell, existed a secret fount. Revered by the Indians in the region, its waters had mysterious properties conferring lasting vigor, beauty, and youth to all who drank them. His quest, he knew, was to claim that fountain for Spain's king, Ferdinand II, and to bring that elixir home for the royal families of Europe.

Four centuries later, in a laboratory outside Miami, a white-coated cell biologist straightens up from her computer terminal. On its green phosphor screen, she has been mapping the very secrets that the Spanish explorer had dreamed of. Her quest focuses, not on the flowing waters of a mythical fountain, but on much more intimate ones: the biochemical fluids locked within the human immune cell.

It is in these waters, she knows, that the real secrets of aging are to be found, etched in a complex code of DNA.

The book you hold in your hands is the culmination of a journey begun long ago, well before Ponce de León. It represents a dream that has tempted the human species ever since we lived in caves— the dream of a life without aging, without senescence or decay, where we stay forever young (well, *almost* forever—but then again, who wants to live to be 647 years old, anyway?).

Throughout human history, prolonging youth has been the province of magic and myth. Today, in the final decade of the twentieth century, it has become one of science and certainty. For the first time ever, we have the opportunity to realize that dream.

> Aging, as we have always known it, may no longer be inevitable or irrevocable. Breakthroughs all across the frontier of biomedical science make it increasingly feasible to hope that we may hold back the ravages of senescence—even to abolish many of the degenerative symptoms of the hitherto-universal disease called old age. For nearly every symptom of aging . . . there are remedies and preventive measures being actively investigated.
>
> —Albert Rosenfeld, in *Prolongevity*

Today, thanks to research developments in the last decade, the deepest secrets of biological aging lie within our grasp. Again and again in these pages, you will find yourself confronting one central truth: *We now know enough to alter significantly the course of how—and how fast—we age.* Ours is the first generation that has a very real, very practical chance of staying younger, longer, than ever before. That is a chance you must be willing to take, or you would not have purchased this book.

A decade ago this book could not have been written, for many of the specific steps we will cover were then unknown. I can sit down to write it today because now we hold hard medical science in hand, promising and fascinating nuggets buried in papers from research labs the world over. Some of these steps may seem familiar, others will be completely new to you. But by combining them all together in one cohesive program, you will realize all of the advantages that medical science can provide. You will have a simple, stepwise program to put these principles to work in your own life—starting this minute.

How realistic is that? Well, according to one eminent specialist on the aging process, writing in the *Proceedings of the National Academy of Sciences,*

> It is not unreasonable to expect on the basis of present data that the healthy life span can be increased by 5–10 or more years. . . .

That is our task in the pages that follow. You and I will bring those discoveries out of cloistered biochemistry laboratories and into your life—so you can begin to benefit from what scientists have pieced together. We will see what is surely the most exciting series of breakthroughs of the age, discoveries that go beyond simply unraveling any one disease or condition. Rather, these scientific advances address the whole spectrum of changes that occur—in our brains and biochemistry, in our cells and synapses—as our bodies age. Correctly and judiciously applied, the specific techniques in these pages are a prescription for remaining vital, healthy, and active until the very end of a long, productive life.

Welcome—to the Longevity Revolution

The prescription you are about to write for yourself draws from a diverse range of topics and disciplines: medicine, nutrition, immunology, cancer prevention, even exercise physiology. For what has happened in the last few years—and the main reason I could write this book—is that a number of scientific disciplines have converged. As that has happened, we have undergone what many call the "Longevity Revolution."

For many years, researchers in these fields had labored in relative isolation. Like so many blind men describing the same elephant, each beheld a small piece: aging as it happened in the cardiovascular system and the immune system, bone and skeletal changes, the chronological development of the brain.

But then, as laboratory scientists and clinical practitioners began to share information across disciplines, they started to find common ground, realizing that in many respects they were working on different pieces of the same vast puzzle. Their work started to coalesce; findings piled upon findings, reinforcing, substantiating, proving and disproving. Piece by painstaking piece, enough information has been assembled from medical science to make possible a book like this, dedicated to putting all of these findings in one place, with one common goal: keeping you younger.

Hardly a month goes by that I do not read of yet another research report, another vital piece of the puzzle about how we can slow—even, in some cases, reverse—the cellular processes of decay. The concrete signs of the pace of research in this area abound:

- The budget of the National Institute on Aging will reach an impressive $194 million this fiscal year, funding some 697 separate research projects.
- America now boasts some dozen scientific institutions devoted solely to anti-aging research and study.
- If you go to the nearest medical research library, you will find more than thirty-four journals devoted to findings on various aspects of aging—and aging prevention.

When I sat down to write this book, my first step was to key into a medical research computer bank the broad topic of "aging research." The answer it gave me testifies to the meteoric growth in this field—it selected more than 45,000 scientific papers for me to review!

All of this points in one very hopeful direction. We are now able to lengthen our lives, prolong our healthy and vital years, and reduce the procession of chronic, debilitating illnesses that have come to define old age. We have inched forward in our understanding of just what aging is, how it works, and—most important of all—what you can do about it.

"Youth Preservation": A Science Is Born

It is at this fertile crossroad that the science of "Youth Preservation" has come into being. Or at least, that's the term I use for it. Unfortunately, you will not yet find those exact words listed in the curricula at medical schools or in official proceedings. It remains a hybrid field, a mosaic of cell biology, genetics, biochemistry, oncology, geriatrics, and several other disciplines. But although we don't yet have an agreed-upon name for this science, it is clear that each of these disciplines is a part of the larger picture, and that this larger picture points the way to a younger, more vital you.

A certain part of this revolution is as simple as the fact that we have grown much more skilled at preventing a whole family of specific diseases of old age. It is a biological fact that just a handful of diseases—cancer, coronary artery disease, stroke, diabetes, kidney failure, obstructive lung disease, pneumonia, and the flu account for 85 percent of the debilitating illnesses of old age. Heart disease all by itself accounts for fully one out of every two deaths of older Americans, and high blood pressure directly causes or contributes to 15 percent of all deaths.

Yet amazingly, we can already control many of these diseases. Listen to the expert testimony of former Secretary of Health, Education and Welfare Joseph A. Califano, Jr., before the United States Senate:

"67% of all disease and premature death is preventable."

- Dr. Peter Greenwald, director of Cancer Prevention and Control at the National Cancer Institute, says that 80 percent of cancer cases are linked to how we live our lives—so can be controlled.
- Margaret Heckler, former Secretary of Health and Human Services, says, "Changes in lifestyle and behavior could save 95,000 lives per year by the year 2000."

What these experts are telling us is clear: If you did nothing else but focus on these high-risk diseases—by knowing how to eat, exercise, and live your life so you can lower your risk for them—you would automatically improve your odds for a reprieve from the most common, and obvious, causes of debility, premature aging, and death.

Research shows again and again that many of the problems we have come to expect as part of "just getting old" have more to do with *how* we live than how *long*.

- Coronary artery disease accounts for half of all deaths in those over sixty-five. But there is clear research showing that athero-sclerosis—the artery clogging that is the main culprit in prema-ture heart disease—is not a necessary part of aging. In most mammals, and even in some human societies, it doesn't happen. In Chapter 6 I give you six "young-at-heart" guidelines to make sure it won't happen to you either.
- High blood pressure, as any doctor in this country will tell you, rises with age—a rise of about 15 percent is considered "average." But among the inhabitants of Easter Island, these changes in blood pressure don't happen. Clearly, if they can avoid this dam-aging rise, we can too.
- Bone weakening (osteoporosis) causes 1.2 million hip fractures every year among older women, and some 40,000 deaths. Yet in China and Japan, such fractures are extremely rare—because of factors like diet and exercise. We will review the four crucial bone builder tips in Chapter 8.

In these cases, as in many others, the more we look, the more we see that many of the diseases we associate with age are highly avoid-able. As we add more diseases, one by one, to the list of those we can most likely avoid, we tip the balance in our favor to live longer, more active lives.

Family Health History Quiz

To understand what these specific discoveries may mean for you, take a moment to do the following exercise. It is most applicable if you are in your midthirties or above.

If you have lost parents, grandparents, or other older relatives, consider a few simple questions:

What did your father die from?_____

What did your mother die from?_____

What did your grandfather die from?_____

What did your grandmother die from?_____

What have other older relatives died from?_____

Without doubt, your list included such conditions as cancer, heart disease, pneumonia, and infections. Now imagine how your own medical future is changed by striking out those candidates from the list—because you have built them out of your life! By reducing your chances that those conditions will happen to you, you have already joined the Longevity Revolution!

Outwitting Mr. Gompertz

How old are you? Older than thirty-five? If so, Benjamin Gompertz has some disturbing news for you. Gompertz was a British scientist, population expert, and statistician who lived and wrote in the early years of the nineteenth century. In a famous formulation, which has come to be known as Gompertz Constant, he estimated that the probability of dying increases exponentially every year after age thirty-five. Scientists have relied on the Gompertz Constant for years as they attempt to push back the limits of aging and death.

Just three years ago, Nobel Prize-winning biochemist Linus Pauling reexamined Gompertz's calculations and found that for most of us, the chance of death increases by almost 9 percent *each* year after age thirty-five.

Since your statistical chance of dying doubles every eight years and ten weeks, if you celebrated your thirty-fifth birthday today, that means the odds of your dying double by your forty-third birthday, and quadruple by your fifty-second birthday!

But there is a silver lining to this gloomy Gompertzian cloud.

These numbers, remember, are based on an actuarial average. By the very act of picking up this book, and of launching yourself into a Youth Preservation Program, you are leapfrogging ahead of the population on whom such predictions are based. The many specific steps throughout this book help you take strong, positive action to outwit Mr. Gompertz's dismal numbers—and stay forever young.

The Longevity Revolution comes not a moment too soon. More people can benefit from such research than ever before—for the very simple reason that never before has our country had so many people getting older. Look around you. Statistics reflect that fact from every corner:

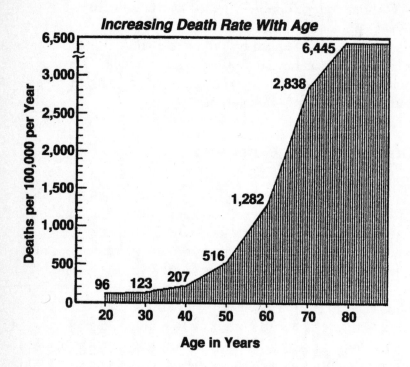

Life Span According to State

Statistically, your chances for a long and healthy life vary significantly depending on where you live. Just for your information, you may find it interesting to find the average life span in your state:

State	Age		State	Age
1. HAWAII	77.02		27. INDIANA	73.84
2. MINNESOTA	76.15		28. MISSOURI	73.84
3. IOWA	75.81		29. ARKANSAS	73.72
4. UTAH	75.76		30. NEW YORK	73.70
5. NORTH DAKOTA	75.71		31. MICHIGAN	73.67
6. NEBRASKA	75.49		32. OKLAHOMA	73.67
7. WISCONSIN	75.35		33. TEXAS	73.64
8. KANSAS	75.31		34. PENNSYLVANIA	73.58
9. COLORADO	75.30		35. OHIO	73.49
10. IDAHO	75.19		36. VIRGINIA	73.43
11. WASHINGTON	75.13		37. ILLINOIS	73.37
12. CONNECTICUT	75.12		38. MARYLAND	73.32
13. MASSACHUSETTS	75.01		39. TENNESSEE	73.30
14. OREGON	74.99		40. DELAWARE	73.21
15. NEW HAMPSHIRE	74.98		41. KENTUCKY	73.06
16. SOUTH DAKOTA	74.97		42. NORTH CAROLINA	72.96
17. VERMONT	74.79		43. WEST VIRGINIA	72.84
18. RHODE ISLAND	74.78		44. NEVADA	72.64
19. MAINE	74.59		45. ALABAMA	72.53
20. CALIFORNIA	74.57		46. ALASKA	72.24
21. ARIZONA	74.30		47. GEORGIA	72.22
22. NEW MEXICO	74.01		48. MISSISSIPPI	71.98
23. FLORIDA	74.00		49. SOUTH CAROLINA	71.85
24. NEW JERSEY	74.00		50. LOUISIANA	71.74
25. MONTANA	73.93		51. DISTRICT OF	69.20
26. WYOMING	73.85		COLUMBIA	

SOURCE: National Center for Health Statistics

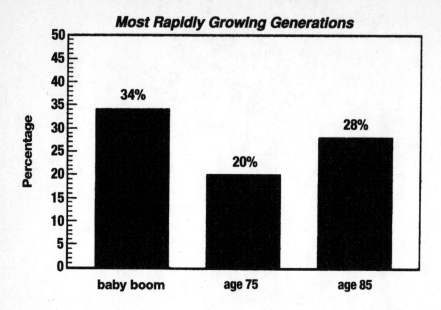

Most Rapidly Growing Generations

• This April, the U. S. Census Bureau reported that the nation's median age is at its highest point since they began tracking it 160 years ago. Today, one American in eight is over sixty-five—some thirty-two million people. That number is greater than the entire population of Australia, Belgium, and Israel combined! By the year 2030, the number will have doubled, to sixty-five million, or one American in five.

• The fastest-growing population segment is the baby boom generation, now aged thirty-five to forty-four. Next come seniors, seventy-five and older.

Still not convinced? Then just look at the shape of things to come, according to the National Institute on Aging.

Such clear pictures are worth thousands of erudite words. The trend to an entire society living longer is unprecedented in our history—or, for that matter, in the history of the human race.

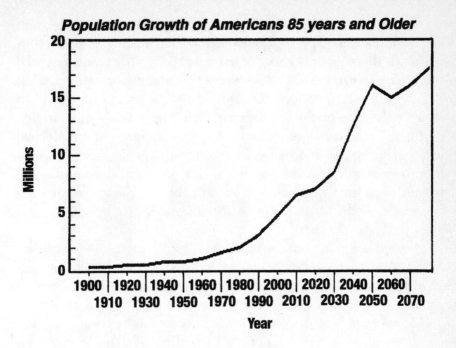

Population Growth of Americans 85 years and Older

Not Just How Long, How Well

"A major objective now and in the future should be maximizing health and well-being . . . so as to make life worth living for as long as possible. This will require a more careful application of "preventive medicine."

> —Dr. Denham Harman,
> biochemical
> gerontologist

"Adding life to years, not just years to life, is the goal of aging research."

> —Dr. Edward Schneider,
> Dean, Gerontology
> Center,
> University of Southern
> California

Of course, there's more to longevity than just the sheer number of years you can manage to squeeze out. What counts as much—or more—is their quality. Those of us under sixty—the group in which you count yourself, I suspect—face a fundamental question: What quality of life can we look forward to? Do we intend to spend our later years in a twilight existence of failing health and vitality, paying the medical price for having ignored fundamental biological verities during our first half century, or will we take steps to trans- form ourselves into a culture of the healthiest, most youthful sep- tuagenarians the world has ever known, able to take for granted the verve and vitality that is now associated with people ten, twenty, even thirty years younger?

I hear these questions being asked—and answered—every day. Many of my acquaintances, members of the baby boom, are just starting to feel the encroaching nibbles of age. Every day as I talk to patients and friends, as I lecture around the country and work with colleagues from New York to Hawaii, I become more convinced that the issue of what can be done to lengthen life and improve its quality is of unparalleled importance to the overwhelming majority of Americans.

What all of those people share—and this is true whether you are thirty-six or sixty-three—is a fervent desire to slow the rate at which their bodies are aging. Not just to live longer, but to live better. They seek a way to avoid the chronic diseases, encroaching fatigue, and degrading changes that seem to characterize old age. As a nation, we are looking to find what we can do to make our lives better, extend our most healthy, vibrant, active years, and shorten the time of weakness and failing health. We are a people ripe and ready to join the Longevity Revolution.

The goal is to put you on the dotted curve above—to compress the time you spend ailing and frail, and extend the time you spend in full, robust, and energetic health.

For each of us, the realization of aging surfaces in different ways. Are you:

- Between twenty-five and thirty-five, just beginning to feel the first subtle twinges of growing older? You notice you sleep later on weekends than you once did. Maybe you can't stay out as late

Two Views of Aging

without feeling some ill effects. You may have watched your weight rise slightly, pounds getting easier to put on and harder to lose, as your metabolism changed. Perhaps sometime in the last year you suffered a minor sprain or injury in some athletic pursuit —an injury that you would have shrugged off five years ago.

- Between thirty-five and forty-five, having seen a friend, parent, or family member struck down with some serious disease? That experience may have made you start reading the health pages with a little extra care. Perhaps your doctor has found a condition like heart disease, diabetes, or obesity that "bears watching." Or maybe you are a parent, enjoying the new life you have brought into the world, but being reminded that you have a finite amount of time left in your own life.

- Between fifty-five and sixty-five? You may feel in good shape, but have started to take a certain amount of impairment for granted? You tire more easily, and have grown used to living with the arthritis, or gout, or heart condition your doctor diagnosed. You cannot help but hope that you will avoid the seriously deteriorating health that seems to have overtaken many of your contemporaries. You want to make sure you spend your next years enjoying what you have worked for instead of fighting discomfort, decay, and disease.

If you see yourself described here, or if you have simply wondered if there isn't something you ought to be doing to increase your health and longevity, I think you will find much to interest you in the pages that follow.

Among the important breakthroughs you will discover in these chapters:

- Your own health and life-style test to help you design an anti-aging program that is just right for you (Chapter 4)
- How you can best use the newest anti-aging skin-care treatments (Chapter 5)
- The nutritional keys you can use *now* to decrease the aging of your skin (Chapter 5)
- The just-discovered nutrient that promises a bone-rejuvenation breakthrough (Chapter 8)
- A specific nutritional plan to take you off the danger list for cardiac problems (Chapter 6)
- The effect that one simple change may have on reversing skeletal aging (Chapter 8)
- The "Antiviral Cocktail," first developed for AIDS, that can help increase your immune strength (Chapter 9)
- The safe vitamin treatment your doctor can give you to help restore your immune system to its youthful vigor (Chapter 9)
- The simple principles you can use to keep your brain younger, longer (Chapter 10)
- The dietary key to reducing the cellular changes leading to old age, and an eating plan to help you use it (Chapter 11)
- The new findings about the difference between exercise and activity—and how they affect your longevity (Chapter 11)
- The one single change some of you can make that is *100 percent guaranteed* to extend your healthy lives (Chapter 7)
- A step-by-step plan to reprogram the internal computer that may be aging you prematurely (Chapter 13)

My 20-20 Pledge to You

In health there are no absolute guarantees. But by following the twenty-plus specific health counsels in these pages, I can assure you that:

1. You will be following the best, most scientifically sound attempt you can make at present to stay younger, longer.
2. You will find them practical, real, do-able with inexpensive tools you have at your disposal.
3. By following these steps for twenty weeks, you will already feel and see a significant change in your appearance, health, and vitality.
4. The steps in these chapters will definitely help you feel better, with more energy and less likelihood of chronic disease.
5. By *not* heeding these principles, you will certainly shorten your healthy, productive life span.

I hope you take the 20-20 pledge: *That by following the twenty-plus guidelines throughout this book, you feel better in twenty weeks—and could add up to twenty years of productive, healthy, vigorous life.*

In return, I have to ask for one promise: that you will do your best to start thinking differently. Like Ponce de León, you need to become something of an explorer. But unlike his fantastic quest, yours has a sure chance of success, for it is based on science, not on speculation.

Being an explorer means you will have to get used to a whole new way of thinking. Perhaps the most significant changes of aging happen, not in your arteries, muscles, and bones, but in that marvelous organ nestled between your ears. When it comes to Youth Preservation, it is clear that the biggest differences lie in the choices we make many times each day: decisions about what we will eat, how we move, how we treat ourselves, even what inner tapes we play as we drift to sleep at night. Being around enjoying life in thirty, forty, or fifty years means having a strong inner commitment to longevity, starting right now.

You may find that hard at first because we are all so conditioned to see our lives in terms of the allotted threescore years and ten. Society has accustomed us to expect to live that length of time and no more, and I believe that at a very profound level we actually "program" ourselves to make it come true. I'll get to the specifics in Chapter 13, but the main point to keep in mind as you read this book is that you may be called upon to make a radical shift in that "programming," in how you see your life now, where you are headed, and what your future will look like.

If you've thought of retirement, of dropping out and taking it easy, of "coasting out" your last golden decade and a half, you may find yourself wanting to reconsider. I hope you will come to see retirement as just one of your options, along with other scenarios that have you working productively and energetically, physically and mentally active for more years than you had ever dared hope.

That's the kind of thinking I hope you'll do a lot of throughout this book. Because if you conscientiously apply the principles in it, you'd better have a good plan for how you want to spend all that extra time you'll be building into your life!

More on this subject later, but for now I just ask you to keep your heart and mind open to changing the way you see yourself and your life path, and to consider that a work in progress as you read the pages ahead.

So if I have that promise from you, and you have these pledges from me, let us not waste another minute that you could be using to grow younger. Come along, and together we'll take up where Ponce de León left off and finish that noble quest begun so many centuries ago. I hope you *are* looking forward—to growing younger!

2.

Fables, Fountains,
and Facts

All the days of Methuselah were nine hundred sixty
and nine years: and he died.
                                        —Genesis 5:27

Do not try to live forever; you will not succeed.
                                        —George Bernard Shaw

George Bernard Shaw was right. Obviously, I can't promise
you that after you read this book, you can look forward to an added
nine centuries of life. (Even back in Methuselah's time, when miracles like burning bushes and parting seas were everyday occurrences,
living to his ripe age of 969 was considered pretty out of the ordinary.) More common, according to the very next chapter of Genesis,
was that Man's "days shall be an hundred and twenty years"—the
very age, by coincidence, that Moses died.

It turns out that those biblical "biologists" were pretty accurate—
even today, the biological maximum life of *Homo sapiens* is generally
agreed by most aging experts to be in the range of 115 to 120 years.
That may seem strange, at first. After all, how many people do you
know who live to be 115? Well, the factor to keep in mind is that
such a figure represents, not the average, but the likely utmost top
limit. That number has not changed appreciably since ancient
Rome, when Pliny the Elder wrote that centenarians were, if not
common, not unknown either. He even described a popular actress

who was then one hundred years old. Today, the oldest documented living person is 114 years old; the oldest person ever authenticated lived to the age of 120. And while biomedical science may succeed in pushing back that limit, extending the hypothetical upper limit is not the main focus of this book.

I hold a much more practical—and, I believe, more easily achieved—goal. Obviously, most of us don't live anywhere near our 115-year limit. What the biblical scholars estimated as threescore and ten has been refined by latter-day biostatisticians as 74.7 years —the average life expectancy today in America. But the real question is: What happens in that gap between 74.7 years and 115?

Closing the gap is what this book is all about. Together, we can give you the edge so that you can more fully achieve your inbred biological maximum. It is the same goal that Wilder Penfield, the famed American neurosurgeon, envisioned when he wrote that he foresaw a day when "more men and women reach life's true goal, fulfilling the cycle set for us, bypassing the plagues, disease and famine."

We want to take his advice, to *take maximum biological advantage* of the preset limit built into our body's aging time clock—and to do it in such a way that what time we do have will be the healthiest, happiest possible. We first need to know what aging really is—and that, in turn, means debunking a few fables about what it most certainly is not.

First, the Fables . . .

Through the centuries, mankind's preoccupation with the subject of aging has been matched only by its collective imagination in devising ways to deal with it. The history of Youth Preservation spans several millennia of wild expectations, dashed hopes, and failed promises.

Five thousand years ago, in the oldest tale of Western civilization, the Babylonians told of the king Gilgamesh, who wanted to live forever. To do so, he was told by a sage, he must eat a certain plant growing under water, whose powers "restore lost youth to a man. . . . By its virtue a man may win back all his former strength. Its name shall be 'The-Old-Men-Are-Young-Again.'" Gilgamesh vowed to eat it and "return to what I was in my youth."

While that may have been the first time this idea arose, it was certainly not the last. For thousands of years, across many of the world's great cultures, the quest continued. The Chinese, the ancient Hebrews, Greeks, and Romans, medieval monks and twentieth-century Swiss doctors, each offered their own unique contributions to the pursuit of elusive immortality. Several thousand years ago, Chinese apothecaries whipped up an anti-aging cocktail called "tan," compounded from gold and the mercury-containing ore cinnabar (given the proven toxic effects of both metals, it is likely this "youth-preserving" formula hastened the deaths of those who swallowed it).

The Taoist religion held as a central goal the prolonging of life through nutrition, meditation, sports, and even sex. In biblical times many Middle Eastern societies believed that living to a ripe old age was God's reward for right-living and faith. For them, the key to remaining youthful—or at least alive—was not an elixir, but one's behavior. Those fortunate few who lived long enough to show the effects of age—no scant feat in an era when most people died by age forty—were considered models of appropriate living, deserving honor and reverence by virtue of their longevity. The Arabs spoke of a Well of Life that, like Ponce de León's fountain two millennia later, would confer glorious youth on those who enjoyed its waters.

In Europe during the Middle Ages, the practice of alchemy held as a goal, not to turn lead into gold—as is popularly believed—but to create nostrums that would forestall aging. The topic continued to fascinate Europeans for several hundred years. One scholarly work, written in the sixteenth century, explained that aging was the result of the loss of "vital particles" that we exhale with each breath. The way to stay young, it suggested, had been discovered by the occupant of an ancient Egyptian tomb who had lived an impressive 115 years. According to the inscription on the burial vault, he owed his longevity to "the Breath of Young Women." A colorful prescription, to be sure (and one that more than a few of my male patients would gladly accept!), but hardly accurate.

In our own century, the quest has taken a more scientific turn. In the 1920s, it was believed that the secret to prolonging vigor in men at least was to transplant into them the testicles of virile apes. Needless to say, this fanciful treatment did not yield any positive results (but I can't help wondering if the elderly male patients showed any increased craving for bananas!).

During the next decade, longevity again captured the popular imagination, in the form of the immensely popular book *Lost Horizon*. The tale told of Shangri-La, a city high up in the mountains, where the secret to infinite youth was to be found.

Not long thereafter, this time in the mountains of Central Europe, a researcher named Ana Aslan discovered what she thought was the cure to aging. In the early 1950s, this Rumanian biochemist created a drug called Gerovital-H3, which she claimed would reduce the changes of aging. It set off a flurry of research, and scores of eager patients flocked from the world over to her clinic at the Geriatric Institute in Bucharest. Today, some thirty-five years later, research has shown that the initial hopes for the drug were over-optimistic, and that the drug does not have any significant anti-aging effects.

Not far away, in Switzerland, you can still check into one of the most renowned (and expensive) clinics and be injected in the rump with a puree made from the cells of lamb fetuses. These cells are claimed to inspire your old decrepit cells to be younger—a dramatic notion, to be sure, but there is no evidence in any credible scientific journal to suggest it works.

In recent years the anti-aging doctors have trotted out an alphabet soup of different chemical compounds—BHT, SOD, L-DOPA, NDGA, to name a few—to chemically forestall the cellular damage of aging and so keep us younger. While several of these compounds initially appeared to show promise, none has given us the magic key to aging that their inventors hoped.

And Now, the Facts

After many long centuries of fanciful theorizing, it is only in the last few years that we have advanced to the point of pinning down the true causes and mechanisms of aging—and with them, the clues to staying young.

The rest of this chapter is dedicated to bringing you up to date on some of the most current thinking. I hope you'll read it because it will help you understand the rationale for the steps we will undertake together in later chapters—the self-help core of this book.

However, I understand that you may be a doer, not a student, and may be impatient to get started on your twenty-week plan for improving your health and extending your life. You may be less interested in the theory than in beginning your own specific anti-aging steps *now*. If that is you, you are welcome to skip the rest of this chapter and go directly to the next chapter, which begins the interactive self-assessment for your own Youth Preservation Program. But if you do that, promise me one more thing—you will come back and read this chapter later . . . please?

A key event happened in 1964 when a premier microbiologist named Leonard Hayflick made a basic but crucial discovery. The human cells he was looking at would divide only about fifty times, then die—and little could be done to change that pattern. Hayflick's discovery took us a major step forward because it focused the debate on aging away from the larger organ systems to the innermost workings of the body's trillions of cells. It became a cornerstone in the whole new scientific discipline of biogerontology, the biological study of aging.

Today it is a scientific truism that we will not understand aging until we understand the astoundingly complex mechanics that happen within our cells. However, if everybody agrees that the cell is the "scene of the crime," there is less accord about exactly what happens inside it when we grow older.

There is no shortage of theories. Look at a recent list compiled by the National Institute on Aging:

Wear-and-tear theory
Rate-of-living theory
Metabolic theory
Endocrine theory
Free-radical theory
Collagen theory
Somatic mutation theory
Programmed senescence theory

Error catastrophe theory
Cross-linking theory
Immunological theory
Redundant message theory
Codon restriction theory
Transcriptional event theory

Behind each of these intriguing names are learned scientists, thoughtful adherents, and detractors. To give you an idea of all those theories would require several volumes and a graduate course, and that is hardly our goal here. But it is useful to get a basic familiarity with a few of the most common theories, because it is on this work that much of this book is based.

Most of the backers of the prime theories fall into one of two broad camps: those I call the "Entropists" and those I term the "Genetic Fatalists."

The Entropy of Age

Newton's Second Law of Thermodynamics, known to physicists as "entropy," states that things cool off over time. Scientists tell us that means that any organized system tends to move from order to chaos. (Anyone who has ever seen my workdesk at home—or, for that matter, any parent who has tried to keep a child-filled household tidy—knows exactly what I'm talking about!)

The same principle of entropy holds true, too, at a biological level. Every living organism is engaged in a constant struggle with the forces of entropy and disorder. That struggle is what aging is. Not only do our cells, and organs, and functioning become more disorderly with every passing year, the fact is, we literally "cool off" —our body temperature will have dropped by an average of two degrees by age seventy! In a very real sense, being alive means being engaged in a constant struggle against disorder, and our final capitulation to chaos comes only when we expire.

There is a whole school of thought that relies on entropy as the most likely explanation of aging. The Entropists say that it is wear and tear, the accumulating clutter of living that does us in. They postulate that the aging of the body's cells is much like the decay of, say, an old barn. Little by little, different things break down, damaged by the ravages of time. A hinge may fail there, a coat of paint peel here, a window sag somewhere else, and *voilà*—soon we are experiencing the creaky, slow, throbbing decrepitude of old age.

Although experts agree that such a gradual process occurs, they do not all agree about where to place most of the blame. Some say the "scene of the crime" is DNA, the genetic code that lies at the heart of human cells. Because of exposure to toxins, chemicals and ultraviolet light filtering through the skin, these complex chains of information-carrying chemicals may break, twist, become transposed, or otherwise get out of order. When they do, goes the theory, the cells are not able to pass along their genetic blueprints accurately, and key chemical reactions within the body's cells begin to go haywire. When enough of these cells break down, the scientists hypothesize, the changes accumulate into serious deficits that weaken whole organs. It is an intriguing proof for this theory that those animals whose cells repair DNA damage quickly and efficiently are also those who live the longest.

Another theory focuses more on the enzymes our cells produce. Sometimes they become faulty, and instead of the well-ordered cellular chemical production lines that Nature designed, our cells start to look like a crazed, disorderly factory floor, turning out too much of some things and not enough of others.

Another popular theory that researchers have focused on has been termed the "error catastrophe" theory. It suggests that defective proteins in the body's cells accumulate into an intracellular chemical soup that interferes with the cells' proper biochemical tasks and thus weakens them. Others suggest it is not that the chemicals are made wrong, but that they never get broken down and recycled properly. The image these biologists paint is one in which the cells' "work space" grows increasingly chaotic because its "janitors" are out on strike.

A "Radical" Theory of Aging

The most compelling of the many aging theories advanced by cell biologists is called the "free-radical" theory. It is this theory that underlies many of the nutritional counsels throughout this book— and it plays a role in many of the twenty-four rejuvenation steps we will explore.

This dramatic-sounding name, with its overtones of terrorists and saboteurs, may remind you of something from political theory instead of biology. Indeed, from your cells' point of view, that is almost exactly right. *Free radicals* are very reactive chemical by-products that are created as oxygen is burned as fuel in our cells. (For that reason, chemists also know them as "oxidation products.") Chemically, they are molecules out of electrical balance. Unfortunately, the only way they know to rebalance themselves is to steal an electron belonging to another molecule, thereby unbalancing it. And so the chain reaction goes, unleashing all sorts of havoc.

Free radicals can interact with fatty molecules, lipids, in your cells. Then, they create a pollutant, a sort of intracellular sludge called "lipofuscin," a pigment that can change the color of skin. However, their damage is far more than cosmetic. As they react explosively with many of your cells' natural chemicals, these free-radical reactions can inflict severe damage on the fragile equilibrium of the cells. (In fact, the damage they do is the same that occurs when you are exposed to radiation—except it is happening all the time, from the inside, instead of from an external radiation source.)

Free radicals destroy key cell enzymes, fats, and proteins. If they borrow electrons from fat molecules in the critical membrane wall of a cell, they can actually destroy the integrity of the cell. Too, they can interfere with the elegant intermeshing ballet of DNA and RNA that is responsible for cell division. As these miscreants do their dirty work, trouble begins to spread far and wide. They can trigger inflammation, damage lung cells and blood vessels, and lead to mutations, cell destruction, degenerative diseases, and even cancer. In terms of the destruction they cause, free radicals are the biological equivalent of a terrorist bomber gone berserk in the control room of a nuclear reactor. As enough of the cells' vital mecha-nisms are damaged, the cell can become less efficient, malfunction, or even die.

And when enough of *that* happens, there is a cascade of biological damage. The cumulative levels of oxidation radicals put millions, even billions, of cells out of commission. As you read this sentence, free radicals are slowly building up and being destroyed in your body. But as you age, their numbers certainly increase, and as they do, the chances also increase that these cellular saboteurs can do greater and greater harm to the "works" of your cells.

One school of thought, based on the breakthrough research of the eminent biologist Dr. Denham Harman, believes that the cumula-tive effect of free-radical damage is the root of cell aging—and all the debilitating, difficult diseases that often come with increasing years. The researchers are quite unequivocal: "Chances are 99% that free radicals are the basis for aging," says biochemist Harman, the father of free-radical theory. "Aging is the ever-increasing accumu-lation of changes caused or contributed to by free radicals." These scientists blame free radicals for many common degenerative dis-eases: arthritis, diabetes, hardening of the arteries, heart and kidney ailments, Parkinson's disease, even cataracts. As I was writing this chapter, the largest group of free-radical scientists in history met in an international colloquium to review the newest findings about these agents—and how to disable them. You will find some of their findings—particularly those about antioxidant nutritional defenses —in the chapters to come.

HOW NOT TO BE NATURE'S GUINEA PIG

Why on earth would Mother Nature have evolved us to have such potentially damaging chemical reactions? Denham Harman suggests two reasons: First, the same free radicals that cause aging and cancer also make it pos-sible for all of the biological mutations that Nature has used over billions of years to make you the terrific, nearly perfect person you are. You can thank free radicals for the fact that you no longer swing from trees and walk on all fours! In that respect, free radicals are biological wild cards, thrown in to keep the evolutionary game interesting and moving along.

Second, the fact that free-radical oxidation plays a part in aging and cancer "may play a useful role, possibly a necessary one . . . by aiding in the disposal of old organisms after they have provided new 'experiments' for evaluation against the environment." Gulp. We are, of course, the "old organisms" Harman is talking about. But just in case you don't like the idea of being one of Nature's guinea pigs as your free radicals run wild, you will find suggestions for a potent antioxidant plan in the twenty-two steps throughout this book.

Although scientists may disagree whether the aging culprit is DNA, free radicals, defective cell enzymes, or some combination of these and other factors, what links all of them is a belief that losing our youthful vigor is a process of entropy, the result of the wear and tear of existence. They tell us it is when our cells grow increasingly snarled, jumbled, and generally muddled with chemical clutter that we start to look, act, and feel old.

Old age is like a plane flying through a storm. Once you are aboard, there is nothing you can do.
—Golda Meir

The second major school of theorists says there is more to aging than mere entropy. These scientists are the Genetic Fatalists, whose credo, as voiced by one of their proponents, runs: "Life is a terminal disease." Their idea is simple. The human body is programmed to self-destruct, and the code to do so is written in our genes.

A concise view of this theory was written by the eminent immunobiologist Lewis Thomas in his *Medusa and the Snail*: "This is . . . what happens when a healthy old creature, old man or old mayfly, dies. The dying is built into the system so that it can occur at once, at the end of a genetically pre-determined allotment of living."

The possibility of genetic programming certainly goes a long way to explaining why the human species seems to have a fixed upper age of about 115 years. That presumably represents the maximum age our genes are "set" to. The adherents of such a theory cite the evidence of evolution: In order to continue the species, humans need survive only about thirty years—just enough time to have children. From an evolutionary perspective, the following seventy years are just so much window dressing, which confers little survival advantage for the species. They cite, too, the fact that the way our bodies change as we age—even down to such physical changes as our ears lengthening and our noses widening—as evidence for cellular programming to distribute fat, connective tissue, and even bone mass differently. Why then, they ask, could we not also be programmed to expire?

Some experts postulate that certain organs or organ systems control the body's internal clock. Noting that the immune system loses 90 percent of its power between the ages of fourteen and seventy, many biogerontologists have suggested that this complex system of cells, organs, and chemical messengers may be the body's "longevity timer." Others point to one part of the immune system, the thymus gland, as our biological pacemaker. Whether the cause is to be found in the whole or the part, what seems clear is that when our immune system weakens past a certain point, we succumb to the cancer or infections which a younger person would fight off.

The pathologist Roy Walford, a preeminent researcher at the University of California at Los Angeles, believes that immune system decline is probably controlled by a group of genes with the tongue-twisting name of major histocompatibility complex—MHC, for short. The MHC may affect breakage and repair of DNA, the levels of free radicals, even the pace at which our tissues develop and regenerate.

I have even heard other researchers point out that what may seem like built-in immune programming to grow older may in fact be due to the foods we eat throughout our lifetime. They believe that our immune system can be overtaxed by creating antibodies to deal with the many foreign proteins in the foods we consume. In the long haul, they argue, a steady barrage of foreign substances exhausts our B cells, T cells, and the natural killer cells of our immune defenses so that eventually they become depleted and cannot rise to the challenge when we need them—to fight off infections and cancers.

Tower of Biological Babel?

By now, you may feel that you are listening to the tower of scientific babel—or do I mean babble?—and can't distinguish a word that seems helpful. When the truth is finally sorted out, it may turn out that both sides are right. Our species' upper age limit of 115 years may be set by genetic limits locked into our genes, but we may rarely reach it because of the daily wear and tear that damages our cells long before then.

For you, who just want to live better and longer, this is something of an abstract discussion. When the experts seem so far apart, postulating such disparate mechanisms as genetic programming, DNA damage, accumulated cell toxins, even the food we eat, how can you make sense of it all? After all, if we don't know just what causes aging, how can we slow the process down?

Although I would be the first to admit that we do not yet have the final theoretical answer, I hope you aren't feeling dismayed. There is a relatively easy answer here: What you need to keep in mind is that there are several quite clear things that are helpful to focus on.

If you can increase your life expectancy from the seventy-four years that the statisticians tell us is now the norm even *halfway* up to the theoretical current maximum of 115 years, you would lengthen your life by 27 percent—more than one quarter. This may sound like an ambitious goal—indeed it is. But it doesn't mean it is not practical. Linus Pauling, three-time Nobel Prize-winning biochemist, estimates in *How to Live Longer and Feel Better* that using health measures presently available, we can increase our life expectancy from twenty-five to thirty-five years. Gerontologists Denham Harman and Roy Walford have estimated the potential additional time as five to ten years, which gives us a life span of about eighty-five years. Even the august National Institute on Aging, a mainline institution if there ever was one, published a paper saying that certain interventions "can improve heart and lung function, staving off normal age-related decrements by as much as 10 years."

People in developed countries have already added an astounding twenty-eight years to their average life span since the beginning of the twentieth century. *There is no reason whatsoever for not continuing that progress,* extending your life span even further.

The major point to keep in mind is that such an increase requires no fundamental change in scientific understanding, no major conceptual breakthroughs of the sort that researchers work and worry over. It doesn't necessarily matter, in fact, *which* of the many theories ultimately prove right.

All that it requires is following the steps detailed throughout these chapters. As you do so, you will build risk factors and unnecessary toxins out of your life; you will give your cells a chance to rebuild themselves. Your goal is to eliminate the factors that could prematurely truncate your life long before its true biological deadline. By doing so, you will let your body take advantage of the wonderful longevity that Nature originally designed into it.

74—THE MAGIC NUMBER?

If you live to the age of a hundred, you have it made, because very few people die past the age of a hundred.
—George Burns

There is a grain of truth to the venerable comedian's counsel. If you are about to celebrate your seventy-fourth birthday, don't dust off your will just yet. Yes, seventy-four may be the average age, but that is a statistical confusion. It really reflects the large numbers of people who die prematurely from diseases and accidents. The thing to keep in mind is that, if you are healthy enough to live to a healthy, vital seventy, the chances are you will live another decade longer!

The System Is the Secret

What has become increasingly clear is that the answer to staying young will be found, not in one magic bullet, but in a connected web of behavior—how we eat, sleep, work, exercise, even think. That understanding is the basis of the more than twenty longevity steps you will find throughout this book, and that together make up a "systems approach" to keep you young.

It was the famed British physician Sir James Crichton-Browne who wrote: "There is no short-cut to longevity. To win it is the work of a lifetime, and the promotion of it a branch of preventive medicine." I couldn't agree more, and it is that principle that underlies the changes I will be asking you to make in your life over the next twenty weeks.

I hope you don't see those twenty weeks as a shortcut to longevity —they are not. Instead, you should think of them as a training period, a time for you to explore, acquire, and learn the new habits that you will incorporate into your life and carry for a lifetime. If you do that, you will reap a handsome dividend in terms of the length, the quality, and the pure enjoyment of your years ahead.

3.

The Changes of Aging

To me, old age is always fifteen years older than I
am.
　　　　　　　　　　　　　　—Bernard Baruch

Every one of your body's systems, from your hair to your
toenails, will undergo predictable changes as you age.

To stay young and vital for as long as possible, you need some idea
of what really happens as a body grows older (keep in mind this isn't
just *anybody* we're talking about—it's *your* body!). So put on your
physician's white coat and let's look at the physiological changes
that lie ahead for you. Only by understanding what Nature has in
store for us can we hope to control the aging process.

"An adult is a person who has ceased to grow vertically, but not
horizontally."

This change is called the "Great Metabolism Shift," and it starts
somewhere around the beginning of your fourth decade. Your energy
furnaces start to burn differently, and Nature begins to swaddle you
with an extra layer of fat. As fat increases, you also lose lean muscle

39

mass; so your fat-to-muscle ratio increases significantly over the years, as shown on the charts on page 41.

The Incredible Shrinking Woman

In recent years, no disease has gotten more notice than osteoporosis. Few people realize that this is not just a disease of bones that break, but also of *bones that actually shrink*.

By the time you are sixty-five, your body is only about half as efficient as it once was in absorbing mineral nutrients from foods. Instead of your body taking minerals like calcium, magnesium and potassium from your food, it borrows them from your bones. The bones weaken, losing, on average, 25 percent of their density.

This bone loss can take a significant toll on your height. For most people, the average length of the vertebral column is relatively constant—about 24 inches for women and 27 inches for men. That means, if you subtract the height of the leg bones, we are rather similar in height.

TALLNESS TEST

The next time you find yourself in a group of people of different height, observe carefully what happens as you sit down. When you sit, you are all more or less eye to eye, even though you may have to look up or down at them when you stand up. The differences in people's height are due mostly to the length of the leg bones.

As your body borrows minerals stored in the spinal vertebrae, those bones actually begin to collapse and compact, falling in on themselves. As your spinal column shrinks, you gradually lose the 24 inches or 27 inches of spine length you once had, and you become a "little old lady" or a "little old man."

The average American man can expect to lose up to 2¾ inches in height between the ages of 25 and 70; women, a less drastic 1⅞ inches. Sometimes, the loss is not so gradual: The collapse of just one of the vertebrae in the middle of the back can remove as much as 1⅛ inches of height.

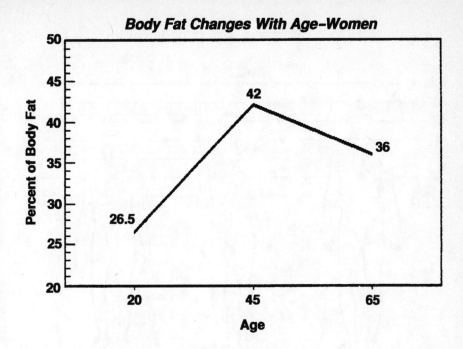

Body Fat Changes With Age–Women

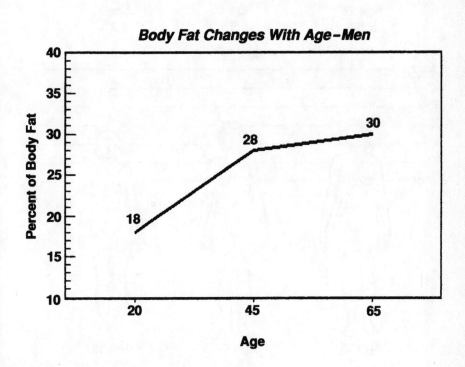

Body Fat Changes With Age–Men

Over the years, you can expect something like this:

MALE

6 foot
10"
8"
6"
4"
2"
5 foot

Age 25
5'10"

Age 45
5'9⅛"

Age 65
5'7⅜"

FEMALE

6 foot
10"
8"
6"
4"
2"
5 foot

Age 25
5'7"

Age 45
5'6½"

Age 65
5'5½"

OUT OF ARM'S WAY . . .

Even your arms shrink as you age. Your arm span, measured from fingertip to fingertip with your arms outstretched, will be one-half less at age sixty-five than it is today. But through an interesting biological optical illusion, they appear to lengthen with age. The reason? Your arms shrink far less than your spine, so that as they hang next to your body, they will appear relatively longer.

The changes go all the way to your fingertips. Right now, if you are twenty years old, your nails take an average of one third less time to grow out than they will at age sixty. After another decade of getting older, by age seventy, they will grow less than half as fast as they do now.

But if you're worried that every part of you will shrink with age, don't—your feet, at least, actually become longer and enlarge as you age.

Face to Face with Age

At age 50, every man has the face he deserves.
—George Orwell

Orwell was talking about the obvious, outward changes that are most noticeable in the face. Rather than reading all the biological details, in this case, you'll see the picture on page 44 is worth a thousand words.

Hair Today, Gone Tomorrow?

Not necessarily. It is true that hair undergoes major changes with age because it is one of the fastest-replicating tissues of the body. There are three primary changes you can expect:

- For both men and women, the hair becomes much finer. Each strand loses about one fifth of its thickness.

Facial Changes With Age

Aging spots appear, due to accumulation of fatty waste product, lipofuscin, in cells

Eyes seem "shrunken" as fat surrounding them diminishes

Eyes become more far-sighted

Skin loses overall uniform pigmentation

Skull increases in diameter

Bags form as fat pouches accumulate below the eyes

Ears lengthen

Cheek and jowl skin sags with cumulative effect of gravity

Nose widens and lengthens

Cheeks may sink in as significant number of teeth are lost

Lines in forehead, around mouth and eyes are established, due to habitual facial expressions

- Hair color comes from the pigment contained in each hair shaft. As you age, the coarse, pigmented hair is replaced by nonpigmented strands—and when you look in the mirror, you find more (gasp!) gray hairs.
- The density of individual hair follicles—how thickly your head is "forested"—drops from a high of six hundred follicles per square centimeter on your thirtieth birthday to half that number by age fifty.
- If you are a *man*, your hair will probably change its pattern of distribution, even if you do not go bald. You can expect to lose hair around your temples, the result of your male hormones. Whether you will also manifest the creeping hair loss of a receding hairline and a widening bald area on the crown of your pate, well, that depends on your genes.
- If you are a *woman*, there is a one-in-six chance that you will have lost most of your body and pubic hair by age sixty (unless you come from Japanese stock, in which case it is virtually 100 percent likely).

Hear Today, Gone Tomorrow?

> . . . One man in his time plays many parts,
> His acts being seven ages.
> The sixth age . . . his big manly voice,
> turning again toward childish treble, pipes
> And whistles in his sound.
>
> —*As You Like It,* Act II,
> scene vii

We now understand medically what the Bard meant. As your vocal cords pull taut with age, they resonate higher. The result:

"HUM" TEST

Hum softly the first notes of "Greensleeves" ("The Sounds of Silence" will do for the younger generation). The difference between the first and second notes is the difference between your speaking voice now and at age seventy. Or, to put it another way, if at seventy you start to hum the tune you will naturally begin on the same pitch that the second note falls on today.

Your speaking voice—in both men and women—rises about twenty-five cycles per second. To get an idea of how your speaking voice will rise, try the "hum" test.

More Than Skin Deep . . .

Perhaps the most profound changes happen where you can't see or hear them, deep within your cellular and organ systems. In virtually every niche and cranny of your body, aging means the power and strength of your organs and cells are gradual waning.

Losing Our Immunity?

> Aging is the progressive accumulation of changes with time . . . associated with or responsible for the ever-increasing susceptibility to disease and death which accompanies old age.
> —Dr. Denham Harman,
> "The Aging Process,"
> *Proceedings of the*
> *National Academy*
> *of Science,*
> November 1978.

The vulnerability he speaks of is intimately linked to the immune system. During your twenties and thirties, and particularly after age forty or so, your immune system begins to wane in several ways:

- Certain types of immune sentries—T cells, B cells, and neutrophils—become less efficient at protecting you from bacteria, viruses, and cancer.

- By age seventy, your immune system has lost 80 percent to 90 percent of the vigor and germ-fighting reserve it had when you were fifteen.
- Your body becomes less vigilant about fighting off threats to your health, leaving you more vulnerable to infections and cancer.
- Your immune troops become careless and imprecise, failing to distinguish adequately between enemy targets and friendly targets they should leave alone. When this happens, in what doctors call an "autoimmune response" ("auto" means "self"), your body starts to fight itself, even your most vital organs. When the armies that Nature gave you to defend your body turn mutinous, you pay a steep price.

WHEN IMMUNE CELLS ATTACK . . .   *YOU GET . . .*

Joint linings	Rheumatoid arthritis
Pancreas cells	Diabetes
Nerve fibers	Multiple sclerosis
Stomach lining	Pernicious anemia
Liver	Chronic active hepatitis
Thyroid gland	Graves' disease

An aging immune system, then, is one that has grown both weak and careless.

Plumbing Problems

You can expect your urinary system to lose fully one half its efficiency between age thirty and age eighty. That means your kidneys filter only half as much blood waste per hour. At the same time, the walls of your bladder change, and its capacity diminishes. The result? Rest-room stops become more and more frequent—and urgent.

The body's electrical system, the nerves, also show signs of wear. Your overall muscle coordination and reflexes drop by one third to one quarter. Some of that is due to the speed of electrical nerve signals along the body, which slows down a few percent each decade. By your midsixties, those signals are traveling about 15 percent slower than they used to.

Neuro-Muscular Changes With Age

**15% slower
nerve reaction**

**25-33% slower
muscle reaction**

Are You All Wet?

Even your body's cells themselves change. For instance, do you believe that the body's cells become more or less moist with age? The answer may seem obvious: They actually lose moisture with each passing year, dropping from 42 percent to 33 percent of your body's composition from age twenty-five to seventy-five. This dryness may be part of what accounts for the general sensation of losing the suppleness and silkiness of youth.

There is a very important practical consideration you should know about. As you age, you need to take smaller drug doses to get the same effect. Partly that is due to the fact that your liver and kidneys perform less efficiently. But we know now that part is also due to the greater concentration of drugs in your cells, which in older adults are less diluted by cellular fluids.

Oxygen Changes

One of the most profound changes comes in how your body processes oxygen. Oxygen, of course, is the fuel that stokes your cellular energy furnaces. As the years pass, the oxygen processing mechanism changes in two main ways:

Oxygen Processing Losses With Age

| —50% loss of lung capacity | + | —33% loss of heart pumping action | = | 50% less oxygen delivered to cells |

- Your lung capacity drops from six to three quarts of air with each breath. Right there, less oxygen is available to your bloodstream.
- Then, the average American heart loses up to a third of its pumping capacity, due to the damage caused by disease processes that appear with increasing age. The pumping rate may drop from a high of almost four quarts a minute at age twenty-five to only two and a half quarts at age sixty-five.

This adds up to a significant double whammy: By retirement age, your cells may be getting just half the oxygen they were getting

when you graduated college. Small wonder every set of stairs seems
to get steeper!

Lowering the Energy Throttle

The common perception of "losing energy" with age reflects a profound biologic truth. Your *basal metabolism*—the rate at which your
body burns fuel—drops almost 3 percent every decade. By age seventy, it has tapered off by about one fifth from its peak when you
were young. In effect, your body's engines throttle themselves down,
bit by inevitable bit.

Time for "Young Blood"?

You probably don't think of your blood as a part of your body that
ages particularly, but it does. All of your blood cells are constantly
being replaced, and of the approximately twenty-odd trillion blood
cells in your body right now, none is older than about four months.
However, the real shift comes in the overall chemical profile of the
four quarts (men, make that six) of red stuff in your arteries.

Reading Your Own "Blood Age Print"

As you age, the combination of chemicals in your blood changes
significantly. If you are a healthy thirty-four-year-old, how your
blood profile looks today has little in common with how it will look
at age sixty. That means the blood system carries its own rough "age
print" which a blood expert (hematologist) can "read" to get a
rough idea of how far along you are in the aging process. To cite just
four vital measures:

- Blood chemicals, like the hormone renin aldosterone and the
  blood component albumin, drop as we age. Others, like glucose,
  uric acid, and the abnormal protein called rheumatoid factor, rise.
- Your blood pressure creeps up over the years, so that what would
  be a worrisome elevation in a twenty-five-year-old is just about

average for his or her mother. Most of us can expect our overall blood pressure to increase about 15 percent between the ages of thirty and sixty-five.

- Likewise, you can expect your cholesterol to rise—for a while. A level of 220 would be of some concern in a twenty-five-year-old, but just about normal at age fifty. But then, after about age fifty-five, it starts inching its way back down again.
- Your blood level of abnormal proteins increases. One of these proteins, rheumatoid factor, is implicated in arthritic inflammation of the joints.

Come to Your Senses . . .

[The] last scene of all . . .
Sans teeth, sans eyes, sans taste, sans everything.
                              —*As You Like It,* Act II,
                                       scene vii

It is a common view that our older years should be a time to "stop and smell the roses," but unfortunately Nature has built in an obstacle. Experiments suggest that the sense of smell declines significantly with age, particularly for men.

Happily, though, Nature does not rob you of all senses equally. Shakespeare notwithstanding, the sense of taste is very little affected directly by age.

TAKE THE TONGUE TEST

Look at your tongue in the mirror, you will see that it is covered with small bumps, or *papillae.* If you looked at these bumps under a microscope, you would see that each contains a total of between two thousand and nine thousand taste buds—the nerve endings that register sweet, sour, salt, and bitter, and tell you the difference between lime sherbet, fresh peaches, and chopped liver.

Starting at age fifty, the taste buds become less able to regenerate. Within about twenty years, perhaps 70 percent have died off, leaving a scanty seventy-five taste buds on each papilla.

We become less sensitive to the four basic tastes after age fifty. Happily, this loss doesn't lead to a corresponding two-thirds drop in your tasting enjoyment, because Nature has built in redundancy to the human body. If you do lose some sense of taste with age, it is most likely due to some other reason—drugs, sickness, even changes in nerve-transmitter chemicals in the brain.

Ah yes, the brain. Most of us think of the brain as one of the most vulnerable organs to the ravages of age. From a biological perspective, that is accurate: Your brain shrinks, losing about 10 percent of its sixteen billion nerve cells by age seventy, and about 40 percent of its weight.

Loss of Taste Buds With Age

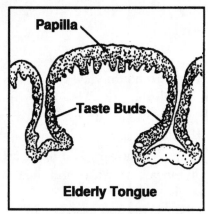

It is a rough-and-ready rule of thumb that if aging is left to its own course you can count on it robbing your body of about 1 percent of its overall functional capacity each year after about age 35. Notice that I said "left to its own course"—after all, you wouldn't be reading this book if you were planning to leave aging to its own course!

Your Body's Functional Capacity

> There is a wicked inclination in most people to
> suppose an old man decayed in his intellects. If a
> young or middle-aged man, when leaving a
> company, does not recollect where he laid his hat, it
> is nothing; but let the same inattention be
> discovered in an old man and people shrug and say,
> "His memory is going."
>
> —Samuel Johnson

Samuel Johnson's wise observation is echoed by the newest brain research. Despite physical losses, it just isn't true that we face an inevitable loss of our thinking and brainpower as we age, and it most certainly doesn't have to happen to you. Consider recent research findings:

"Despite the common belief, thinking can actually improve with age."—New York Hospital–Cornell Medical Center.

"In every age group, even among the oldest, individuals were found whose performance on mental tasks did not decline with age, but was indistinguishable from that of younger adults." —*Handbook of the Biology of Aging*, 1985.

"At all ages the majority of people maintain their levels of intellectual competence—or actually improve—as they grow older." — National Institute on Aging.

ADD IT ALL UP AND WHAT DO YOU GET?

Brain weight	decreases 40% by age 70
Number of nerve trunk fibers	decreases 37% by age 70
Blood flow to brain	decreases 20% by age 70
Speed of blood equilibrium mechanism	decreases 83% by age 70

Basal metabolic rate	decreases 20% by age 70
Kidney filtration rate	decreases 50% by age 70
Body water content	decreases 15% by age 70
Resting heart output	decreases 30% by age 70
Handgrip strength	decreases 45% by age 70
Oxygen uptake while exercising	decreases 60% by age 70
Lung volume during exercise	decreases 47% by age 70

My medical training showed me firsthand just how one can keep intellectual abilities sharp into the most advanced age. I will never forget the staggering intellect of one of my medical professors, a man who is now on the near side of eighty. He was held in awe for his razor-sharp intellect and total recall, which were terribly intimidating to my cadre of green medical students. Woe to the poor young intern who made the mistake of supposing that Dr. Weinstein had lost any of his faculties!

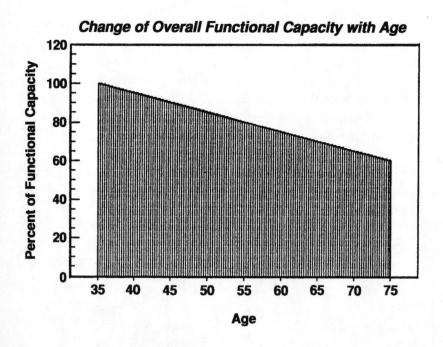

Change of Overall Functional Capacity with Age

Aging Overview

Brain weight decreases 40%

Speed of blood equilibrium mechanism decreases 83%

Blood flow to brain decreases 20%

Lung volume during exercise decreases 47%

Basal metabolic rate decreases 20%

Resting heart ouput decreases 30%

Oxygen uptake while exercising decreases 60%

Handgrip strength decreases 45%

Number of nerve trunk fibers decreases 37%

Kidney filtration rate decreases 50%

Body water content decreases 15%

By Age 70

Sex and the Seventy-Year-Old

> One other bit of good news: Obviously, a woman's hormonal profile changes dramatically with menopause, and it has long been thought that men's hormones showed a similar waning in their later years. Happily, current research indicates that the levels of the male sex hormones testosterone and androgen in older men remain equal to those of their sons, even grandsons.
>
> The best part of this prescription is that the levels of sex hormones stay highest among those men who have the highest level of sexual activity.

The Anti-aging Motto: Use It or Lose It

We now understand that to a great extent the body operates on a "use it or lose it" principle. That is true of heart, mind, and muscles. That means that there are ways to make sure you will be as sharp, vital, and alive in thirty years as you are right now.

If there is one youth secret that runs through all the research on growth and aging, and throughout this book, it is summed up in those five words—use it or lose it. You possess the keys to staying young and vital—if you choose to use them.

Let's Get Personal

Let's bring this down to a very personal level and look at how these changes will touch *your* life (how much more personal can you get than inside your own body?). You will dust off your crystal ball and peer into the decades ahead.

Using some basic medical tools, you can in effect project your medical future with some educated guesses about what your body will look, act, and feel like as you age.

Dear Old Mom and Dad—
Your Aging Blueprint

You already own the simplest tool to give you a hint about your medical future—the family photo album. Take a look at a picture of your parents or grandparents when they were your age. Look at their hairlines, their body shape, their weight distribution, their faces—then and now. Do you see something of yourself in them (or, more accurately, vice-versa)?

Now compare earlier photographs of them with later ones. In a very real way, the differences your parents have manifested over two decades are a blueprint for the changes you can reasonably expect to experience as you grow older.

- Did your mother develop the bent-over "dowager's hump" that signals osteoporosis?
- Did your father's joints swell with rheumatoid arthritis?
- Did they lose their looks and vitality, or stay hale and hearty until relatively late in life?

There is a solid scientific reason for this exercise. Your parents, after all, are practically your closest genetic match—they just have a twenty- or thirty-year jump on you in how long they've aged, and are the best living examples of how your basic gene set is likely to age.

Aging Forecaster

The second method is more scientific, based on data gathered in examining thousands of people. It takes into account certain average changes that come with age. These data are based on a statistical golden mean, and there is no guarantee that you will age exactly the same way, but it certainly gives you a general idea about what the decades ahead may hold for you.

Fill in as many of the answers in the lefthand column as you can.

Then follow the instructions in the middle column, and behold! the righthand column will give you a reasonable extrapolation of where you might be yourself a few years from now.

Certain aspects affecting your health are such important variables that they merit a more in-depth, and more precise, prediction.

Your Personal Aging Forecaster

Your current:	Factor in these biological changes:	Personal prediction at age 70:
Weight _____	Men: Subtract 7% Women: Add 4%	_____
Height _____	Men: subtract 2½" Women: subtract 1¾"	_____
Number of teeth: _____ (32, if none are lost yet)	Subtract 1 tooth per decade	_____
Blood pressure _____	Men: add 20/10 Women: add 30/10	_____
Overall functional capacity, start with 100% at age 25 _____	Subtract 10% for each decade	_____
Body temperature _____	Subtract 1.5 degrees	_____
Cholesterol _____	Men add 40 points Women add 50 points	_____

BLOOD PRESSURE PREDICTOR

Biostatistics let us create a more accurate model to predict possible changes in your blood pressure over the coming years. To predict your possible blood pressure at a given age, use the charts on page 59.

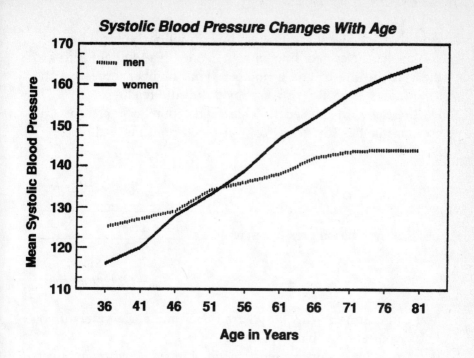

Systolic Blood Pressure Changes With Age

men
women

Mean Systolic Blood Pressure

Age in Years

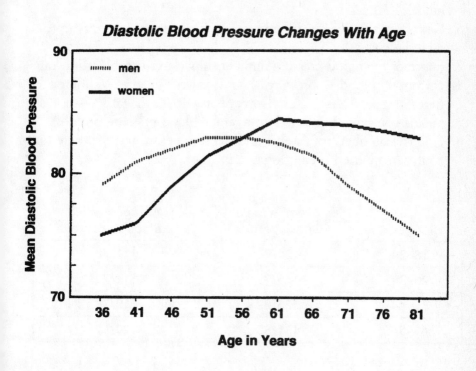

Diastolic Blood Pressure Changes With Age

men
women

Mean Diastolic Blood Pressure

Age in Years

1. Find that age along the line at the bottom of the first chart.
2. Looking at the correct line for your gender, read straight across to the vertical line to find a number. That number represents the top number (systolic) of your blood pressure reading.
3. Do the same on the second chart. That number represents the bottom number (diastolic) of your blood pressure reading.
4. Now for your final result:

Number from
top chart

At age ＿＿my blood pressure may be:＿＿＿＿＿＿＿＿＿＿

Number from
bottom chart

You can customize this for yourself even more accurately if you know your current blood pressure.

5. If you know your current blood pressure, write numbers here:＿＿＿＿
6. Next, find the average blood pressure for your age category in the table below.
7. Subtract the blood pressure number shown in the table from your current blood pressure and write the difference here:＿＿＿＿＿＿＿＿ (Don't worry if it's negative—it just means you have a lower-than-average blood pressure profile.)
8. Add the number from step 7 and the number from step 4 here for your personalized prediction:＿＿＿

Age	Average Male Blood Pressure	Average Female Blood Pressure
18–24	124/76	111/70
25–34	125/79	112/73
35–44	126/82	119/78
45–54	131/85	129/82

GUESS YOUR WEIGHT

Unlike getting on the scales down at the local drugstore, this is done with the help of medical epidemiology. Use the chart on page 63.

YOUR CHOLESTEROL COMPUTER

If your doctor has told you what your cholesterol level is, you can proceed with this test.

1. Find your age on the chart opposite, depending on your gender.
2. If your current cholesterol level is approximately equal to that indicated for your age and gender, you can follow this curve up to get a rough average prediction of your cholesterol later in life.
3. If your current cholesterol level differs widely from that shown in the chart, determine the difference. (For example, a thirty-year-old woman should have a level of no more than 190. If yours is 205, the difference is 15 points.)
4. Add the point difference from step 3 to the age-adjusted value you found in step 2. This gives an approximate range that you might hit at that age—providing you don't make changes in your diet, exercise, or medications.

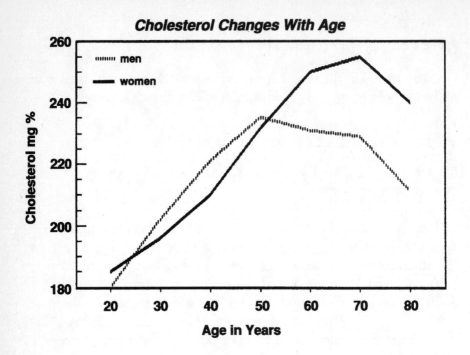

You may want to copy down these predictive results and file them away. Twenty weeks from now, when you have had a chance to incorporate many of the basic longevity steps outlined in this book into your life, you might want to consult these results. If you do, I think you may find a pleasant surprise: Thanks to this book, and the changes you have made in your life, you will have improved your score on these variables. But more important than your test score is how you feel, look, and act. Because in those twenty weeks you will have started making yourself biologically younger than your present chronological age.

So next time you hear someone say, "You're not getting any younger," remember your twenty-two longevity steps and smile—because you'll know better.

Ideal Weight Chart

YOUR HEIGHT		AGE				
		18–24	25–34	35–44	45–54	55–64
4'10"	Women	114	123	133	132	135
4'11"	Women	118	126	136	136	138
5'0"	Women	121	130	139	139	142
5'1"	Women	124	133	144	143	145
5'2"	Men	130	139	146	148	147
5'2"	Women	128	136	144	146	148
5'3"	Men	135	145	149	154	151
5'3"	Women	131	139	146	150	151
5'4"	Men	139	151	155	158	156
5'4"	Women	134	142	149	153	154
5'5"	Men	143	155	159	163	160
5'5"	Women	137	146	151	157	157
5'6"	Men	148	159	164	167	165
5'6"	Women	141	149	154	160	161
5'7"	Men	152	164	169	171	170
5'7"	Women	144	152	156	164	164
5'8"	Men	157	168	174	176	174
5'8"	Women	147	155	159	168	167
5'9"	Men	162	173	178	180	178
5'10"	Men	166	177	183	185	183
5'11"	Men	171	182	188	190	187
6'0"	Men	175	186	192	194	192
6'1"	Men	180	191	197	198	197
6'2"	Men	185	196	202	204	201

Calculated from: U.S. Center for Health Statistics, North American Association Study of Obesity.

4.

How Old Are You, Really?

"This is it. This is what fifty looks like."
—Gloria Steinem, on
being told how
young she looked on
her fiftieth birthday

If you are to commit to making yourself younger, you have to know where to start—to know how old your body systems are right now. That seems easy—you know how old you are, right? Medically speaking, that isn't necessarily accurate.

A range of biological factors makes the body's real biological age —where its physical systems fall along the continuum from birth to death—only loosely related to the number of years since birth. From your body's perspective, your age is an absolutely relative, approximate measure. You have surely heard a "youthful" seventy-year-old say of a young person that he is "old beyond his years," or have watched a friend age quickly in a few months' time. In each of those instances, you have picked up on a series of subtle—and not-to-subtle—clues about the energy, vitality, mental acuity, general fitness, and sharpness of these people's senses and reflexes, as well as a broad range of different elements about their biological, social, and psychological functioning.

Too, not all parts of your body age at the same rate. You may have a heart that functions at a level "younger" than the age shown on your driver's license, thanks to careful diet and exercise. Yet your skin, liver, or other organs may function like the organs of someone much older because of genetic weakness or stresses they have endured.

Reckoning how the body's systems work is what I do with my patients, and what your own family doctor does during your physical. As your physician checks out your heart and lungs, bones and mobility, blood pressure and lab results, she or he is in effect assessing how you are doing relative to others of the same approximate age. It is when you fall outside the range of age-adjusted values that you are diagnosed with some problem.

In this chapter, you will do much the same thing, assessing your body's relative biological age—what I call your "Youth Quotient."

YOUR PERSONAL "YOUTH QUOTIENT" ASSESSMENT

Your Physiology

1. Is your blood pressure: _____
   A. In the range of 120/80–140/90 (1)
   B. Above 140/90 (10)
   C. Above 95/60 but below 120/80 (−10)
   D. Less than 95/60 (10)
2. Is your blood cholesterol level: _____
   A. More than 260 (15)
   B. Between 230 and 260 (10)
   C. Between 180 and 220 (1)
   D. Between 140 and 180 (−10)
   E. Below 140 (−5)
3. Is your resting pulse: _____
   A. Less than 60 beats per minute (−10)
   B. 60–70 beats per minute (1)
   C. 70–90 beats per minute (10)
   D. More than 90 beats per minute (15)

4. Has your doctor ever told you that you are ane-
   mic?   _____
   A. Yes (10)
   B. No (1)
5. Are you: _____
   A. 20% or more above desired weight (10)
   B. 5%–20% overweight (5)
   C. About right for your height (1)
   D. 5%–20% underweight (5)
   E. 20% or more under (8)
6. Compared to this time last year, your weight: _____
   A. Is pretty much the same (1)
   B. Has risen or fallen, but you can control it
   with diet and exercise (5)
   C. Is rising or falling now, and is very hard to
   maintain (10)

Family History

7. Do any family members have diabetes, hyperten-
   sion, or heart disease?   _____
   A. No (1)
   B. Yes (10)
8. Has anyone in your family ever been diagnosed
   with cancer?   _____
   A. No (1)
   B. Yes (5)
9. Do others in your family have severe allergies?   _____
   A. No, not that I know of (1)
   B. Yes, mostly hay fever (3)
   C. Yes, significant allergies to foods or environ-
   ment (5)
10. Do you have trouble breathing, shortness of
    breath?   _____
    A. No (1)
    B. Sometimes, but infrequently (5)
    C. This is a regular or common feeling (10)

11. Do you cough when you wake up in the morning?

    A. Almost never, except when I have flu or a cold (1)

    B. Sometimes, but it passes quickly (5)

    C. This happens regularly (10)

Immune Function

12. Do you frequently catch cold, flu, or other illnesses?

    A. Never—or very rarely (1)

    B. 2–4 times a year (5)

    C. More than 4 times a year (10)

13. When you get sick, how long does it usually take to recover fully?

    A. 3–4 days (1)

    B. About 10 days (5)

    C. I haven't felt really well for a very long time (10)

    D. Can't remember the last time I was sick (−10)

14. Do you have a history of chronic illness?

    A. No (−10)

    B. Yes, but for less than 5 years (5)

    C. Yes, for 5 or more years (10)

15. When you get a cut or bruise, does it heal quickly?

    A. Yes, it usually heals completely in a few days (1)

    B. I have noticed that I heal more slowly than I used to (5)

    C. Bruises stay a long time; cuts leave a visible mark (10)

16. Your overall health is:

    A. Excellent—I am very satisfied (1)

    B. Usually all right, but could be better (5)

    C. Fair to poor—I wish it were better (10)

Specific Symptoms

17. Have you noticed any problems with walking, balance, or coordination?   _____
    A. No (1)
    B. Yes, ongoing minor problems (5)
    C. Yes, they significantly impair my movement (10)
18. How is your skin?   _____
    A. Smooth and supple, not scaly or irritated (1)
    B. Rough, cracked, dry in some months. Occasional problem patches (5)
    C. Chronically dry, itchy, flaky, or irritated (10)
19. Do you have headaches?   _____
    A. A few times a year, or less (1)
    B. Often, but they go away quickly (5)
    C. Often, and they are painful and debilitating (10)
20. Do you experience leg or arm muscle cramps?   _____
    A. No, almost never (1)
    B. Occasionally—sometimes when I am sleeping (5)
    C. Yes, frequently, especially when I walk or exercise (10)
21. Do you have arthritis, joint pain, or pain in your feet and hands?   _____
    A. Only rarely (1)
    B. My joints sometimes seem stiff; I notice pain in my hands and feet more (5)
    C. Pain in joints and extremities has really limited my mobility or actions (10)
22. Do you have pain in your back, especially down low?   _____
    A. Only rarely, and it goes away (1)
    B. Twinges, but not debilitating (5)
    C. It is a constant feeling, and affects my mobility, actions, or mood (10)

23. Do your extremities ever feel cold, numb, or tingly?   _____
    A. No, I do not experience those feelings (1)
    B. They happen sometimes, but not regularly (5)
    C. Yes, I have noticed those sensations regularly (10)

24. Do you get diarrhea, constipation, or digestion problems?   _____
    A. No, or only when I am ill or have eaten the wrong foods (1)
    B. Yes, but the problems are more irritating than serious (5)
    C. These are frequent problems; I watch carefully what I eat (10)

Exercise

25. When was the last time you did any strenuous exercise?   _____
    A. Within the last 5 days (−10)
    B. Only within the last month (1)
    C. Longer than a month (10)

26. Do you get out of breath?   _____
    A. When I do strenuous aerobic exercise for more than a few minutes (−10)
    B. Whenever I exercise or have a short exertion like running for a bus or playing with a child for a little while (5)
    C. When I climb stairs or carry parcels (10)

27. Do your legs cramp when you walk more than a few minutes?   _____
    A. As a regular occurrence (10)
    B. Sometimes, but rarely (5)
    C. No (1)

28. Have you had any broken bones in the last year?   _____
    A. No (1)
    B. Yes, one incident (5)
    C. Two or more separate times (10)

29. Your general energy level is: _____
    A. Variable—some days I feel fine, but mostly I
    could use more energy (5)
    B. Great—I have lots of energy (1)
    C. Constantly sluggish. I often want to sleep.
    When I do, I often don't awake refreshed (10)

Nutrition and Diet

30. When it comes to fiber in your food, you: _____
    A. Consciously eat raw vegetables and fruits,
    grains; and legumes (−10)
    B. Usually eat at least a salad once a day, whole
    grains or equivalent (1)
    C. Eat mostly frozen or canned vegetables (5)
    D. I don't like vegetables or grains (10)
31. Does *most* of your protein come from: _____
    A. Veal, white-meat chicken (5)
    B. Vegetable sources (nuts, grains, or legumes) or
    fish (−5)
    C. Red meat (10)
32. How often do you eat fried foods, butter, or
    other cholesterol-containing foods?   _____
    A. More than once a day (10)
    B. About once a day (5)
    C. Less than once a day (−5)
33. Do you eat cruciferous vegetables (cauliflower,
    broccoli, Brussels sprouts)?   _____
    A. At least once a week, fresh (−5)
    B. No more than occasionally (5)
    C. Hardly ever or never (10)
34. What about calcium?   _____
    A. I know the calcium content of foods and
    make an effort to eat calcium-rich foods (−5)
    B. I take calcium supplements (1)
    C. I don't make any special effort (10)

35. Do you eat more: _____
    A. Simple carbohydrates (candy, sweets, jelly,
    desserts) (10)
    B. Complex carbohydrates (pasta, bread, grains)
    (−5)
36. Do you salt your food: _____
    A. Heavily (10)
    B. Lightly (5)
    C. Not at all (1)
37. Have you noticed allergies to any food or drink?   _____
    A. No, nothing obvious (1)
    B. Yes, to 1 or 2 specific items (5)
    C. Yes, to 3 or more food or drink items (10)

Life-Style and Habits

38. Do you drink alcohol?   _____
    A. More than 2 drinks per day (10)
    B. 2 drinks per day (3)
    C. Occasionally, less than 2 drinks daily (−5)
    D. No (−10)
39. Do you always wear seat belts?   _____
    A. Yes (1)
    B. No (10)
40. Do you smoke cigars, pipes, or cigarettes?   _____
    A. Yes (10)
    B. No (−10)
41. Do you breathe others' smoke at home or at
    work?   _____
    A. Yes (10)
    B. No (1)
42. If you are light-skinned, do you take measures to
    protect your skin from the sun?   _____
    A. Yes, I stay out of the sun or remain thor-
    oughly covered (1)
    B. Yes, I wear sunscreen (5)
    C. No, I like looking tanned and healthy (10)

43. Which best describes your sleeping habits?   _____
    A. I usually get 6–8 hours of sleep a night; I
    awaken refreshed (1)
    B. I don't always get enough sleep, but catch up
    on weekends (5)
    C. I have problems falling asleep, wake through
    the night, have trouble waking in the morning,
    or don't feel rested (10)
44. When it comes to worrying: _____
    A. Once I make up my mind, I don't look back.
    Fretting is not my style. I leave problems at
    work (1)
    B. Like most people, I have a lot on my mind
    sometimes, but not usually (5)
    C. I often worry about things that haven't hap-
    pened yet. I replay what I should have said or
    done in situations (10)
45. How many prescription drugs do you take?   _____
    A. None, have never taken them regularly (1)
    B. 1–3 types of drugs now or in the last year (5)
    C. At least 4 types now or in the last year (10)

Emotional Status

46. About your work life and career choice: _____
    A. I really enjoy my job and the challenge it
    brings me (1)
    B. I am generally satisfied, but sometimes it gives
    me real problems (5)
    C. My job is a chore, I wish I were somewhere
    else (10)
47. Is there someone in your life you trust absolutely
    and can tell your deepest secrets to?   _____
    A. Yes, my mate or best friend (−10)
    B. Usually, but I don't often bother people with
    my problems (5)
    C. There is no one in my life I can confide in
    right now, I tend to be a loner (10)

48. In life:
    A. I am quite independent in making decisions that affect me (1)
    B. Much of what I do depends on my mate, boss, family, or others. Sometimes I don't feel in control (5)
    C. My life is very constrained by others (10)

49. Does your life allow you to really enjoy your friends and hobbies?
    A. Yes, I am pretty happy with my balanced life-style (−5)
    B. My time is mostly dedicated to obligations and duties (5)
    C. I can't remember the last time I really had great fun (10)

50. Right now, you would describe your emotional state as:
    A. Pretty upbeat and stable, all things considered (1)
    B. It varies, but I don't get too down or stay that way (5)
    C. My life feels pretty bleak and out of control (10)

51. Your sexual relations are:
    A. Satisfying and positive (1)
    B. Some areas definitely need help (5)
    C. A significant issue—I have no satisfying sexual outlet (10)

52. Choose the phrase that best describes you:
    A. Calm, even-tempered and generally happy. Friends comment on it (1)
    B. A "hard worker" with high standards at work, school, in relationships. Trying to keep everything under control, I don't always succeed (5)
    C. I am under heavy stress. I am quick to anger (10)

53. Your relations with others tend to be: _____
    A. Satisfying, with clear lines of communica-
    tion (1)
    B. A strain. I often feel like I can't connect (5)
    C. Often short-lived and marked by disputes
    (10)
54. When you look in a mirror, you feel: _____
    A. I look good for someone my age, as well as I
    feel (−5)
    B. I could look better with some work on diet,
    exercise, etc. (1)
    C. To look good is a major, difficult effort (10)

Scoring:

Total score for your biological age: _____

1. Write your chronological age here: _____
2. Look up your total score to find your biological
   age and your Youth Preservation Level: _____

Pay Special Attention to Your
Youth Preservation Level

That letter is your key to the Youth Preservation steps you will be
making in every chapter from now on. If you are in Level A, you will
have a different regime than if you are in Level D throughout this
book. You need to know your Youth Preservation Level in order to
tailor the Youth Preservation steps to you.

Score	Your Biological Age	Youth Preservation Level
–82 to 43	Subtract 5 Years from Chronological Age	A
43 to 170	Subtract 2 years from Chronological Age	B
170 to 296	Keep Chronological Age Unchanged	C
296 to 423	Add 2 Years to Chronological Age	D
423 to 550	Add 5 Years to Chronological Age	E

Grand total for Your Biological Age: _____

If you don't like what you see right now, as you add up the grand total, remember: The farther behind you are, the greater your potential to make tremendous, positive changes in your health and life expectancy. You may want to take this quiz again after you have made the life-style changes in the chapters that follow. I guarantee that you will score "younger"—because biologically your body's processes will actually *be* younger.

5.

Keeping the Outer You
Looking Young

T he first place to start making yourself younger is where it is
most obvious—with the body that greets you in the mirror and
which everybody sees. This chapter focuses on that outer you, your
skin and face. It gives you six easy steps that you can do, right now,
to make yourself look younger and regain the glow of youthful,
radiant skin. Follow these steps, and in ten weeks from now you will
start to see results. By the time you are twenty weeks into the
program, I expect you will see a significant improvement in your
skin's health and appearance.

But first, let's settle one thing once and for all. Many of my
patients, when they first consult me for ways to make themselves
look more youthful, confide this to me as though it were a dirty little
secret. They think the idea of taking care of themselves is vain
somehow. I disagree. Our society places an obsessive value on youth
and vitality. Much of our power as individuals, and our self-worth, is
intimately related to how youthful we, and others, feel we look.
Appearance is the face you present to the world and, as such, it is

very important. Outward appearances are far more than empty vanity.

Happily, mainstream medicine is now coming to agree. Note this editorial in the *Journal of the American Medical Association*:

> It is increasingly apparent that appearance, certainly including cutaneous appearance, contributes to society's evaluation of an individual's competence and to that individual's sense of self-worth and well-being. . . . The prospect of [an] effective anti-aging product for the skin may have direct medical benefit beyond its effect on premalignant lesions.
>
> —*Journal of the American Medical Association*, 1/22/88, Vol. 259, No. 4, p. 569

Translation: Experts realize that *looking as young as you feel is a vital part of being a vital person.*

The public has understood this fact longer than the doctors have. In the time it takes you to read this page, Americans will have spent $19,000 on skin preparations—a rate that adds up to a whopping $27 million every day! It's not just women; men, too, are finally starting to understand that looking their best makes them feel their best.

At the same time, scientists have found a fascinating relation between how old somebody looks to an observer and their scores on a battery of laboratory tests that measure aging throughout the body's systems. It seems that youthful-looking people have bodies that function biologically below their chronological age, and the reverse is true of people who look prematurely aged—independent of their chronological age. Clearly, inside and out, looking young is part of what it is to *be* young.

What's in Store for Your Skin?

Consider the difference between old and young skin.

As your skin ages, here's what happens biologically:

- You lose elasticity.
- You lose 10% to 20% of your skin's pigment cells each decade (that's why very old people seem to have such light, almost translucent skin).
- You lose 50 percent of the Langerhans cells, immune cells that protect against skin cancer.
- Your skin gets rougher and less evenly pigmented (age spots).
- Your skin turns from a rosy color to a more yellowish hue.

Just a Pinch . . .

The Pinch Test is an approximate way to test your skin's age. Put your hand flat on a table, back side up. Pinch a fingerful of loose skin on the back of your hand between thumb and forefinger of your other hand, then let it go. Note how long it takes until the area you pinched has flattened out completely. That time suggests a reading of your skin's relative age.

Time for Pinch to Return to Normal

Women	Men	Skin Age
0 sec	0 sec	10–19
0 sec	0 sec	20–29
1 sec	<.5 sec	30–39
3 sec	1 sec	40–49
12 sec	4 sec	50–59
21 sec	20 sec	60–69
1 min	43 sec	Over 70

That's a picture of what happens if Nature takes its course. Now let's see what you can do about it—the good news here. Today, there is an array of quite effective ways to keep your skin young and supple. Best of all, they are ways that work! Let's look at the six skin-care principles, combining nutrition, several new developments in skin products, and a few commonsense changes. With them, you can not only dramatically slow the rate of your skin's aging, but actually *reverse* some of the ravages that time has wrought.

Step One: The Tretinoin "Miracle"

You have probably heard of last year's dermatologic superstar, topical tretinoin, or Retin-A. Just last year, the *Journal of the American Medical Association* caused an immense public stir when it published a study showing that this vitamin A-derived cream actually seems to reverse some of the changes caused by aging, renewing and rebuilding skin cells so the skin is less rough, mottled, and wrinkled. Where most creams merely hydrate your skin—that is, restore lost water and puff it up—Retin-A goes deeper into the dermal layers and actually stimulates new cell growth. The result? Your skin gains a new lease on life, actually filling in small creases and wrinkles, smoothing out rough spots. Since this discovery, Retin-A has been flying off pharmacists' shelves, and dermatologists have hardly been able to keep up with the demand.

The excitement is because Retin-A is the first product that can demonstrably, dependably make skin look younger. It smoothes out fine wrinkles, sun spots, and skin blemishes. It clearly promotes the growth of new, healthy skin, lifts the top surface of the skin away from deeper layers, and increases the rate of formation of new skin cells. The result is that Retin-A-treated skin is rejuvenated; creating not just new skin but more healthy, rosy, and fresh-looking skin. It is no miracle cure, surely, but one of the best tools to soften and lighten the patina of age that starts taking its toll on our faces after age thirty. I have seen Retin-A make positive changes in many patients after just several months.

You can expect it to:

- Help minor wrinkles, such as those around the nose and eyes
- Reduce blemishes, discoloration, or sun spots
- Help give your skin a better tone
- Make your skin somewhat softer and smoother
- Restore a more rosy glow to your skin

But don't expect a complete face-lift in a tube. Deep wrinkles and furrows will remain unchanged. And do be patient. After all, what Nature did in decades you can't expect to undo in weeks. You will probably require six months of daily applications to begin to appreciate fully the noticeable improvement in your skin's texture and luster.

ARE YOU A RETIN-A CANDIDATE?

Some people are ideal Retin-A candidates because of their skin type. Are you:

- Of Celtic origin (Irish, Scottish, English)?
- With blond or red hair?
- With fair skin?
- With blue eyes?
- One who spends any time in the sun?

If your answer to several of these questions is yes, congratulations: You are the ideal candidate to reverse the damages of skin aging by Retin-A. That doesn't mean other people won't be helped, too. It's just that they are most sensitive to the kind of sunlight damage that Retin-A works best on. But since almost all of us have some degree of photoaging, we, too, can be candidates for "saving face" with Retin-A.

PUTTING IT TO WORK IN YOUR OWN LIFE

If you are interested in Retin-A for you, the first step is to discuss it with a knowledgeable dermatologist. He or she will probably start you off with the 0.1 percent dosage concentration that is most widely used. Nine out of ten people have a reaction when they first use the cream—discomfort, peeling, or irritation. Don't worry— that is an expected and customary phase of your body's adaptation to the biological power of Retin-A.

Then, as you get used to the treatment, many doctors including Dr. Albert Kligman, professor emeritus of dermatology at the University of Pennsylvania, who discovered Retin-A's anti-aging properties, recommend increasing the dosage concentration to 0.2 percent or 0.5 percent after a period of time, if your skin can tolerate it.

To help make Retin-A available to everybody who could benefit from it, the makers of Retin-A have just announced that they will manufacture a special quarter-strength .025 percent version. This formulation should be available in your pharmacy by the time you read this. This means that many people with sensitive skin, who might have problems tolerating the full-strength 0.1 percent-formulation Retin-A, can still take advantage of its real wrinkle-smoothing benefits.

Retin-A is almost as easy to use as cold cream. Just spread a pea-sized dab of it each night on your face and neck. I usually start patients on an every-other-day regimen, to let their skin get used to the cream. If you tolerate it well, you can then slowly increase the frequency to once a day. If your skin gets irritated, ask your doctor for a lower concentration or use the cream every third day, until the redness goes away, then try returning to a more frequent schedule.

The latest research suggests that you should get the most significant cosmetic results in the first year and a half that you use Retin-A. At that point, the improvement seems to level off, and you can go on a less frequent maintenance regime that keeps the positive changes you have gained so far.

RETIN-A HINTS

You can dramatically improve the chance of Retin-A working for you by following a few simple guidelines:

- I recommend you apply Retin-A at night, before bed; then wash or shower it off in the morning.
- A few minutes before applying Retin-A, wash your face with a mild, nonastringent cleanser.
- Because Retin-A makes your skin effectively younger, and promotes the growth of new skin cells, your face also becomes that much more sensitive to sunlight. That means it is *essential* that you protect your new, tender (and youthful!) skin. *Always* wear an SPF (sun protection factor) 15 sunblock when you go out in the

sun—even for a quick shopping trip. I tell my patients to get in the habit of putting on a sunblock each morning before they go out.

- It may also help to use a moisturizer each morning after you have removed the Retin-A. If you do, make sure it is a hypoallergenic product, to avoid irritating the tender new skin.
- If you are pregnant or nursing, do not use Retin-A.
- One consumers' advisory: Make sure you use the real thing. With the avalanche of press attention to tretinoin, several companies have jumped into the market to get their share of the pie, offering confusingly named products that are a far cry from what the doctor ordered. One such ersatz product calls itself Retinol-A, another Retinyl-A, and several others may have sprouted up by the time you read this. The truth is, there is no generic Retin-A, and the name of the only real product, made by Ortho Pharmaceutical Corporation, is Retin-A.

Retin-A has not yet been carefully tested in controlled experiments on large numbers of people, so we are still learning about its long-term effects. But it is already clear that Retin-A represents a quantum step in anti-aging skin care. It is an exciting step, and one which can make a difference in your own life and in the face that you see in the mirror! But keep three cardinal rules in mind:

- DON'T expect miraculous changes to happen overnight.
- DO expect an irritation reaction, particularly in the beginning.
- DO make Retin-A part of an overall skin-care team—not the only player.

What's Next?

Retin-A is only the first of what promises to be a new generation of skin-care creams. These products, the "cosmaceuticals," actually have proven medical effects and are more than simple moisturizers. Several other promising possibilities are now coming through the research pipeline, and will be appearing in the coming years.

Now that you have made Retin-A the first step of your young-skin program, let's look at what else you can do right now to keep your skin youthful.

Step Two: Moisturizers

When it comes to moisturizers, there is good news and bad news. First, the bad: None of the $10 billion worth of commercial cosmetics we buy each year really reverse the damages of age at the cellular level. Now the good news: They may make you look as if they do.

Moisturizers work on a simple principle. They keep water next to your skin, and as the moistened skin swells, it masks small wrinkles, blemishes, and imperfections. Wrinkles don't really go away, of course, because no real repair has been done. When you rinse off the cream, or the moisture evaporates, they are still there. Still, for simple cosmetic value, these products may deliver a lot of illusory bang for the buck. For that reason, there is no reason not to continue using them, if you like the way you look.

You should know, however, that none of the "high-priced spreads" containing exotic oils and ingredients necessarily do a much better job than such old-fashioned stand-bys as basic cold cream and petroleum jelly. Nivea and Vaseline are hardly romantic, but these heavy oils do as good a job as any to keep the skin moist.

Summary Moisturizers have a place in your young-skin regime, but none of them, neither the basics nor the most elegant and expensive concoctions, actually do anything to repair the underlying problem.

Step Three: C Is for Collagen

There is, however, one kind of cream that may be an exception to this rule because laboratory science suggests it gets to the root of the problem. A prime component of skin is the connective protein collagen. It now appears that vitamin C may actually strengthen and rejuvenate the collagen in your skin in several ways.

For ten years, laboratory researchers at Duke University have been working with vitamin C and skin cells. Their work suggests that in the test tube a topical application of vitamin C cream works to help skin synthesize vital new collagen, the essential component that is damaged by aging. While we do not yet have absolute proof that vitamin C works in the body, at least one cosmetic manufacturer, Avon, has created a vitamin C-based skin cream that delivers the ascorbic acid (vitamin C) where it does the most good: right on the aging skin cells. Similarly, vitamin C has been shown to inhibit certain skin cancers.

Summary Vitamin C cream can't hurt, and may be a valuable addition to your young-skin regimen.

Step Four: Youth-Preserving Skin Nutrition

In addition to vitamin C, there are two other vitamins that play an important role in making your skin young from the inside out. To understand why, it's necessary to understand the phenomenon called "cross-linking." When you are young and your skin is at its most supple, the strings of collagen protein it contains are relatively well formed and neat. But as you age, the accumulated damage of sun, chemicals, wind, smoke, and biological toxins tangle those protein strings. In cross-linking, the proteins can grab on to each other, linking molecules where they should not and generally getting very tangled. When that happens, your skin loses its elasticity and becomes rigid.

A good way to visualize cross-linking is imagine hanging twenty strips of sticky adhesive tape from your hand, and vigorously moving them around. As the tape strips touch, they stick and become tangled, until soon they bear very little resemblance to the twenty neat rows you started with. With this happening throughout your skin's connective tissue, no wonder it loses its youthful suppleness!

Scientists now believe that the antioxidant vitamins C, A, and E can help prevent and undo the cellular damage of cross-linking. They work, not just in your skin, but in all the body's tissues where cross-linking can occur: connective tissues, tendons, blood vessels, corneas, bones, and many organs. These vitamins can also help promote skin healing, reduce the formation of scar tissue, and give your skin and mucosal tissues the elements they need to grow healthily and smoothly.

THEY FORM THE CORE OF YOUR YOUTH PRESERVA- TION PROGRAM, and are essential for your skin's youthful appear- ance and long-term health. *Your vitamin-supplement program is based on your score from the personal "Youth Quotient" Assessment quiz you took in Chapter 4.* Turn to page 75, at the end of Chapter 4, to find your Youth Preservation Category. That category determines the level of nutritional help your skin needs.

Youth Preservation Category	Vitamin C	Vitamin E	Beta-carotene*
A	2 grams	400 I.U.	12,000 I.U.
B	3 grams	400 I.U.	15,000 I.U.
C	4 grams	600 I.U.	17,500 I.U.
D	4 grams	600 I.U.	18,000 I.U.
E	5 grams	600 I.U.	20,000 I.U.

* An entirely safe form of vitamin A

Vitamin A vs. Beta-carotene

You may wonder if there is something missing from this picture. Why don't I prescribe vitamin A? After all, A is important for keeping your skin, eyes, and the mucosal linings of your body healthy. Even your nails, glands, hair, and teeth need enough A to stay healthy and attractive. Studies show that four out of ten Ameri- cans—especially blacks and Hispanics—do not consume the RDA (Recommended Daily Allowance) for vitamin A.

However, vitamin A can also be toxic. Because this fat-soluble vitamin is stored in your fat and liver, it can build up to dangerously high levels. Too much vitamin A can create severe complications, like gout, anemia, and worse. Happily, there is a safer way to make sure you get enough.

"Better Than A": Beta-carotene

The truth is, not all vitamin A is created equal. Ready-made vitamin A, called retinol, comes from animal sources. Another form, the carotenoids, is present also in plants. The most important of carotenoids is beta-carotene. This orange chemical is a first-stage form of vitamin A, called a "precursor." Your body converts beta-carotene into the vitamin A it needs. That means you can make beta-carotene into the vitamin A, enjoy its vital youth benefits, yet avoid the possible toxicity of regular vitamin A. (One study, at Harvard University, had 11,000 physicians taking as much as 30 milligrams of beta-carotene each day. I don't recommend such huge doses—but when it comes to safety, 11,000 Harvard doctors can't be too wrong!)

The point is, your body will convert just how much beta-carotene it needs into usable vitamin A, while naturally protecting you against a toxic overdose. This makes beta-carotene an "A-Plus" nutrient—all the benefits of vitamin A PLUS complete safety. That's why you should get used to taking the harmless, beta-carotene form of vitamin A.

Beta-carotene, like the other skin nutrients vitamins E and C, is a powerful antioxidant. It fights the free radicals that cause aging in your skin and throughout your body. At Harvard researchers have shown that beta-carotene may prevent or slow the development of skin cancer. Not only does beta-carotene fight biological damage to our cells as we age, it has even been shown to extend life expectancy in animals, from mice to men. That's why you must make sure to get enough of it.

You can boost your beta-carotene by eating foods like those shown below:

BETA-CAROTENE-RICH FOODS

Beets	*Greens:*
Broccoli	Chicory
Butternut squash	Watercress

Carrots	Dandelion
Kale	Mustard
Parsnips	Radish
Pumpkins	Collard
Spinach	
Sweet potatoes	*Others:*
Tomatoes	Cantaloupe
	Papaya
	Vegetable soups
	Milk
	Fresh tomato sauce

If you follow the plan and eat at least one 3-ounce serving of green, red, or yellow vegetables a day, you'll be giving yourself enough beta-carotene to make your skin and your whole body look younger. Because beta-carotene helps protect against cancer and aging, it is one of the easiest and most delicious parts of your Youth Preservation prescription.

Summary Get sufficient vitamins C and E and beta-carotene from food and from the supplement regime I suggest, based on your Youth Preservation Category.

Step Five: The Sin of Sun

> Mad dogs and Englishmen
> go out in the midday sun.
> —Noel Coward

This step has little to do with research breakthroughs or exotic treatments. It's news you've surely heard before. Yet it is *your single best and most effective way to keep your skin young.* The tip? Stay out of the sun. Period.

Sunlight—that seemingly promotes a "healthy" tan—works like a destructive time machine, giving you the skin of a person many decades older. When rays of light enter the skin cells, they react with oxygen, creating the free radicals we discussed earlier. These unstable oxygen molecules, in turn, damage virtually every aspect of your cells: membranes, fats, the proteins the cells need to operate, and the DNA and RNA they need to replicate. This process, called "photoaging," damages your skin in ways that normal aging does not:

- Changing its color from rosy red to yellowish
- Toughening, roughening, and wrinkling extensively
- Spotting with brown patches, red spidery veins, and warty growths
- Accelerates by many times the normal loss of elasticity

Of course, this is just the damage you can see. At the same time, overexposure to the sun increases your risk for three kinds of skin cancer, one of which, malignant melanoma, is especially deadly. If you think you've heard most of this before, stay tuned anyway because you probably haven't heard about two new wrinkles under the sun—more reasons that scientists have found that sunlight is bad news for those who want young skin.

TRY THE "CHEEK-TO-CHEEK TEST"

Many of what we usually think of as the inevitable changes of aging are, in truth, the results of photoaging. You can see the dramatic proof of that through what I call the "cheek-to-cheek test." Compare the skin on your buttocks (that is, if you're not a habitual sunbather *au naturel*) with the skin on your face, arms, and hands. The skin that was covered shows what the "inevitable" and normal skin-aging process looks like. The difference between that and the more exposed skin areas is the price of indiscriminate photoaging—a price that is avoidable.

OZONE AND AGING

The ozone layer, ten to twenty miles above the planet's surface, may not seem very relevant to your life. But we now know it directly affects your chances of ending up with cancer and prematurely aged skin. The ozone layer works like a layer of sunscreen over the whole planet. This chemical blanket absorbs large amounts of ultraviolet radiation, preventing our sensitive skin from being bombarded by it.

Unfortunately, planet Earth's sunscreen is dissolving even as you read this. The protective ozone layer has decreased 3 percent in recent years, bringing a 15 percent rise in skin cancer cases. That means, 78,000 more people will get skin cancer, and more than 1,000 will die. It is because of the decrease in the ozone layer that the rate of skin cancer has never been higher. If the trend continues, as experts predict, we will see tens of thousands of new skin cancer cases, and thousands of needless, avoidable deaths.

Also, a Cornell Medical School study shows that too much sun can deplete your body's stores of the very beta-carotene that protects it. Another reason (if you needed one) to make sure you take adequate beta-carotene supplements.

Clearly, it is more important than ever to control the amount of sun your skin gets. However, that is probably not news to you. The real news is how to do it most effectively.

Summary Stay out of the sun as much as possible.

Step Six: Sunscreen, the Skin Savior

Most sunscreens do a good job of absorbing certain kinds of light rays—called "ultraviolet B (UVB)." That is the type of sunlight that gives you a burn. The UVB rays only penetrate your skin's top layers, and with most protective sunscreens, much of this radiation can be blocked. How much is blocked is what is meant by the sun protection factor (SPF) on the label of the bottle or tube.

But that's only half the story. Experts have recently come to understand that there is another villain responsible for sun aging,

Skin Penetration of Light Rays

Paba vs. Natural Melanin Ultraviolet Protection

ultraviolet A (UVA) light. Where the UVB rays penetrate only the top layers of the skin, the more powerful UVA rays penetrate even deeper, damaging the deepest layers of the skin and the supporting collagen tissues.

Unfortunately, many of the commercial sunscreens use PABA (para-aminobenzoic acid), which stops UVB but still lets most of the dangerous UVA penetrate to your skin's deepest levels. These creams prevent visible burning, so can lull you into a false sense of security: You stay out longer, exposed to harmful UVA rays. These rays not only increase the risk of skin cancer, but accelerate the aging of the deepest layers of the skin.

The only moderately effective sunscreens that work against UVA and UVB rays are those containing both PABA and a chemical called oxybenzone (by the time you read this, these preparations will be the majority on the market). Such "wide-spectrum" preparations represent the state-of-the-art in sun protection.

However, there is one thing you need to know about wide-spectrum creams. *The sun protection factor listed on the bottle or tube applies only to their UVB (sunburn) protection.* When it comes to the damaging UVA rays, their protection value is equivalent to about a 2. That means you have to use them with great care, for though they keep you from burning up to fifteen to thirty times longer, they only give you minimal protection against invisible aging damage, no matter what number is shown on the label. So, until more powerful wide-spectrum blockers are available, limiting sun exposure mechanically —with clothes, hats, and shade—is still the way to keep your skin supple, smooth, and young.

A NOTE ABOUT ALLERGIES . . .

You may have tried sunscreens with PABA or oxybenzone, found that you had a severe inflammation, or a burning or itching sensation when you went out into the sun, and concluded that you were allergic to PABA. You're probably half right—you may have an allergy but most likely, it's not to these ingredients. Laboratory tests show that fewer than one person in a thousand have documented allergic reactions to PABA.

But if you feel you are that one person, or you have especially sensitive skin that does have problems, you can shop around for products without PABA. It doesn't matter which other UVB sunscreen they contain: So long as you choose a suitable SPF, you'll be protected. I recommend that you try Sundown Broad Spectrum, because it uses titanium, which blocks UVA rays, and is free of PABA. However, if you have problems with one brand, always experiment with another until you find one you tolerate better.

Summary If you must be in the sun, use wide-spectrum sunscreens containing PABA and oxybenzone. If the PABA bothers your skin, switch to another sunscreen with an equal SPF number, and preferably one that contains oxybenzone for UVA protection.

Looking Ahead to Tomorrow's Breakthroughs . . .

Part of the task of this book is to alert you to research developments that, if they are not here yet, may be available soon. In the burgeoning field of anti-aging skin products, Retin-A represents only the first generation of true anti-aging treatments that actually reverse the process. The science of skin rejuvenation is exploding with even more exciting developments. As this book goes to press, a ferocious war is going on in research laboratories the world over to develop other, more powerful ways to rejuvenate the skin. Let me share with you some of the research breakthroughs that will change your life (or at least your skin's life) in the next few years. Remember —you heard it here first!

FACTOR X

From biomedical researchers in Denmark comes word of what may be the most promising new substance on the research horizon. Developed by the British biotechnology laboratory Senetek, it has a name that conjures images of secret laboratories and mysterious ingredients: Factor X. If early reports prove out, it may indeed be a stunning breakthrough in anti-aging treatment. Factor X may be nothing less than the biochemical fountain of youth that can prevent the changes that age causes in skin cell structure.

Normally, as the body's cells live longer, they change shape and their volume increases, so fewer of them can fit in the same space. The result is that the body's tissues become less compact—and biochemically less efficient. At the same time, older cells in the skin dramatically slow their production of critical cell proteins, such as elastin, that your skin needs to stay flexible, supple, and healthy.

Enter Factor X. When this extract is added to the cells and they are observed under a microscope, the changes that normally happen in older cells seem not to happen. They remain compact looking and, acting like younger cells, continue to churn out the critical proteins that help the skin stay young.

Clearly, such a product, if it proved viable, would represent a stunning breakthrough in the chemical treatment of aging—not just for the skin, but for cells throughout the body. Thus far, it is very hard to get much information about the project, and key details remain shrouded in secrecy. Dr. Nick Coppard, one of the biochemists in charge of the project, says only that they hope to begin human trials with an anti-aging skin lotion within the next year. They may have even begun by the time this book goes to press. Keep your eyes open for late-breaking news about how you can use Factor X to keep your skin looking younger, longer.

Looking ahead to future developments, there are several new products that could revolutionize how our skin ages.

Full-spectrum sunscreens that block the full range of skin-damaging ultraviolet light will be available. Versions of these that are already on the market are relatively crude; as we learn more about the UVA skin aging, we can expect to see safer and more effective sunscreens that will afford you high-range protection for the entire spectrum of ultraviolet radiation.

Genetically engineered sunscreen is being developed by a California laboratory called Advanced Polymer Systems. Utilizing a remarkable fusion of high-tech and natural approaches, this sunscreen contains the strongest natural sun protection known, the skin pigment melanin.

Melanin is the perfect sunscreen you would come up with if you were as smart as Mother Nature and had tens of millions of years to work in. This pigment shields you from wavelengths of ultraviolet light in direct proportion to their damaging effect on your skin. Studies show that black Africans, who have very high levels of natural melanin in their skin, have a "built-in" sun protection factor of 15. Soon, you may be able to benefit from the same protection.

Unfortunately, melanin has been too scarce to use—until now. California researchers have found a way to produce large quantities of natural, safe melanin using genetic engineering. However, melanin doesn't work effectively if you just slather it on, so other researchers have come up with an astonishing way to apply it where it does the most good.

They encapsulate it in tiny microscopic sponges, so infinitesimal that a single one measures about $1/1000$th of an inch and weighs about $1/4$ *billionth* of an ounce! These "microsponges" trap the genetically engineered melanin next to the skin, creating an effective, safe layer of the natural pigment that Nature meant you to have.

This radical approach promises a safer, more effective, natural sunscreen. Though the project is still on the drawing board, look for the first melanin products in the early 1990s.

Sun protection in a pill. What would have sounded like science fiction just a few years ago is being investigated and developed in research centers around the country. The goal: sunscreen products you swallow instead of applying.

Researchers at the University of Arizona Medical Center are working on a way to boost your body's own sun-protection mechanism: a tanning hormone that increases the natural melanin. They have created a superactive analog of a natural hormone called "melanocyte stimulating hormone" (MSH), which "instructs" the body to manufacture more pigment cells in the skin. Biochemically, it is the same reaction that occurs when a chameleon changes color—or when you get a natural tan. This hormone would make your skin look as if you had been at the beach all summer—but with none of the serious aging effects that would create. The goal is not just to make you look naturally healthy and fit (though you would), but to block sunlight so it doesn't penetrate to damage and age the deeper skin tissues. Early tests suggest that the hormone product is nontoxic and could be swallowed like a pill.

The protective tan MSH creates may last as long as several months—guarding you against the sun, reducing your risk of skin cancer, and giving you a glowing, appealing tan. The research is only in its earliest phase in animals, so don't expect to see these products on the market for at least six or seven years. But if MSH works, it will be among the hottest news on the scientific horizon.

Scientists at Harvard Medical School are trying a very different approach. Instead of blocking the sun from striking the skin cells, as with lotions, or filtering it with the skin's own pigment, they are trying to help the body repair the damage that light can cause within the skin itself. A photobiologist in Boston reports early laboratory research based on the theory of anti-oxidants, which are thought to be key to many of the body's aging processes. The goal is to neutralize the deadly oxygen by-products—the free radicals—which are created in your cells by exposure to ultraviolet light. Because free radicals cause skin aging, cross-linking, and skin cancer, researchers hope that by chemically inactivating these destructive oxygen molecules, tissue damage can be prevented before it happens. They envision using this kind of pill not as a replacement for the bottle of sunscreen at the beach, but as protection against limited short-duration exposures to sun.

"Sun protection in a pill" is one of the most exciting and creative ideas on the anti-aging horizon. Laboratories are trying to perfect the first generation of oral sun protectors. The medical evidence all points to one inescapable conclusion: *Within the next few years, we will have a stunning new array of tools that not only control, but reverse disfiguring skin aging.*

The Six-Step Skin-Care Program

However, in order to take full advantage of these new developments, you must do all you can now to keep your skin young, using every tool at your disposal today. Your prescription is to heed the six vital steps to skin rejuvenation . . . starting right now! Include these six crucial steps in your younger-skin regimen:

1. Ask your doctor if you are a candidate for Retin-A cream.
2. If you use a basic moisturizer, do it only for cosmetic, not thera-peutic, results.
3. Consider using a nutrient-enriched (vitamin C) skin cream.
4. Take an appropriate Youth Preservation nutrient regime (as de-termined by your personal Youth Preservation Quotient), and keep your diet high in beta-carotene.
5. Keep out of the sun as much as possible. Period.
6. If you use a sunblock, use one that contains a wide-spectrum PABA-oxybenzone agent.

6.

Young at Heart: Building Yourself a State-of-the-Art Heart

Heart disease before eighty is our own fault, not God's or Nature's will.

—Harvard University cardiac specialist Paul Dudley White, M.D.

Energy. Fitness. Vigor. They are synonymous with all it means to be youthful. For true biological youth has little to do with how many birthdays you have chalked up. What counts is your vitality, how you can bound up a flight of stairs or enjoy playing with a child or grandchild with energy and full enjoyment. It means waking to each day brimming with vigor and enthusiasm, knowing you can count on your body to perform what you demand of it, knowing it will deliver the energy, vitality, and stamina you need to lead an active life.

All of that depends on one muscle—the one beating in your chest right now. You are only as youthful as your heart is, and this essential muscle determines your vitality, how young you feel, and whether you will have the breath, energy, and stamina to meet life on your terms. It is an essential component not just of longevity, but of a truly healthy, vital existence.

A too-old heart makes you too old to enjoy the wonderful bounty that life holds for those who have the vitality to seize it. Premature heart aging robs more than five million Americans of this vitality, makes them sluggish and sedentary, and steals years from their productive, active lives. They weaken or die too young with a heart that is too old; the victims of 100 percent preventable, 100 percent unnecessary cardiovascular aging.

But this unnecessary killer disease doesn't happen so much to people in other societies, and it won't happen to you if you follow the guidelines I recommend. Below are the six easy steps you need to keep your heart strong and sound, pumping forcefully and faithfully, assuring you of decades of active, positive life. They are the state-of-the-medical art in preventive cardiology, geared to add several years to the life of your heart. Follow them and I promise you: One year from today, your heart will be "younger" than it is today. You will have a 100 percent state-of-the-art heart!

1. STOP SMOKING NOW, TO REJUVENATE YOUR HEART.
2. EAT A "HEART-SMART" DIET THAT REDUCES SATURATED FATS.
3. CONSUME FISH AS A MAIN MEAL AT LEAST TWICE WEEKLY. AVOID FRIED FISH.
4. EAT FIBER TO REDUCE FATS AND CHOLESTEROL.
5. TAKE TIME EACH DAY TO RELAX AND REDUCE STRESS.
6. GET MODERATE EXERCISE AND ACTIVITY SEVERAL TIMES A WEEK.

With these steps you can do *more* than just prevent your heart from aging. You can actually *reverse* destructive heart and artery changes that may have already occurred.

Much of this may sound familiar. That's fine. Our goal is to help you incorporate these cardio-fitness rules into a life-prolonging, health-prolonging plan—to make you 100 percent "young at heart."

A Heart Choice

It has been said that the average American's heart loses up to one third of its pumping capacity by age seventy. *But new research shows that such a cardiac decline is neither inevitable nor necessarily built in.* Maintain your heart right, and it will work about as well at age eighty as it did at twenty. Heart decay occurs, not because of normal aging, but because of a lifetime of cardiac ignorance, mistreatment, or abuse. It's up to you: Which lifeline do *you* want to be on?

Summary The loss of heart function with age is not "natural." It *is* preventable. Staying young at heart is up to you.

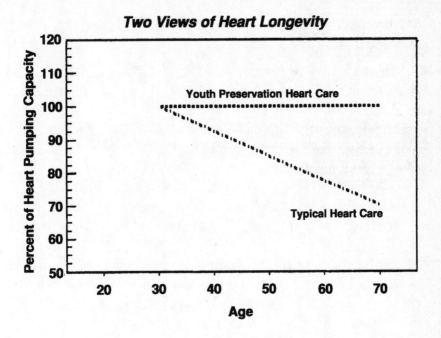

Two Views of Heart Longevity

Test Yourself: How Old Is Your Heart?

The greater your present risk for cardiac disease, the older the effective age of your heart and cardiovascular system. Are you:

Group A:

From a family with a history of heart disease?   _____
A smoker?   _____
With cholesterol above 230?   _____
With blood pressure above 140/90? (If so, see special
  note on page 111.)   _____

Group B:

A diabetic?   _____
More than 15% overweight?   _____
A survivor of one or more heart attacks?   _____
Ever diagnosed with angina?   _____
Suffering occasional sharp chest pains?   _____
A competitive, hard-driving personality?   _____
Sedentary and inactive?   _____

For each Yes answer in Group A, add two years to your cardiac age.
For each Yes answer in Group B, add one year to your cardiac age.

If you have any of the factors in Group A, your risk for having heart disease, and perhaps a heart attack, is two to four times higher than if you don't. The factors in Group B are less severe, but also increase your risk for heart disease. Combine factors in both groups, and the risk increases that much more. A person with high blood pressure and high cholesterol who smokes is *eight times* more likely to have a heart attack than one who has none of these factors.

The good news is that *you can change most of these factors*. You have the chance to reap the wonderful rewards of being youthful, energetic, and strong at heart for many years to come!

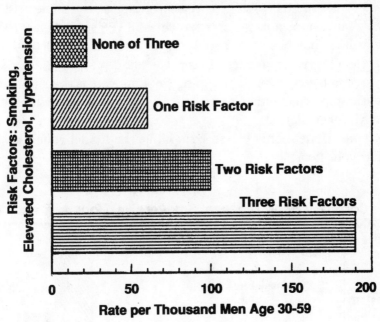

Risk Factors for Coronary Heart Disease

Risk Factors: Smoking, Elevated Cholesterol, Hypertension

None of Three

One Risk Factor

Two Risk Factors

Three Risk Factors

0   50   100   150   200

Rate per Thousand Men Age 30-59

Young-at-Heart Step One: Where There's Smoke, There's Danger

Do you know the *single most effective* way to reduce your heart's age? Stop smoking. Right now. There is no better way to dramatically and significantly lower the effective age of your entire cardiovascular system. Consider:

- The heart disease rate is twice as high in smokers than in non-smokers—four times as high for heavy smokers.
- Smokers are at higher risk for sudden death, heart attack, artery disease, and aneurysm, and are twice as likely to have a stroke as nonsmokers.
- Smoking ages virtually every part of the cardiovascular system prematurely and unnecessarily.

Happily, just as soon as you stop smoking, your risk begins dropping sharply; so that after five years you are at no higher risk for stroke than a nonsmoker. After ten years, if you smoked less than a pack a day, your heart risk would be virtually identical to that of someone who never smoked. *Every day you don't smoke, your heart heals itself and gets younger!* Stopping smoking *now* is the single most dramatic step you can take to make your cardiovascular system effectively younger. Period.

Summary The sooner you stop smoking, the sooner your body will rebuild your heart.

Coronary Heart Disease, Smokers vs. Nonsmokers

Young-at-Heart Step Two:
Clean out Those Pipes

> Diet can influence your long-term health prospects
> more than any other action. Of greatest concern is
> our intake of dietary fat for chronic diseases such as
> coronary artery disease . . . and strokes.
> —U.S. Surgeon General's
> Report on Nutrition
> and Health, 1988

The Surgeon General, our highest health authority, has finally said what many have known for some time: Diet is the most important tool against heart aging. National health authorities have now made "less fat" America's number-one diet priority.

Yet the National Institutes of Health reports that most Americans' cholesterol levels are still too high. That means that, although the basic goal is clear, people are confused about how to put dietary recommendations into practice. They hear "high-density lipoproteins" and "low-density lipoproteins"; "triglycerides" versus "cholesterol"; "saturated," "polyunsaturated," and "monosaturated" fats— and end up befuddled about what they ought to eat, *right now*, to make a difference.

Enough. If you want to keep your cardiovascular system young, if you want to enjoy the health and longevity advantages of a state-of-the-art heart, remember this one simple principle: *Keep your pipes clear and clean.*

A young circulatory system is one whose arterial pipelines are smooth and unblocked, with the least possible arterial thickening and blood-blocking plaque deposits. The cleaner, more fat-free you keep your blood, the more you reverse aging in arteries, veins, and heart. Every percent you lower your blood cholesterol means a 2 percent drop in your heart-attack risk. What could be simpler?

Below are nine basic diet principles, based on recommendations of the National Institutes of Health, the American Heart Association, and virtually every responsible cardio-health authority. Follow these rules, and every bite you take will help you strip away years from the biological age of your cardiovascular system.

This plan has helped thousands of my patients give themselves a cardiac "retread." It has given them state-of-the-art hearts to make them feel more buoyant and energetic, more alive and vigorous. They feel more alive, can exercise (some for the first time in years!) and have more energy for work, hobbies, and family. With these nine diet rules you can turn back the clock on aging, remove previously deposited fats from your artery walls, give your cardiovascular system a "retread"—and ensure a longer, more vigorous life. You can see why I want *you* to start experiencing such terrific benefits!

NINE DIET RULES FOR A STATE-OF-THE-ART HEART

1. Increase your intake of complex carbohydrates (starches).
2. Greatly reduce red meats and animal fats and trim off all visible fat.
3. Eat fewer eggs or eggs without the yolks.
4. Eat more fish. Try for three times each week.
5. When you do eat fats, make sure they are monosaturated, not saturated or polyunsaturated (see Appendix A, "Cardiac Longevity Foods").
6. Increase your fiber intake—whole grains, fresh fruits, and vegetables. You should eat fiber with every meal.
7. Reduce consumption of highly refined foods, including refined sugar.
8. Instead of fried foods, eat broiled, baked or boiled foods.
9. Reduce your intake of coffee.

Summary Reduce saturated fats and cholesterol in your diet.

Turning Back the Clock

By themselves, these tips aren't radical. What is radical is how they can actually reverse heart and arterial damage that may have already occurred, and effectively drop your cardiac age.

Cholesterol Transport in the Body

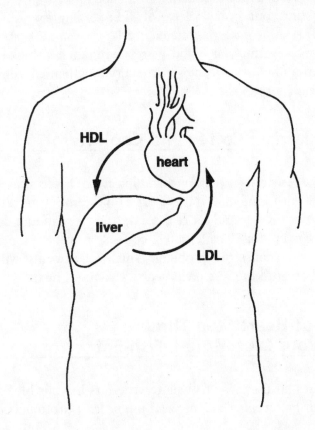

Let me explain. Cholesterol circulates in your body by piggy-backing on one of two one-way messengers: LDL (low-density lipo-protein) moves cholesterol from your liver to your tissues and organs (like your cardiac vessels); HDL (high-density lipoprotein) trans-ports it back. By changing the ratio of those elements, with more HDL carrying cholesterol back to the liver and less LDL carrying it out to the blood vessels, you can halt the process that ages the heart and arteries. The single best way to do that is through the ratio of saturated fat and cholesterol you eat.

Research shows that if you lower your LDL level to below 100, your body can actually start pulling deposited fats and cholesterol out of your blood vessel walls, so they can heal themselves and return to a smoother, "younger" state. That means heart rejuvenation, pure and simple, allowing your heart and arteries to function as long and well as Nature designed them to.

By lowering your total cholesterol and reducing your LDL, *you can actually reverse the damage accumulated before you ever picked up this book!* In six months your blood vessels will actually look smoother, more open and elastic—*younger* in every biochemical sense—than they are right now.

New Surprise: Coffee and Cholesterol?

Brand-new research in the *American Journal of Epidemiology* suggests that coffee drinking may raise your cholesterol. Interestingly, no such link has been found for tea, colas, or other caffeine-containing drinks, or even for decaffeinated coffee. However, something in coffee seems to cause this problem. Until we know just what it is, it appears that drinking less java means a younger heart.

Young-at-Heart Step Three: Make Your Diet More E-Fish-Ent

Next comes an easy way to balance the fats in your blood. *Starting today, with this evening's dinner, eat fish at least two times each week.* Doctor's orders.

Fish contains the best fats, the Omega-3 fatty acids, among them EPA (eicosapentaenoic acid) and DHA (docosahexaenoic acid). Among their many positive effects, they:

- Make your blood platelets less sticky
- Reduce several chemical steps that lead to arterial lesions
- Reduce LDL levels
- Reduce overall cholesterol
- Reduce blood pressure
- Minimize inflammation

They are your key to achieving a clean, smooth, youthful heart and blood system. You will greatly reduce your risk of early death from coronary disease. Fish oils have also been shown to help people who have had their arteries opened surgically to keep them clear, and young. Obviously, you should have your fish dishes broiled, baked, poached, or boiled—not fried.

Fish oil works best when it is eaten as fish rather than as pills. There is less risk of side effects or overdosing; you have one less pill to take, and using fish as your protein source means you will be eating less meat, whose saturated fats boost cholesterol. And fish is so much more delicious!

Summary Eat fish as a main meal at least twice weekly. Avoid fried fish.

Young-at-Heart Step Four: Fiber for Your Heart

You may think fiber helps with bowel regularity, or weight loss, or even as cancer protection—and it does. But it also reduces excess blood fats and cholesterol.

Fiber helps prevent your body from absorbing the wrong fats from foods. Its chemical and mechanical action sweeps unhealthy fats out of your intestines, reducing cholesterol that would otherwise gum up your blood, blood vessels, and heart.

People in societies that consume high levels of fiber have significantly younger hearts and low rates of cardiovascular aging. The Japanese, who eat more fiber per capita than any other nation, lose one seventh as many people to heart attacks as we do in the United States, which has one of the world's lowest rates of fiber consumption. In America vegetarians who eat a lot of fiber have less fat in their blood, and lower average blood pressures, than people with low-fiber intake. A high-fiber diet can lower triglycerides and cholesterol by one fifth to one third, slowing down the aging of your entire cardiac system.

When it comes to clearing out fat, not all fiber is created equal. I especially recommend:

- Soybean fiber, which has been shown to significantly decrease cholesterol in people with moderately high levels.

- Oat bran, which is also highly effective. Get in the habit of starting your day with a bowl of regular (not instant) oatmeal.
- Corn fiber, which is one of the newest food supplements, and has been shown to reduce cholesterol by an average of 20 percent, and other blood fats by more than 30 percent. Even better, this insoluble fiber has very few calories.
- Guar gum is another terrific blood fat-fighter. A Stanford University study shows that guar-gum supplements reduce both the overall cholesterol level and the specific type of cholesterol (LDL) most implicated in aging your heart and blood vessels. I have given many of my patients these supplements to reduce high cholesterol, blood fats, and with them, the age of their cardiovascular system.
- A natural fiber preparation called "psyllium hydrophilic mucilloid," available at your local pharmacy, is also effective in lowering cholesterol.

Other fiber sources that can extend the life of your heart are:

Fiber Sources to Fight Cardio-aging		
Fiber class	Found in these foods	Absorbs fats & cholesterol
Pectin	Apples, grapes, potatoes, squash, oranges, lemons, grapefruit	Yes
Gum	Oats, oat bran, barley, lentils, chick-peas, black-eyed peas, pinto beans, navy beans, split peas	Yes
Mucilage	Seeds	Yes

In addition, many fiber foods are good sources of vitamins, such as vitamin C and the B vitamin inositol, which your body needs to fight fats and cholesterol.

Diet Before Drugs

Eating the proper food is always your first and best line of defense against early heart aging. Only if you cannot achieve results with diet alone should your doctor prescribe drugs to help lower your cholesterol. Some of these drugs (called "bile-sequestrants," such as cholestyramine or colestipol) prevent the cholesterol from being absorbed from your digestive tract in the first place, and some of them (such as lovastatin) work in the bloodstream itself.

You should ask your doctor for the first kind. According to the National Heart, Lung, and Blood Institute, bile-sequestrant drugs should be the first treatment after diet; they are preferable to drugs that work in the bloodstream. If you must use medication, discuss the different options with your doctor.

But remember: By following the guidelines in this chapter, you should need no drugs at all. To get you started, I have included a special appendix section at the end of this book, with a specific state-of-the-art heart diet, and extensive information on heart-preservative fiber-rich foods.

Summary Use fiber and diet—not drugs—to reduce fats and cholesterol.

SPECIAL NOTE FOR HYPERTENSIVES . . .

We can't talk about keeping your heart young without a word about blood pressure. If you answered yes to the question about blood pressure in the self-test on page 102, you may be the one in six Americans who has hypertension. That puts you at higher risk for several diseases, including heart attack and stroke. In addition, your cardiovascular system is aging faster than it should.

Usually you can do something about high blood pressure. With your doctor's help, you can probably remove yourself from this risk group completely. But to start, here are three heart-helping hints to lower your blood pressure, your risk for stroke and heart attack—and your biological age.

BLOOD PRESSURE MYTH

Many people seem to think you can tell persons with high blood pressure because they are nervous, jittery, or tense. That is more myth than medicine. Hypertension and personality bear no relation to each other. People with high blood pressure can be tense and anxious or placid and laid-back.

First—Reduce the alcohol you drink. If it's two drinks a day, make it one. Try some nonalcoholic beverages, or dilute the alcohol you do drink with mixers. This is an absolutely necessary step to reducing the excess blood pressure that is prematurely aging your circulatory system.

Second—Stop using salt on your food, and start paying careful attention to the salt content of the prepared, frozen, and canned foods you eat. Make sodium-free salt substitutes a part of your diet. Expand your taste in seasoning to include garlic, onions, and herbs in place of salt in every dish. You've probably heard those two tips before (from your own physician, I hope!), but you may not have heard this final recommendation.

Third—Eat more fiber, the natural way to control blood pressure. It has been shown that when low-fiber eaters include more of it in their diet for one month, their blood pressure drops significantly. Many natural forms of fiber—vegetables and grains—also include minerals like magnesium, calcium, and potassium, which also help stabilize blood pressure.

All three of these heart-helping hints are essential to controlling this insidious and common factor responsible for aging your body before its time. After following these tips for a month, check yourself against the chart at right.

If your blood pressure is still too high, talk with your doctor to see if you are a candidate for blood-pressure-lowering medicine. Remember: You *can* eliminate high blood pressure, and by removing this premature aging factor from your life, you take a large step toward extending your most healthy and vigorous years.

Age	Average Male Blood Pressure	Average Female Blood Pressure
25	124/76 E	
30	125/76 E	
35	125/80 E	115/75 F
40	128/82 F 129/81 E	119/75 F
45	130/83 F	125/78 F
50	134/83	130/81 F
55	134/83 F	139/83 F
60	136/82 F 140/83 E	148/84 F

Young-at-Heart Step Five: A Calm Heart Is a Young Heart

The next step is both simple and very difficult. Relax. We have long known that too much stress puts you at risk for heart attack. Who can't recall being under stress and feeling their heart thumping or racing? Unfortunately, that is just the visible sign of the serious long-term effects stress puts on your heart:

- Men with what doctors term the "Type A" personality—hard-driving, impatient, achieving, competitive—are twice as likely to develop heart disease as their calmer, "Type B" fellows.
- Those who have lost a spouse to death are much more at risk for heart attack than are their same-age friends who have not experienced emotional trauma.
- Residents near major airports, living with the steady stress of aircraft noise, have high rates of heart disease and hypertension.
- From the *New England Journal of Medicine*, research shows that everyday stresses—acts as simple as talking about an emotional subject, doing math problems, or speaking in public—could trig-

ger episodes of oxygen deprivation and erratic heartbeat. Though silent and painless, these episodes are nonetheless damaging.

● As this chapter went to press, a report in the *American Heart Journal* showed that psychological stress can lead to heart-rhythm abnormalities, and even fatal heart malfunction.

The evidence is clear: Stress weakens your heart, aging it before its time. Heart youth means reducing stress, to rejuvenate your heart.

WHAT'S YOUR "STRESS LOAD"?

Stress is very individual. What may seem a killing amount for one person might seem just about average for a second, and not bother a third person at all. We even require a certain amount of stress in our lives to feel motivated and stimulated. It is not the absolute level of stress that counts, but how you experience it—your "stress load." This following quiz was designed for the U.S. Department of Health and Human Services to help you assess your stress load:

1. Do you have a supportive family?   Yes____(10)   No____(0)
2. Do you belong to a nonfamily social activity group, meeting at least once each month?   Yes____(10)   No____(0)
3. In a week, do you do something you really enjoy that is just for you?   Yes____(5)   No____(0)
4. At home, do you have a place to relax or be by yourself?   Yes____(10)   No____(0)
5. How often do you bring work home at night?   ____(multiply by −5)
6. Do you actively pursue a hobby?   Yes____(10)   No____(0)
7. Do you engage in deep relaxation (meditation, yoga, etc.) at least three times each week?   Yes____(15)   No____(0)

8. How many packs of cigarettes do you smoke each day? (multiply by 10)

None	＿＿
One	＿＿
Two	＿＿
Three or more	＿＿

9. How many evenings each week do you use a drug or a drink to help fall asleep?

＿＿(multiply by −5)

10. Do you use a drug or drinks to help calm down during the day?

＿＿(multiply by −10)

11. How many times do you exercise 30 minutes or longer in a given week?

I don't	＿＿(0)
One	＿＿(5)
Two	＿＿(10)
Three	＿＿(15)
Four or more	＿＿(20)

12. How many nutritionally balanced and wholesome meals do you eat each day?

None	＿＿(0)
One	＿＿(5)
Two	＿＿(10)
Three	＿＿(15)

13. Are you within five pounds of your "ideal" body weight for your age and bone type?

Yes＿＿(15) No＿＿(0)

14. Do you practice time management techniques in your daily life?

Yes＿＿(10) No＿＿(0)

TOTAL SCORE:＿＿＿＿＿

Scoring:

100–120   Congratulations! You take care of your stress load well enough that you are not a candidate for stress-related heart aging.

60–100   You deal with stress adequately, but you have room to improve. Your heart could be having stress damage.

Below 60   Your stress levels are unhealthy. You risk aging your heart prematurely.

*   *   *

Now, let's improve things. Go back and look at the test questions. Each suggests a way you can build stress out of your life and give yourself a younger heart! You might:

1. Take up a hobby you enjoy.
2. Join a group that lets you get out with friends regularly.
3. Work to bring yourself within five pounds of your "ideal" weight.
4. Do some form of deep relaxation (meditation, yoga, biofeedback, etc.)
5. Make sure you get exercise every few days.
6. Learn to eat nutritionally balanced and wholesome meals.
7. Take time each week to do something special just for yourself.
8. Create a place to relax or be by yourself at home or nearby.
9. Learn and use time management techniques in your daily life.
10. Stop smoking (but you knew that!).
11. Learn to use relaxation exercises instead of alcohol or drugs to unwind before sleep.
12. Don't bring work home at night.

Do such measures work? Yes, says an intriguing study released from the Medical School of Athens. Epidemiologists, ruling out other known risk factors, found that men who took a half-hour nap daily to control stress were 30 percent less likely to suffer from coronary disease than men who didn't! Studies at Harvard show that relaxation exercises can help regulate irregular heartbeats in people with heart damage. Obviously, you don't have to take a siesta each day religiously, but some form of stress control will help take years off your heart.

Summary Taking time each day to relax and reduce stress keeps your heart young.

Young-at-Heart Step Six: Exercise

This last is a very simple, and very essential, point. *Every hour that you sit or lie around instead of being active shortens your life.* Period. While almost every part of your body benefits from exercise, by far the most good comes in your heart and circulatory system. Exercise can:

- Reduce bad LDL fats and increase good HDL fats.
- Reduce blood pressure in sedentary people.
- Help vanquish angina (heart pain due to lack of oxygen).
- Lower the risk of heart attack by more than half.
- Decrease excess body fat, which otherwise weakens your heart and shortens your life.
- Help you live longer.

Workers in high-activity jobs have less coronary artery disease than their low-activity colleagues. In the words of one textbook: "When people remain active, their body . . . tends to resemble that of younger people." The research message is clear—need I say more?

Well, yes. There are two myths about exercise that may be preventing you from taking advantage of its full heart-rejuvenating potential. Let's put them to rest.

Exercise Myth #1: "You have to do serious aerobic workouts, marathons, and the like to benefit. I'm no athlete."

You don't have to be. The fact is, any exercise is better than none. Among the kinds of exercise that have been shown effective are:

Playing with children
Walking to errands
Cleaning windows
Vacuuming or mopping the floor
Bowling
Golf
Cleaning out the attic or cellar
Pruning trees
Body surfing

Gardening
Raking leaves
Dancing
Taking a hike
Playing
Climbing stairs
Mowing the lawn
Walking the dog
Swimming

This list proves the point: Any time spent being active is better than time spent not being active. If you expend even 1,000 calories each week above your daily needs, you begin to derive clear health benefits. You don't have to be a Greg Louganis or Carl Lewis, you just have to *not* be a couch potato. To be sure, if you are a more avid athlete, your potential benefit is that much greater. But just because you can't run a marathon is no reason to give up on the solid benefits of moderate activity to keep your heart young.

Exercise Myth #2: "I'm too old to exercise. I can't make up for a life of not exercising."

Banish another myth. In truth, a reasonable program of activity and exercise will make you younger at any age. Researchers from the Palo Alto (California) Clinic measured age against one common laboratory standard of aging, the maximum oxygen uptake (VO_2Max), and found:

> If an inactive 70-year old were to begin an exercise program of "moderate activity," the result would be a gain of 15 years. . . . If the subject were to achieve the "athlete" level of conditioning, there would be a potential improvement of *40 years* [emphasis in original].
>
> —*Journal of American Geriatrics*

If that can work for seventy-year olds, think what it can do for you! As I sat down to write this chapter, a study was just published from the famed Honolulu Heart Program at Kauakini Medical Center. They found that even among people forty-five to sixty-four years old, those who led active lives had almost one third less coronary heart disease than their inactive counterparts. Those men have functionally younger hearts, and can expect to live longer and better. Tennis, anyone?

Summary Moderate exercise and activity are crucial to giving yourself a state-of-the-art heart.

Looking Ahead:
Tomorrow's State-of-the-Art Heart

- One of the most innovative and exciting weapons in our fight against high cholesterol came recently when the FDA approved a new "cholesterol card" test. You simply prick your finger and squeeze a drop of blood on the card, which changes color to signal if your cholesterol levels are in the low/safe, medium/normal, or high/danger range. As of this writing, the card is available only to doctors. But there are plans to license it for home use as well, and I hope it will be available by the time you read this. It is a quick, almost painless, and inexpensive means of assessing your own cholesterol risk.

- From Boston University and Harvard medical schools, a new discovery uses the natural vegetable compound beta-carotene to boost the most advanced laser-surgery techniques for clogged arteries. Powerful laser scalpels have proven difficult to use to open clogged arteries because they can also damage the surrounding blood vessel walls. But by treating patients with beta-carotene before surgery, doctors can alter the fatty deposits in the heart arteries, making them more vulnerable to laser light. Combining this natural vitamin and high-tech lasers, surgeons can vaporize dangerous fat deposits more easily without harming adjacent blood vessel walls.

- Some 500,000 Americans have an inherited defect in their cholesterol regulation system that predisposes them to heart attack. At the University of California at San Diego, researchers are working on a gene transplant that would replace those defective genes with biologically correct ones. If the experiment works, they will be able to inject these "corrected" genes, to be incorporated into a person's own genetic code. The hope is that as these new genes grow to replace an individual's own faulty genes, they will help clear excess cholesterol from the body.

- Scientists at Johns Hopkins University are working to develop a new breed of diagnostic tool, a miniaturized electronic capsule that can be swallowed. Like a tiny internal satellite, once inside the body it sends radio signals that trace the heartbeat from the inside out. Such capsules may just be a first step: One day, electronics that you swallow may give you and your physician a more accurate, in-depth look at cardiac functioning than is now possible. The earliest prototypes may undergo testing in three years.

- Promising new drug research may hold good news for the sixty million Americans with high blood pressure. Radically different kinds of drugs, called "renin blockers," are now being perfected in Upjohn's research laboratories. They work on a new principle: They bind a million times more strongly to blood pressure enzymes than the body's own natural chemicals do, so they interfere with the runaway hypertension syndrome—before it turns dangerous. This drug may be generally available approximately five years from now.

Young-at-Heart Review

Remember the basic building blocks of a state-of-the-art heart:

1. THE LOSS OF HEART FUNCTION WITH AGE IS NOT "NATURAL." IT *IS* LARGELY PREVENTABLE.
2. STOP SMOKING NOW, TO REJUVENATE YOUR HEART.
3. REDUCE SATURATED FATS IN YOUR DIET.
4. EAT FISH AS A MAIN MEAL AT LEAST TWICE WEEKLY. AVOID FRIED FISH.
5. USE FIBER TO REDUCE FATS AND CHOLESTEROL.
6. TAKE TIME EACH DAY TO RELAX AND REDUCE STRESS.
7. GET MODERATE EXERCISE AND ACTIVITY SEVERAL TIMES A WEEK.

7.

Where There's Smoke . . . There's Aging

Cigarettes are the most important individual health risk in this country, responsible for more premature deaths and disability than any other known agent.
—C. Everett Koop, M.D.
U.S. Surgeon General

Welcome to the briefest chapter of this book. If you are one of the fifty-four million Americans who still smoke, I wrote it just for you. If you're not, you can read it if you wish or skip ahead to the next chapter.

You may not be surprised that the message of this short chapter can be reduced to two short words: Stop Now. Simply put, smoking is one of the most effective ways to age your body prematurely and cause you to die too young. *This means that to stop smoking is one of the most effective steps you can take to slow the aging process throughout your body.*

Smoking works against every single principle of this book, and defeats your goal of living longer and more healthily. If you have a two-pack-a-day habit, you have a 70 percent greater chance of dying of disease than your friends who don't smoke, and you can expect to shorten your life by eight to nine years. In this case, the charts on the next page are worth a thousand words.

I expect you already know all of this. But what you may not know is that there is a real silver lining for you behind these grim statistics. *As a smoker, you are in a unique position to make an immense positive change in your life expectancy.* If this book motivates you to do nothing but stop smoking, that one change means a 100 percent guaranteed, 100 percent positive impact on your longevity. By that single act, you will have won yourself more years of life and better years of health than through any other life change you can make.

Age That You Stop Smoking

Of course, it isn't just how long you live, but how well. By stopping smoking now you will have more stamina and endurance, clearer breathing, fewer infections and colds, younger-looking skin, and significantly better physical energy and vitality.

Summary Stopping smoking guarantees better health and longevity.

I don't want to dwell on what you've already heard about the dangers of smoking. Instead, I want to give you some information that you may not have heard—and a specific four-part program to help you stop.

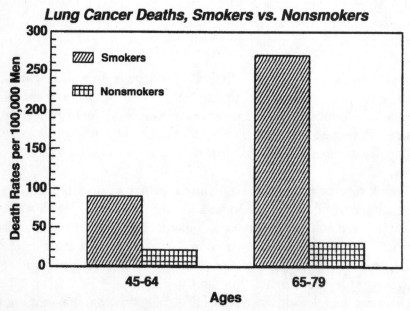

Lung Cancer Deaths, Smokers vs. Nonsmokers

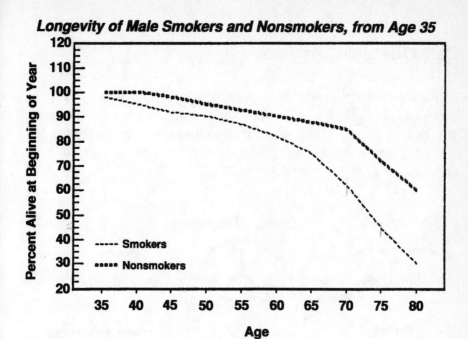

Longevity of Male Smokers and Nonsmokers, from Age 35

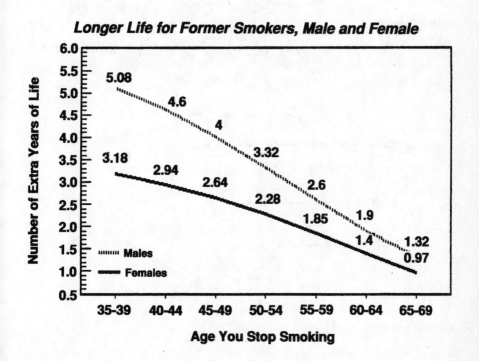

Longer Life for Former Smokers, Male and Female

Part One: Just the Facts

Research shows that accurate information is a big part of helping you stop smoking. So, your first step to enjoying a healthy, long, smoke-free life is to get the most well-rounded picture of what smoking does to your health. *This information is the first step in your commitment to stopping smoking.*

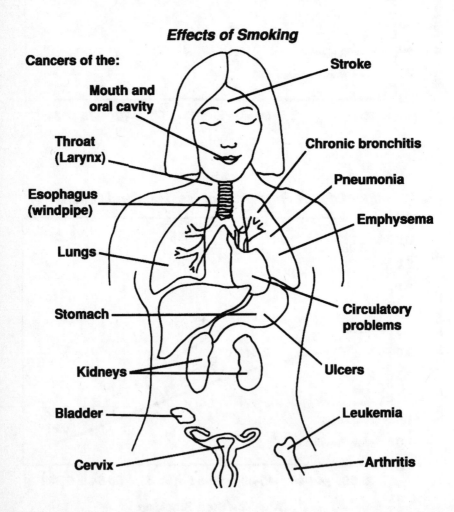

Effects of Smoking

Cancers of the:

Mouth and oral cavity

Throat (Larynx)

Esophagus (windpipe)

Lungs

Stomach

Kidneys

Bladder

Cervix

Stroke

Chronic bronchitis

Pneumonia

Emphysema

Circulatory problems

Ulcers

Leukemia

Arthritis

You know that quitting now will give you a younger heart and cardiovascular system. You probably know, too, that the same is true of your lungs. Because smoking increases your risk for lung cancer between ten and twenty-five times, stopping now removes you from these risk groups—increasing your longevity potential still further.

While stopping smoking rejuvenates your heart and lungs, and increases your life span, it also decreases the risks shown on page 124.

What better way to rejuvenate and protect so many areas of the body—Just Say No to Tobacco!

FOR MOTHERS ONLY

For pregnant women, smoking has special risks (below).

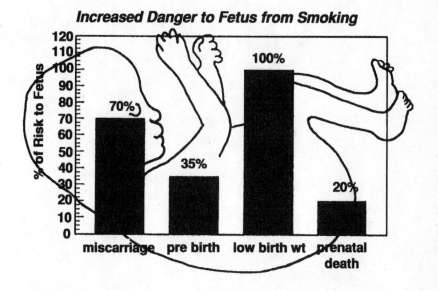

Increased Danger to Fetus from Smoking

Add these factors up, then figure in the severe aging effects smoking has on your heart and blood vessels, and you begin to see why it is the single most pernicious cause of early mortality we know, one that takes 315,000 lives every year. But more important, it points the way to *the obvious step you can take right now* to easily, simply, give yourself years of extra-quality life. Knowing the whole health story, you know that *you can choose to build these problems out of your life*. So what are you waiting for?

Summary Knowing all the facts is the first part to quitting.

Part Two: Addiction

So now you are convinced you should stop smoking. You're in good company—so have the thirty-seven million people who actually have dropped the habit in the last twenty years. However, what keeps one in three Americans smoking today is a question of addiction, pure and simple.

You don't need lectures about an addiction you can't help. What you need are some useful tools to help you break that addictive pattern, and give the single biggest boost to your longevity, vitality, and health. That means understanding your physiological relation to smoking—what it does to your body's biochemistry. This quiz was developed by the Public Health Service of the National Institutes of Health to help you gauge your nicotine tolerance.

NICOTINE TOLERANCE QUIZ

1. How soon after wakening do you first light a cigarette?
   A. Within 30 minutes
   B. After 30 minutes

2. Is it hard for you to obey the "no smoking" rules in areas like the doctor's office, theaters, or restaurants?
   A. No
   B. Yes

3. Which is the most satisfying cigarette you smoke all day?
   A. The first one of the day
   B. Some one other than the first

4. How many cigarettes do you smoke in a typical day?
   A. 1–15
   B. 16–25
   C. More than 25

5. Do you smoke more before noon than during the rest of the day?
   A. No
   B. Yes

6. Do you smoke when you are ill and staying in bed most of the day?
   A. Yes
   B. No

7. Is your cigarette brand's content of nicotine and tar:
   A. High (1.3 mg or more)
   B. Medium (1.0–1.2 mg)
   C. Low (0.9 mg or less?)

8. Do you inhale:
   A. Never
   B. Sometimes
   C. Always

Scoring:

1 A = 1 point, B = 0 point
2 A = 0 point, B = 1 point
3 A = 1 point, B = 0 point
4 A = 0 point, B = 1 point, C = 2 points
5 A = 0 point, B = 1 point
6 A = 1 point, B = 0 point
7 A = 2 points, B = 1 point, C = 0 point
8 A = 0 point, B = 1 point, C = 2 points

Total:____5____

If you score 6 points or more, consider yourself as tolerant to nicotine. For you, quitting may involve some degree of physical discomfort as your body adjusts.

If you score below 6 points, you are not likely to be physically addicted yet, so quitting should be easier.

Summary Knowing your physical tolerance is a necessary step so you know what to expect when you quit.

Part Three: What's in it for You?

Good—you have taken yet another step on your road to a smoke-free, youthful body. But as any smoker knows, physical needs are only a part of the picture. Now that you have assessed your physiological tolerance, this section will help you understand the psychological benefits you get out of smoking. The following is another test developed by the National Institutes of Health to help you do that. It is your next step. Make sure you answer every question by circling the number in the column that applies.

For each category below, a score of 11 or more is high, 8 to 10 is medium, and 7 or less is low.

Stimulation Category: Total your answers to A, G, and M. If the total is more than 9, you rely on cigarettes to stimulate and enliven you, to help you work, organize, or be creative. You are a good candidate for a substitute of another kind of "high": five minutes of exercise in your office, a brisk walk.

Tactile Category: Total your answers to B, H, and N. If the total is 9 or above, an important aspect of your smoking is the feel of it. Try substituting a pen or pencil, doodling, or occupying yourself with a small toy. You may want to squeeze a tennis ball or handgrip exerciser, or even hold a plastic cigarette.

Pleasure Category: Total your answers to C, I, and O. A high score suggests that you are one of the people for whom cigarettes provide some real pleasure. If this is you, you are a particularly good candidate to stop because you can substitute other pleasurable outlets—reasonable eating, or social, sports, or physical activities—for smoking.

Tension Category: Total your answers to D, J, and P. Those who score high here use tobacco as a crutch, to reduce negative feelings, relieve problems, much like a tranquilizer. You are likely to find it easy to quit when things are going well, but staying off is harder in bad times. For you, the key is to find other activities that also work to reduce negative feelings; dancing, meditation, yoga, sports or exercise, meals, or social activities work for many such smokers.

Addiction Category: Total your answers to E, K, and Q. Quitting is hard for those who score high in this group because you are probably psychologically addicted and crave cigarettes. You aren't likely to succeed by tapering off gradually. Instead, try smoking more than usual for a day or two, until the craving dulls, then drop it cold turkey, and *isolate yourself* from cigarettes for a long period. There is good news, though: Once your craving is broken, you are less likely to relapse because you won't want to go through that distress again.

Habit Category: Total your answers to F, L, and R. High scores indicate that you are a "reflex" smoker. For you, quitting may be relatively easy. Your goal is to break the link between smoking and your own triggering events—food, a cup of coffee, sitting down to work. Think of tapering off gradually. Each time you reach for a cigarette, stop and ask yourself *out loud:* "Do I really want this cigarette?" If you answer no, then skip it.

	Always	Usually	Sometimes	Seldom	Never
A. I smoke cigarettes to keep myself from slowing down.	5	4	3	2	1
B. Handling and touching a cigarette is part of enjoying smoking.	5	4	3	2	1
C. I feel pleasant and relaxed when I smoke.	5	4	3	2	1
D. I light up when I feel tense or mad about something.	5	4	3	2	1
E. When I run out of cigarettes, I can hardly stand it until I get more.	5	4	3	2	1
F. I smoke automatically, I am not always aware when I am smoking.	5	4	3	2	1
G. Smoking helps me feel stimulated, turned on, creative.	5	4	3	2	1
H. Part of my enjoyment comes in the steps I take to light up.	5	4	3	2	1
I. For me, cigarettes are simply pleasurable.	5	4	3	2	1
J. I light up when I feel upset or uncomfortable about something.	5	4	3	2	1
K. I am quite aware of it when I am not smoking a cigarette.	5	4	3	2	1
L. I may light up not realizing that I still have a cigarette burning in the ashtray.	5	4	3	2	1
M. I smoke because cigarettes give me a "lift."	5	4	3	2	1

	Always	Usually	Sometimes	Seldom	Never
N. Part of the pleasure of smoking is watching the smoke as I exhale.	5	4	3	2	(1)
O. I want a cigarette most when I am relaxed and comfortable.	5	4	(3)	2	1
P. I smoke when I am blue or want to take my mind off my worries.	(5)	4	3	2	1
Q. I get "hungry" for a cigarette when I have not smoked for a while.	(5)	4	3	2	1
R. I often find a cigarette in my mouth and don't remember putting it there.	5	4	3	2	(1)

The higher your score in each category, the more that factor plays a role in your smoking. If you score low in all the categories, you probably aren't a long-term smoker. Congratulations—you have the best chance of getting off and staying off.

Combined high scores across several categories suggest that you get several kinds of rewards from smoking. For you, stopping may mean you need to try several different tactics. Being a high scorer in both TENSION and ADDICTION is a particularly tough combination. You *can* quit—many such people have—but it may be more difficult for you than for others. If you score high in STIMULATION and ADDICTION, however, you may benefit from changing your patterns of smoking as you cut down. Smoke less often, or only smoke each cigarette partway, inhale less, use tapering filters or low-tar/nicotine brands.

Summary Knowing why you smoke will help you know how best to stop.

Part Four: How Best to Quit

Just as people smoke for different reasons, they also stop for different reasons and in different ways. Today, the field of smoking cessation has become a whole new topic of study among behavioral psychologists, psychiatrists, and practicing physicians. The range of possible interventions is both broad and effective, so that virtually every person who is motivated can find a way to stop.

For instance, you may not have fully appreciated the staggering range of techniques and approaches that have been tried. All are available to help you stop smoking:

Nicotine chewing gum*	Acupuncture
Graduated smoke filters	Individual therapy
Hypnosis (group or individual)*	Rapid smoking
Education/motivation lectures*	Relaxation therapy
Aversive conditioning	Electric shock therapy
Doctor's intervention	Satiation smoking*
Physician and psychologist intervention*	Group counseling
Medication	Stress management
Educational	Biofeedback
Self-help books	No-smoking clinics
Audio and videotapes	No-smoking contracts

Hundreds of test studies have shown that most of these methods help between one third and one half of their subjects to stop smoking. Only a handful of methods, those I have marked with an asterisk, seem to show greater-than-average effectiveness. Through all this research, several principles have become clear:

1. Different ways work for different people.
2. The best ways tend to combine several approaches.
3. Groups can be helpful.
4. If you can stay off cigarettes for a year, you probably won't relapse.
5. If you are sufficiently motivated to stop, you will.

Summary You can find an effective method to stop smoking.

Doing It Your Way . . .

Despite all these available avenues, research shows that most smokers simply prefer to kick the habit on their own, and that many millions have been successful doing so.

Here are the addresses of some of the best no-smoking programs and kits available, and those which you can usually obtain free of charge:

The American Cancer Society—7 Day Quitter's Guide
3340 Peachtree N.E.
Atlanta, GA 30326

Information Resources Branch
Office of Cancer Communications
National Cancer Institute
Building 31, Room 10A
Bethesda, MD 20892
or call: 1-800-4-CANCER

Your local chapter of The American Lung Association (listed in the White Pages) or:
The American Lung Association
P.O. Box 596DN
New York, NY 10001

You now possess everything that I can give you in a book to help you stop smoking. You have the basic information, data about your nicotine tolerance, a psychological smoking profile, and information about what means are available to help you stop. The next move is up to you. Take the single biggest step you can to promote your health, extend your life, and make sure the years you add to that life will be more worth living.

Keep in mind all you stand to gain:

- Better wind, stamina, and endurance
- Increased capacity for exercise
- Better and more restful sleep
- Fewer colds and infections
- Reduced respiratory symptoms (coughing, mucus, asthma)
- Stronger heart and circulatory system
- Reduced unsightly aging of the skin
- Lower risk of cancer and debilitating disease
- More energy and vitality
- Extra years of life

I hope you will do yourself the biggest health- and youth-preserving favor you can. Make today the first day of your wonderfully long, wonderfully healthy, *smoke-free* life.

In review, the key points of this chapter are:

1. STOPPING SMOKING GUARANTEES BETTER HEALTH AND LONGEVITY.
2. KNOWING ALL THE FACTS IS THE FIRST STEP TO QUITTING.
3. KNOWING YOUR PHYSICAL TOLERANCE HELPS YOU KNOW WHAT TO EXPECT WHEN YOU QUIT.
4. KNOWING WHY YOU SMOKE WILL HELP YOU KNOW HOW BEST TO STOP.
5. YOU CAN FIND AN EFFECTIVE METHOD TO STOP SMOKING.

8.

Keeping Your Bones Young

Can you recall how it felt to move when you were young? Think back to a time when your every movement seemed free, fluid, easy. Your gait had a buoyant energy, your walk was steady and vigorous. You stood erect and alert, yet relaxed. It felt natural to bend, reach, and flex with easy grace. You took for granted an energetic strength. In all of your motions, from the smallest gesture to the most athletic jump, you felt a wonderful, free confidence, knowing that your body would do what you asked without complaint.

One of the joys of youth is that we enjoy every ounce of the natural physical grace that Nature designed into our bodies. Yet too often, we see that grace and flexibility diminish as we age. It may start with creaks and stiffness in the joints, or the twinges of an ailing back. Gradually you feel your joints become stiffer and less pliant. Maybe you cut down on sports or any activity that requires significant movement. No more can you count on bursts of speed, for you have lost confidence in how your body will react. With the passing of each year, you may watch the person in the mirror become more stooped; your walk becomes stiffer and more halting. As this continues, bit by inevitable bit, you will eventually take on the cramped movements, unsteady gait, and stooped posture of an old person.

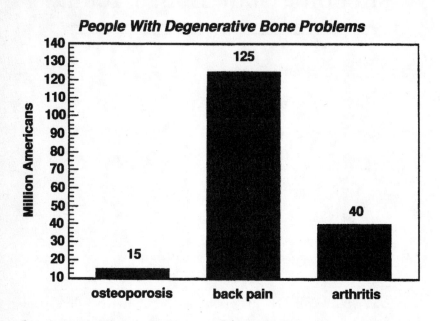

People With Degenerative Bone Problems

It is a rare adult indeed in this country who does not suffer from one or more common skeletal problems, including the stiffness and swollen joints of arthritis, the debilitating agony of lower back pain, or the bone-wasting syndrome of osteoporosis.

But that doesn't have to be your future. And it won't be because this chapter includes the four key "bone-builder" steps you need to keep your bones healthy, hard, and young for decades to come. These steps will help you prevent or forestall common degenerative problems that weaken your body's bony frame. These bone builders are your key to maintaining strength and youthful fitness, increasing your ease of movement, and generally keeping your frame young and supple. More than that, they are your assurance that you will retain the lively walk, grace of movement, and general vigor that spells YOUTH.

Modern laboratory research on nutrients and cell chemistry suggests that most skeletal aging that occurs is not only preventable but reversible. Scientists are learning how to keep our musculoskeletal system strong and supple far longer than we ever thought possible. With the right care and attention, you can expect to stay spry and active into your sixth, seventh, and eighth decades of life. However, to enjoy that kind of health twenty years from now means you have to take simple steps today.

The Basics on Bones

You may think of your bones as the rock-hard, permanent supports for your muscles and organs. That is only partly true. Biologically your bones are more like bank accounts in a constant state of shifting deposits and withdrawals. But instead of money, they bank the minerals your body needs: calcium, magnesium, phosphorus, silicon, fluoride, and copper.

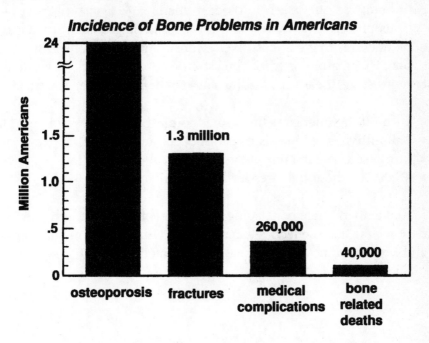

If you are in your midtwenties, those accounts are currently the strongest, and most mineral-rich, they will ever be. But by age forty, both men and women become less efficient at absorbing mineral nutrients from food. By age sixty-five, your body is only half as efficient as it once was. So, if it can't get minerals like calcium, magnesium, and potassium from the food you eat, it borrows them from your bones. As this borrowing syndrome continues, your bones become depleted, porous, and brittle, and you develop *osteoporosis*. Over a lifetime, this process can rob an average of 25 percent of your bones' density. *Bone aging is almost entirely due to the gradual loss of vital skeletal minerals.*

Porous bones age prematurely, collapsing and compacting. It becomes a particular problem in the spine; postmenopausal women lose up to 5 percent of spinal bone mass every year! Soon this aging actually shrinks the spinal column. By age seventy, the average American man can expect to lose as much as $2^3/4$ inches in height; women, a less drastic $1^7/8$ inches. The change can be sudden: The collapse of one cervical vertebra can cost you an inch in height in a week! As the spinal vertebrae collapse, you start to show the dowager's hump, so often seen in older women.

Osteoporosis is far more than just a cosmetic problem. It leads to bone fractures that can cost lives. More common than heart attack, stroke, rheumatoid arthritis, breast cancer, or diabetes, this silent, bone-wasting disease is a leading cause of death in older Americans.

- 24 million Americans have some form of osteoporosis (1 in 11).
- 1.3 million osteoporosis fractures occur annually.
- 1 in 5 of those fractures develop medical complications.
- 40,000 of those fractures lead to death.

Remember: Since bone aging means loss of bone strength, rejuvenating your bones effectively makes your entire skeleton younger— and keeps you moving well, easily, and safely.

Are You at Risk?

In order to keep your skeletal frame as young and strong as possible, your first step is to find out if you are a likely candidate for premature bone aging and weakening. Do you fit into any of these risk groups:

1. Are you a woman?
2. Do you have small bones and a slight build?
3. Are you of Asian or Latin American heritage?
4. Do you smoke?
5. Did you have menopause before forty-five?
6. Do you have light (blond or reddish) coloring or hair?
7. Are your eyes any color other than brown?
8. Did you ever take oral steroids (such as prednisone) for more than six months?
9. Did your mother or sister break a wrist, hip, or vertebra other than in a serious accident?
10. Do you drink a lot of coffee or cola?
11. Do you get almost no exercise at all?
12. Do you get highly strenuous and prolonged exercise or have you ever exercised so much that you stopped menstruating?
13. Have you ever suffered from anorexia or dieted so much that you stopped menstruating?
14. Have you ever suffered from alcoholism?
15. Do you have a visible spinal curvature (dowager's hump)?
16. Do you now take, or have you routinely taken, diuretics, insulin, steroids, antiulcer, anticoagulant, or anticonvulsant medicines?

A yes answer to one of the above questions suggests you could be at risk for osteoporosis, but if you answered yes to two, three, or more of them, you should definitely begin incorporating the bone builder hints as soon as possible.

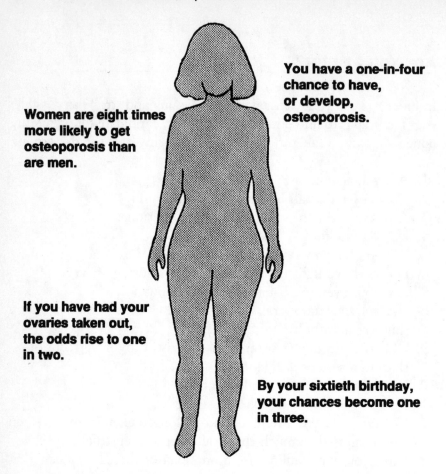

Women are eight times more likely to get osteoporosis than are men.

You have a one-in-four chance to have, or develop, osteoporosis.

If you have had your ovaries taken out, the odds rise to one in two.

By your sixtieth birthday, your chances become one in three.

AS A WOMAN:

- Women are eight times more likely to get osteoporosis than are men.
- You have a one-in-four chance to have, or develop, osteoporosis.
- By your sixtieth birthday, your chances become one in three.
- If you have had your ovaries taken out, the odds rise to one in two.

Bone Builder Step One: Micronutrients

The first step to rejuvenating your bones is a micronutrient plan to make sure you get all the minerals and vitamins your body needs. The plan starts with two essential bone-building vitamins. They work in different ways to help your bones maintain their strong, youthful mineral balance.

Daily Bone-Building Micronutrient Mix

Vitamin C	1gram
Vitamin D	400I.U.
Vitamin B_{12}	100mcg
Manganese	1mg

Next comes *calcium*. I recommend:

If You Are . . .	You Should Take:
Male:	1,000 mg
Female:	
Teens	1,200 mg
Premenopausal/taking estrogen	1,000 mg
Postmenopausal or over 60	1,500 mg
In a risk group:	
Fair-skinned Caucasian	1,500 mg
Asian	
Small-boned	
Smoker	
Drinks much alcohol	
Pregnant or nursing, 19 and older	1,400 mg
Pregnant or nursing, younger than 19	2,000 mg

Remember: Just taking calcium alone is not enough to reverse bone aging. But it is an essential component of any bone-building plan.

Bone Builder Step Two:
Eat the Right Minerals

The next step is to make certain that you get enough of certain bone-building minerals in the food you eat. That means eating a variety of whole foods that contain the following minerals to promote skeletal longevity.

Magnesium is a key bone builder. Unfortunately, most refined American diets are low in good sources of this vital mineral. Ironically, the diet your great-grandparents ate a century ago was two or three times richer in magnesium than diets today, thanks to all the magnesium-laden fresh vegetables and whole grains they ate. You should do the same.

Manganese also fights premature bone aging. I have listed some of the best manganese-rich foods below.

Boron. It is rare that we discover a wholly new nutrient, but that is what this bone-building mineral seems to be. The news on boron is by far the most exciting to appear on the bone-rejuvenation horizon recently. And recent it is—the pivotal findings about boron, its role in bone strengthening hitherto unsuspected, came just as I was assembling the research for this book!

A recent landmark study from the Grand Forks Human Nutrition Laboratory of the U.S. Department of Agriculture (USDA) shows that the mineral element boron, long overlooked, can play a key role in promoting and maintaining bone health—and in protecting our bones against aging and weakness.

This new bone builder is doubly powerful because it does double duty. First, it works as a team player, helping the body absorb other crucial bone-building nutrients from the food we eat. Research suggests that women who get enough boron in their food—3 milligrams per day, the amount you would get by eating moderate amounts of fresh fruits and vegetables—showed *significant improvement* in how their bodies absorbed calcium and magnesium. That means it works a bit like a catalyst—enough boron in your diet helps assure that your body will properly metabolize the other bone nutrients you need.

Boron also seems to work on another level, too. It can play a role in raising the levels of your hormones. This is helpful because these hormones, including estrogen and testosterone, are *directly related* to your bones' strength and resiliency. They are chemicals Nature uses to keep your bones healthy and young. That's why bone loss usually occurs after menopause, and why the most commonly accepted treatment for postmenopausal bone weakening is to prescribe female hormones. The hope is that boron may work to boost these hormone levels naturally, conferring the same kind of protection that hormone treatments would.

Because this news about boron is so recent, there is still much we have to learn about it. Laboratory scientists at USDA and elsewhere must determine optimal and safe boron-supplement levels. It may be that we can get enough boron from our diet, or that special supplements are recommended for people at risk for premature bone weakening. I expect that there will be a lot more news about this bone-longevity breakthrough appearing in research journals soon. I expect that boron will take its place in the bone-strengthening nutritional armamentarium within five years.

But you don't have to wait. You can start taking advantage of boron now—by including it in your diet, today. *The single best way to get enough boron* is to eat plenty of fresh fruits and fresh vegetables. They are Nature's prime, safe sources of this key bone builder. By eating a balanced diet of boron-rich foods, you can give yourself the same dose of boron that was used in the pioneering studies.

Below is a list of the best bone-building foods for an optimal balance of nutrients—including boron.

Good sources of:

Calcium: dairy products, low-fat yogurt, sardines (with bones), salmon, tofu, broccoli, spinach, collard greens, sesame seeds, seaweeds (used in Japanese cooking)

Magnesium: Dark green vegetables, broccoli, Brussels sprouts, spinach, dark-green lettuce

Manganese: Legumes, sunflower seeds, meat, dark-green lettuce, cloves, spinach, wheat germ, and black beans

Boron: Tofu, plums, peaches, grapes, raisins, apples, wine, prunes, almonds, pears, peanuts, dates, green leafy vegetables.

With all these minerals, the rule is "diet before drugs." Studies show that vegetarians suffer from osteoporosis much less than nonvegetarians. By including a good balance of fresh fruits and vegetables in your diet (which, of course, you are doing after having read the young-at-heart chapter) you will automatically—and deliciously!—help your bones get enough of the vital minerals they need to stay youthful and strong.

Bone Builder Step Three: Nutritional Tips

In addition to eating the right foods, here are some special dietary tips to help prevent destructive bone aging.

- Eat a lot of fiber, but in natural, not supplemented, forms: whole grains, brown rice, oatmeal, and bulgur are better than refined wheat bran.
- Limit the amount of concentrated animal protein you eat. A very high-protein diet causes minerals to be flushed from the body—among them bone minerals. A more balanced, lower-protein diet helps guard against mineral depletion.
- Drink fewer carbonated drinks. They are acidic, which can upset your mineral balance.
- Both rhubarb and spinach contain oxalic acid, which can block mineral absorption.
- Reduce alcohol consumption to avoid flushing out minerals.
- Cigarettes have been shown to reduce estrogen levels and hasten menopause—another great reason to stop smoking.
- Avoid special very low-calorie diets, especially those with incomplete nutrients (weight-loss powders, drinks, or one-item diet programs).

Bone Builder Step Four: Exercise

Exercise is the vital fourth component to adding years to the life of your bones. It is now generally accepted that certain kinds of weight-bearing exercise are Nature's way of keeping your bones strong, healthy, and young. Check the guide below.

Weight-Bearing Exercise	*Nonweight-Bearing Exercise*
Impact aerobics	Biking
Basketball	No-impact aerobics
Dancing	Swimming
Football	Yoga
Gymnastics	
Hiking	
Lacrosse	
Running	
Skiing	
Squash	
Tennis	
Volleyball	
Walking	
Weight lifting	

If you are not now exercising, you should start gradually. Your goal should be to exercise for an hour or so, three to four times each week. Whether that means a session at the spa, a brisk after-dinner walk, or a racquetball game with a friend, you will be making an important contribution to your body's longevity.

But remember: Exercise by itself won't dramatically reduce the effective age of your bones. However, taken along with supplements and dietary bone builders, it is of vital importance to prolonging the life of your skeleton.

Your Doctor Can Help

The four bone-building steps outlined above will almost certainly help you rejuvenate your bones, lower the effective age of your skeletal frame, and protect against bone aging. But the key is to start the steps early enough in life so that your bones have not already started to weaken. However, since you may have already suffered significant bone aging, and so may need even more help, your doctor has a large array of treatments to reverse this age-related weakening. Treatment options include:

Time-release sodium fluoride
Fluoride calcium therapy
Estrogen replacement
Low-dose estrogen and calcium
Parathyroid hormone
Calcitonin
Growth hormone

If you follow the bone-building steps I've described, especially if you start now, the odds are you will never need any medical treatment because you will have effectively reduced the age of your entire skeletal system.

Good-bye, Creaky Joints!

Scientists have described some 110 forms of arthritis, all of which can contribute to premature aging, loss of mobility, and to a general feeling of being old before your time. Arthritis is the most common chronic disease in men, and the single leading cause of disability in old age. So, if you want to ensure yourself a more mobile, more active, more youthful life, there are some tips that can help keep arthritis at bay.

Keeping your joints young and pain-free requires two kinds of attention: physical and dietary. First, let's get physical.

It is the large, weight-bearing joints—knees, hips, and spine—
that are most vulnerable to arthritis. That means you need to take
special care during activities that use those joints, and this should be
a focus of your arthritis-prevention efforts:

- *Sitting* places more stress and strain on the back than any other
  position. The basic law is: Don't sit longer than thirty minutes
  without getting up and stretching your back and legs. If your work
  involves sitting for long periods, make sure your chair supports
  your lower back, has armrests, and keeps your knees raised to a
  level slightly above your hips. If necessary, you may want to raise
  your feet on a small wooden box so that your knees are slightly
  higher than your hips.
- *Standing* can create joint stress as well. To relieve stress from
  standing, lift one leg so that hip and knee bend, and place one
  foot up on a short step or stool. After a few minutes, put that foot
  down and raise the other foot.
- *Lifting* often ignites serious lower-back pain. Always lift by bend-
  ing your knees and keep your back as straight as possible. Try to
  lift and carry objects close to your body.
- *Sleeping* can be the most restful position for various joints if it is
  done correctly. Lie on your back with one to two pillows under
  your knees so that your hips and knees are bent, or on your side
  with hips bent so that your knees are pulled up toward your chest
  (fetal position), and with a pillow placed between your knees.
- *Muscles, ligaments, and tendons lose fibers with age,* which restricts
  the movement of your joints. One way to avoid damaging those
  joints is always to begin any strenuous exercise with a warm-up
  period of slow, easy, gradual stretches.

Diet also plays a key role in the joint pain that makes you old and
creaky before your time. Your diet can help keep your joints young
and supple in the following ways:

- Fish oils work as anti-inflammatory agents, helping alleviate the
  pain and premature aging of arthritis. Fish oils don't actually
  lubricate the joints themselves, but they chemically change the
  blood and reduce the body's own chemicals that lead to painful

joint tenderness, swelling, and inflammation. Thus they break the chain of pain and inflammation that leads to arthritis. As we saw in the chapter on heart youth, you don't have to take fish oils in pill form; you will derive more overall benefit by eating fish. Certain varieties of fish have higher levels of the essential fatty acids that help protect your joints. Among the richest sources are: tuna, salmon, sardines, mackerel, sable, whitefish, bluefish, swordfish, rainbow trout, eels, herring, and squid.

- When it comes to keeping your joints young and agile, what you don't eat can be as important as what you do eat. It is clear that diet plays a role in preventing and relieving crippling arthritis pain. British researchers conducted a study on fifty-three patients with serious, crippling rheumatoid arthritis. When specific foods were eliminated from the diets of these patients, they reported "significant improvement" in joint symptoms. They had less morning stiffness, joint pain, and walked better. In other words— their joints and movement got effectively "younger."

I read about a mother of three children who suffered from progressive, crippling rheumatoid arthritis for some ten years. Then, her doctors asked her to abstain from eating dairy products, especially milk and cheese. Within three weeks her symptoms abated dramatically. For the first time in years, she was able to walk without pain, felt herself regaining strength in her hands, and could stop taking anti-inflammatory drugs. When, as a test, she started eating dairy products again, her severe arthritic symptoms returned within twelve hours. She has now been living symptom-free for several months.

You can put your diet to work in the same way to forestall the premature aging of joint pain. If arthritis is a problem, I suggest you avoid eating large quantities of foods in the nightshade family, since these are known to trigger or exacerbate joint inflammation. These foods include: zucchini, eggplants, tomatoes, bell peppers, white onions, potatoes, squash, and paprika.

- Incorporate this anti-arthritis formula into your daily plan:

Vitamin B$_3$ (niacinamide)	100 mg
Vitamin B$_{12}$	150 mcg

Vitamin B₅ (pantothenic acid)	250 mg
Vitamin B₆	100 mg
Vitamin C	3 grams
Zinc	75 mg
Evening primrose oil or linseed oil	Use in cooking and on salads

For a Better Back

You can't feel young with a crippled back. Today, 195 million Americans have had some back problems, and fully three in ten have a severe, chronic back ailment. These people know only too well that the agonizing pain of spinal or disk degeneration robs you of the freedom and movement of youth, casts a pall over your life, can even debilitate you.

To continue to enjoy the free and easy movement of youth during your whole lifetime, you have to avoid this most common crippling malady. Beginning on page 150 is a series of exercises and tips that you may want to incorporate into your daily regimen. These are used at the New York Hospital for Joint Diseases Orthopedic Institute, and were designed by Neil Kahanovitz, M.D., and Kathleen Viola, RPT. These exercises are your single best insurance against forfeiting youthful mobility to an aching back.

At the Medical Frontier

Here are some of the most exciting research developments that will be available soon to help us protect and rejuvenate our bones and joints, so we can keep our body moving easily and well throughout life:

Screening tests for bone aging are being perfected at Columbia University. A test, called a "GnRH-agonist test," has been developed that can reliably predict if a woman is likely to develop age-related bone wasting after menopause. The hope is that you could eventually get the test as part of a routine physical. A positive result would

PELVIC LIFT

Lie on your back. Bend both knees so feet are flat on the floor. Squeeze your buttocks together and lift your hips off the floor.

Objective: *to strengthen the buttock muscles.*

BACK STRENGTHENING EXERCISE

Assume all-four's position. Lift one arm and one leg on the opposite sides, hold and relax. Alternate sides.

Objective: *improve coordination balance and strength of the back and supportive muscles.*

PELVIC TILT

Lie on your back, knees bent, feet on the floor. Tighten the muscles in your stomach and squeeze your buttocks together, pushing your back into the floor.

Objective: *to strengthen the lower abdominal muscles.*

PECTORAL STRETCH

Stand facing a corner. Extend your arms and place your palms against the wall. With your body straight, lean toward the wall, keeping your legs straight and your heels firmly on the floor. Repeat, gradually increasing your distance from the wall.

Objective: *to stretch the chest and calf muscles.*

ARCH AND CURVE

Assume an all-four's position with your head in neutral position. Allow your back to arch. Then, curve your back upwards at the waist level, tightening your stomach muscles.

Objective: *to stretch and strengthen the back and abdominal muscles.*

alert you and your doctor that special treatment is necessary to keep your bones young and strong.

A tantalizing *bone-rejuvenation breakthrough* may depend on something as simple as the time of day, according to studies done by Dr. David Simmons, an orthopedic researcher at the University of Texas Medical Branch. There, doctors are exploiting the fluctuations of the body's own internal clock—what are called "circadian rhythms" —to keep bones at their strongest.

The researchers suspect that the peak time when the human body builds bone may be in the evening, before midnight. That's when the levels of crucial bone-forming hormones, such as parathyroid and growth hormones, are at their highest. (As parents and pediatricians know, nighttime is also when children suffer most from the growing pains that are linked to bone growth.)

This suggests that drugs that help to increase bone growth, like testosterone and estrogen, or to inhibit bone shrinkage, like calcitonin, may work more powerfully during prime time than during the wee hours of the morning or during the workday.

These discoveries suggest that one common medication used to reverse bone aging builds more bone when it is administered in the morning, has little effect when taken at noon, and may actually decrease bone strength when taken late in the day.

The idea is so new that researchers are testing it only in lab animals, comparing a medication schedule of 8:00 A.M., high noon, and 4:00 P.M. If the animals show a difference in bone growth, the findings could be applied to humans, who could take a pill or even an inhalable spray of bone-strengthening drugs at the most propitious hours.

This simple discovery could prove to be one of those buried nuggets of medical lore that need only a perceptive medical mind to unearth them. If it proves out, it will be significant news on the anti-aging front. Simply watching the clock might give us a new, entirely cost-free way to avoid, and treat, bone aging. The sophisticated notion of cooperating, not competing, with the body's own internal hormonal rhythms may suggest that we should eat certain bone-strengthening foods at certain meals, to ensure that their nutrients are available when our body needs them most to build strong bones.

A *new radiation drug*, dysprosium-165, promises relief to many of the six million sufferers of rheumatoid arthritis. Created by physicians in Boston, this short-lived, safe radioactive drug can be injected into damaged joints. It does with radiation what a surgeon would do with a scalpel, eliminating the damaged and inflamed tissue that creates crippling arthritis pain. Used in the knee joints, the procedure has relieved pain and restored free movement to more than three hundred patients so far, with virtually no side effects, for a fraction of the cost of surgery. It is now in clinical trials only in Boston and New York, but is hoped to become available to arthritis sufferers in fourteen major cities throughout the United States within the next year.

In Israel an *electronic therapy*, called "transcutaneous electrical nerve stimulation," is being studied to relieve arthritis pain. It appears that the electrical fields diminish the body's inflammatory process in arthritic joints, and so reduce joint pain.

But remember: Rather than use such futuristic developments to remedy joint and skeletal pain, you can use the tips in this chapter to keep your bones and muscles young, supple, and strong—and avoid problems altogether!

9.

Make Yourself Immune to Age

If you want to assure that you live a long, healthy life, nothing is more crucial than your immune system. This network of blood cells, antibodies, and chemicals is your body's protection against the diseases that age us all. It fights germs, from common bacteria to exotic parasites to the deadliest viruses. It is also your sole guardian against the malignant, often deadly, growth of cancer. Your immune system is all that stands between you and diseases that can sap your energy, threaten your life, and make your body weak and infirm many years too soon.

Unaided, your immune system will lose almost 90 percent of its strength between the ages of twenty and seventy. As the years pass and those losses accumulate, your dulled immune defenses allow you to catch infections more easily. The body's energy is sapped in a chronic low-level fight against illness. As it weakens further, you may be one of the approximately seventy-five million Americans who will develop cancer in their lifetime.

Immune Rejuvenation means turning that process around. And

you can. *There is no reason you can't have a superpotent immune system your whole life long.* By keeping your immune defenders intact and well armed, working at peak strength, you help make yourself "immune to age."

The steps in this chapter are drawn from several areas of research to help you do that. Some are based on the most complete findings about immune nutrients and anticancer diets published by the National Cancer Institute. Other suggestions in this chapter come from research being done, here and abroad, on how to strengthen the immune system of people suffering from the devastating disease AIDS. The "Antiviral Cocktail," which I will describe in this chapter, is based on findings from clinics and laboratories that show promise in helping strengthen the immune system. The intravenous vitamin C treatments are the ones that I am currently most excited about. Having used these with many, many patients, I have seen quite astounding results.

Together, these steps make up a solid prescription for immune longevity. That adds up to fewer infections, less debilitating illness, and less time wasted feeling subpar. Immune Rejuvenation is your biological insurance policy that you will fight off disease, stay strong against cancer, and always enjoy the high energy and radiant health that Nature gave you.

That is 100 percent achievable if you follow the basic steps outlined below. Remember: You can give your body's disease-fighting troops a big advantage in their effort to keep you healthy and youthful, free of diseases and full of vitality.

The three steps to keeping your immune system young are:

1. Build *out* cancer from your life.
2. Build *up* your immune system to keep it young and healthy.
3. Build *in* added protection against disease-causing viruses.

Step One: Eat to Conquer Cancer

Believe it or not, you can conquer cancer in your life. Right now, statistics show that you have a three-in-ten chance of getting cancer during your lifetime, and that someone in your family has a three-in-four chance of being touched by cancer. With odds like that, you could well be among the almost one million Americans who will be diagnosed with some form of cancer this year. But if you could *remove* yourself from the list of "cancer candidates," this would give a tremendous boost to both your longevity and the quality of your life.

You can avoid being a "cancer candidate." The National Cancer Institute estimates that 80 percent of all cancers come from how we live. We know an *enormous* amount about how to build cancer risk out of our lives. According to the *New England Journal of Medicine*, diet is "second only to cigarette smoking as a determinant of cancer in this country." So, *just by eliminating cancer-risk habits, you can give yourself an 80 percent chance of avoiding cancer entirely.* This one step alone potentially offers you several extra decades of productive, healthy life. Yet despite all we know, only one American in seven has ever discussed with a doctor about putting these principles to work in his/her own life. In 1988 a survey showed that while 68 percent of Americans believe there is a link between diet and cancer, the great majority don't know what to do about it.

Fortunately, you don't have to count yourself among them. That's because many of the same health tips we have already discussed— your keys to rejuvenating your skin, heart, and bones—dramatically lower your cancer risk. If you are:

- Eating more fiber . . .
- Eating less fat . . .
- Eating more mineral- and vitamin-rich fresh vegetables . . .
- Stopping smoking . . .
- Moderating alcohol consumption to a reasonable level . . .

. . . then congratulations! You have already taken the most significant and positive steps to put cancer out of your life!

Of these health tips, reducing fat is particularly crucial. It has been shown that lowering cholesterol levels help the phagocytes, a vital type of immune cell, and that a generally low-fat diet not only reduces the free radicals that cause cancer, but actually helps the immune system work better.

You should know about one other important anticancer counsel.

Make sure that you eat some of the following vegetables at least once each week:

Broccoli	Kale
Brussels sprouts	Kohlrabi
Cabbage	Mustard greens
Cauliflower	Rutabaga
Chinese cabbage	Turnips
Collards	

New research shows that these vegetables, which belong to the cruciferous family, contain chemical compounds called indoles, which are thought to help reduce cancer, particularly colon cancer.

By making these changes in your living habits, you will be doing exactly what the nation's foremost cancer experts, from the National Cancer Institute to the National Research Council to the Surgeon General himself, recommend. Before long, you will begin to reap the benefits: a younger heart, cleaner arteries, and stronger bones. But the best benefit is to your long-term health and peace of mind, for you will have cut your vulnerability to deadly cancer by a factor of eight or more, and made a major improvement in the quality and length of your life! Amazing, isn't it, how changing a few health habits can do so much good to so much of your body?

Step Two: Your Personal Nutrition Plan for Immune Youth

A change of diet is half the cancer battle. The other half involves a pro-active, balanced supplement plan to make sure that your cellular defense system has all the micronutrients it needs to fight off cancer and keep part of your immune armies strong. One way to do that is with a balanced program of antioxidant nutrients, to fight the biological changes that damage your immune system. Clearly, a finely tuned immune system is essential to radiant health and long life.

Which may be why women, who tend to have stronger immune systems than men, usually live longer.

Scientists at Memorial Sloan-Kettering Cancer Center in New York City have shown that nutritional deficiencies, especially of key immune-health nutrients, weaken the immune system. To keep your immune health at its youthful peak, your body's trillion or so immune cells need the right balance of vitamins, minerals, and amino acids. Yet study after study show that many millions of Americans are low on at least one key immune-boosting vitamin or mineral, like vitamin A, vitamin C, or zinc. It is no accident that the group with the lowest immune function—the elderly—is also the most likely to lack key immune nutrients. To avoid the premature aging that cripples so many people, here are the ingredients you need:

Vitamin A. Known to broadly strengthen the immune system, boost immune cells' reactions, and aid the body's fight against cancer, especially lung cancer. People who get more vitamin A have a lower incidence of cancer, and A specifically works as an antioxidant and anticarcinogen in the body. Instead of taking the pure form of A, which you can overdose on, I recommend beta-carotene, a harmless substance that your body converts into usable vitamin A.

Vitamin B_{12} (cobalamine). One of the most important of the B-vitamin family when taken for immune health. It helps immune cells directly, and low levels are known to impair immunity.

Vitamin C (ascorbic acid). The number-one immune-boosting vitamin, C is known to increase several different kinds of immune-cell components, strengthen the cellular arm of the immune defenses, and increase production of the body's natural germ-fighting chemical interferon.

Vitamin E (alpha tocopherol). Plays a crucial role in preventing cancer directly, neutralizing cancer-causing chemicals, and generally boosting the immune system, according to research from Harvard Medical School, Tufts Medical School, the U.S. Department of Agriculture, and many other laboratories. It strengthens both arms of the immune system, protects against infection, and soaks up dangerous cancer-causing chemicals in your cells. High levels of E can reverse the age-related decline in immune strength, and low levels are associated with increased cancer risk.

Selenium. One of the two key mineral protectors against cancer, according to research being conducted at the University of California and the National Cancer Institute. Like vitamin E, selenium has been found to increase immune response, and people living in areas with sufficient selenium in their diets show a lower cancer incidence.

Zinc. The other primary immune mineral. The *American Journal of Clinical Nutrition* and researchers at M.I.T. have reported that zinc is necessary for the body's overall immune strength and that it seems to enhance the vital immune cells lymphocytes. In particular, zinc helps the anticancer activity of the body's immune T cells.

Organic germanium. A powerful immune stimulant long used by the Japanese, which has only recently been introduced into this country. It boosts the body's levels of interferon, increases several kinds of immune cells, including the body's natural killer and macrophage cells, and acts as an antiviral. It also has been found to fight tumors in both humans and animals.

Now, let's put that general information to work so you can *greatly extend your young and healthy years.*

Youth-Preservation Immune Doses:	Your Correct Category:	
A	Beta-carotene	20,000 I.U.
	B_{12}	200 mcg
	Vitamin C	2,000 mg
	Vitamin E	400 I.U.
	Zinc	50 mg
	Selenium	100 mcg
	Organic germanium	150 mg
B	Beta-carotene	20,000 I.U.
	B_{12}	250 mcg
	Vitamin C	3,000 mg
	Vitamin E	400 I.U.
	Zinc	50 mg
	Selenium	150 mcg
	Organic germanium	200 mg

Youth-Preservation Immune Doses:	Your Correct Category:	
C*	Beta-carotene	25,000 I.U.
	B_{12}	300 mcg
	Vitamin C	4,000 mg
	Vitamin E	600 I.U.
	Zinc	75 mg
	Selenium	200 mcg
	Copper	0.1 mg
	Organic germanium	150 mg
D*	Beta-carotene	25,000 I.U.
	B_{12}	400 mcg
	Vitamin C	5,000 mg
	Vitamin E	600 I.U.
	Zinc	75 mg
	Selenium	200 mcg
	Copper	0.1 mg
	Organic germanium	300 mg
E*	Beta-carotene	30,000 I.U.
	B_{12}	500 mcg
	Vitamin C	6,000 mg
	Vitamin E	800 I.U.
	Zinc	100 mg
	Selenium	200 mcg
	Copper	0.2 mg
	Organic germanium	300 mg

* Important: For categories C, D, and E, take the dose for only three weeks, then go to category B for three weeks, then use category A levels for your maintenance dose.

Each of the steps I have discussed includes a basic combination of key immune micronutrients—vitamins, minerals, and amino acids. In Chapter 4 you established your Youth Preservation Category (see page 75). Use the level you achieved there to determine your correct immune-supplement regime.

"DRIP" Your Way to Immune Youth

Although most of this book is geared to things that you can do yourself at home, there is one powerful immune booster that you should know about, and that requires working with a physician. It is one I frequently use with my patients for its spectacular results in boosting immune function and effectively lowering immune age.

It involves many of the same immunonutrients listed in the table, but it is given in intravenous ("drip injection") form. The treatment has made a dramatic difference in a wide range of significant immune-related problems: the chronic, virally induced fatigue syndrome; the nearly ubiquitous infection of cytomegalovirus, which afflicts several million Americans; and long-term Epstein-Barr infection. These diseases can impair the absorption of vitamins, so that you are unable to take in the very nutrients you most need to fight off debilitating viruses.

To break this vicious viral cycle, a treatment was developed by Dr. Robert Cathcart, a pioneering orthopedic surgeon in California, who made his reputation as a premier orthopedic specialist at Stanford Medical Center. The treatment uses an injectable immune "cocktail" consisting of several key immune nutrients. I have found the best results by including vitamins C, B_5, and B_{12}, and zinc and manganese in the "cocktail." The elements must be carefully measured in appropriate proportions, and balanced and adjusted carefully to match the body's acid-alkaline chemistry. Then the mixture is gradually dripped into a vein in the arm. The treatment is painless, safe, and lasts only an hour or ninety minutes.

Similar intravenous immune-nutrient regimes are now being used internationally. Because these treatments can produce truly impressive changes in people's immune health, freeing them from chronic infections and illness, more and more doctors in the United States are using vitamin C intravenously in the fight against the immune-weakening diseases, including chronic viral infections, environmental and chemical allergies, AIDS, and cancer.

With my own patients, I have seen truly astounding improvements in overall vigor and health. They become seemingly younger and healthier in a matter of days with intravenous treatments. The results have brought about many complete cures among people who had tried numerous other approaches with no success. After a course of immune-boosting infusions, these patients have left my office, not only free of the viral disease that had plagued them for years, but with an immune system that is, in every functional way, stronger and dramatically rejuvenated.

I have taken drip injections to boost and strengthen my own immune system, and I urge you to think seriously about trying such treatments. If you are interested, look for a nutritionally aware physician in your area who can offer this nutrient-based intravenous approach.

Step Three: To Stay Young, Vanquish Viruses!

You have already seen how to conquer cancer and boost your overall immune power. You have come to the final frontier of true Immune Rejuvenation: vanquishing the viruses that age you too soon and too fast.

Viruses play a large part in how and why we lose function and age too soon. Each time a virus makes us sick, it ages our body. In part, at least, the reason that we lose function with age has to do with an accumulation of years of viral insults. I can't count how often I have heard patients say, "I haven't quite been the same ever since I was sick last winter." You may have said it yourself, feeling that some part of your vitality has disappeared in the wake of an infection, mononucleosis, or even a bad season of the winter flu. You may have witnessed how a particularly serious illness can age a person shockingly fast.

We are learning, too, that viruses play a much larger role than we ever suspected in a wide range of diseases, including:

- Chronic-fatigue syndrome
- Leukemia
- Epstein-Barr syndrome
- Cervical cancer
- Uterine cancer

- Burkitt's lymphoma
- Liver cancer
- Lymphoma
- Meningitis
- Herpes
- Encephalitis

Each illness takes a little extra toll on our overall health, and makes us look, act, and feel older. That, in turn, leaves us more vulnerable to the next viral attack.

With viruses at the root of so many illnesses, it follows that *the best way to break that cycle is to protect ourselves against them, so that they don't make us sick and old before our time.*

The best hope to do that comes from research on a new treatment for the deadly viral disease AIDS, and it involves a substance called "egg lecithin lipids" (you may also have heard it called AL-721). Developed in Israel, this food product—derived from three ingredients found in egg yolks—seems to work like a natural antiviral agent, helping to reverse the immune-system damage done by the AIDS virus. Some patients taking daily doses of the lecithin lipid paste report dramatic improvements in their immune system. It may work, in part, because it restores certain characteristics of young cell membranes and makes the cells' metabolism run more efficiently. There is much we still have to learn about the antiviral potential of lecithin lipids, and research is ongoing as I write this.

You don't have to have AIDS to put the antiviral power of this

"The Vicious Viral Cycle of Aging"

1. VIRAL INFECTION

2. ILLNESS

3. AGING

4. INCREASED SUSCEPTIBILITY

wonderful new treatment to work for you. Just as the "Antiviral Cocktail" shown below may work against the AIDS virus, it is believed to help control several other kinds of viruses—herpes, the ubiquitous cytomegalovirus, and the Epstein-Barr virus implicated in chronic-fatigue syndrome. Because all these viruses can damage your organs, sap your energy, and age you prematurely, it makes sense that an antiviral mixture can provide a good safeguard against their ravages.

Since the "Antiviral Cocktail" is made entirely from natural food products, it is very safe, and you can make your own "home brew" formula. For the lecithin, this version uses a soy product instead of cholesterol-laden eggs, and it doesn't carry a pharmaceutical brand name, but biologically it can be used as a generic, home-brew equivalent of the promising Israeli antiviral treatment.

Many of my patients have used this home-brew formula to derive many of the same beneficial antiviral effects of lecithin lipids. You should find that it can make a real difference in arming your body to fight the viruses that would otherwise accelerate your aging process.

"ANTIVIRAL COCKTAIL"

1. At a health-food store, purchase PC-55 lecithin, a high-strength soy-lecithin concentrate.
2. Add 1 tablespoon of PC-55 to 1 cup of orange or other fruit juice.
3. Let mixture sit 5 minutes, then blend until well mixed.
4. Add 1 generous tablespoon of olive oil or peanut oil, and blend thoroughly for several minutes.
5. The cocktail is best taken in the morning on an empty stomach. IT SHOULD NOT BE EATEN AS PART OF A BREAKFAST CONTAINING ANY FATS (eggs, whole milk, butter, margarine, cheese, or yogurt). You can drink it with fat-free cereals and 100 percent skim milk, or fresh fruit.
6. I recommend that you drink this mixture every third day. The vegetable oil should be kept in a refrigerator between uses. CAUTION: IF YOU HAVE CANCER AND ARE UNDERGOING TREATMENT FOR IT, OR HAVE HIGH CHOLESTEROL, YOU SHOULD NOT DRINK THIS COCKTAIL.

Tomorrow's Immune Health

By following the three-step process in this chapter—anticancer nutrition, immune boosters, and the "Antiviral Cocktail"—you will be doing everything now known about how to make your body's immune system younger, and your health more vital. Believe me, you will feel, and show, the results.

There is no other field where the changes are coming so quickly and dramatically as in immune health and rejuvenation. Among the developments that hold the most promise for the next five years:

At Harvard University Medical School, scientists have created what they call "antibody bridges," molecules that work like tiny guided missiles, attaching one end of themselves to cancerous cells that the immune system may miss. These molecules then attach their other end to killer immune cells, forming a bridge between the immune cell and the cancer cell. Then the killer immune cells activate and destroy the cancer cells before they can grow into a deadly tumor.

A major step in understanding the immune system occurred the week I sat down to write this chapter, when researchers at the University of California discovered a brand-new, unsuspected kind of immune helper cell. This fundamental biological discovery deepens our understanding about how the body fights bacteria and viruses, and will help us design more effective treatments against them and promote wound healing.

One of the best immune boosters now under investigation may be entirely natural, cost-free, and wonderfully enjoyable: that old standby, the belly laugh. For years, there have been anecdotes and books suggesting that laughter helps boost the immune system. Two new experiments have helped lend scientific proof to that assertion. In one, researchers measured the levels of immune proteins in the saliva of people before they watched a film of a hilarious stand-up comedian. The researchers found that the immune factors, essential components in the body's first-line defense against viruses, rose dramatically after the subjects viewed funny videos, and stayed stable after they viewed more serious videos.

This finding coincides with other research showing that students who scored highly on questionnaires designed to measure humor have higher levels of virus-fighting antibodies in their saliva than do their more sober friends, and tend to react to a funny film with pronounced changes in antibody levels.

One of the most intriguing avenues of research involves borrowing from Nature to restore youthful vigor and power to the immune system. The idea is simply to restore certain of the body's own chemicals, which are in abundance when the immune system is at its peak—in youth and adolescence—but which decline with age. Researchers at Veterans Administration hospitals in Wisconsin have found that the failing immune systems of elderly veterans are not fully capable of mounting a strong response when they are given seasonal influenza shots. However, their immunity was improved when the flu shots were "boosted" with a synthetic immune substance called "thymic hormone." This is based on a natural immune-boosting substance that a healthy body produces at high levels when young, but tapers off with age. Tests are under way to learn whether resupplying the body with this pro-immune hormone can effectively rejuvenate the age-weakened immune system.

Another hormone, called DHA, may also play a role as a potential immune regulator. At the University of Southwestern Texas Medical School, a researcher has already used it to extend the life spans of laboratory animals. This scientist took a breed of mouse with the inborn immune disease systemic lupus erythematosus, which usually begins to die after six months of life, and injected the mice with DHA hormone. About half the mice survived as long as ordinary, disease-free mice—and even longer. Other reports suggest that the same hormone also extends the life span of immunodeficient animals. The next step is to test DHA in animals with an AIDS-like immune condition. These studies offer hope that the answer to revitalizing the age-weakened immune system may be largely a matter of putting back hormones that age has taken away.

Scientists have long argued that the blueprints for how we age are written in our DNA. They suggest that a genetic self-destruct mechanism built into our cells affects crucial bodily processes, creating aging and even death. If that is true, researchers hope, then we can isolate those genes and actually manipulate the aging centers that right now are ticking away in our body's cells. Researchers in Irvine, California, have taken a major step to doing just that. They have studied the genetic code of a simple creature, a roundworm, and have determined a single, crucial gene, labeled "Age-1 (hx 546)." When researchers changed that one gene and reimplanted it into a generation of worms, those worms lived two thirds longer than their ordinary siblings. That's the equivalent of a human being able to live 125 years! The research is a terrifically exciting first step, as it suggests where we can look to find similar genes in humans. One of the researchers predicts "a huge payoff twenty years down the road." The next step to be taken by the National Institute on Aging is to apply this same finding to other, more complex animals. If that experiment succeeds, it will bring us one step closer to being able to do it for the most complex animal of all—*you.*

10.

Smart Beyond Your Years: Making Your Brain Younger

Any adult who has spent time with teenagers can't help but feel a certain envy of their sheer, clear brainpower. At such a young age, before the predations of age, disease, and chemicals have set in, their minds seem to function at a biological peak. They work like natural learning machines, effortlessly absorbing facts and impressions instantly. Unlike adults, they rarely grope for a name or recollection. Their brains are razor-sharp and retentive; new intellectual challenges, whether learning a language or memorizing information for an exam, come with ease.

Few of us keep that keen mental edge. As the years pass, our mental faculties seem to lose their original power, clarity, and speed. Subtle errors creep in; a stealthy forgetfulness, a creeping inattention appear in our third decade. Names, facts, and ideas take longer to recall, and we cannot absorb, retain, and remember things in the same effortless way we once did. To ease the load on our mind and memory, we surround ourselves with various devices like Rolodexes, calendars, calculators.

But it doesn't have to be this way. By using the newest brain-youth tools you can do much to retain sharp, youthful brain and mental functions. A host of research teams has shown that you can bring your brain to its biological maximum, stimulate greater alertness, heightened concentration, and a surer, more confident recall. With no pain and no expensive treatments, you can give yourself a functionally younger brain, regain the mental powers you once took for granted, and enjoy the benefits longer than you ever thought possible. That is, you can be smart beyond your years.

The real excitement comes when the experts show that it is possible to retain our intellectual faculties until a very advanced age, and even to reverse certain intellectual declines that have already started. Keeping your brain young is essential to reaping the rewards of an alert, enjoyable life. That is the life you deserve, brimming with interest, opportunity, and spice. The Youth Preservation tools that follow will help you keep your brain finely tuned, retentive, and sharp.

Young Between the Ears

You need to know something of the physical changes that occur in that gray globe between your ears as you age. Over the next few decades, your brain will shrink constantly. It will lose neurons, those connections between brain cells that allow you to think, feel, reason, even to understand the words on this page. By age seventy, most people have lost more than one billion of their ten billion nerve cells. By age ninety, some parts of your brain may have lost up to 40 percent of their nerve-cell connections!

Happily, though, we don't lose 40 percent of our brainpower. If we did, we'd be in real trouble. Nature has cleverly designed it so that as some brain cells die, the remaining ones actually expand, filling in and making new nerve connections to fill the gaps. The medical name for this process is "reactive synaptogenesis," or "resprouting," but you can think of it as just like a forest—as one tree falls, its neighbors expand, their branches taking over, enlarging to fill the vacant space. In the amazingly complex forest of your brain, that same process is occurring right now as new cells expand to make new connections and take over functions that are lost when old cells die.

New research has even indicated that the devastating changes of Alzheimer's disease may simply be an acceleration of the normal aging process that happens to us all—only the thinning out of the nerve synapses is magnified and speeded up to a tragic degree.

This means that the first step to keeping your brain strong and youthful must occur at a physical level. You must use diet and nutritional tools to slow the rate of the cellular changes in your brain, reduce brain-cell loss, and encourage regrowth of cells.

Step One: Food for Thought

It has been proven that nutritional status affects brain function. Therefore, the first step to keeping your brain working at full, youthful efficiency is to get adequate nutritional support. Here are certain nutritional basics to give your brain the maximum chance to stay young:

- High levels of dietary fat have been shown to lower brain function in animals—yet more evidence that it is a good idea to keep dietary-fat levels low.
- Antioxidants seem to play a clear role in keeping your brain at its peak. The brain has many fat-containing cells, which are particularly vulnerable to the oxidation damage caused by free radicals, which increase with age in the brain and cause certain brain-aging changes. A solid regime of antioxidants—beta-carotene, vitamins C and E, zinc, and selenium—can inactivate those destructive chemicals and prevent the premature aging of brain cells.
- Zinc is essential to the growth, development, and functioning of the brain. Levels of the mineral affect neurotransmitters, brain wave patterns, the brain's physical structures, even the thinking process. As brain cells are lost with age, they need to be rejuvenated, so adequate zinc is essential for lasting brain health.
- Lecithin is a food product containing choline, which has been shown repeatedly to improve mental-test results, help memory,

and maximize brain function. In experiments, doses of choline made animals actually perform like much younger animals on mental tests! Lecithin seems to work by increasing one of the brain's key neurotransmitters, acetylcholine.

Of course, all these nutritional basics share one thing in common: You should already be following them. Zinc, lecithin, antioxidants, less fat in the diet—each of these counsels also appeared in the chapters on immune youth and cardiac rejuvenation. So, by following the programs already outlined, you will also be helping to keep your brain young—all with no extra work!

There are three other brain-boosting tips you should know about:

- The B vitamins—especially B_3, B_5, B_6, B_{12}, thiamine, and folacin —are critical to healthy brain functioning. They have been found to protect against mental slowness, memory defects, and mood disorders. Studies are now showing that deficiencies of B vitamins may impair recent memory, produce depression, create apprehension, hyperirritability, and emotional instability. These deficiencies appear to be much more common among older Americans than we have ever recognized. It may be more than a coincidence that this is exactly the group with the most serious problems in mental functioning. For that reason, I prescribe a solid B-complex vitamin supplement to many of my patients of all ages.
- Copper, iodine, and manganese are critical brain-nutrient minerals. They can affect brain functioning and mood, boost mental alertness and sharpness, improve memory, reduce nervous anxiety, and generally keep the mental status stable. Accordingly, make sure your diet includes foods that are a good source of these minerals, including dried beans, peas, shrimp, oysters and most seafood, seaweed, onions, whole grains (including the bran), green leafy vegetables, prunes, dark chocolate, seeds, nuts, fruits, and many other unprocessed foods.

Metals and Memory

Of course, not all minerals help the brain. The "heavy metals"—among them aluminum, mercury, lead, and cadmium—can be very toxic to the brain. Lead poisoning can cause mental sluggishness and even retardation. Cadmium can lead to significant memory loss and diminished mental function. Both aluminum and cadmium are thought to be factors in the tragic brain-wasting of Alzheimer's disease. Memory problems can be a symptom of heavy-metal poisoning, which you may be exposed to in many ways. Do you:

- Live in an area with a lot of environmental pollution, including smog or smoke?
- Live next to a major roadway or airport? German researchers have found that people living next to roadways have dangerously high levels of lead.
- Cook or eat food from aluminum pots or use aluminum foil? Certain acidic foods—tomato juice, lemonade, vinegar, orange juice—can draw the aluminum into them.
- Use ceramic bowls and dishes? Glazes used in some pottery can leach lead into certain foods.
- Have silver fillings in your mouth? Scientists in The Netherlands show that tooth fillings can release toxic metals into the body.
- Regularly take over-the-counter antacid remedies? If so, look on the label: One of the main ingredients is aluminum. If you've been taking them for a long time, you can be getting too much aluminum.
- Use an aluminum-containing antiperspirant? If so, you may be chronically absorbing excess aluminum through your skin.

If you fit into several of these categories, I recommend that you go on a special detoxifying regimen, in addition to the supplements we discussed earlier, to help keep your brain young and clear. This once-a-day, four-week program will help clear out heavy-metal residues before they can create a toxic buildup in your brain. Take

50 milligrams of glutathione
500 milligrams of cysteine

These amino acids bind heavy metals to help your body flush
them out. The vitamin C and selenium that you are already taking
will also help remove lead from your brain, and help your body
eliminate heavy metals.

Step Two: Train Your Brain

The nutritional counsels above are only half the solution. With
them, you have started to make your brain more physically youthful.
Now comes the next step: to keep your brain young and to realize its
maximum biological potential. That requires mental exercises and
imagery to constantly train, expand, and hone the brain.

Modern research suggests that we need to exercise our brain to
stay youthful and strong. We know that such training has a profound
impact on how much, and how fast, our brain ages—or, better, on
how young it stays. This process—termed "cognitive training"—is
the best way to maximize our biological potential and keep our brain
strong and sharp far longer than otherwise. The most exciting studies show that you can even *reverse* the brain's physical deterioration
that may have already started!

- A score of research papers have shown that continual brain training and learning can offset and even reverse brain aging. Older
  animals that live in rich and varied environments, with the opportunity for constant learning, actually show organic changes in
  their brains. The nerve connections grow more complex, with
  more synapses, and more closely resemble the brains of healthy
  younger animals.
- A study of four thousand older volunteers showed that many of
  them could greatly improve two kinds of brain skills that had
  declined with age, simply by using brain-training techniques. Two
  out of five subjects made so much progress that they actually
  regained the performance levels they had shown fourteen years

earlier, in effect turning back the clock a decade and a half in their brain's functional age!

- A report by a National Institute on Aging task force showed that one in five older people with intellectual impairment may be able to reverse the downward slide.
- Cognitive training was found to increase older people's accuracy on standard mental-function tests, so they scored as though they were "younger."

The picture is clear: You don't have to lose brainpower as you age, and some of what you may have lost already can be retrieved and retrained. Rather, our intellectual skills, like muscles, seem to atrophy with disuse. Just as we need a physical workout, we need a mental one as well. With sufficient practice and stimulation, you can do much to reverse the "inevitable" mental declines of old age.

Putting It to Work for You

How can you take advantage of these new findings, and give your brain the mental workout it needs to stay younger, stronger, and more alert? One good way is by taking tests designed to sharpen specific skills of spatial orientation and inductive reasoning. Research suggests that practicing on such tests can help you sharpen those skills, and effectively lower the functional age of your brain.

Just doing these tests one time won't, of course, take years off the age of your brain. The key is consistency. You need to build into your life these kind of challenging mental exercises on a regular basis. There are several ways I tell my patients to do that:

- Get in the habit of doing games, tests, quizzes, puzzles, or brain twisters. You can pick up a collection at your local bookstore. Scrabble, word jumbles, acrostics, even crossword puzzles give the brain necessary exercise. Card games are particularly helpful for training reasoning and retention.
- Take a course at a local college or adult-education center. The practice you get in memorization, inductive or deductive reason-

ing, spatial orientation, or calculation will help give you the
mental exercise you need.

- Pick up any one of the scores of preparation books for the SAT or
  other standardized scholastic tests. They are treasure troves of
  exactly the kind of varied, stimulating mental exercises that can
  help your brain stay young.
- If there is a university near you, its psychology department may
  have a specialist in psychometric testing. He or she may be able to
  help you obtain hundreds of brain-expanding tests and test instruments.
- Look in the "psychometrics" section of your local library for test
  instruments you can use as brain-training tools.

Step Three: "Memory Magnifiers"

There is no more important way to keep your brain young and
powerful than to boost the power of your memory. Loss of memory is
the first sign we associate with failing faculties, and a good memory
is one of the most impressive aspects of clear mental functioning as
we grow older. Happily, it is also one of the mental processes on
which you can have the most significant, and dramatic, impact.

To boost memory requires no specialized tests at all. Here are four
"memory magnifier" techniques that you can do on your own, as you
go about your everyday life, with no tools or expense. Practice them
and apply them diligently, and you can expect to see a dramatic rise
in your retention and recollection abilities.

Mnemonics and acronyms are the techniques of creating a word
or sentence, each letter of which stands for one of the words you
want to recall. Every Good Boy Does Fine has enabled countless
music students to remember the letters of the treble clef musical staff
E, G, B, D, F. This technique is used by every doctor to survive
medical school. To retain the overwhelming crush of information
physicians required—such as the names of the myriad nerves serving one part of the face—you make up a word whose letters are
associated with each item. This technique works well with a shop-

ping list, the names of your spouses or extended relatives, the signs of the zodiac, your boss's children.

Rhyme association. Who can forget the first-grade spelling rule "I before E except after C"? And who hasn't reckoned the length of months by repeating "Thirty days hath September . . ."? The trick still works: Match an item you want to recall with a rhyming word, and you won't forget it. For best results, make up your own personal rhyme: ["Mish, mash, take out the trash."]

Visual association. Pairing each item you want to recall with an associated visual cue is a powerful memory builder. You'll remember Mrs. Greenbottom, Mr. Brooks, and Ms. Burns much better if you turn their names into images. The more outrageous and improbable the images, the more firmly they will lodge in your memory banks. That's why I'll bet you remember Mrs. Greenbottom longest of the three! This technique also helps experienced card players recall the flow of cards. They create a visual image of which number cards in which suits have been played, then they recall, say, a gap in the lower middle of the spades, or a solid run in the face cards in hearts. With each new play, they adjust their internal picture accordingly. That way, they only have to remember four groups of one suit each, rather than fifty-two separate cards.

Loci association is a well-proven memory-enhancing technique. To recall a list of things, you envision an area you know well. It may be your bedroom, your office, or your street. Then you mentally "place" each item on the list at a different spot in the familiar landscape. To recollect the items, you simply take a tour through that area, picking up each item as you see it.

The technique works to organize any serial list: one's thoughts for a speech, Saturday's planned errands, or what you want to take on an upcoming trip.

The key in all of these techniques is the process of association itself. Memory is nothing more than associating the item we want to remember with a cue. Studies show that the more effort that we put into the act of perceiving or remembering something, the better we recall it. Your goal is to make that process conscious, pairing every item with a tangible and unexpected cue. Whether it is a rhyme, a word, a place, or an object doesn't matter. What counts is the effort you put into it. That's why devices you make up yourself work better than those you copy from others, and also why the best memory joggers are often the most outrageous ones.

At first, you may find this association process awkward, but it soon becomes second nature. As it does, you will notice a marked improvement in your memory. You will begin to make the physical changes in your brain's neuronal structure that strengthen memory. But most of all, you will give yourself a younger, more retentive mind, and reduce your effective mental age, making your brain younger in every sense of the word.

Looking Ahead—Super Brains?

Tomorrow's brain clinics may offer pills, shots, or treatments that greatly increase your brainpower, or at least help give the brain a chemical overhaul, restoring retention, alertness, and analytic capacity seemingly lost years before. Neurobiochemists are pursuing several promising avenues of research, including:

The hormone DHEA may strengthen the brain as well, according to current research. Scientists surmise that DHEA is such a powerful bioregulator because the body can use it to synthesize more than a dozen distinct steroid hormones. In the brain, it seems to help cells grow in a more organized, interconnected fashion. Injected into test animals, it created dramatic improvements in their performance on laboratory mazes—in some cases allowing old mice, who had previously performed poorly, to run the mazes as well as young mice. It appears to work by helping the animals retain what they have learned from previous attempts.

Test animals are getting smarter at the University of Rochester too, according to a paper published in the journal *Brain Research*. Neurochemists took rats with seriously failing memories and infused their brains with a chemical, norepinephrine, found in a normal, healthy brain. Immediately the rats began performing almost like much younger rats. To test the idea, the researchers then implanted into the rats' brains, cells that release the chemical. In several months, when the cellular transplants "took," there was a marked improvement in the rats' memories.

There is a feeling of great excitement in neurobiology laboratories around the country. There is a clear sense that we are closer than ever before to unlocking the chemical keys that will allow us to stay more alert, more retentive—just plain smarter—longer. We may even be able to reverse the most common degradations in brain-power, keep a razor-sharp intellect and memory ten, twenty, or thirty years longer than we can today.

Until then, is there any way you can prepare yourself for these new findings? Absolutely. By giving your brain adequate nutritional support, in terms of micronutrients, vitamins, minerals, and amino acids, protecting it against accumulated toxins like heavy metals, and giving it the exercise it needs to stay young—in other words, by following the three brain-longevity steps in this chapter!

11.

Can't Live Without It: Activity and Aging

Teach us to live that we may dread
Unnecessary time in bed
Get people up and we may save
Our patients from an early grave.

—British Medical Journal,
1947

A physically active life may allow us to approach our
true biogenetic potential for longevity.

—Journal of the
American Medical
Association, 1980

Suppose I told you that you have available *today* a powerful,
proven method to stay young and vigorous longer. This single measure could ensure that for many more years you will meet life on your
own terms, unencumbered by ill health or fading energy. It would
help you greet each day with renewed energy and vitality, and give
you the strength and vigor to do and be all you can. Even better, this
technique is:

- Cost-free
- Enjoyable
- Free of special diets, treatments, or medication
- Easily incorporated into your life
- Guaranteed to have a positive impact on your health and longev-
  ity

The "secret" ingredient that makes this all possible? It is as simple as *regular physical activity*.

But you knew that, right? After all, we've already seen in other chapters how activity and exercise help the heart, circulatory system, and bones. But before you dismiss it as too simple, let's look at what you may *not* have known—because the news is just now breaking in scientific journals. Among the surprising and hopeful findings:

- There is a direct activity-longevity link.
- Your physical activity will determine your freedom from illness.
- There is new evidence on how much activity, and what kind, gives you the "longevity effect."
- You may need *less* exercise than you think to live better and longer.

Make no mistake: There is real news here. Most exciting of all, these findings represent a real advance from what we thought just a few years ago. I recall a recent newswire about a new medical advisory publication from the Canadian government. "If people are to live as long as possible without serious health problems," it said, doctors should prescribe exercise for patients. "The use of activity rather than bed rest in medical treatment is a real revolution in the 80's, . . . but doctors don't routinely prescribe exercise . . . because they just don't know." It may be years before this revolution trickles down to the average doctor's office, but there is every reason for you to put it to work *now* to feel, act, and look younger, longer.

All of this research boils down to a simple principle: Increasing your physical activity will add years to your life and life to your years, *even without strenuous exercise*. This short chapter reviews our state-of-the-art understanding of the activity-longevity link, and shows how you can use this knowledge in your own life.

The Activity-Longevity Link

For a long time, physicians have known that activity and exercise help specific parts of our body—the heart, the bones, etc. Now they have extended this research to show conclusively that *activity and exercise may be your single biggest defense against the changes of age.* To cite just a few voices from respected medical journals:

"Many of the changes commonly attributed to aging can be retarded by an active exercise program. . . . A high degree of physical fitness should offset age changes."—*Journal of the American Geriatric Association*

"A portion of the changes commonly attributed to aging is in reality caused by disuse and . . . is subject to correction."—*Journal of the American Medical Association*

"When people remain active, their body composition tends to resemble that of younger people."—*Handbook of the Biology of Aging*

"Physical activity discourages disease, the absence of exercise invites disease."—*Predictive Medicine, A Study in Strategy*

"Increased activity is associated with increased life expectancy. There is no doubt whatsoever that inactivity will shorten your life."—*The Physician and Sports Medicine*

"Exercise results in improved survival . . . countering deleterious effects of a sedentary life."—*Society of Experimental Biology Journal*

"By age 80 . . . additional life attributable to adequate exercise . . . was more than two years . . ." *New England Journal of Medicine*

The latest research has proven beyond a trace of doubt what generations of mothers and gym teachers have long suspected:
ACTIVITY IS LONGEVITY.

NOT JUST LONGER . . . BETTER

Increased longevity is only half the battle. What counts as much as how long you live is how *well*. None of us wants to live for many years being feeble and doddering, our energy and faculties sapped. Our goal, rather, is to realize the longest possible "well-span"—years of being fully alert, energetic, and radiantly alive. I know your goal is to extend this period of life as long as possible, to keep the sparkle in your eyes, the spring in your step, and the joy in your heart for many decades to come. Plain and simple, it is your level of physical activity that will let you do that. If you want . . .

- Less chance of heart attack, chest pain, and artery disease
- Less likelihood of broken bones due to osteoporosis
- More muscle strength
- Less fat and more lean body mass
- More stable blood sugar
- More energy and better breathing
- Less joint pain
- More flexibility
- Less depression
- Better mental functioning, better memory, improved reasoning and confidence
- Better, more restful sleep

. . . then activity and exercise are the keys. A dramatic demonstration of how exercise makes you biologically younger was reported in the *Journal of American Geriatrics*. Doctors measured biological age through a common laboratory standard of the level of oxygen uptake of the lungs. They compared the scores of seventy-year-olds and younger subjects, who did and did not exercise, and found that when inactive seventy-year-olds started "moderate activity," their physiological profiles showed up to fifteen years younger. Those who continued to the "athlete" level of conditioning had a potential reduction of *forty years* in their age. It may be that the mythical Fountain of Youth is as close as the nearest health club!

If exercise rejuvenates the body, you'd expect inactivity to age it —which is just what studies show. When healthy people are forced to take bed rest or be confined, their biochemical profile starts to resemble that of someone much older. On certain physiological tests, people aged ten years during only thirty-six weeks of bed rest! Research with hospital patients, prisoners, and astronauts shows that inactivity takes a measurable toll on the immune system, the blood, cholesterol, heart function, bones, nerves, body composition, even brain waves. The moral is clear: Exercising is your best bet to stay supple, energetic, and alert, to keep your mood high, your muscles strong, and your mind clear. It is the best way to take years off your body's age, and to make sure that the years ahead will be the most enjoyable, vigorous, and healthy ever.

Be an Activist, Not an Athlete

By now, you know *why* you should be more active. For your life span, and your enjoyment of it, the benefits of increasing activity levels are beyond dispute. But wait just one minute, I hear you say. "Even if I have resolved that my days as a couch potato are numbered, I am also a far cry from being an athlete." Perhaps even the thought of running shoes makes you tired, and the idea of heavy, gasping, sweaty workouts makes you want to just curl up with a good book. You may be one of the millions who have tried exercising, only to give up in frustration after being unable to stick to a rigorous program. Does that mean you should turn to the next chapter and write off your chances for Youth Preservation through exercise?

Once upon a time, medical science might have said yes. But now I have good news—just for people like you. The latest research tells a very different, and much more hopeful, story. You may notice that throughout this chapter, I have referred to "exercise" together with "activity." Not long ago, the conventional wisdom held that one had to be a marathoner or a serious athlete, or at least a health-club habitué to gain longevity benefit from exercise. Exercise was thought to be an "all or nothing" proposition.

But the newest findings suggest that you can benefit, not just from grueling exercise, but also from more moderate levels of regular activity in your weekly routine. Just by increasing your basic levels of weekly activity, you increase your life expectancy. Conversely, says a Harvard Medical School researcher, "There's no doubt whatever that insufficient activity will shorten your life."

The key here—the real news you should know from the most recent findings—is that what counts is activity, not just athletics. Studies have shown that regardless of the strenuous exercise they do or do not get, men whose jobs require them to walk more, lift more, and generally be more active have fewer health problems and live longer.

These tidings mean that it's worth acquiring some new habits: Walk those extra few blocks to the store, take the stairs instead of the elevator, and do whatever you can to build-in occasions to be active rather than sedentary as you go about your daily life. Moderate activity will do. If you expend more than about 1,000 calories each week beyond your basic needs, you will cross the threshold to achieving better health and longevity. Best of all, think of all the pleasant ways to do that:

Gardening   Going for a swim
Dancing   Bowling
Playing with children   Chopping wood
Riding a bike   Walking the dog
Taking a Saturday hike

Even washing windows, scrubbing floors, and cutting the lawn—while not perhaps high on your "recreation" list—burn up calories and count toward your activity levels. Just think, this coming week you could make the house look terrific, treat yourself to an hour's walk afterward, play with the kids—and feel virtuous while doing it, knowing you are adding years—healthy ones—to your life!

This "activity revolution" provides real hope for a lot of us who may have sat out the "fitness revolution." *We who cannot dedicate ourselves to strenuous athletics can still reap many health and life-span benefits—just by staying moderately active.*

Exercise and Mortality

A few years ago, the Secretary of Health and Human Services issued a report showing that less than 20 percent of Americans exercise strenuously and often enough to meet popular aerobic fitness standards. Now we know that there is some hope for the 200 million-plus who haven't achieved star-athlete level of fitness training: For all the rest of us, then, these new findings offer great promise for longer, healthier lives.

Summary Regular activity, not just strenuous exercise, is the key to health and longevity.

Feel Free to Exercise . . .

Although activity does more than we once supposed, I do not mean to discourage you from more intense exercise. It can extend your health and longevity benefits still further. The chart opposite, based on epidemiological research, tells the whole story.

Certainly, those who get more exercise show the most dramatic improvements in longevity. But the real story is the one told by the rest of the curve. *The greatest benefits come when you change from no activity to moderate activity, rather than from moderate activity to high activity.*

Confucius said, "Every journey begins with a single step," and so it is with the activity-exercise continuum. If you are like most of my patients, you may find that by an easy increase in your general activity level, the next step gets easier and more pleasant. You may never end up a decathlon champion—but you will end up healthier and biologically younger.

That is really the moral of this chapter, and what I hope you take away with you. The more activity and exercise you get, the better (so long as you do not have physical limitations that make exercise unwise). But because you can't bench-press three hundred pounds doesn't mean you can't start increasing your levels of basic daily activity. Keep in mind that regular activity is just as important as hard exercise—and for many of us, much more realistic. So remember: Activity *is* longevity. To ensure yourself a long and healthy life, you really *can't* live without it.

12.

Less Is More: The VLC Plan for Long Life

If you are a seriously dedicated, die-hard Youth Preservationist, this chapter is for you. It is something of a "graduate course" in the ways you can preserve your youth and lengthen your life. The information it contains may not be something that everybody wants to use, but I do want you to know about it.

So far, we have emphasized those elements you need to *add* to your diet or life-style to live longer and feel much better. But if you were to ask virtually any reputable longevity biologist in any of the world's premier laboratories, you would soon learn that the greatest impact on your life may come, not from what you *add* to your diet, but from what you *subtract*.

All those eminent scientists know that there exists one undisputable, sure-fire route to preserving youth and vitality. It is one you can follow starting right now, and it is *virtually guaranteed* to add years, perhaps even decades, of healthy time to your life. Best of all, they would tell you, it is amazingly simple and costs you nothing.

You may be thinking that such a powerful technique must be a closely guarded secret, right? Not at all. It has been proven and reproven over more than fifty years of laboratory studies, published in hundreds of papers, proven and replicated around the world.

Does this sound too good to be true? It's not. Allow me to let you in on the "secret" the experts know. The single surest way to guaranteeing yourself a longer, healthier life span boils down to three letters; VLC, and they stand for Very Low Calories.

It is a scientific truism that *animals live significantly longer by dramatically reducing the number of calories they eat.* And the animal to whom that means the most is . . . *you.*

The experimental evidence for the VLC phenomenon is rock solid and beyond dispute. Among its astounding, proven benefits, such a diet:

- Extends life spans in lab experiments
- Lowers blood pressure
- Reduces destructive antibodies that attack the brain
- Reduces the loss of certain brain cells
- Strengthens the immune system
- Slows the aging process
- Lowers cholesterol and heart-disease risk
- Reduces muscle oxygen loss, and improves muscle function
- Reduces free-radical damage to the body's tissues
- Helps stabilize the blood sugar imbalance in diabetes
- Helps the body run at peak metabolic efficiency

Most dramatic of all, scores of studies show that animals on VLC diets live dramatically longer, without disease, with longevity increases of 50 percent, 65 percent, even 83 percent! In the words of one expert in the life-prolonging science of VLC diets: "Food restriction is unique in . . . the extent to which life is extended."

We do not yet understand just why and how a VLC diet prolongs life so dramatically. In part, it may work because it reduces body fat, which in turn diminishes toxic free radicals, and lowers cancer and heart-disease risk. But the longevity payoff of a VLC program goes beyond just these differences. Whatever the precise mechanism involved in VLC turns out to be, many generations of ancient, healthy laboratory mice are (long) living proof that it works!

VLC is not just a matter of eating "lite" foods, a few low-cal snacks, and skipping the occasional lunch. Not by a long shot. VLC diets that have been tested have involved a reduction in daily calorie intake down to about 60 percent of normal. In a typical group of test animals, this meant getting fed only every other day. It also meant they ate in such a way that vital nutrients were concentrated, and every single bit of food energy was used where it did the most good. As their reward for eating less and eating more efficiently, these particular animals lived 83 percent longer than their normal-feeding companions. In human terms, this would translate into living to the ripe old age of 137!

Of Mice and Man

Now you, of course, are not a laboratory mouse. But you don't need to be. If there is one thing all the experts agree on, it is the view expressed in one major paper, which reviewed a number of scientific studies on VLC diets: "The basic aging processes of all mammals are similar . . . nutritional manipulations that slow the aging process in rats will do the same in humans."

In other words, there is every genetic and biological reason to think that what works for laboratory animals works for the human animal. There is enough learned consensus that it will work for humans that several prominent gerontological scientists are enthusiastic about proposing VLC diets for humans. One eminent physician, a member of the medical school faculty at the University of California, Los Angeles, has been on such a very low-calorie longevity regimen for years—he is still going strong today and fully expects to enjoy buoyant energy and health for many decades to come.

Although the odds are that such a program works for the human animal, for most of us the problem is one of motivation. Few of us are eager to cut our diet so deeply. (I can hardly imagine anyone eager to go on an every-other-day eating program!) In order to get the maximum longevity benefit, and match the dramatic results of those studies, you would eventually need to cut back to a level of about 60 percent of the calories you now take in. For women, who normally need 2,000 calories per day, that would mean gradually dropping to 1,300; for men, it would mean a reduction from 2,700 to 1,650 calories. Gulp!

But when it comes to a VLC program, there is a much *easier* way. I don't really recommend such a drastic calorie reduction, because I find it is simply too hard for people to stay on such a restricted diet. In addition, trying to keep track of actual calories can be a tedious and painstaking process. But since the calories you eat usually translate directly into weight, let your pounds be your guide. Find yourself on the VLC Target Weight Table on the opposite page.

Normally, you probably weigh approximately 20 percent more than the value shown on the chart. For example, a woman who is 5 feet 7 inches tall, between age 55 and age 64, might weigh 155 pounds—or 20 percent more than the values in the VLC Target Weight Table. In any safe and appropriate VLC program, your goal is to reduce your weight to 20 percent below what you usually think of as normal for your age and height—that is what the values in the chart represent. Obviously weight is not the only thing that counts —it is also important that you eat the right foods to give your body the longevity nutrients it needs.

Do You Have to Go "All the Way"?

Many of my patients want to know if there is some way to gain some of the longevity benefits without such a severe diet—and without being a mealtime maniac. They ask: "Is there any reasonable way I can benefit from the VLC effect that has helped those Methuselah mice?"

My answer is: "Absolutely." Even if you don't want to go "all the way" to a strict VLC diet, you can still use its sound biological principles to extend your life and improve your health.

The VLC diet is simply the logical conclusion of many of the ideas in this book. The basic anticancer, heart-smart, pro-longevity steps we have discussed so far—less fat, less meat, more fish and filling fibers, less refined sugar and alcohol, appropriate vitamin and mineral supplements, and regular activity—are all 100 percent compatible with reducing the body's excess calories. You may decide to shoot for a personal weight reduction goal of 5 percent, 10 percent, or 12 percent below your current weight—but whatever your goal, you cannot help but gain—in health and in longevity.

VLC Target Weight Table

YOUR HEIGHT		AGE 18–24	25–34	35–44	45–54	55–64
4′ 10″	Women	92	99	107	106	108
4′ 11″	Women	95	101	109	109	110
5′ 0″	Women	97	104	111	111	114
5′ 1″	Women	99	106	113	114	116
5′ 2″	Men	104	111	117	118	117
	Women	102	109	115	117	118
5′ 3″	Men	108	116	119	123	121
	Women	105	111	117	120	121
5′ 4″	Men	111	121	124	126	124
	Women	107	114	119	122	123
5′ 5″	Men	114	124	127	130	128
	Women	110	117	121	126	126
5′ 6″	Men	118	127	131	134	132
	Women	113	119	123	128	129
5′ 7″	Men	122	131	135	137	136
	Women	115	122	125	131	131
5′ 8″	Men	126	134	139	141	139
	Women	118	124	127	134	134
5′ 9″	Men	130	138	142	144	142
5′ 10″	Men	133	142	146	148	146
5′ 11″	Men	134	146	150	152	150
6′ 0″	Men	140	149	154	155	154
6′ 1″	Men	144	153	158	158	158
6′ 2″	Men	148	157	162	163	161

Calculated from: U.S. Center for Health Statistics, North American Association Study of Obesity

The VLC High-Efficiency Diet

If you are interested in trying a VLC regime, there are three principles to remember:

1. In general, the fewer calories you eat, the more years you add to your life.
2. The less you eat, the more *efficient* your diet must be.
3. You must undertake such a plan gradually and correctly or you can do yourself more harm than good.

In other words, the best way to use VLC is with a little TLC—the Tender Loving Care you must have to give your body what it needs, while removing what it doesn't.

Six VLC Tips

If you are interested in trying a VLC diet, here are six primary principles to keep in mind:

1. *Make every calorie count!* EFFICIENCY is the name of the game in a VLC diet. With so many fewer allowable calories, those you do eat must give you the most possible nutritive "bang for your buck." Your goal is to assure that you get enough energy and protein to stay vigorous, and nothing extra. That means:

- NO refined or highly processed foods. Simple carbohydrates and sugars must be cut to an absolute low.
- Eat about 80 grams of protein daily, and make sure your protein and carbohydrate sources are as "pure" and fat-free as possible.
- Keep fat to a bare-bones minimum—*no more than 20 percent of total calories.*
- Eat no more than 300 grams of dietary cholesterol daily.

2. *Go for bulk.* It is easy to cut down on food if you eat things that help you feel full. You will want to balance your diet to include a lot

of fiber and bulky foods—ideally those that pass through your system undigested, yet give you a feeling of having eaten. As a goal, aim to eat at least 50 grams of fiber each day.

3. *Use a fullness enhancer.* Another way to give you the feeling of fullness you need to stay on a VLC plan is to use a substance like guar gum. Guar gum is nondigestible, nonnutritive, and comes in liquid form. Once in your stomach, it expands to help you feel full. I have put hundreds of patients on guar-gum supplements to lose weight—it is a crucial component in any VLC diet.

4. *Don't spare those nutritional supplements.* Because you are eating so little food, you could short-change yourself on essential vitamins, minerals, and amino acids. On any VLC plan, you must take a strong, wide-spectrum micronutrient supplement to make sure your body gets all it needs to stay healthy on a reduced calorie diet. Micronutrient supplements won't add to your calorie intake, but they will give your body the necessary nutritional support. You will find an example of such a supplement plan in Appendix B, to give you an idea of the optimal levels to use if you are on a VLC diet.

5. *Ease into a VLC program very gradually.* If you try to drop to 80 percent of your weight immediately, you will be ravenous for a few days, and then fall off the VLC wagon with a resounding thump. It is far better to reduce your weight in gradual steps. You may want to establish a goal of a pound of weight loss every two weeks for the first five pounds, then a pound a month until you get down to the proper VLC maintenance level. It may take some time to achieve your target, true—but it is the best way to ensure you will stay with the program. *A drastic and transient weight loss WILL NOT enhance your longevity or health, and it WILL make it harder to achieve your VLC target.*

6. *Prepare yourself for a change in your appearance.* Your VLC efficiency diet will cause a real change in your body. You will lose excess fat—in places you didn't even know you had it. As you become lean, your body's metabolism will adapt to your new dietary levels, becoming ever more efficient. Your body's engines will run more cleanly and efficiently, extracting maximum energy from every bit you eat. You should be prepared for the new, lean person that emerges.

* * *

For those of you who are sincerely interested in going on a VLC diet, I have included my own sample diet in Appendix C. It brings you to a level of 1,600 calories for women and slightly higher for men, a significant reduction of calories—AND A SIGNIFICANT STEP ON YOUR WAY TO A LIFE-PROLONGING DIET!

One Final Note

Let's talk frankly. I understand that you may not want to undertake a difficult regimen like a full-fledged VLC diet. That's fine. After all, by reading this book, you have already taken steps to give yourself not just many more years of life, but *better* years of life. I can guarantee that you will enjoy increased benefits—in health, vigor, energy, and well-being—regardless of whether you go all the way and adopt a rigorous VLC program.

My goal in this chapter, like my goal in this entire book, is to tell you about what tools exist right now that allow you to make a real, significant difference in the quantity and quality of your life. In that spirit, I want at least to make sure that you know about the proven life-improving promise of VLC high-efficiency diets. But beyond that, the choice is up to you. Different tools work differently for different people, and I am not saying you have to put yourself on a severe VLC diet. You can take advantage of many of these benefits by going part way—that is, by setting your own personal VLC target. You may choose a weight goal different from the value in the VLC Target Weight Table, maybe halfway between the number on the table and your normal weight. What I do want you to understand is that *whatever weight reduction you make is a change for the better*. You will still derive real benefits from the program because every step toward your VLC target gives you greater longevity and health benefits.

That's what this book is all about: feeling better, looking better, living longer. These benefits can all be yours if you decide to make the "secret" of the high-efficiency, extra-longevity VLC diet a part of your life.

13.

Reprogramming Your Aging Computer

You have often heard it said that "you are only as old as you think you are." I prefer to phrase it slightly differently: We are as *young* as we think we are. When it comes to staying young and leading a full exuberant life, it is not just your brain that counts, but your mind. That may be the single most important element, and it is the focus of this short final chapter.

According to a new field of research that has opened up in the last few years, your mind may be both the simplest, and the most powerful, weapon in your fight against premature aging. This new discipline is called "psychoneuroimmunology," or PNI for short. It charts the links between what goes on in our mind—our emotions, attitudes, and beliefs—and the health and vitality of our organs and physiological systems. The goal of PNI scientists is to unravel the mind-body connection that has perplexed and tantalized humans for millennia. Over the next two decades, I believe, this discipline will hold the most exciting and promising keys to longevity and long-term health.

However, far more important is what it means for you right now. It offers you nothing less than the keys to reprogramming the master computer that is ultimately responsible for aging—your mind.

The last five years have brought a torrent of fascinating and exciting findings from PNI researchers worldwide. They have shown that:

- In both men and women, mental programming for hope, hopelessness, or depression affects one's chances of getting, and surviving, many kinds of cancer, including lung, breast, cervical, and skin cancers.
- The personality programming you received as a child can affect your likelihood of developing cancer later in life.
- Animals given control over their environment fight off tumors better and live longer than animals with no control.
- Institutionalized people who have more control over their lives show dramatic improvements in overall health, even reversing bodily changes due to aging.
- Personality type may play a role in a person's susceptibility to diseases like asthma, peptic ulcers, arthritis, diabetes, multiple sclerosis, even heart disease and cancer.
- Brain chemicals that regulate happiness, sex drive, mental functioning, sleep, depression, aggression, and all of our other brain functions, have been found to activate specific immune fighters such as scavenger cells, T killer cells, antibody-producing cells, and immune boosters like interferon and interleukin-2.
- Our immune system's strength reflects our emotional and mental coping mechanisms. Life-style and psychological stresses can weaken our immune defenses, increase the likelihood of catching infections, and raise our risk for many kinds of diseases.
- People with strong psychological coping skills have been found to have more powerful immune systems, and higher levels of killer immune cells, than people with poor coping skills.
- Grieving, stress, and depression have all been proven to lower your body's immunological fighter cells dramatically.
- Research at Vanderbilt University Medical Center shows that patients who are programmed to expect a slow recovery after

surgery exhibit more physical problems, and those who expect to leave the hospital quickly are much more likely to.

- By programming themselves with mental-relaxation tools, people can lower blood pressure and reduce the frequency of heart-rhythm abnormalities.
- George Washington University physicians found that patients can use mental imagery to change the levels of certain immune cells necessary to fight cancer.
- It has been discovered that people with multiple personalities have dramatically different physical reactions with their different personas. The changes include tolerance to medications, eyesight and sensory acuity, allergies, right- or lefthandedness, and neurological characteristics. Mental programming for each personality transforms the same individual into many measurably different biological "beings."

The list of discoveries is long and varied, touching on virtually every aspect of our body's functioning. This information avalanche points to one inescapable conclusion. From our hearts and blood pressure to our immune system, from our resistance to the common cold or to the deadliest cancer, every bodily process responds to some conscious mental and emotional control.

Your mind is the computer that controls the biological processes that age you. Even more astounding, we have learned that each of us holds the tools to *reprogram that computer* so we can retard the aging process and extend our young, healthy years. This represents a mind-boggling scientific awakening. We are just learning to harness the mind's awesome potential. I have no doubt that this is the medicine that will be practiced in the twenty-first century—but you can start using it now.

Who's Running This Computer, Anyway?

Your body's master aging computer already lies within you, and it is running even as you read this. In fact, it is already executing a complex and detailed "program" that will control your rates of aging, of fitness, and health. Your longevity program is the sum total of your expectations about what the next half century holds for you. It includes how you envision what your state of health will be, what you anticipate doing and being able to do, how you expect to feel, what physical limitations you see lying ahead for you, even when you expect to die.

Unfortunately, if you are like most people, *right now, you are running a longevity program that is fatally flawed.* It's not your fault. One cannot grow up in our culture without "programming in" some very negative expectations about aging. We are surrounded by a national conspiracy to sell ourselves short when it comes to growing older. For example, you probably see yourself on a slow downward curve after the age of fifty. You expect to lose your faculties, feel less energetic, move more slowly and with less ease, get sick more often. Perhaps you've seen older relatives grow infirm and frail for the last decade of their lives, so you may anticipate that course for yourself. You probably plan to retire, have some leisure time, and then find yourself on a slippery slope where you sicken, weaken, and eventually die. I expect that you see each change in your bodily state as a part of a diminishing, inevitable pattern of decay. Such negative images surround us, reinforced by experiencing how people used to age in previous generations, and by the national media and a culture that disseminates much nonsense about what it is like to be on the far side of sixty.

The mind-body scientists have demonstrated that your mental aging computer commands many powerful ways to *make those expectations come true*—slowly, gradually, and inevitably—through its control over your bodily processes. And it will do it, unless you rewrite the program. Now, for the first time, you have a chance to take conscious control of this extraordinarily powerful anti-aging tool and put it on your side.

PNI has shown us that we have the ability to create a "longevity conspiracy," linking our mind and our body's physiological systems for better health, more vigorous years, longer youth. Science has given us the tools, and it is up to each of us to believe in them, stop selling our future short, and put them to work right now.

Four Steps to a New Longevity Program

Fortunately, there are some simple and easy ways to reprogram your aging computer. Because, sophisticated as it is, it only operates on what you tell it. If you repeatedly remind your computer that you plan to live a long and healthy life, and that frailty and decrepitude have no place in your life, it will react accordingly. Here is a set of positive visualization exercises to help you do that.

Longevity Visualization Exercises

I. RELAXATION IMAGERY

1. *Relax* two or three times each day, sitting calmly for ten minutes in a comfortable chair, with your feet flat on the ground. Imagine yourself at ninety, being active, energetic, full of life.

2. *Create* your own internal "movie" of how you want to feel. Picture yourself among friends, enjoying yourself, feeling strong and wise. Imagine being surrounded by many people who love you and value your long lifetime of experience.

3. *Repeat* twenty times in succession, twice daily, an affirmation like: "I feel myself getting stronger, healthier every day. I will live to be a healthy, vigorous ninety-eight-year-old."

II. LIFE GOALS

At least once each week, I hope you can take some time out to ponder the following topics:

- Give some serious thought to the most major life change you plan to make after age seventy. Will you continue to work? Will you volunteer to help people? Perhaps you will branch out completely and start something you have always wanted to do. Will your goal be to make money, to serve people, to have a very creative or helpful career? At what age do you expect to change? What do you have to do now to prepare for it?

- Draw a timeline of your life, numbering each decade. Put a short label on each decade, describing its main feature or accomplishment. Now place yourself along the line. Notice at what age you ended the line. Now extend it another twenty years, and fill in the extra decades with what you want them to hold.
- Sit down and write up exactly what you want to do to celebrate your ninety-fifth birthday. Where will you be? Who will you be with? What will be the most special thing about it? Figure out what kind of physical exercise you will enjoy most in the next twenty years, and in the twenty years after that. Make a list of something special you want to do in each five-year period for the next thirty years.
- Contemplate which friends you expect to be closest to in your eighties. Sit down with them now and share with them your thoughts and hopes about what you will be doing together.
- Discuss with your family, spouse, or lover what you are looking forward to most about living another forty years. As ideas occur to you, describe in detail what you will be doing in the year 2025.
- Think about the young people now in your life. Imagine what wisdom you will want to share with them when you are ninety.
- Spend a moment thinking about the aspects of your life that will be better, more fulfilled, or more interesting thirty years from now.
- Think about where you expect to be living in your late eighties. Is there a part of the country or of the world where you have always wanted to live? At what age do you plan to move there?
- If you see a negative image about aging, say to yourself, "That doesn't apply to me, because I am going to be a healthy ninety-year-old."
- Contemplate the most exciting project you want to have accomplished by the time you are one hundred.
- Take a moment to sit quietly and relax, and decide what age—at least ninety—you expect to live until. Get used to that age and remember it every time you hear, read, talk, or think about the future.

These are just a few ideas to inspire your own creative efforts. Your goal is to replace every one of your current negative images about what the future holds with positive, health-affirming, longevity-boosting scenarios, in which you are active, energetic, and healthy. This may seem awkward or strange at first, but it will soon become automatic. What you want to do is reshape your expectations so that you continuously desire, believe, and expect the image of yourself to come true. Your mental computer will help make sure that it does.

III. PHYSIOLOGICAL CHANGES

These changes are designed to give you specific, concrete images to help specific physiological systems in your body.

1. For two minutes, visualize a positive change taking place in your own skin, arteries, spine and bones, and brain.
2. Visualize that image as many times as you can each day.
3. After a week, change to another image of another part of your body.

IV. LONGEVITY ROLE MODELS

To remind you what your future could hold, I suggest you copy out this list and post it someplace where you will see it often:

- Sophocles wrote *Oedipus at Colonus* at age 92.
- Frank Lloyd Wright designed award-winning buildings into his nineties.
- Bob Hope, age 90, entertains and travels around the world.
- George Burns, age 96, appears in films and on television.
- Martha Graham, at age 95, continued her work as a choreographer.
- Louis Nizer, at age 87, continued to win cases in his law practice in New York City.

These are the best reminders that we all can be candidates for this list in our nineties!

Remember: Your longevity program can only keep you as young as the expectations you feed into it.

14.

Putting It All Together

A major objective now and in the future should be to maximize health and well-being during our essentially fixed span of life.

> —Dr. Denham Harman,
> gerontological
> researcher

We have come a long way together since we began our journey long ago on the deck of Ponce de León's ship. You now possess Youth Preservation techniques and formulas to extend the benefits of youth in many of your body's vital biological systems. You have improved your skin and appearance, your bones, muscles, blood, heart, and brain. You have reviewed the benefits of exercise and activity, learned the principles of a VLC diet plan, and gotten the tools to reprogram your mind's longevity computer. That is a lot of learning, and a lot to be proud of!

We have covered a lot of ground, so it might be useful to review the basic longevity steps, the key components in your twenty-two-point plan to better health, longer life, and increased well-being.

FOR A YOUNG OUTER YOU:

1. ASK YOUR DOCTOR ABOUT RETIN-A CREAM.
2. TAKE THE YOUTH PRESERVATION NUTRIENTS BETA-CARO-TENE, VITAMIN C, and VITAMIN E.
3. KEEP OUT OF THE SUN AS MUCH AS POSSIBLE.
4. USE A WIDE-SPECTRUM, PABA-OXYBENZONE SUNSCREEN.

TO STAY "YOUNG AT HEART" (CARDIAC LONGEVITY)

5. STOP SMOKING NOW TO REJUVENATE YOUR HEART AND LUNGS.
6. CUT SATURATED FATS TO A BARE MINIMUM IN YOUR DIET.
7. EAT FISH AS A MAIN MEAL AT LEAST TWICE WEEKLY.
8. EAT FIBER TO REDUCE FATS AND CHOLESTEROL.
9. TAKE TIME EACH DAY TO RELAX AND REDUCE STRESS.
10. DO MODERATE EXERCISE OR A BASIC DAILY ACTIVITY, SEVERAL TIMES EACH WEEK.

FOR YOUNG BONES (SKELETAL LONGEVITY)

11. USE THE DAILY BONE-BUILDING MICRONUTRIENT FOR-MULA.
12. INCLUDE THE NEWEST BONE BUILDER BORON IN YOUR DIET.
13. REDUCE ALCOHOL CONSUMPTION TO AVOID FLUSHING OUT MINERALS.
14. DO EXERCISES TO STRENGTHEN JOINTS AND BACK.
15. USE THE ANTI-ARTHRITIS NUTRITIONAL SUPPLEMENT PLAN.

STAYING "IMMUNE TO AGE"
(IMMUNE LONGEVITY)

16. OBSERVE THE ANTICANCER EATING GUIDELINES.
17. CONSIDER INTRAVENOUS VITAMIN C TREATMENTS.
18. USE THE "ANTIVIRAL COCKTAIL" TO REDUCE VIRAL ILL-NESS.

YOUNG BETWEEN THE EARS
(BRAIN LONGEVITY)

19. FOLLOW THE FOOD-FOR-THOUGHT EATING GUIDELINES, INCLUDING ANTIOXIDANTS.
20. KEEP MENTALLY ACTIVE AND USE MEMORY MAGNIFIERS TO TRAIN YOUR BRAIN FOR LONG-TERM HEALTH.
21. CONSIDER GOING ON THE LONGEVITY-PROMOTING VLC DIET.
22. USE MENTAL IMAGES TO REPROGRAM YOUR INTERNAL AGING COMPUTER.

These twenty-two steps represent the most comprehensive, hopeful prescription available today for longevity. If you incorporate them diligently into your life, I am 100 percent certain that in twenty weeks, you will feel better, look better, think more clearly, and enjoy more energy and vitality. Best of all, you will have put yourself on the road to a significant longevity boost. Twenty-two steps, twenty weeks, can give you twenty months (or years!) of extra, *healthy* life.

Putting It All Together

Throughout this book, we have explored very concrete, very specific steps necessary to add years to your life. However, I don't want to leave you with the notion that your key to long and healthy life is twenty-two distinct, disjointed fragments. We are now at the point where we can put it all together—because you are, after all, more than simply the sum of your biological parts.

Keeping yourself young, beautiful, and vital longer is not a matter of checking items off a list, but of creating one healthy, unified whole.

We have examined various branches of health—immune, cardiac, skin, neurological, skeletal, and mental. It is true that each of those branches must be healthy for the whole tree to flourish. But as any gardener knows, the roots are as important as the individual branches.

In your case, the root of true, healthy longevity lies deep within your cells. All of the changes we have talked about, in one way or another, go back to that fundamental cause of aging.

At the beginning of this book, we discussed several theories of aging. The most compelling, the free-radical theory, suggests very clearly that the losses of age are due to accumulated damage to trillions of your body's cells. That accumulated damage is the real cause of aging—and the real source of potential longevity.

If you look back at the twenty-two steps outlined above, as well as reviewing many of the other counsels given throughout this book, most of them share one thing in common: *They help fight the basic aging processes in your cells.* They give your body the antioxidant nutrients it needs, and minimize your exposure to damaging fats, toxins, and ultraviolet light. They create an environment where your cells work cleanly, without interference, as Nature designed them. Taken together, they focus longevity changes where they do the most good: at the root of aging, in the innermost machinery of your cells.

It is no biological coincidence that several basic steps in your twenty-two-point plan work synergistically in several different parts of the body. Eating fiber has benefits for your heart, your blood vessels, and your bones; antioxidants help your immunity, your skin, and bones; exercise helps your heart and bones and brain; and so forth. When you bear in mind that each of these steps is aimed at having an effect at the basic level of your cells, it makes sense that they will improve many different aspects of your well-being.

It should be clear by now that there is no thirty-words-or-less formula for resetting your cells' innermost biological clock. As we have seen again and again, such a formula can never be just one simple answer, nor one magic bullet. If you could ask virtually any responsible thinker in this exciting field about what each of us can do *right now* to stay young, you would hear that it involves a combination of different interventions, programs, and practices. That advice is at the core of the twenty-two steps you have been given. These steps let you do everything possible *now* to rejuvenate and reenergize the systems that keep you young and alive—from the deepest cells of your long bones to the most hidden folds of your brain, to the outermost surfaces of your skin. Taken together, these twenty-two steps could quite possibly add twenty years to your life— years of healthy, energetic living.

Prepare Yourself for Tomorrow's Breakthroughs

There is one last thing to think about. Throughout this book, I have tried to keep you informed about the terrifically exciting news that is waiting just on the medical horizon. In the course of writing this book, several new major findings have been announced. Others, I'm sure, will have been announced by the time you read this. Such is the breakneck pace of change in the field of rejuvenation.

Does that make this book obsolete? Just the reverse. The twenty-two steps in this book will keep you in tip-top shape to benefit from new research breakthroughs. It will do you little good to pick up the morning paper on, say, March 4, 2003, and find out there is a new magic youth pill if you are already wasted from cancer, bedridden with heart disease, stooped over with arthritis and osteoporosis, addled with Alzheimer's disease, or debilitated by any of a host of other chronic and crippling maladies! The twenty-two points we've discussed are changes you can make *today* so you can keep in the youngest shape possible for what science learns *tomorrow*.

On a More Personal Note

I hope you will congratulate yourself on the changes you have made in coming this far. Give yourself credit for being smart enough to see that you *can* fight your own war against the decay of aging, and assure yourself of youthful energy and health. You already know you can make a real difference in your well-being and longevity by simply putting the knowledge you already have to work. That is the realization we started with in the first chapter, and it seems a fitting place to close this part of our adventure.

In truth, an adventure like this is never ended. Our only solid guarantee is that the Youth Revolution will continue, that discoveries will broaden, and that more and more people will wake up and start to follow the kinds of changes we have discussed. Until they do, you are in the vanguard of those making changes now to ensure dramatically more, and dramatically *better*, years of vigorous life.

My very personal thanks for coming this far on this exciting journey. Through these pages, you have joined the growing club of far-sighted visionaries who are smart enough to start putting these state-of-the-art ideas to work now. Together, we will finish the quest that our ancestors started so long ago.

I have no doubt that we will see wonderful research developments in the next five, ten, or twenty years. Best of all, you will have the satisfaction of being in the best possible shape to take advantage of them because of the changes you have already made.

I wish you luck, and I know you will not be sorry, for you now have the potential to live a better, more vigorous and healthy life than ever before.

To help you realize that potential, I want to extend you the special invitation below. I am planning to host a wonderful free party—a reunion for readers of this book—on New Year's Day in the year 2045 (that's a Sunday). So, put the date in your calendar now, stay in touch . . . and I expect to see you there, ready to dance.

Until then, be well, and be youthful.

> Your healthy presence
> is cordially requested at
> a gala celebration
> of long life,
> strong health,
> and extended youth.
>
> To be given by
> Dr. Stuart M. Berger, MD.
>
> Sunday, January 1, 2045
> 12:00 noon
> Place to be announced

Appendix A

Sample Cardiac Longevity Menu

Here is a very specific five-day diet for a state-of-the-art heart. The low levels of fat in this menu are first steps to reducing the toll that age takes on your heart and blood vessels. If you wish to pursue this subject in greater detail, I refer you to my book *How to Be Your Own Nutritionist.*

DAY 1:

Breakfast:

Low-sodium tomato juice
Whole-wheat toast with unsweetened jam
Low-fat yogurt with berries

Lunch:

Vegetarian chili topped with low-fat yogurt
Tossed green salad
Banana

Dinner:

Poached salmon
Brown rice and herbs
Salad of romaine lettuce, green peppers, tomato,
alfalfa sprouts, or: broccoli in garlic sauce
Pineapple spears and strawberries

DAY 2:

Breakfast:

Bowl unsalted, unsweetened oatmeal
Skim milk
1 sliced banana or other fruit
2 slices whole-wheat toast or bran muffin
Herbal tea

Lunch:

Carrot and celery sticks
Sardines in tomato sauce
Whole-grain crackers
Peach
Skim or low-fat milk

Dinner:

Lean veal chops
Barley pilaf
Chicory and chopped celery salad
Steamed baby carrots
Broiled grapefruit

DAY 3:

Breakfast:

Carrot juice
Whole-wheat cereal with skim milk
Blueberries

Lunch:

Low-fat cottage cheese with vegetables and kidney
beans
Rice cakes
Nectarine

Dinner:

Vegetable sticks
Broiled brook trout

Parsleyed wild rice
Fresh spinach and garlic
Fresh fruit sorbet

DAY 4:

Breakfast:

Low-fat cottage cheese
Grapefruit slices
Whole-wheat bagel

Lunch:

Hearty minestrone soup
Whole-grain roll
Skim or low-fat milk
Plums

Dinner:

Pasta primavera
Salad of tomato, cucumber, red onion
Poached pear

DAY 5:

Breakfast:

Low-sodium tomato or vegetable juice
Oatmeal with cinnamon and apple
Skim or low-fat milk

Lunch:

Tuna-vegetable salad on whole-wheat toast
Lettuce and tomato
Pear

Dinner:

Broiled chicken
Baked potato with yogurt and chives
Salad of spinach, onions, carrots, mushrooms

String beans amandine
Kiwi fruit and berries
1 piece low-fat, low sodium cheese

For Dressings and Seasonings Use:

Vegetable oils   Lemon juice
Low-fat yogurt   Garlic
Low-fat cottage cheese   Onion
Vinegar   Herbs

Cardiac Longevity Foods

Foods That Preserve Your Heart	*Foods That Age Your Heart*
Fish high in essential oils:	
Salmon	Deep-fried fish
Mackerel	Fish in cream or butter sauces
Tuna	
Trout	
Haddock	
Cod	
Other fish:	
Sole	
Snapper	
Lean meats:	*Fatty meats:*
White-meat poultry without skin	Dark-meat poultry
Veal	Fried chicken
Lean beef	Duck
	Ham
	Pork
	Fatty beef
	Luncheon meats

Foods That Preserve *Your Heart*	*Foods That Age* *Your Heart*
	Hot dogs Bacon Spare ribs Lamb Sausage Liver Kidneys

Low-fat or skim dairy products:	*High-fat dairy products:*
Skim milk, or 1% or low-fat milk Farmer cheese Low-fat yogurt and cottage cheese Low-fat low-sodium cheeses Part-skim ricotta Part-skim mozzarella Ice milk Skim-milk buttermilk	Cream, regular milk Half-and-half Nondairy creamers Regular yogurt Regular cottage cheese Hard and semisoft cheeses Ice cream, sour cream Eggs

Fruits and vegetables:	
Leafy green vegetables Fresh vegetables Fresh fruits	Canned vegetables Canned fruits in syrup Coconut

Grains:	
Whole grains Brown rice Whole-wheat flour Kasha Couscous Millet Bulgur	Processed grains White rice Refined flour

Beans:	
Pinto Navy Kidney	Pork and beans

Foods That Preserve Your Heart	Foods That Age Your Heart

Polyunsaturated oils:

Safflower oil	Saturated fats
Sunflower oil	Animal fats
Corn oil	Hydrogenated fats
	Coconut oil
	Palm oil

Monosaturated oils:

Salts:

Peanut oil	Soy sauce
Olive oil	Mayonnaise
	Pickled foods

Snack foods:

Chips
Candy
Cake
Pastry

Fiber Content of Common Foods

Food	Serving Size	Fiber Content (in grams)

Grains

• Wheat bran	• 1/3 cup	• 6.5
• Oat bran	• 1/3 cup	• 4
• Popcorn	• 2 cups	• 3

Vegetables

• Spinach	• 1/2 cup	• 6
• Sweet potato	• "	• 4
• Brussels sprouts	• "	• 4
• Corn	• 1/2 cup	• 4
• Baked potato (med.)	• "	• 3.5
• Turnips/rutabagas	• " (cooked)	• 3

Food	Serving Size	Fiber Content (in grams)

Legumes

• Lentils	• ½ cup uncooked	• 11
• Kidney beans	• ½ cup cooked	• 6
• Pinto beans	• "	• 5
• Split peas	• "	• 5
• White beans	• "	• 5
• Lima beans	• "	• 5
• Peas (green)	• ½ cup cooked	• 4

Fruits and Nuts

• Apricots (dried)	• ½ cup	• 15
• Prunes (stewed)	• ½ cup	• 15
• Almonds	• ½ cup	• 10
• Peanuts	• ½ cup	• 6
• Blackberries	• ½ cup	• 4.5
• Raspberries	• ½ cup	• 4.5
• Prunes	• 4	• 4

Cereals

• All-Bran (with extra fiber)	• 1 ounce	• 13
• Fiber One	• "	• 12
• 100% Bran	• "	• 9
• All-Bran	• "	• 9
• Bran Buds	• "	• 8
• Corn Bran	• "	• 6
• Bran Chex	• "	• 5
• Natural Bran Flakes	• "	• 5
• 40% Bran Flakes	• 1 ounce	• 4
• Cracklin' Oat Bran	• "	• 4
• Fruit 'n' Fiber	• "	• 4
• Fruitful Bran	• "	• 4
• Shredded Wheat & Bran	• "	• 4
• Wheatena	• "	• 4

Appendix B

Sample Supplementation Plan for VLC Diet

On a VLC diet, it is essential to include a strong, balanced micronutrient-supplement plan. This ensures that your reduced level of calories will not lead to a deficiency of the vital micronutrient elements you need.

Vitamins:

Vitamin A	20,000 I.U.
Beta-carotene	20,000 I.U.
Vitamin B_1 (thiamine)	100 mg
Vitamin B_2 (riboflavin)	100 mg
Vitamin B_3 (niacin)	100 mg
Vitamin B_5 (pantothenic acid)	200 mg
Vitamin B_6 (pyridoxine)	50 mg
Vitamin B_{12}	200 mcg
Folic acid	400 mcg
Choline	200 mg
Inositol	200 mg
Biotin	100 mcg
Vitamin C	2,000 mg
Vitamin D	400 I.U.
Vitamin E	200 I.U.
Bioflavinoids:	
Rutin	400 mg
Hesperidin	400 mg

Minerals:

Calcium	400	mg
Magnesium	200	mg
Iron	10	mg
Zinc	50	mg
Selenium	100	mcg

Appendix C

Sample VLC Diet Plan

Here is your sample menu plan for twenty-one days of a prolongevity VLC regimen. This plan is exactly balanced to give you the optimal mix of nutrients you need to take advantage of the strong life-span- and health-promoting benefits of VLC eating.

Be a bit generous with your servings of vegetables and salads, but be very stingy in using oil or fat in cooking or serving. If you do both those things, this plan provides approximately 60 percent carbohydrate, 20 percent protein, 20 percent fat—and for women, 1,600 calories each day. Men following the plan should eat the same foods, except they can increase their servings of salads and carbohydrates within reason, to allow for the extra calories the male body needs.

DAY 1:

Breakfast:

2 large buckwheat pancakes, topped with berries
and wheat bran
1 cup skim milk

Lunch:

Tuna salad made with:
water-packed tuna, celery, onion, low-fat yogurt on
2 slices whole-wheat bread
1 peach

Dinner:

Mixed salad with oil, vinegar, and herbs
1 large baked potato with low-fat yogurt and chives
3-oz chicken cutlet sautéed with peppers, tomatoes,
and onion in very little oil

Snack:

4 rye crackers
Carrot sticks
Large apple

DAY 2:

Breakfast:

$^1/_2$ grapefruit
1 poached egg
2 slices whole-wheat toast with unsweetened preserves

Lunch:

Vegetarian chef salad made with:
$^1/_2$ cup kidney beans,
$^1/_2$ cup chick-peas, oil, vinegar, and herbs
1 cup skim milk
$^1/_2$ grapefruit

Dinner:

Endive salad with oil, vinegar, and herbs
1 cup herbed brown rice
1 cup broccoli
5 oz poached salmon

Snack:

4 rice cakes
1 cup low-fat yogurt with strawberries

DAY 3:

Breakfast:

1 cup cooked oatmeal
1 banana
1 cup skim milk

Lunch:

Tofu with bean sprouts, lettuce, and tomato on
2 slices whole-wheat bread
1 apple

Dinner:

Spinach salad with low-fat yogurt-based dressing with dill
Small butternut squash
1 cup French-cut green beans
4 oz lamb chop
1 whole-wheat roll with 1 tsp butter

Snack:

2 whole-wheat matzohs
A few almonds
1 orange

DAY 4:

Breakfast:

Canteloupe wedge
Whole-wheat bagel with
1 oz melted low-fat cheese

Lunch:

Taco shell, stuffed with lettuce and tomato
1/2 cup beans
1/2 cup grapes

Dinner:

Mixed salad with oil, vinegar, and herbs
1 cup mashed potatoes
1 cup baby carrots
5 oz broiled sole

Snack:

4 Wasa crackers
½ cup low-fat cottage cheese
1 tangerine

DAY 5:

Breakfast:

1 cup puffed rice with blueberries
1 cup skim milk

Lunch:

1½ cups minestrone soup
1 slice whole-wheat toast with
1 oz melted low-fat cheese
1 apple

Dinner:

Arugula salad with oil, vinegar, and herbs
1 large sweet potato with 1 tsp butter
1 cup Brussels sprouts
4 oz sliced baked turkey breast

Snack:

2 rice cakes with
2 tbs natural peanut butter
1 banana

DAY 6:

Breakfast:

1 large bran muffin
½ cup low-fat cottage cheese
10 orange slices

Lunch:

Tomato stuffed with chicken salad
1 whole-wheat bagel
Mixed fruit with low-fat yogurt

Dinner:

Spinach salad with oil, vinegar, and herbs
1 acorn squash
1 cup cauliflower
5 oz broiled brook trout
1 whole-wheat roll

Snack:

2 cups air-popped corn
1 pear

DAY 7:

Breakfast:

1 cup bran flakes
1 banana
1 cup skim milk

Lunch:

1 cup black-bean soup
1 oz low-fat cheese
2 slices 7-grain bread
1 tsp butter

Dinner:

Arugula salad with oil, vinegar, and herbs
1 cup rice
5 oz lean steak, with peppers, onions, tomatoes
1 whole-wheat roll

Snack:

Carrot sticks
A few cashews
1 small papaya

DAY 8:

Breakfast:

1 cup cooked Wheatena
3–4 dried apricots
1 cup skim milk

Lunch:

Cucumber salad with low-fat yogurt and chives
2 pieces whole-wheat pita bread with
Hummus
Sprouts

Dinner:

Mixed green salad with oil, vinegar, and herbs
1 cup minestrone soup
Escarole
2 cups whole-wheat pasta and
Red clam sauce

Snack:

A few hazelnuts
1 banana

DAY 9:

Breakfast:

Citrus salad
1 soft-boiled egg
2 slices whole-wheat toast with
1 tsp butter

Lunch:

1½ cups whole-wheat pasta salad with vegetables
1 cup cabbage slaw
2 rye crackers

Dinner:

Endive salad with oil, vinegar, and herbs
1 cup boiled new potatoes with 1 tsp butter and herbs
1 cup cooked spinach
4 oz grilled salmon

Snack:

4 rice cakes
2 oz low-fat cheese
3 dried figs

DAY 10:

Breakfast:

1 cup puffed corn with blueberries
1 cup skim milk

Lunch:

½ grapefruit
½ cup low-fat cottage cheese with chopped vegetables
1 whole-wheat biscuit

Dinner:

Chinese vegetable soup
1½ cups rice
5 oz chicken cutlet, stir-fried with
Chinese vegetables

Snack:

2 whole-wheat matzohs
A few almonds
1 mango

DAY 11:

Breakfast:

1 large oat-bran muffin with unsweetened preserves
1 cup skim milk
1 apple

Lunch:

1½ cups 3-bean salad on
Bed of lettuce
1 cup chilled steamed broccoli
2 rice cakes

Dinner:

Spinach salad with
Low-fat yogurt-based dressing with dry mustard
1 cup whole-wheat pasta marinara
1 cup green beans
5 oz veal cutlet with mushroom wine sauce

Snack:

1 cup low-fat yogurt with
Mixed fruit topped with
Wheat germ

DAY 12:

Breakfast:

1 cup shredded wheat
1 banana
1 cup skim milk

Lunch:

2 slices 7-grain bread with
1 oz melted low-fat cheese
Lettuce and tomato

Dinner:

Arugula salad with oil, vinegar, and herbs
1 cup herbed barley and peapods
5 oz broiled mackerel

Snack:

4 Wasa crackers
Small amount of nut butter
1 apple

DAY 13:

Breakfast:

1 cup cream of rye with
1 tsp butter
$1/2$ cup low-fat cottage cheese with herbs
1 orange

Lunch:

Tuna salad in whole-wheat
Pita with chopped vegetables

Dinner:

Mixed green salad with oil, vinegar, and herbs
1 cup lentil soup
1½ cups whole-wheat pasta primavera
2 pieces whole-wheat Italian bread

Snack:

½ cup low-fat cottage cheese with
Mixed citrus fruit
A few cashews

DAY 14:

Breakfast:

2 whole-wheat waffles topped with
Low-fat yogurt and strawberries

Lunch:

Mixed green salad with oil, vinegar, and herbs
1 cup tabouli salad with a few pine nuts
1 apple

Dinner:

Endive salad with oil, vinegar, and herbs
1 cup zucchini and tomato
9 shrimp sautéed in olive oil and garlic over 1 cup rice

Snack:

4 rice cakes
1 oz low-fat cottage cheese
1 orange

DAY 15:

Breakfast:

1 cup puffed wheat
1 peach
1 cup skim milk

Lunch:

Spinach salad with oil, vinegar, and herbs
1 cup rice with chopped vegetables
1 pear

Dinner:

Mixed salad with oil, vinegar, and herbs
1 large baked potato
1 cup wax beans
5 oz liver and onions

Snack:

1 cup low-fat yogurt with
Dried fruit and wheat bran
1 slice whole-wheat bread with small amount of nut butter
Unsweetened preserves

DAY 16:

Breakfast:

1 melon wedge
1 egg yolk, 2 egg whites, as omelet or scrambled
2 whole-wheat biscuits with
1 tsp butter

Lunch:

1½ cups minestrone soup
2 pieces 7-grain bread with
1 oz melted low-fat cheese

Dinner:

Spinach salad with
Low-fat yogurt-based dressing with dry mustard
1 cup Italian green beans
2 cups whole-wheat pasta with mussels marinara

Snack:

2 Wasa crackers
Small amount of nut butter
1 banana

DAY 17:

Breakfast:

1 cup Nutri-Grain
1 banana
1 cup skim milk

Lunch:

1½ cups vegetarian chili
1 oz low-fat cheese

Dinner:

Arugula salad with oil, vinegar, and herbs
1 cup buckwheat pilaf and corn
1 cup Brussels sprouts
5 oz red snapper

Snack:

2 cups air-popped corn
Celery sticks
A few cashews
3 dried figs

DAY 18:

Breakfast:

1 cup cooked oat bran
1 apple
1 cup skim milk

Lunch:

1½ cups rice and beans with
Chopped vegetables

Dinner:

Mixed green salad with oil, vinegar, and herbs
1 large sweet potato
1 cup cauliflower
5 oz sliced baked turkey breast
Fresh cranberry sauce

Snack:

4 rice cakes
1 oz low-fat cheese
A few hazelnuts
1 pear

DAY 19:

Breakfast:

1 large corn muffin
1 oz low-fat cheese
1 pear

Lunch:

4 oz sardines in water or tomato sauce
2 slices whole-wheat bread
Lettuce and tomato
1 orange

Dinner:

Endive salad with oil, vinegar, and herbs
1 cup broccoli
2 cups vegetable lasagna with low-fat ricotta
1 piece whole-wheat Italian bread

Snack:

½ cup unsweetened granola with
Dates and nuts

DAY 20:

Breakfast:

1 cup puffed millet
1 nectarine
1 cup skim milk

Lunch:

Mixed salad with oil, vinegar, and herbs
1½ cups whole-wheat pasta salad with vegetables
and
Grated low-fat cheese

Dinner:

Arugula salad with oil, vinegar, and herbs
1 cup rice and herbs
1 zucchini, steamed
5 oz broiled lobster tail

Snack:

4 rye crackers
Small amount of nut butter
1 apple

DAY 21:

Breakfast:

1 cup cream of rice
3 prunes
1 cup skim milk

Lunch:

Large spinach salad with lemon and herbs
1 hard-boiled egg
2 slices whole-wheat bread
1 apple

Dinner:

Vegetable soup
1½ cups oven-baked french fries
3 oz lean hamburger
Whole-wheat roll
Lettuce and tomato

Snack:

3 rice cakes
1 cup low-fat yogurt
Mixed fruit

HOW TO BE YOUR OWN NUTRITIONIST

I dedicate this book to my parents,
Otto and Rachel,
whose commitment to good nutrition
and exercise allows them
a healthy life today.

Acknowledgments

This book could not have been written without Linda Murray, who has done the actual writing. Also, my deep appreciation to David Nimmons and Charlene Laino, whose special knowledge and expertise have made this book possible.

For their enduring support and friendship, my thanks to Lorna Darmour, Scott Meredith, Oscar Dystel, Walter Anderson, Roger Wood, and Pat Miller.

I am grateful to Sherry Arden, Pat Golbitz, Lela Rolontz, Cheryl Asherman, and Rena Wolner for their help in the publication of this book.

And special thanks to my patients, friends, and colleagues, who have always been a source of great excitement and inspiration.

Contents

1.

How To Be Your
Own Nutritionist

"If I am not for myself,
who shall be for me?
And if not now, when?"

—Rabbi Hillel, third century

Have you been searching for a caring, competent health-care expert, someone who can give you a nutritional plan based on your own unique needs? Look no longer. You've just found that person— yourself! Are you surprised? That's only the first of many surprises you will find in this book.

You are about to discover a whole new way of taking charge of your health. I don't say that lightly. I have designed this *entire* book from the ground up to teach you how to become your own nutritionist, your own expert. You're going to learn things about yourself and your nutrition that you've never known before. And you will learn them in a totally new way.

So What Brings *You* Here?

That is usually the first question I ask my patients, as we get down to the business of making them well. So let me ask you the same thing: Just why *did* you buy this book?

Was it because of a vague sense of dissatisfaction? Maybe you've never felt quite the robust health you feel you should. Remember that total at-home-ness in your body you felt as a child? We didn't think of our bodies then; we just took for granted the ease of movement, the bounding energy. Even as adults, some rare individuals seem still to have that special spark of vitality and energy, a *joie de vivre* that lets them savor every drop of life's rich enjoyment. Yet the great majority of us spend most of our time feeling that we lack that special edge of exuberant health.

You may be reading this because you sense that your body is functioning just a notch below its true peak. You're not sick, but over the years you have collected an assortment of twinges, aches, pains, and creakings that tell you your body is aging like a rusty machine. You miss the easy, fluid way you once moved, the grace and lightness as you walk down the street. You picked this book up in the hopes of once again feeling your body, strong and supple, at your command. You may have heard of thousands of people who have seen truly remarkable improvements from my *Immune Power Diet*—or you may be one of those people yourself! —and you want to go the next step in assuring yourself strong and lasting health.

Or maybe you bought this book because you finally got tired of flinching each time you looked in a mirror. You have had enough of seeing yourself bulging with too many pounds, too much flesh. You're tired of feeling that you're a failure because, try as you may, you simply can't seem to control your weight. You're tired of puffing up stairs, of having to squeeze into seats, of choosing your clothes to hide the extra baggage you carry. You're tired of feeling ashamed of your body.

More than that, you are worried, because you know the toll these pounds take on your health, your happiness, and your chances for a long life. For you, becoming your own nutritionist means taking charge, once and for all, of how much you want to weigh.

Or maybe you are simply feeling weary. You may be one of the millions who feel a gray cloud covering their whole lives, who must make a great effort to drag from one long day to the next. You realize you never hear yourself let loose with a great bellylaugh anymore.

It's been so long since you've felt really excited or stimulated in your life that it's become a real effort to feel enthusiastic about anything. For you, this book means the chance to take charge of your nutrition, and again awaken enthusiastic, full of energy to face the day ahead.

If you see yourself in any of these statements, this book was written for you. The plan I outline in these pages will show you in detail how to take control of your nutritional health—and in so doing, say good-bye to sickness, good-bye to fat, good-bye to depression and stress. You will see astounding improvements in your health and vitality, your weight, your mood, and, most of all, your sense of enjoyment and enthusiasm for the world.

You'll find out how nutritional health can give you the key to each and every one of these areas. This book will give you insights into what is already known about nutrition as well as introducing you to brand-new discoveries. When you've finished, you'll be able to integrate this new knowledge and use it as the basis for mapping out your own nutritional program.

In fact, by the time you've finished this book, I think it is safe to say that your understanding of nutrition—and of the role it plays in keeping you strong, healthy, and vital—will be way beyond the average doctor's. That means you'll have the tools to make yourself feel better, more alert and responsive, more free of chronic complaints, than you've ever felt in your life. I'm sure enough of this that I have included a contract in the last chapter: If you really learn the principles of *How to Be Your Own Nutritionist* you will be a happier, healthier, more alive person.

You don't believe it? That's understandable. It's an ambitious pledge. But I can make it because I know this book will teach you how to write your own nutritional prescription—one designed by you, for you. You'll be able to decide exactly what foods you should eat, which ones aren't right for you, what vitamins and minerals you need to take, which to avoid, and why. You are going to base those decisions on all the factors that make you unique—your age, sex, genes, life-style, your stress and activity levels, and medical status.

How can I make you such a guarantee? Because I know this approach *works*. I've tried and tested it in my own private practice.

For though you may have purchased this book brand-new, in one way it is a "used" book. Quite a few people have already been exposed to the ideas in this book—fourteen thousand of them, in fact. So who has seen it already? The more than seven thousand patients I have treated in over a decade of clinical practice. All of these people—each with his or her own unique set of medical or psychological complaints—have succeeded in taking control of their own nutrition and turning that ability into bountiful good health. With all that patient pre-testing, this is one book that is actually better "used" than new!

Many of the ideas in these pages are based on brand-new theories from the revolutionary science of *preventive nutrition*. If you read a lot about nutrition, you may have read this term. You may have heard it bandied about but never adequately defined. In the simplest, most direct language, it means that you are what you eat and what you eat can make you healthier and stronger than you had ever imagined. Its main emphasis is on *prevention*, not on waiting until you come down with symptoms to get yourself to a doctor to *treat* those symptoms.

Beyond *Immune Power*

In my last book, *Dr. Berger's Immune Power Diet*, you learned about one very specific piece of the health puzzle—preventive immunology and the innovative techniques you can master to bolster your body's immune system, designed to ward off infection. There, I told you about food allergies that cause everything from headaches, asthma, and arthritis to anxiety, eczema, and swollen ankles. These sensitivities can even make you fat and keep you fat, and can wreak havoc with the immune system that is designed to protect you. We saw in the *Immune Power Diet* how many people are allergic to particular foods and don't know it.

I told you in that book how to identify your food sensitivities safely at home. We talked about the Sinister Seven foods that account for about 85 percent of the food reactions I've documented in my years of treating patients. Readers learned how to eliminate the

Sinister Seven from their diets, then reintroduce them one by one and observe their effects. They saw how, by adjusting their food, they could boost their immune systems to fight off all kinds of medical problems—from common colds to cancer.

After I wrote that book, I received letters from hundreds of readers, telling me how immune power had changed their lives. Let me share with you a few of those touching comments:

I wish I could thank you personally for the changes—*all positive*—which have made it possible for our daughter to live a normal life. Since we visited you in October and embarked on your program, she has had no respiratory failure, no pneumonia, and has been able to reduce her cortisone intake. When we came to you in desperation after four years of severe asthma, the year prior to visiting your office was horrendous and I hope will never be repeated. Since October, she has steadily improved. Today, our daughter is a delightful, beautiful almost sixteen year old, who gets up every morning with a smile on her face. Her allergies are almost nonexistent. We cannot thank you enough. . . .

—Mrs. S. B., Alberta, Canada

. . . I am six weeks into the diet and have experienced the following:

1. In four weeks I lost 13 pounds, without once feeling hungry or suffering any of the discomforts associated with diet.

2. I discovered that lettuce and wheat are responsible for my eczema, and have eliminated my itching problem by eliminating them from my diet.

3. I have eliminated 90% of my migraine problem by eliminating those foods.

4. I have thrown away my acne medicine.

5. My blood pressure dropped from 140/100 to 130/84, which marks the first time in twenty years that it has dropped.

6. I have never experienced the feeling of vitality that I now feel.

—Mr. R. H., Nashville, Tenn.

. . . We had never heard of this revolutionary theory, but it really works! My husband has lived most of his days with mild stomach aches and upsets, nausea, evening headaches, and night sweats which doctors . . . diagnose with little or no success. During the 21 days of the diet, my husband did not have one headache, or stomach ache, upset stomach, or night sweats. Now we are elimi-nating the two culprit foods, corn and soy, and we know for sure how much better he feels without the pain and discomfort he used to suffer almost every day. . . .

—Mrs. F. M., Niagara Falls, N.Y.

This book picks up where my *Immune Power Diet* left off. It rounds out every aspect of full-body health. This book goes beyond the immune system to show you how to nutritionally boost all of your body's systems: heart, lungs, blood vessels, digestion, brain, nerves, and glands.

THE BODY-SYSTEM CHECKUP

To know where you want to go, you have to start with where you are now. Take out a pencil and complete this Body-System Checkup. Then, when you have completed the book and designed your own nutritional regimen, you can take this again, and chart your im-provement.

1. Do you have trouble breathing, shortness of breath?
   1) No.
   2) Sometimes, but infrequently.
   3) This is a regular feeling for me.
2. Do you have to cough when you wake up in the morning?
   1) Almost never, except when I am sick.
   2) Sometimes, but it passes quickly.
   3) This happens regularly.
3. Do you frequently catch cold, flu, or other illnesses?
   1) Never—or very rarely.
   2) Two to four times a year.
   3) More than four times a year.

4. When you get sick, how long does it take you to fully recover?
   1) Three to four days.
   2) At least a week.
   3) I don't feel really well for a very long time.
5. When you get a cut or bruise, does it heal quickly?
   1) Yes, heals completely in a few days.
   2) I have noticed that I heal more slowly than I used to.
   3) Bruises stay a long time; cuts leave a visible scar.
6. Have you noticed any problem with walking, balance, or coordination?
   1) No.
   2) Yes, ongoing minor problems.
   3) Yes, they significantly impair my movement.
7. Describe your eyesight.
   1) Fine, with no correction.
   2) I wear prescription glasses or contact lenses.
   3) I have ongoing problems with glaucoma, cataracts, infections.
8. Is your hair thin and lacking shine?
   1) No, I am satisfied with it.
   2) It could be better, but it's no problem.
   3) Yes, its appearance has significantly deteriorated.
9. Describe your skin:
   1) Smooth and silky, not scaly or irritated.
   2) Rough and dry in some months; occasional problem patches.
   3) Often itchy, flaky, or irritated.
10. Do you have headaches?
    1) Once every two months or less.
    2) Yes, often, but they go away easily.
    3) They are painful and debilitating.
11. Do you get leg, arm, or recurring muscle cramps?
    1) No, almost never.
    2) Occasionally—sometimes when I am sleeping.
    3) Yes, frequently, especially when I exercise.
12. Are you troubled by arthritis or joint pain?
    1) No.
    2) Joints sometimes seem stiff, and I notice them more.
    3) Yes, it has really limited my mobility or actions.

13. Do you bleed or bruise easily?
    1) Not that I have noticed.
    2) Yes, but it is not a problem.
    3) Yes, I get bruised by the slightest thing or bleed profusely.

14. Are your extremities ever cold, numb, or tingly-feeling?
    1) No, I do not experience that feeling.
    2) It happens sometimes, but not regularly.
    3) Yes, I have noticed this regularly.

15. When was the last time you did any strenuous exercise?
    1) Within the last five days.
    2) Within the last month.
    3) Within the last year or less.

16. Have you had a broken bone in the last year?
    1) No.
    2) Yes, one incident.
    3) Two or more separate times.

17. Do you get diarrhea, constipation, or digestion problems?
    1) No, or only rarely.
    2) Only when I am ill or have eaten the wrong foods.
    3) This is a frequent problem; I watch carefully what I eat.

18. Do you frequently get indigestion, flatulence, or heartburn?
    1) No.
    2) Occasionally.
    3) It is a regular problem with me.

19. What happens when you don't eat on a regular schedule, or miss a meal?
    1) It doesn't make much difference.
    2) I feel hungry and cranky.
    3) I feel weak, giddy, shaky, or nauseated.

20. Which best describes your sleeping habits?
    1) I usually get six to eight hours of sleep a night; I awake refreshed.
    2) I don't always get enough sleep, but catch up on weekends.
    3) I have problems falling asleep, wake through the night, or have trouble waking in the morning.

21. What is your weight?
    1) About right for my height.
    2) At least ten pounds over my correct weight; my doctor has told me to reduce.
    3) I am currently overweight and it is affecting my health and energy level.
22. Have any family members had diabetes, hypertension, or heart disease?
    1) No, nobody closer than grandparents.
    2) Yes, one or both parents.
    3) Yes, parents and/or a sibling.
23. Have any family members had cancer?
    1) No, nobody closer than grandparents.
    2) Yes, one or both parents.
    3) Yes, parents and/or a sibling.
24. How many prescription drugs do you take?
    1) None, never have taken them regularly.
    2) One to three types of drugs now or in the last year.
    3) At least 4 types now or in the last year.
25. Have you ever been a patient in a hospital?
    1) No.
    2) Once more than a year ago, or for a minor problem, or childbirth.
    3) More than once for a minor problem or have had major problem/surgery.
26. How is your general energy level?
    1) Great—I have lots of energy.
    2) My energy comes in spurts—some days I feel marvelous, but mostly I could use more energy.
    3) Consistent low energy. I often feel I need to sleep, and sometimes even when I do, I don't awake refreshed.
27. Do you have environmental allergies?
    1) No, not that I know of.
    2) Occasionally itchy eyes, runny nose in spring and summer.
    3) It is a constant or frequent problem for me.
28. Have you noticed allergies to any food or drink?
    1) No, nothing I know of.

2) Yes, to one or two specific items.

3) Yes, to three or more food or drink items.

29. Do family members have allergies?

    1) No, not that I know of.

    2) Yes, mostly hay fever.

    3) Yes, significant allergies to foods or environment.

30. How about your work life and career choice?

    1) I really enjoy my job and the challenge it brings me.

    2) I am generally satisfied, but sometimes it gives me real problems.

    3) My job is a chore; I want to leave. I do not work.

31. Is there someone in your life you trust absolutely and can tell your deepest secrets to?

    1) Yes, my mate.

    2) It would depend on the secret.

    3) There is not really anyone in my life I can confide in right now. I am a loner.

32. Do you take time to really enjoy your life, friends, hobbies?

    1) Yes, I am absolutely happy with my balanced life-style.

    2) My time is mostly dedicated to daily chores/family problems.

    3) I can't remember the last time I really had great fun.

33. How is your overall health?

    1) Excellent—I am very satisfied.

    2) Usually all right, but could be better.

    3) Only fair to poor—I wish it were better.

34. Do you have an exercise program?

    1) At least three times a week aerobic exercise, two times a week calisthenics or weight lifting.

    2) I get exercise less than one or two times a week.

    3) Walking is my main exercise, or I get no exercise at all.

35. Choose the one that best describes you:

    1) Calm, even-tempered and generally happy.

    2) I try to keep everything under control, don't always succeed.

    3) I cannot control my temper, am under heavy stress.

36. When you look in a mirror, how do you feel?

    1) That I look good for someone my age, as well as I feel.

2) That it is an effort to feel and look good.

3) I feel I need an entire body makeover.

Now, add up all the numbers you have circled.

If Your Overall Score Is:	Then You Are:
40 or less	Probably in very good shape. You can use this book to help improve your health knowledge even further.
41–80	Basically healthy, could be better. You can expect to see significant improvement with this health program
81 and above	In need of real health changes. You stand to achieve the most dramatic benefits of any group by following the principles in this book.

This is a good general guideline to help you chart progress throughout the book. Keep these questions and categories in mind, and be aware of your own improvement as you tailor your own nutrition plan.

This book goes much farther than *Immune Power*. Preventive nutrition is the true medicine of the next century. The discoveries that make this possible are emerging every day from scientific laboratories all over the world. Just in the two years since I wrote that book, we have seen more significant breakthroughs in this field than in all the other health sciences combined. I know that preventive nutrition is going to have a fundamental impact on longevity and on the quality of life we all live. And I know future generations will take it for granted the way we now accept vaccines and antibiotics as part of everyday life. But why wait until then? Tomorrow's findings won't help you today. You don't have time to spend hours buried in some medical library, sifting the kernels of truth from the many intriguing but ultimately meaningless reports of experimental findings. I have already done that for you.

This book puts the practical gems of that research at your fingertips, beginning only a few pages away. This book brings all of this exciting research together in a way that enables you to make use of it. It is this whole new philosophy of health care that makes this book what it is—*the most advanced, complete nutritional program ever formulated.*

You Are The Expert

You probably already know that you're good at a lot of things in your life—maybe dealing with your family or job or creating special relationships with friends. Maybe you play piano or ski or have some other hobby you do well. But you're probably not used to thinking of yourself as a nutritional expert. After all, that sounds very difficult. That field takes special expertise, doesn't it? On the contrary, that is the basic idea of this book—that nobody is better qualified to design a nutritional plan for you than you are.

No matter how many doctors you've consulted over the years, no matter how long you've seen them, and how many bills you have paid, the fact is that you know something they don't. You alone have intimate knowledge of all the aspects of your health—mental and physical. You know your habits, both good and bad. You know your family history, your environment, your job, your stresses—in short, all the factors that make you unique. These are aspects of your life no doctor, no expert, will fully explore in depth. But this specialized knowledge is what we will tap into together in this book to put *you* at the center, squarely in charge of your own health. You will make *yourself* the expert.

PERSONAL EXPERTISE QUIZ

Each one of us has aspects of our physical and psychological makeup that make us unique. I want you to start getting used to knowing just what those are—in other words, thinking like a medical diagnostician. This exercise has two parts: First, on a sheet of paper, list all the things you can think about yourself that are special and that could possibly have a bearing on your nutritional status. List every-

thing you can think of. There is no one universal set of right answers
—the idea is to get you used to thinking about things that may be
relevant to your own nutritional profile.

The second part is simple: I have given you a checklist that
includes a wide range of factors that you could have chosen. Compare your list against my Personal Inventory list, which follows. Are
there some factors on my list you didn't have on yours? I suggest you
put a check by those categories you believe are particularly relevant
to you. Then you can use this master list—your own personal-
nutrition-factor checklist—as a reminder to guide you as you work
through this book.

Personal Inventory

I am a man _____

I am a woman _____

I am pregnant/lactating _____

I am a woman between 14 and 45 _____

I am past menopause _____

I am an adolescent _____

I am over 60 years old _____

Family history of:

Cancer _____

Heart disease _____

Lung problems _____

Kidney disease _____

High blood pressure _____

Blood disorders _____

Obesity _____

Bone problems _____

Digestive disease _____

Substance abuse _____

Diabetes _____

Diet:

I eat red meat daily _____

I eat fish twice a week _____

I am a vegetarian _____
I eat to lose weight _____
I sometimes binge eat _____
I have two drinks a day _____
I eat a lot of fresh fruits and produce _____
I often eat fast foods _____
I use salt on my food _____
I drink coffee regularly _____
I eat butter regularly _____
I eat cured/smoked meats _____
I am often depressed _____
I am often tired _____
I am often tense _____
I have a stressful life _____
I lack appetite _____
I often don't sleep well _____
I have several different sexual partners _____
I exercise 3 times a week _____
I get less than 1 hour of sunlight a week _____
I get more than 3 hours of sunlight a week _____

Current medical status:

I have:
A heart problem _____
High blood pressure _____
High cholesterol or triglycerides _____
Severe allergies _____
Kidney problems _____
Cancer _____
Diabetes _____
Gastrointestinal problems _____
Hypoglycemia _____
Food allergies _____
Ulcers _____
Numbness or tingling in my extremities _____
Premenstrual problems _____

Periodontal disease   _____
Insomnia   _____
Chronic infections   _____
Arthritis   _____
Constipation   _____

I take:

Blood-pressure medicine   _____
Oral contraceptives   _____
Psychoactive drugs   _____
Diuretics   _____
Insulin   _____
Heart drugs   _____
Antacids   _____
Aspirin   _____

I am a smoker   _____
I work mainly at a desk   _____
I work around chemicals   _____
I work at a computer   _____
I am scheduled for/recovering from surgery   _____
I am an alcoholic   _____
I live in an extremely hot/cold climate   _____
I am 10 percent or more overweight   _____

A SPECIAL NOTE ABOUT SECRETS

Throughout this book, you'll find yourself asking a lot of detailed, sometimes personal questions. Please, don't be bashful in your answers. Just as you have to tell your physician the absolute, unvarnished truth to get the best care, you have to be absolutely honest with yourself on these quizzes. Maybe you have some "secrets": Are you on the Pill? Are you taking some mood-altering medicine, like antidepressants? Do you have a "hidden" medical condition like a colostomy or psoriasis?

Any of these could have an effect on your optimal nutrition plan. And because you know them, they are part of what make you such an expert on yourself. That means you have to take them into account if you are to get the most out of this book.

Nobody else can read any of your answers for I have purposely designed these tests so that you will write your answers on a separate sheet, and only you know where they are and what they refer to. So, with that protection, remember: Honesty is the best medicine!

Enough "Near-Miss" Medicine!

Try this simple experiment. Walk into any local bookstore on your next lunch hour and find the Health and Nutrition section. Look at the books you see there: The California Diet, the Beverly Hills Diet, the Stillman Diet, the Scarsdale Diet, the Eat-To-Win Diet. They all have fancy covers and fancy titles, and their authors may have impressive credentials.

There are now more than fifteen hundred nutrition books in print in hardcover and countless more in paperback. But if you look closely at those books, if you pick up every one on that shelf in the bookstore, you'll see that they all have one thing in common. They rely on the same basic plan for all their readers. They are one-size-fits-all plans. They promise to be all things to all people, ignoring that each person's needs and life-style are vastly different. The fact is, they assume that you are exactly like everybody else, or they try to convince you that the differences don't matter, or they ignore the question entirely.

Think about that for a moment. What would you say if you went into a clothing store and they had fifteen hundred suits, all in the exact same style, size, and color? Do you think you would find one that looked best on you?

These books are just the same. Why should the same prescription work for a nineteen-year-old college student who stays up all night to study for exams and plays on the football team as well as for his forty-four-year-old mother who works as a librarian and leads a sedentary life? Do you suppose the construction worker who begins his day at 6 A.M., smokes constantly and drinks beer on the job has the same nutritional needs as the fifty-year-old office executive who works at her computer terminal under artificial lights and visits her health club three times a week?

All of these diets rely on what I call "near-miss" medicine—they offer an average, off-the-shelf system that will work for *most* people. But not for all. They are designed to work for the average, the median, the mean. They do not take special life-style, medical, and dietary factors into account—how can they? Instead, they rely on the hope that their rules will be right for most of the people who buy that book.

But if there is one thing I have learned from seeing thousands of patients, it is that when it comes to nutrition, there are many more "exceptions" than "rules." So what do those books offer for the rest of us—for those of us with any special considerations? What if you smoke, or are overweight, or have a family history of heart problems? What if you are pregnant, or a runner, or under a lot of stress? You have already seen your own personal expertise list—you know that the number of factors affecting your health goes on and on. Yet those other plans would have you forget all that and settle for a program that *almost* works, that is *nearly* right—that is, at best, a near-miss.

But it isn't just diet books that depend on near-miss medicine. Everybody has heard of the Recommended Dietary Allowance of vitamins and minerals, right? Well, those standards—the most influential and widely used nutritional standards in the country—are based on . . . you guessed it, our old friend, the near-miss principle. They are designed for two people: one, a woman five feet four inches tall, weighing 120 pounds. The other, a man five feet ten inches tall, weighing 154 pounds. Those are the reference "normals." If that describes you 100 percent, absolutely, then those RDAs are talking to you.

But what about the other 224 million of us? What if you are a smaller man, or a taller woman? Or what if you are overweight? Or smoke, exercise regularly, take oral contraceptives, eat vegetarian, have high blood pressure, get a lot of sun, get no sun, are over sixty-five, are pregnant, or . . . well, you begin to get the idea. The RDA simply has no way to take that into account.

This book ends the era of near-miss medicine. Since you are going to become your own expert, you can start by asking yourself the question I pose to every one of my patients: Does this near-miss approach make sense to you?

Of course not—you know that. You don't need an advanced degree to figure that out. Each of us needs different vitamins and minerals, amounts of carbohydrates, as well as amino acids and other nutritional substances. You didn't buy this book to get an approximate solution. You bought it to get real answers that work for you. True health *for you* can come only from a specific program *tailored to you*. Anything else is, well, nutritional nonsense.

If that was the answer you came up with, you are already one step ahead of many of the so-called experts. You are now ready to embark on your own journey to personalized nutritional fitness—to find the nutritional truths that are right for you. Let me be honest from the start. If you've come to this book for a magic cure-all, a one-size-fits-all prescription, you're out of luck. Those are the out-moded concepts of near-miss medicine—formulas that work for most people but are not necessarily right for you.

You're going to leave all that behind. Forget the idea of following blindly in someone else's footsteps. Instead, if you're willing to learn and take responsibility for your own health, you have found the right source and guide. You will learn to map your own path to health, not rely on somebody else's solutions. You will arm yourself with your own personalized knowledge. In short, you have already taken the first step to becoming your own nutritionist.

The Nutrition Workout

Make no mistake. Success doesn't come easily. You're going to have to work at it in a nutritional workout every bit as intense as a Nautilus regimen.

You already know two ways in which this book is unique. The first principle is *personal responsibility*. From now on, you, and you alone, are responsible for your health care.

The second step is *education*. This book distills for you a wide range of nutritional truths. They run from the most tried and true, proven methods to highly innovative, groundbreaking research at the very frontier of preventive nutrition.

But it is the third way this book is different from any others you may have read that is the most important. The nutrition workout is a workbook. Flip through the pages now and you'll see that every chapter has quizzes, charts, and self-assessment quotients. I have included a series of self-scoring profiles for you to evaluate your own highly specific needs based on diet, age, sex, stress and activity levels, medical status, and life-style. They have been designed using the same logic as a branching program on a computer. They may suggest other facts, or sections you ought to reread, or remind you of special personalized factors. Through all of these measures, by using this book as your own health computer, you will be able to calculate your personalized nutrient needs.

Put The Experts At Your Elbow

Through this integrated series of self-tests, this book provides something you could never get in real life—a private, personalized consultation with the world's leading experts on nutrition. You have the chance to follow your own leads, chart your own course, even to train your own thinking to become a better nutrition sleuth.

The key to this book is that it allows you to *interact*, answer questions, find yourself on charts and scales, compare and analyze symptoms. Answering these questions is crucial. At the end, the answers you have given will help you integrate the scores into a grand finale. They will point the way for you to design your own safe, professional, and totally personalized nutritional program.

My Commitment To You

Does it sound difficult? Maybe even impossible? It's not. This same plan has proved do-able, practical—and effective—for thousands of my patients before you. And I promise I will be there at your side through this whole book, helping guide you just as I was in my *Immune Power Diet.*

Together, we will build a patient-proven, sane way to bring all the systems of your body into synchrony. This book will show you how to rebalance nutritional elements and rebuild your body's own health-keeping mechanisms. It will help you take control of yourself to improve your health, appearance, and energy.

Every day, I see for myself how the nutritional wisdom in these pages can make good health available for any person in a more total, dramatic, and *safe* way than ever before.

In documented cases of my seven thousand patients—and you'll meet some of them in these pages—this comprehensive nutritional approach has relieved migraines, arthritis, depression, skin and nerve disorders, anxiety, and numerous other complaints and illnesses. Moreover, it's given significant and lasting weight loss and brought about dramatic improvements in mood, health, stamina, and vitality.

That's why I guarantee that any reader who follows its principles will feel and look better, get sick less, and enjoy improved mood and vitality.

Are you ready? Then let's begin!

Oh, one more thing—get up right now and go get your calendar. Find today, and mark it in red. Why? Because you will look back on it as the day you took your first step to lifelong nutritional health. And when you see the terrific differences this day will make in your energy, appearance—in every phase of your life—I know you'll agree: This is a day to celebrate!

2.

Step Into—And Out Of—
The Nutritional Jungle

Shakespeare certainly didn't have nutrition in mind when he wrote those lines, but he might as well have. I can think of few better descriptions of the current state of nutritional knowledge. To show you what I mean, let me take you behind the scenes to view the work of a prestigious committee of nutritional scientists whose findings you may have seen in the headlines last year.

For five long years, the country's most eminent nutritional researchers had worked to review the existing RDAs—the Recommended Dietary Allowances that are the backbone of our nation's nutritional rules. These members of the nutrition elite weigh all the scientific evidence—old and new—to decide if and how the RDAs should be changed.

The decision of this small group of scientists would send tremors throughout the nutrition world. Doctors follow the RDAs to tell their patients what to include in their diets, food and supplement manufacturers use them to determine the nutritive content of foods, and as consumers, we all rely on them every time we read a food label. The RDAs are supposed to represent the consensus of our best scientific opinion.

Accordingly, those on the panel are truly the high priests of nutrition. They hold impeccable credentials. Participating in the debate were a highly renowned professor of bio-chemistry at Duke University, the president of the National Academy of Sciences, the chief of the Gastrointestinal Unit at Massachusetts-General Hospital and a professor emeritus of nutrition at Harvard Medical School. Fine scientists like these, with such sterling credentials, should certainly be able to agree on these important standards, right? Wrong. In fact, they couldn't manage to find common ground on what the RDAs should even *do*. The debaters divided into two camps: the Illness Avoiders and the Wellness Champions. The Avoiders believe nutritional guidelines are only supposed to guard us against deficiencies. So long as we don't suffer from deficiency diseases like scurvy (not enough vitamin C) and rickets (a lack of vitamin D)—we have enough vitamins. So long as we skirt the edge of gross clinical disease, the RDAs are doing their job.

The Wellness Champions take another approach. They follow the newest research showing how we can use nutrition to prevent cancer, heart disease, and many other chronic illnesses. They think we should use our nutrients to boost our health, not just stave off sickness. Absolute optimum health is their quest, and nutrition, their weapon.

The Avoiders wanted to reduce the amounts of vitamins A and C in the RDAs. Yet this directly contradicted a report issued by the same Academy of Sciences only a few years ago: In *Diet, Nutrition and Cancer*, the Academy reported that vitamins A and C may help prevent cancerous tumors and recommended eating more foods containing those nutrients. The chairman of the Academy's Food and Nutrition Board, Kurt Isselbacher, M.D., cited studies under way showing that vitamin C can have an antitumor effect, and asked point-blank, "Wouldn't it be more responsible to wait for the results of these studies than to arbitrarily lower the RDA now and then increase it later?"

Others, like Dr. Stephen Tannenbaum, a professor at MIT, maintained that "the current RDA for vitamin C is already rock bottom."

He recommended raising it substantially "in order to prevent the development of cancer."

As the debate continued, the words became heated: At one point, the recommendations were termed "absolutely ridiculous and an insult to the scientific community." Another speaker, the professor emeritus from Harvard, put the matter in a nutshell: "The Academy would look foolish if in one report it recommended taking more of a vitamin, and . . . a few years later, it recommended taking less of the same vitamin. Where the hell do we stand on this?"

Yet under all the hoopla, the differences really boiled down to mere milligrams. The most striking changes were those proposed for vitamins A and C. Yet, by just eating one large carrot or a small orange each day, you might more than make up for the tiny RDA differences these learned doctors were arguing over. (The RDA committee also wanted to cut the levels of such crucial nutrients as vitamin B_6, magnesium, iron, and zinc and to increase calcium for women.)

Finally, these most eminent scholars had no choice but to shelve their report. These high priests, scientists with scores of years of professional training and research, on whose walls hang every advanced degree, simply could not figure out what to do.

But wait. There's more. As I write this, a brand-new committee of "experts" has been convened to reconsider the same subject: the Recommended Dietary Allowances. In the meantime, they tell us, stick to what the other experts said in 1980.

If you had trouble following the bouncing ball, rest assured that you are not alone. When even the best experts cannot agree, is it any wonder that you feel confused? Welcome . . . to the Nutritional Jungle.

THE C-SAW

You probably have vitamin C on your own medicine shelf. This is the most common, most understood, and most well-studied of all the vitamins. Everybody, from your physician to the federal government to your supermarket checkout clerk, has a different belief about how much C is good for you.

Look for yourself at the various "official" recommendations for this vitamin over the last thirty years:

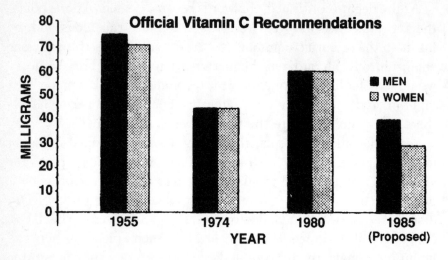

Judge for yourself: Is this the shape of scientific progress?

Deeper Into The Jungle

Every day, you may read something new and allegedly "revolutionary" about nutrition. Then the very next day, you may read something totally contradictory. Sound familiar? If so, you know all too well the rocky terrain, the murkiness, and the quicksand of the Nutritional Jungle.

If you don't believe it is a jungle of contradiction and misinformation out there, look at just a few items I have gathered from the nutritional research frontier in the last few months:

THE OLD SHELL(FISH) GAME

Remember the days—not so long ago—when you weren't supposed to eat shrimp, lobster, or other shellfish because they were high in cholesterol? That seemed reasonable. It was certainly worth it if it helped lower your overall cholesterol and protect you from crippling heart and artery disease. There was only one problem: The information was totally wrong. Now, Alexander Leaf, M.D., chairman of Harvard University's Department of Preventive Medicine, reports that food chemists made a measuring mistake and incorrectly labeled a totally harmless substance as cholesterol! According to him, suddenly we can put shellfish back on the list as an acceptable part of our diet. Ahem.

THE HEIGHT-WEIGHT HOOPLA

Have you ever tried to calculate your ideal weight based on one of the many tables that correlate pounds with height? If so, the result may have surprised you. No wonder, says research in the prestigious *Journal of Nutrition*. It found that two American tables, widely used internationally in assessing nutritional status, completely contradict each other. According to one chart, an eighteen-year-old girl who stands about five feet tall and weighs 101 pounds has an acceptable weight. The same girl, however, is considered 24 percent overweight on the opposite chart! Similarly, if this same teenager weighs about 82 pounds, she falls into the normal range on one chart, but could be classified anorexic according to the other table!

GUESS-YOUR-OWN-WEIGHT EXERCISE

Why do I say "guess"? You can see why for yourself: The table on pages 26–27 has samplings from each of four accepted height-weight charts. Your job is to find yourself on all four—and then calculate the differences among these so-called "authoritative measures." You'll find what most people do—that even at this most basic level, the experts can't agree.

This exercise reminds me of a story told by the late Supreme Court Justice Louis Brandeis: "Back on the farm, when we had to weigh a goat, we'd balance a board on a rock, taking hours to level the board for perfect balance and absolute accuracy. Then we'd carefully place the goat on one end, and very exactingly pile on a precise number of rocks until the board was perfectly in balance. Then, when it was just perfectly still, not moving at all . . ." He'd smile. "We'd guess the weight of the rocks." If the good justice were

Your Ideal Weight According To:

Your Height / Age	Metropolitan Life Insurance Company	U.S. National Center for Health Statistics					North American Association for Study of Obesity	U.S. Department of the Army			
		18–24 years	25–34 years	35–44 years	45–54 years	55–64 years		17–20 years	21–27 years	28–39 years	40+ years
Women											
4'10"	100–131	114	123	133	132	135	114	104	107	110	113
4'11"	101–134	118	126	136	136	138	118	107	110	114	117
5'0"	103–137	121	130	139	139	142	121	111	114	117	121
5'1"	105–140	124	133	141	143	145	124	115	118	121	125
5'2"	108–144	128	136	144	146	148	128	119	123	126	130
5'3"	111–148	131	139	146	150	151	131	123	126	130	134
5'4"	114–152	134	142	149	153	154	134	126	130	134	138
5'5"	117–156	137	146	151	157	157	137	130	134	138	142
5'6"	120–160	141	149	154	160	161	140	135	139	143	147
5'7"	123–164	144	152	156	164	164	144	139	143	148	151
5'8"	126–167	147	155	159	168	167	147	143	147	151	156
5'9"	129–170	—	—	—	—	—	150	147	151	155	160
5'10"	132–173	—	—	—	—	—	153	151	156	160	165

Your Height	Metropolitan Life Insurance Company	U.S. National Center for Health Statistics					North American Association for Study of Obesity	U.S. Department of the Army			
		18–24 years	25–34 years	35–44 years	45–54 years	55–64 years		17–20 years	21–27 years	28–39 years	40 + years
Men											
Age											
5'0"	—	—	—	—	—	—	122	132	136	139	141
5'1"	123–145	—	—	—	—	—	126	136	140	144	146
5'2"	125–148	130	139	146	148	147	131	141	144	148	150
5'3"	127–151	135	145	149	154	151	135	145	149	153	155
5'4"	129–155	139	151	155	158	156	139	150	154	158	160
5'5"	131–159	143	155	159	163	160	144	155	159	163	165
5'6"	133–163	148	159	164	167	165	148	160	163	168	170
5'7"	135–167	152	164	169	171	170	152	165	169	174	176
5'8"	137–171	157	168	174	176	174	157	170	174	179	181
5'9"	139–175	162	173	178	180	178	161	175	179	184	186
5'10"	141–179	166	177	183	185	183	166	180	185	189	192
5'11"	144–183	171	182	188	190	187	171	185	189	194	197
6'0"	147–187	175	186	192	194	192	175	190	195	200	203
6'1"	150–192	180	191	197	198	197	179	195	200	205	208
6'2"	153–197	185	196	202	204	201	184	201	206	211	214

alive today, I think he just might say the same thing about our height-weight tables!

FAST FOOD FEARS

Like most people, you probably grab a quick bite at a fast-food emporium now and then. But did you know that some milk shakes and other fast foods contain yellow dye no. 5? I counsel many of my patients to steer clear of that substance because it can cause allergies. The FDA reports that more than 100,000 Americans may have reactions to the dye, including hives and a dangerous asthmalike response. The dye is used in sodas, ice cream, and a wide range of other foods. Yet those 100,000 people have no way of knowing whether the dye that causes them such acute problems is in their fast foods or not. Why? Because fast foods are currently beyond the arm of FDA requirements that demand that packaged foods be labeled with a nutritional breakdown. Not surprisingly, the National Restaurant Association opposes any changes, claiming that such labeling "would create undue anxiety"! But if fast foods are not labeled, how can you make an informed choice about what you eat? If this sounds like another booby trap in the Nutritional Jungle, you're right.

Yellow dye no. 5 is only one of the many dyes used in our prepackaged foods. There are ten of these common coal-tar dyes that are of questionable safety, and six that are already known to cause cancer in laboratory tests. Yet they remain on sale, in foods like ice cream, maraschino cherries, and a wide variety of children's foods. In fact, FDA figures indicate that over four million children will have consumed more than a pound of these cancer-causing dyes by the time they are twelve years old. And with every bite of these known cancer-causing agents, they increase the risk of serious disease later in life.

CHECK YOUR OWN KITCHEN EXERCISE

Your mission? This exercise has two parts—the second is optional. First, get up right now, go into your kitchen and examine ingredient labels for thirty products. Look at your cans, boxes of prepared mixes —don't forget to look in the refrigerator and freezer. How many of them list artificial colors?

_____	24–30 items	Bad news. Your dietary patterns are almost certainly exposing you to unnecessary cancer-causing substances.
_____	16–23 items	Not great—you can benefit from taking the time to read labels more carefully when you shop.
_____	10–16 items	Average—you probably already take some care, but you are still exposing you and your family to unhealthy levels of additives.
_____	4–9 items	Smart shopper! You obviously watch carefully what you buy. With only a small effort, you could reduce your risk even further.
_____	0–3 items	Congratulations! You obviously make a real effort to control your diet additives and have practically eliminated one source of cancer from your foods!

Remember I said this exercise had two parts? If you are in any of the top four groups, I suggest you go back into the kitchen and discard the color-containing foods. This wins you "extra credit"— not for a grade, but for your commitment to health and nutritional well-being!

FIBER FOLLIES

It's common knowledge that fiber is good for us. Studies have shown that populations that consume a high-fiber diet have much less colon cancer. But we've also been warned by the "experts" that the phytic acid in fiber can interfere with the body's ability to absorb iron and zinc. It now turns out that scientists at the University of Minnesota think that it is precisely this phytic acid—and not the other components of fiber—that helps prevent colon cancer!

The Great Vitamin Rip-Off

How much do you spend on vitamins and mineral supplements? Do you have any idea? Take a minute now and go to your refrigerator or cabinet and add up those prices on the jars. You'll probably be shocked at the total.

Welcome to the club! Each year, Americans spend some $3 billion on supplements. In fact, 40 percent of all people in this country —or about 94 million—determine their own dosages, schedules, and even their own diagnoses. Some of these regimens are pretty complex: More than 10 percent of Americans who take supplements consume between five and fourteen different dietary supplements!

Vitamin C is the most widely consumed nutrient. Almost 91 percent of supplement users take it, either by itself or in combination with other vitamins and minerals. Thiamine is the second most popular, followed by riboflavin, vitamin B_{12}, vitamin B_6, niacin, vitamin E, vitamin A, and vitamin D.

Does this list sound familiar to you? Are you currently taking many of these supplements yourself? No doubt you are using them all with the best motives. It is certainly wise to try to take some responsibility for your own health. You know your food doesn't give you enough nutrients. But uninformed prescribing and ignorant self-dosing are, more often than not, insufficient and ineffective. And at worst, they can be downright dangerous.

Of course, you don't live in a vacuum. There are a number of parties with a strong interest in getting you to take supplements. Many of these are more concerned to stake a reputation for themselves than with the public good. Others put forth untested, half-baked ideas. Too often, convoluted politics influence medical decisions and ideas. It almost amounts to a conspiracy to keep you in a constant state of turmoil. That way, you'll bounce back and forth from one snake-oil solution to another. And all these various factions count on the fact that sooner or later you will be back buying their brand of nutrition.

One particular group to watch out for in the Nutritional Jungle is what I call the Supplement Suckers. They want to suck you into taking supplements and then suck you for all the money they can get. Let's face it: Pharmaceutical companies and vitamin manufacturers spend millions of dollars each year pushing their products— some with alluring brand names that offer all things to all people, packaged in one magic multivitamin. The Supplement Suckers also spend big bucks resisting labeling changes—like the proposed new RDAs. And no wonder—they're making a fortune with things just the way they are.

Another dangerous inhabitant of the Nutritional Jungle is the Pill Glutton. His creed is as simple as it is ill-founded. The Glutton encourages people to dose themselves on the "more is better" premise. "Ten thousand milligrams of vitamin A a day?" they say. "Sounds good. But fifty thousand . . . now that would be even better." This approach is often motivated more by philosophy than by financial greed. Unfortunately, it is also sheer quackery. What the Glutton is inviting you to do is to take megadoses—usually defined as ten times or more of the RDA. Now that, in itself, is not necessarily bad. It's no secret that the RDA is grossly insufficient. The experts we met at the beginning of the chapter told us that, and my own patients demonstrate that every day of the week. But that doesn't necessarily mean that more is better across the board.

The fact is that most nutrients work best in a specific optimal range. That amount depends on all those individual things about you—your life-style, how much you exercise, how you deal with stress, your past medical problems, and many other variables. Just as you can overdose on a drug, you can also O.D. on a vitamin or mineral, ingesting such dangerous levels that you may experience toxic, and sometimes irreversible, side effects.

Still, the Glutton has won plenty of converts. Research shows that for eight common nutrients (thiamine, riboflavin, vitamin C, pantothenic acid, vitamin E, vitamin B_{12}, niacin, and vitamin B_6), millions of consumers take between ten and fifty times the RDA. Most of these people have had no specific work-up, no diagnostics, and don't know how to analyze their own needs. That's not good medicine. On such a program, some pretty frightening things can happen. One of the most abused nutrients is vitamin A. At five to ten times the RDA, this commonly consumed supplement can be toxic. Research from the American Dietetic Association suggests that about four million supplement users in the United States take more than 25,000 international units (I.U.) of vitamin A daily, or five times the RDA. In such high doses, this nutrient can cause birth defects, excess fluid pressure within the skull, headaches, dry skin, bone malformations, an enlarged liver or spleen, loss of appetite, and irritability. Vitamin B_6, otherwise known as pyridoxine, has become a popular treatment to relieve premenstrual symptoms like bloating, headaches, irritability, tender breasts, and the blues. Not only is there little sound evidence that this therapy works, there is also the distinct possibility of dangerous side effects. Researchers have found that an excess of B_6 can cause nervous-system disorders.

That's what happened to my thirty-four-year-old patient Kendra. She is a talented craftsperson, whose beautiful handmade jewelry is in great demand. About two years before she came to my office, she told me, she had heard that vitamin B_6 is the "natural" way to get rid of premenstrual bloating. She began to take 400 milligrams a day. (The RDA allowance is 2 milligrams a day for women.) Over the next few months, she arbitrarily raised her dosage by a factor of ten, to 4 grams a day. Soon she began having trouble with her neck— when she moved it, she got a pins-and-needles sensation that went all the way down her legs to her feet. She started feeling unsteady, had difficulty walking and balancing, and she was having trouble manipulating the tiny tools, gems, and bits of silver she worked with every day.

By the time she got to my office, she could walk only with the aid of a cane. Her physical exam revealed that her sensations of touch, temperature, and vibration were severely impaired. I took her off vitamin B_6 immediately. Only three months later, Kendra had improved so much that she was able to feel sensations again and walk without a cane.

As I told Kendra, she could have been spared all of this agony. We know that we need more B_6 than the mere 2 milligrams a day the RDA recommends. But we also know there is a specific range where this vitamin, like most nutrients, works best. When you do as Kendra did, and write your own prescription without knowing the right facts, it's a straight road to trouble. That's the idea of this book—to give you the facts to write your own prescription, knowledgeably, safely, and effectively.

What Your Doctor Doesn't Know About Nutrition

By now, you're probably thoroughly confused. Where can you turn? You've learned that you can't trust the federal government to tell you how much of each vitamin and mineral you need. You've seen that the nutrition experts are slinging mud at each other, and what was yesterday's nutritional truth is today's tomfoolery. There is a $2 billion industry out there encouraging you to spend your last cent on vitamin and mineral supplements, and a bunch of Gluttons telling you to take as much as you can get.

So whom do people look to? To someone who has been in their lives for years—the trusted family doctor. Perhaps they have a devoted internist, pediatrician, or gynecologist. Surely *they* know the answers, right? The sad truth, I'm sorry to say, is that none of them is really equipped to help you. Would you go to a psychiatrist to set your broken leg? Of course not! So why rely on someone for nutrition advice who hasn't received any specialized training?

Nutrition education in medical schools is, in a word, embarrassing. When the Committee on Nutrition in Medical Education of the National Research Council surveyed 45 of the 127 medical schools in this country, it found that barely one quarter require even *one* course in nutrition. And only 3 to 4 percent of the questions asked by the National Board of Medical Examiners deal with this most crucial topic.

Yet research this year from the prestigious National Research Council implicates nutritional factors in six of ten leading causes of death—heart disease, cerebrovascular disease, cancer, adult diabetes, arteriosclerosis, and alcohol-induced cirrhosis of the liver. That means we should be looking to nutrition to help solve those very problems. No wonder that same study concludes that nutrition education programs are "largely inadequate."

If things stay as they are now, you might soon get better nutritional advice in a three-star restaurant than at your doctor's office. I understand that the crème de la crème of

American cooking schools, the Culinary Institute of America, has instituted a weeklong course in nutrition for its aspiring chefs. That is several days longer than the basic nutrition training at Harvard Medical School. And I'll bet those doctors can't even whip up a soufflé!

Experts are beginning to come to grips with this expertise vacuum: In a recent publication, Tufts Medical School, my alma mater, devoted a whole article to the problem of finding trustworthy nutrition advice. The author wrote: "A mistake that people may make when they want advice about their diets is turning to anyone called 'doctor.' "

It is quite clear that the message about preventive nutrition has not yet reached most practicing physicians. A recent study from the University of Maryland Medical School asked practicing physicians to list actions their own patients could take to improve their health —and barely a *quarter* of the doctors even mentioned taking any vitamin supplements at all! Clearly, old ideas die hard. If your physician doesn't have the answers, perhaps you turn to your pharmacist for advice. Seems reasonable—after all, pharmacists sell over half of all the vitamins in this country. Unfortunately, your friendly neighborhood druggist usually has even less nutrition education than medical students. So where else can you turn? More often than not, the person behind the counter of your local health-food store has not even been certified in any way to dispense nutritional counsel. You'd be better off talking to the local chef!

Now you know why I wrote this book. It will give you the education that your doctor, your pharmacist, your natural healer, or health-food clerk can't. You won't have to wander in the Nutritional Jungle looking for a guide—because you will take on that role yourself!

Every day, my waiting room fills with patients who can't find relief in standard medical care. They get a unique mineral and vitamin program balanced to their own individual medical profile.

But the point is: *This is nothing they couldn't do for themselves.*

My patients see their symptoms disappear; they get stronger, more alert and vital. Most important, they learn to empower themselves for health by becoming their own nutritionists.

As a physician, I know my treatments are based on proven, safe medicine. Having trained in psychiatry, I understand the psychological aspects of good health and positive behavior change. But most of all, as one who spends every day helping people get healthy, I know people can get for themselves the same results I see in my practice.

I consider myself living, vital proof of the results you can get. Since I wrote *Dr. Berger's Immune Power Diet*, I have kept up a schedule that would test the endurance of any professional athlete. I've traveled all over the country, lecturing, appearing on TV talk shows and radio, giving magazine and newspaper interviews, answering questions about the book, consulting with patients and assisting colleagues with professional consultations. Some weeks, I have had to be in three states in two days! As you can imagine, it takes enormous energy and stamina—to say nothing of clearheadedness and vitality—to keep up such a frenetic pace and run my busy practice in New York.

There is simply no way I could have achieved all this and performed well at each task if I had not become my own nutritionist. My patients who are following their own regimens tell me that they too have been able to take on more and accomplish more than they ever dreamed possible. And they don't feel wrung-out or run-down. Neither do I. Far from it. My travels around the country have been exhilarating because so many people have told me that my nutritional guidelines are working for them. The positive responses I have received and continue to receive are among the most gratifying experiences of my life.

Controversy, Controversy, Controversy . . .

But in the midst of all the kudos and encouraging validation of the nutritional principles I use, I have found myself plunged into heated controversy. In each city, I met scores of people who would tell me about the near-miracles they had experienced after following my regimen.

Then I'd return to my office and read articles by the old-line medical establishment who refused to believe it. One reviewer termed my book "filled with unscientific claims and unwarranted advice." Another called it "a collection of quack ideas about food allergies." Jean Mayer, Ph.D., a key figure in American nutrition, had this to say: "In adults, food allergies are rare, tough to diagnose, and should be treated with the help of a registered dietician."

Frankly, I wasn't surprised. The medical establishment has long debated the evidence on food sensitivities and their link to ill health of all kinds. As I've said before, my practice is highly controversial and based on hypotheses only now being proved in the research laboratories.

Dr. Mayer even termed my book "ignorant of the National Academy of Sciences Recommended Dietary Allowances, which were first published over 40 years ago and are periodically updated to reflect the latest evidence on each nutrient."

Now, remember the RDA debate where we started this chapter? That debate occurred only three weeks before Dr. Mayer published his article. Had he even read the newspaper accounts in those weeks, he would have known about the exploding conflict over that "latest evidence." In fact, the very RDA standards he wrote about had been rejected and shelved by none other than the president of the National Academy of Sciences. But even this glaring evidence does not persuade the skeptics. This comes as no surprise to me. Old ideas are easier to hold on to and harder to give up than new ones! Others criticize my recommended dosages because they are above the RDA. They claim that only people with special problems—like alcoholism and genetic malabsorption disorders—have serious deficiencies. If using higher dosages than RDA is the charge, I plead guilty. As I said then, mine is a radical concept of nutrition. It is not enough to keep people perched just over the edge of serious nutritional deficiencies. Instead, we can use powerful, balanced, personalized knowledge to enhance every area of our health and well-being.

I do not doubt that Dr. Mayer and those reviewers reflect the conventional wisdom. But I *do* doubt that they have ever seen, as I have, thousands of patients who show dramatic improvement when their food allergies are taken into account.

The truth is, the newest research has simply left a lot of the traditional thinking behind. Nowhere is this more true than on the subject of food allergies and migraines. I can't help but wonder if the critics are fully familiar with the most recent evidence. In one study, which appeared since my book went to press, a group of 327 British and American migraine-headache experts estimated that up to 20 percent of their patients' migraines were due to dietary factors. Of course, there was some disagreement. A few of the experts estimated the figure ran as high as 80 percent of their patients! The foods most commonly cited as migraine triggers were: chocolate, alcohol, cheese, monosodium glutamate (MSG), nuts, citrus fruit, meat, coffee, nitrates, fish, dairy products, onions, hot dogs, pizza, wheat products, bananas, tomatoes, apples, and various vegetables. If that list sounds familiar, it should. Many of those are the same foods I mention in my earlier work.

MORE NEW PROOF

Another intriguing study has come out since I wrote the *Immune Power Diet*. At the University of Chicago Medical Center, John Crayton, M.D., associate professor of psychiatry, tested twenty-three psychiatric patients with a history of food-reaction complaints. In an eight-day trial comparing them with a control group, 70 percent showed significant mood and behavior responses that made them irritable, anxious, and depressed. And guess which foods were the worst? Wheat and milk—the very same ones I pinpointed in my book. In the laboratory, this same study showed that their blood had significant immune-system abnormalities.

The point is that these studies clearly illustrate the breakneck pace of change in the field of preventive nutrition. Every day we are learning more, and sometimes it takes academic researchers a while to catch up to what many of us who see large numbers of private patients already know.

Happily, the new nutritional thinkers—the Wellness Nutritionists—are making their voices heard. The much-maligned Linus Pauling, Ph.D., winner of two Nobel prizes, has long observed that high doses of vitamins are the key to good health and long life. "They say the RDA is the amount needed to keep the average person in ordinary good health. I say it keeps them in ordinary bad health. I'd like to see persons taking thousands of milligrams a day; they'll lead longer, healthier lives." Of course, it's not enough that any one person should say it, even if he holds two Nobel prizes. We need solid results to support his claims. But I cite Pauling because he is a true nutritional visionary. Based on his vision, scientists who are more far-reaching nutritional thinkers than the old guard, who are not afraid to till intellectual fields, have been encouraged to create a whole new definition of human nutrition—one that goes beyond sickness and treatment to create better health than we ever thought possible. That definition is preventive nutrition.

Nutritional Sanity

So we've come back to where we started this chapter, with the RDA. No doubt you've been making up your own mind about the meaning of that elusive golden rule. By now, you've probably concluded that the RDA means little or nothing for *you* as an individual. You are absolutely right. National averages may work to keep a nation healthy. But you are not a statistic, you are an individual, and averages simply can't work to make *you* as healthy as you can be.

The only approach that makes any sense is individualized nutrition. It provides a unique regimen, not a formula based on statistical averages of large numbers of people. It would be lunatic to base each person's supplements on averages, giving them standardized doses of vitamins, minerals, and amino acids, without even checking to see what their own problems, strengths, and needs are.

It should be clear from this chapter that nobody knows all the facts, and nobody knows what tomorrow's breakthroughs will bring because nutrition is an ever-expanding field. It's going to be quite a while before all the answers are in. I make no claim to be psychic or to have all the answers myself.

But in the meantime, your goal should be to make yourself healthier with all we *do* know, starting today. And your path in that direction, out of the Nutritional Jungle, has to be based on some logic. Isn't it a lot more logical to make some nutritional sense for each individual human being than to try to extrapolate from arbitrary figures for an entire nation? Ultimately, that logic depends on *you.*

I know that sounds like a tall order. Maybe you want to close this book and read some nutritional science fiction that makes it all easier because there are no choices to make and you don't have to take any responsibility. Remember, I said it wasn't going to be easy. Right now, you're probably feeling confused, frightened, maybe even a little panicked. That's only natural. You're afraid of taking the wrong steps. That makes you feel immobilized so you want to do nothing and just sit and stare into space until a magic solution presents itself. Many of my patients have experienced the same feelings. There would be something wrong with you if you didn't feel just this way. After all, you are about to embark on a new journey.

Most new things we take on inspire two contradictory emotions at the same time. One is exhilaration. You feel excited, full of good anticipation of all the wonderful things to come, on the brink of a major positive change in your life.

The other feeling is terror because, by definition, a new experience is totally unfamiliar. You are taking a risk, a challenge. You feel as if your next step may be off the edge of a cliff. So the combination you get is exhilarating terror. You may slip from one side of the continuum to the other and settle anywhere in between for a while.

That's why I am here. My role in this book is to act as your trusted guide and mentor, to show you the way, to make the complex simple and easy to understand—in short, to give you all the emotional support you need on your journey.

You may be confused and not understand many of the things I've talked about so far, but I assure you that by the end of this book, you will have come out on the other side of exhilarating terror where you feel only the exhilaration.

Let's sum up. We've seen that world-renowned experts disagree about nutrition, that doctors don't know enough about the subject, but that you can find nutritional sanity by turning to yourself with my help. In the final analysis, there's really only one question you have to ask yourself: Do you have any choice but to become your own nutritionist?

3.

A View Inside

"Tell me what you eat,
and I will
tell you what you are."

—Anthelme Brillat-Savarin

You're sitting at a corner table at a four-star restaurant. Your waiter brings you your appetizer, a steaming plate of *moules marnière* —mussels cooked in onions and white wine. As he sets them down in front of you, they are still gently sizzling from the kitchen. Your mouth waters, the subtle onion aroma stimulating your nostrils.

You pick up the tiny sterling-silver fork to spear one succulent mussel, twist it away from its pearly shell, and raise it to your mouth. Suddenly, the taste fills your mouth—sweet and delicate. You roll the mussel around your tongue, delighting in the soft, smooth texture.

Every one of your senses is involved. Eating is such a totally sensual experience that one of my patients refers to *Gourmet* magazine as his pornography! As you chew, you are savoring the wine, the meal, and soft lights—and I'll wager nutrition is absolutely the farthest thing from your mind.

But for your body, it's at center stage. From the moment you sat down until long after you have gone to bed tonight, your organs will

285

be working in perfect synchrony, involved in a truly astounding effort—without your even realizing it! Over the next six hours, it will prepare and process all the food you ate, sift the vital nutrients from the waste, unleash thousands of complex biochemical reactions, and transport the fuel from your food to every one of your body's ten trillion cells. And all you have to do is enjoy dinner!

The Great Biological Food Processor

In the first chapter of this book, I promised you *knowledge*. In the second, I guaranteed that together we could clear a path out of the Nutritional Jungle. Now, in this chapter, we will start to make good on both of these pledges.

I want to lead you on a guided tour through the greatest food processor there is—not a Cuisinart, but you. From the inside out, we'll see exactly what happens after you swallow not just those mussels but the filet mignon and baked potato, even your salad and chocolate mousse. We'll follow that meal from your fork to its final destination—watching the nutrients work in each of your body's myriad cells, keeping you vital, fit, and healthy.

Why are we doing this, in a book about nutrition? Simple. When patients come to my office, they are almost always confused about how the food they eat—and the vitamins and minerals they take— really act in their body. When I explain simply how the digestive system works, in a language they can understand, they tell me it is tremendously helpful. I watch their eyes light up as I explain the terms they have heard floating around for so long—but never quite understood. The concepts of "carbohydrates," "proteins," "fats" aren't so complicated, and you don't need a Ph.D. in biochemistry (after all, you hardly have to know optics to watch television, or physics to drive a car).

But understanding them *does* put you in possession of the single most powerful tool you can have to sort out dietary misinformation. Once you have really understood what is in this chapter, you will become much more nutrition savvy. It's much harder for an uninformed or unscrupulous adviser to sell you a bill of goods that such-and-such is a wonder food, when you know that it provides zero nourishment to your cells and is eventually discarded by the body as waste.

IT'S UP TO YOU . . .

Of course, you don't have to read this chapter. If you already have a good blueprint of how things work between your throat and navel, and if you are eager to get on to writing your own nutritional prescription, you can skip to the next chapter, Nutrition 101, on page 54. This book is, remember, a tailor-made nutritional approach, and you have to choose what is right for you.

Still here? Good. A nutritional researcher who is a friend of mine often refers to digestion as "the stomach symphony." She's right, when you understand the incredibly complex chemical symphony that brings together vitamins and minerals, fats, carbohydrates, amino acids, and proteins to construct healthy cells in your blood, organs, and tissue. But if you are to become the director of that symphony, and make it play the way *you* want it to, you have to understand something about how the parts all work together. And, as my patients confirm, once you do, you can make truly beautiful music!

We'll look at how your own body chemically breaks down bits and chunks of your food into pieces small enough to enter your bloodstream; the digestive tricks your body uses to take the bundles of precious nutrients to every corner of your body; how your body keeps its nutrient accounts balanced, and keeps track of supply and demand.

If you are like most of the people I see, you are largely unaware of all the complex machinery that turns food into fuel. It is only when something goes wrong that you sit up—sometimes literally!—and take notice. I know you have suffered at some point from constipation, diarrhea, bad breath, stomach cramps, or heartburn. You may have even had migraine headaches accompanied by nausea or vomiting. All of these problems are unpleasant reminders of the churnings and motions of our digestive system and our overindulgences.

However, by paying careful attention to what you eat and how, you can rid yourself of those symptoms and many others. That is the first sign that you are doing a good job of writing your own nutritional prescription. As you improve and gain confidence, pretty soon you will develop your intuitions, a sort of nutritional sixth sense—about what makes you feel right and what doesn't. Then, when you say "I feel it in my gut," it will be quite literally true.

After The Swallow . . .

No matter what you ate—whether it was mussels, filet mignon, pizza, or ice cream—the next step is the same. The food, mixed with saliva and chewed into soft, moist lumps, is swept by your swallow into the passageway to your stomach—the esophagus. You may sometimes feel that the heavy dinner of lasagne just landed with a thud in your stomach—well, not so. That ten-inch tube is a pipeline of muscle, closed at its lower end by a ring of muscles called a sphincter. That sphincter works like a traffic cop, controlling the flow of food, keeping your digestion running with a steady, even flow.

The sphincter works like a drawstring, staying pinched shut until your food has been properly chewed and mixed with saliva. Only then will the traffic-cop sphincter open to allow the mash to proceed to the next stop: your stomach. The sphincter must work very precisely because your stomach can hold only about a quart of food mash at any one time.

THE BIG, PINK, WAITING ROOM

The first part of your dinner is now arriving in your stomach. But even before the sphincter allows any of it to enter, your stomach has started its work. Back when you first read the menu, when you saw the waiter approach with the fragrant plate of mussels, before you took your first bite, your stomach was on red alert. It began to churn—it may have even emitted a small anticipatory gurgle. At the same time, the front end of the system—your mouth—got ready, secreting the saliva necessary to help you break down and savor the food

—and help your teeth begin the process of chewing your food into mash.

FIND-YOUR-STOMACH EXERCISE

Can you think precisely where your stomach is? Most people don't have a very clear idea of where this organ is located. Stand before a mirror and point to it. If your finger landed somewhere in the middle of your abdomen, slightly above your navel, you're wrong. But nearly everybody makes the same mistake.

Actually, your stomach lies on the left side of your abdomen between the end of your breastbone and your waist. It is a J-shaped pouch, its upper end connected to your esophagus and its lower end connected to your small intestine—again, that portal is ringed by a sphincter muscle.

Most people give the stomach much more credit than it deserves. Very little real digestion happens in the stomach—only certain simple sugars and alcohol enter your bloodstream directly through your stomach. About 20 percent of the alcohol from those mussels went straight into your blood from your stomach. Otherwise, your stomach functions mostly like a food processor, kneading and mixing the rest of your dinner in preparation for the major digestive action of the small intestine.

Of course, the stomach is more than just a mixer that churns your food into a paste. It also adds various chemicals to help break down the food. By far the most powerful is stomach acid, the body's most acidic fluid. This potent liquid kills almost all the harmful bacteria in your food and erodes the cementing material that holds the cells of food together. (It is interesting to note that if you are frightened, angry, or stressed, the gastric juice flows less freely. That's why, if you eat while in a state of emotional turmoil, you may feel stomach discomfort—and why your stomach will do a less efficient job of breaking down nutrients from your food.)

By five hours after you eat, your stomach has done most of its work. The first parts of your meal to leave the stomach are the complex carbohydrates (remember that delicious baked potato?), followed by the proteins and fats. The meal that stays in your stomach longest is one mixed with a lot of protein and fats—the mussels you enjoyed at the beginning of this chapter. Unfortunately, while that may be satisfying, it is not very good for you—the dose of fats and protein it gives you is excessive. It's also why people say you feel hungry again after eating Chinese food—that food often has a near-optimal high-carbohydrate, low-fat balance. That balance is what I recommend for many of my patients, and the basis of the diet suggestions you'll see in Chapter Eleven. But let's not get ahead of the story.

When your stomach has completed the job of breaking down your food part by part, and mixing it into a homogeneous stew, it signals another sphincter, at the lower end of the stomach, to release the mash into the small intestine. The stomach squeezes about a teaspoonful of mash every three seconds into the small intestine, until it has emptied itself—about five hours after you put your fork down in the restaurant. Before long, your stomach is again empty. Soon, in fact, you may hear it start to growl. Doctors don't know precisely why the stomach does that, but it's the signal that your big pink food processor is ready for another meal.

Now the action moves to the small intestine, where the real work of digestion occurs. Don't let the word "small" mislead you. That refers only to its diameter; in truth, there is nothing tiny or insignificant about this organ. In fact, if you stretched it out, it would measure twenty feet long—but thanks to Nature's superb engineering, it is all coiled up inside your abdomen. Its length gives it a huge surface area, to help your body absorb nutrients as quickly and efficiently as possible. If you could look at your own intestine, you would be amazed: Its inner surface is pleated with velvety folds, pimpled with millions of tiny fingers, called *villi*. All the crevices and crannies increase the surface area even more. So much, in fact, that if you were to spread out all these convoluted folds, you would have an area as big as a baseball diamond.

As the food mix is moved along the intestine by muscular contractions (known as *peristalsis*), it gets more processing at every turn. It gets sprayed by a sluice of digestive enzymes from your pancreas and bile from your gallbladder. These both work to break the food up still further, into tiny droplets of chemical fragments, small enough to pass through the blood-rich walls of the intestine. This is the real front line of nutrition, where your dinner finally enters your bloodstream in the form of chemicals, bringing the fuel destined for all the cells of your body. The good parts—the digestible building blocks—of your expensive dinner are now headed directly to where they will do the most good—to your bones, your organs, and your blood, to keep you fit and healthy!

The indigestible material left over after the usable fuel has been absorbed by your small intestine moves farther along, to your large intestine. In the course of digestion your body has used a lot of fluid —two or three quarts—and it can't afford to waste it. So Nature has thoughtfully equipped you with a water-recycling plant: the large intestine.

What's left after the water is wrung out must be expelled as waste. Most of it consists of bacteria, fibers from plant tissue, and gristle or cartilage that your body can't digest. This excess baggage moves downstream to wait in the rectum, ready to be expelled as a bowel movement anywhere from twenty-four to thirty-six hours after you have eaten.

Some bacteria live permanently in the large intestine, feeding on food fragments that pass through. In return for those nutrients and a warm, moist place to dwell, these bacteria perform a vital function. They form vitamins and amino acids that the body needs. For most vitamins, they produce only a fraction of the body's requirements; however, for vitamin K, the crucial vitamin that helps your blood clot properly, these bacteria produce most of your body's supply. If it weren't for those friendly vitamin K-producing bacteria working overtime in your belly, you would soon run low on this essential vitamin, which could cause life-threatening hemorrhage.

Your Chemical Warehouse

Technically, your liver—the largest and heaviest organ in the body, often weighing as much as six pounds—is not really a part of the digestive system. But without it, your entire well-tuned digestive machine would grind to a halt, so I want to talk about it for just a moment. Besides, many of the vitamins and nutrients we will discover in Chapter Eight work in the liver, so it is good to have an understanding of what it does.

The liver is, as much as any organ, key to health and nutrition. It acts as a chemical filter to prevent the bloodstream from being polluted by poisons and toxins. It breaks down red blood cells when they have become damaged and worn-out by their long journey around the bloodstream. It recycles valuable materials like iron, which the body has in short supply, and puts them back in circulation.

Most important, your liver is a magnificent energy "storage battery." It stores the sugar that has been absorbed by the small intestine, and works constantly like an exquisitely tuned energy thermostat. It makes sure your blood is not overrich with sugar—the condition of "hyperglycemia," which may indicate diabetes—or sugar-poor, the well-known condition of hypoglycemia, which can make you feel foggy, fuzzy, and weak.

DIGESTION TIME-LINE QUIZ

Here is an optional quiz to check how well you have understood the digestive phases. I have listed several steps in the digestive process. I want you to number them in the correct order in which they occur when you eat. When you have done that, go back and draw a time line that places the steps in sequence. (Remember, various steps can overlap.) If you aren't sure, go back and read the last few pages.

1. Stomach processes complex carbohydrates_____
2. Esophagus sphincter releases food to stomach_____
3. Stomach growls_____
4. Large intestine re-absorbs water from waste_____
5. Stomach processes proteins and fats_____
6. Stomach sphincter releases food to small intestine_____
7. Liver processes nutrients from intestine_____
8. Vitamin K and amino acids manufactured in large intestine
   _____
9. Saliva glands begin increasing secretions_____
10. Gallbladder and pancreas fluids break down food_____

Answers:

1. 4   2. 3   3. 1   4. 8   5. 5   6. 6   7. 10   8. 9   9. 2   10. 7

That "Gut Feeling"

We have talked a lot about the physiological side of digestion, but of course, not all of the factors are 100 percent physical. There is a psychological side as well. Over and over again, my patients show me that their digestion is a sounding board for their emotions. I know you have experienced a lump in your throat, butterflies in your stomach, or perhaps even diarrhea due to stress or fear. Binge eating can be brought on by your feelings—and so can anorexia, the morbid refusal to eat at all. We have seen how stress makes your digestive machine much less efficient. That is why what you eat, when you eat, and how you feel at the time can affect your body weight, general health, and the value your body derives from your food.

Of course, each of us reacts differently—that is the focus of the individualized nutritive approach of this book. So now that you have a good sense of the general picture, it's time to see how it applies to you—so get out your pencils; it's time for some homework.

KEEP YOUR OWN DIGESTION DIARY

The first thing I had to learn in medical school was to sharpen my eyes and ears, to make sense out of the data my patient's body was giving me. You have to do likewise if you plan to be a good nutritional practitioner for yourself.

You probably know more about the quirks and idiosyncrasies of your digestive system than you realize. When you eat bacon, for instance, do you feel gassy afterward? Do onions have a way of making their presence felt for hours after a meal? You may have noticed that there are particular ingredients or dishes that give you real problems, when your friends, mates, and families report no such reactions.

Those are a part of your digestive "personality." And you must understand that personality intimately—as though your life depended on it, because it does. To get you better acquainted with your digestive system and its specific patterns that make you unique, I want you to use a log sheet like the one on page 100 to keep a very precise account of what you eat for the next week. Write it down in the first column, under the heading FOOD. Be honest now—write down everything, including snacks, nibbles, and noshes. There's no right answer here, so don't hide anything. Besides, nobody is going to see it but you!

The next column—MOOD—is where you record how you felt as you ate. Were you angry at your boss, stressed out because you were rushing to meet a deadline? Or were you calm, leisurely enjoying the sensual experience of a calm, unhurried meal?

The next column—REACTIONS—is where you tune out the world and tune in your digestive system. What signals do you hear? This is the time to use the inner observation skills you learned in Chapter One. Can you feel your stomach churning, kneading, grinding? Are there slight cramps, or a feeling of uncomfortable fullness, anywhere in your belly? Over the next hours, notice any remarkable changes in your bowel movements or urine. Can you relate those to what you ate? I had one patient call only two weeks ago, in a panic because she was having bloody urine. After I calmed her down, I asked what she had eaten the day before. "Well, I had chicken, and a wonderful beet and onion casserole . . ." I reassured her that she had found the culprit—beets often give people a darkish or pinkish tinge to the urine. But if she had been keeping her own Digestive Diary, she would have saved herself not just a phone call but a lot of unnecessary anxiety.

The last column of the Digestive Diary is the most important. "CONCLUSIONS" is where you can play nutritional Sherlock Holmes. Do you see any cause and effect pattern or a trend? Perhaps you feel lighter and more energetic after vegetable meals than after heavy meat-filled meals. Perhaps certain foods make you feel racy, or give you slight headaches or nausea.

By paying close attention, you will learn what foods make your digestive system hum along smoothly and without interruption. You'll also find very quickly what foods force a backup in the system, or even a total breakdown—diarrhea, constipation, or heartburn. Those are the first foods you will learn to avoid or to build into your nutrition schedule in a way that they will not cause distressing symptoms.

You've learned a lot in this chapter, and it's time to give yourself a pat on the back. By understanding the mechanics of your digestive system—what agrees with it, and what raises a ruckus—you have taken another giant step out of the Nutritional Jungle.

Day	Food	Mood	Reactions	Conclusions

4.

Welcome to Nutrition 101

====

"Health has its science, as well as disease."
—Elizabeth Blackwell,
first U.S. woman physician

Somewhere in China, a peasant family sits down to dinner. Ho Si Ping, tired and hungry, has been working the fields all day long. His wife cooks a small scrap of meat along with whatever vegetables she could find that day—black mushrooms, bamboo shoots, and snow peas. She piles the food on heaping mounds of rice and pours cups of tea. The family eats.

Meanwhile, in America, another family sits down to dinner. Before broiling the T-bone steak, Mrs. Allen has carefully trimmed away all the outside fat. As she opens each steaming baked potato, she dabs it with sour cream and chives, then dots the boiled carrots with butter. Four-year-old Sam gets himself a glass of whole milk. His mother asks him to put around the lettuce and tomato salads and get the French dressing and the ketchup. At the end of dinner, Sam pushes back his plate and demands, "What's for dessert?" Apple pie with ice cream, his mother tells him—his favorite.

Now let me ask you: Which family is eating more wisely? Are the Allens, with their several-course balanced meal, getting better nutrition? Actually, Ho Si Ping and his family, who can't read this book and have never shopped in a supermarket, are eating the totally healthy diet.

The Allens' traditional American meal puts them at high risk for a long list of lethal diseases. Hidden in that delicious dinner of steak, sour cream, whole milk, French dressing, butter, and ice cream is a lethal ingredient, one that shortens their lives with every bite—fat. In addition to heart attack, stroke, diabetes, and obesity, that fat has the single strongest link to cancer of anything we eat. Yet 40 percent of the Allens' calories come from various fats, and fully half of the calories of that juicy steak. It all adds up to a deadly, and all too common, fat megadose.

In addition, the poor unsuspecting Allen family ate nowhere near enough complex carbohydrates, and the protein they got came from entirely the wrong sources. As if that weren't bad enough, they put sugar-laden ketchup on their steak and filled up at dessert on more empty calories from refined sugar. Only the apples in the pie—all but unrecognizable after being rolled in sugar and submerged in fatty pastry—provided any of the healthy, natural sugars. In short, they broke almost every rule of good nutrition.

Studies have shown that the average American family gets a massive 40 percent of its calories from fats, and less from carbohydrates—precisely 180 degrees backward! Their intake of fiber is negligible, but sugar from refined sources makes up 18 percent of their daily calories. (It should account for virtually none.) In fact, the only part of the typical American diet that even comes close to the right level is protein—12 percent of the average diet. But unfortunately, most of that comes from the wrong sources.

The problem is that as we have become more affluent in this country, we have gradually consumed more calories. With that has come an increasing incidence of cancer, especially malignancies of the uterus, endometrium (the lining of the uterus), and the gallbladder. In fact, The New England Journal of Medicine reports that 35 percent of cancers in this country may be caused by our diet. Ironically, that means that our diet—the single best tool we can use to stay healthy and fit—is next only to cigarette smoking as a cause of cancer.

While we Americans are far off the nutrition mark, not everybody indulges in such nutritional nonsense. The *Chinese Medical Journal* reports that the average Chinese eats 69 percent carbohydrates, 10 percent protein, and only 21 percent fat. That is much closer to the optimal diet for the human animal. We could take a page from their book, and from the habits of many other cultures, most of them poor and "backward" by our standards, where people eat a much healthier diet than our own. It is ironic that we, who live in the wealthiest country in the world, who are the most abundant food reapers in history, suffer more from certain nutrition-linked ills than some of the poorest, most primitive societies on earth. It's a nutritional embarrassment.

When I tell this story to my patients, you would be surprised how many of them choose the Allens—with all their bad mealtime habits—as a model of nutritional health. That's why this section is crucial. These next three chapters are all about building a safe, solid nutritional foundation. Together, we will cover what you would learn in a good, comprehensive survey course on nutrition—say, Nutrition 101. It is the most important, solid course on sound nutritional health I can offer in the pages of a book. I don't think you will find this course at any college—and certainly not at any medical school. I've designed it to give you the basic nutritional principles for building your own diet.

Nutrition 101 gives you a broad-based nutrition course so you can go from there on your own. Throughout, we discuss the major nutritional groups, the macronutrients. These are the primary building blocks your body needs to perform its many complicated functions and protect you from disease.

As an overview course, Nutrition 101 reviews the scientific consensus on each of the nutritional groups you need for optimal health. Now I can hear you saying: "But, Dr. Berger, I already know the basics." You may feel that you already know enough in these areas and be tempted to skip this section. A word of advice: Don't. For even though you may know parts of this information, and some aspects may seem familiar, I would rather that you got it absolutely right, once and for all.

In my New York practice, I see patients every day who are nutritionally sophisticated. They watch their diets, conscientiously read health magazines, and follow the latest dictums. Yet they still carry tremendous—and dangerous—myths and misconceptions about the macronutrients in their diets. I've been struck over the years by how many patients walk into my office thinking they know all there is to know about diet and health. They assure me that they eat well-balanced meals. But when I sit them down, and they keep a food diary even for only a week, we discover together how they have been unwittingly undermining their health.

It's not their fault. Sorting out the nutrients in foods is a complicated and subtle procedure. I know from experience that this educational process is crucial. If it weren't, people like the Allens would not be eating those steak dinners.

After all this, if you have any doubts—if you still think you ought to "pass out" of Nutrition 101, you may want to take this just-for-fun optional quiz. (Don't worry, nobody will grade this one!) See if you know the difference between nutritional fact and fiction by choosing which of the following statements are true. When you're done, check your answers against those below.

TRUE OR FALSE?

1. For better health, it's a good idea to cut down on starchy foods.
2. A complex carbohydrate is any food like cookies, cake, and ice cream.
3. Since pasta and bread are fattening, they must be avoided on a diet.
4. It's a good idea to avoid grains and cereals because they contain too much sugar.
5. Vegetables and fruits are healthy because they provide roughage.
6. Most people get enough fiber from their diets.
7. If you eat from the major four food groups, you will get all the vitamins and minerals you need.
8. One slice of whole-wheat bread contains about 120 calories.
9. Cholesterol comes mostly from greasy and fried foods.
10. Most of the sugar in our diet comes from soft drinks.
11. Steak contains about 50 percent fat.
12. Protein should make up the bulk of our diet.

13. Short-term fasts are an easy, effective, safe way to lose weight.
14. It is hard to overdose on vitamins and minerals.

Answers

1. False. Eating enough starches is vital to a balanced diet.
2. False. Complex carbohydrates are grains, potatoes, pastas, bread. Foods like cake, candy, and ice cream are full of refined sugars.
3. False. Current medical thinking suggests these foods—in judicious quantities—can actually help you lose weight by helping you feel full.
4. False. By themselves, without artificial processing, grains and cereals are some of the best food you can eat. They contain little sugar—and what sugars they do contain are natural.
5. True. The "roughage," "bulk," or "fiber" of fresh vegetables and fruits are helpful and healthful.
6. False. In America, our refined-food diets supply dietary fiber far below a healthy level.
7. False. While a well-rounded diet is important, most of us have special needs that require supplements for the best levels of vitamins and minerals.
8. False. It contains about 60 calories.
9. False. Greasy and fried foods contain added saturated (animal) fats, but cholesterol occurs naturally in meat, eggs, and dairy products.
10. True. They are the single biggest sugar source in the American diet.
11. True. Over one half of the calories in beefsteak come from saturated fat.
12. False. Protein should make up more like one seventh (15 percent) of a well-balanced diet—most of it should be complex carbohydrates.
13. False. Total abstention from food is an unhealthy, temporary, and inefficient way to lose weight.
14. False. By careless dosing, you can overdose on fat-soluble vitamins (A, D, E, and K), on vitamin B_6, and on many minerals.

Beyond the Basics

I said that this book gives you the basics, but it does more than that. It starts with the proven, widely accepted fundamentals—then goes farther. In many sections, you will also find the latest scientific information about each of the nutritional groups—reports from the frontiers of research that have appeared as this book went to press. Some of this work is still in the experimental stage. Some of these new findings directly disprove long-accepted truths about certain dietary rules. But all of it suggests the exciting, health-promoting dimensions that preventive nutrition is opening to us.

Welcome, then, to Nutrition 101! These are the most important chapters in this book. Please read them carefully. You may even want to go back and reread certain parts. Your time will have been well spent. Once you pass this course, you will have a solid nutritional underpinning to support you as you design your own healthy regimen.

The Monument To Health: The Nutritional Pyramid

We began this chapter at the dinner table. Ideally, the Allens would be eating a much simpler meal, containing just the right balance of the four essential dietary components—carbohydrates, fiber, fats, and protein. With those in the proper balance, your body can keep you mentally alert, hold your weight down, fight infections, and give you abundant physical and mental energy.

These nutritional groups are called *macronutrients*—"macro" because your body needs them in significant amounts. Together, the four macronutrients group into a handy, easy-to-remember device I call the Nutritional Pyramid—a simple, tested way to balance all your nutritional needs with one plan.

At its base is the most essential, the **carbohydrates.** They should make up the bulk of your diet—65 percent of your daily calories. Most of that—ideally, 55 percent—comes from complex carbohydrates or starches, and 10 percent should come from natural sugars like fruit.

Fiber is the next layer of the Pyramid. Although it is technically not a nutrient, fiber plays such a crucial role in preventive nutrition that it holds a special place among the macronutrients of the Nutritional Pyramid. Fiber acts as a potent disease fighter throughout the body, including your heart and blood vessels. But where it really shines is in the intestinal tract, which tends to suffer from a variety of disorders on the highly refined diet most Americans consume.

These two substances together—carbohydrates and fiber—are the foundation of the Nutritional Pyramid—the most important part of your diet. Interestingly, what we now know about these two layers of the Nutritional Pyramid is very different from what was accepted wisdom only a few years ago. Perhaps you can remember when "experts" told you to avoid carbohydrates because they were fattening. When it came to fiber, until recently few nutritional authorities paid much heed one way or the other. Yet our understanding of the key role these elements play has changed 180 degrees since I went to medical school. With things moving so quickly, now do you see why I wanted you to take Nutrition 101?

Next on the Pyramid come **fats.** They should make up no more than 20 percent of your daily calories—about half the level you now eat. If you read a lot of health magazines, you may notice that my recommendation is less than the 30 percent level for dietary fats recommended by the American Heart Association, the American Cancer Society, and the National Academy of Sciences.

In fact, 20 percent—the guideline I set for my patients—is the same level set by many physicians for their patients who already have high blood-cholesterol levels and who are actively trying to lower them. I believe that fat is so potentially destructive to your health that you should keep your consumption down to the bare minimum. In other words, you should eat as though your cholesterol were too high—because, if you eat like most Americans, it is.

This may seem a radical prescription, but it clearly represents the next step in nutritional thinking. In fact, the health results of such low fat levels seem so promising that the National Cancer Institute is now conducting two major long-term studies to see whether such low fat levels can prevent or retard breast cancer.

At the very top of the Pyramid are **proteins.** These should make up a scant 15 percent of your diet. That won't be hard, because that is probably close to the percentage of protein you eat now. The difference, though, is crucial: *The single most important thing to remember about proteins is that they must come from vegetable sources rather than animal sources.* Animal foods like beef, pork, and lamb are concentrated sources of protein, yes, but they are also highly concentrated sources of saturated fats, and harmful drugs and chemicals.

That, in brief, is the Nutritional Pyramid. Four simple elements brought together in a simple shape: carbohydrates, fiber, fats, and protein. It is no accident that I call it a pyramid: the Great Pyramids are the most solid, stable shape we know. Built with good sense and science, they have endured for thousands of years. They are a true wonder of the world.

The same is true of the Nutritional Pyramid. It is the single best combination of dietary factors you can eat, and the most enduring way to rebuild your diet, reduce disease, and promote health. When you think of longtime nutritional stability, you'll *wonder* how in the *world* you ever got along without the Nutritional Pyramid!

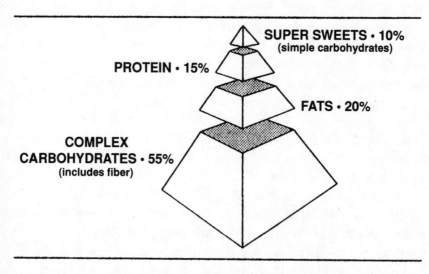

The Secret Power Of The Nutritional Pyramid

The real strength of the four layers of the Nutritional Pyramid—carbohydrates, fiber, fats, and protein—comes from their synergistic effect. They work together to give you more than merely the sum of four ingredients. By combining these elements in this optimal proportion, you will be eating the ideal basic diet to fuel the magnificent machine that is your body. High in carbohydrates and fiber, and low in fats and protein, the Nutritional Pyramid is the best dietary preventive we know for cardiovascular disease, many cancers, high blood pressure, stroke, diabetes, arthritis, bowel and intestinal disease, and overweight.

The perfect balance of the Nutritional Pyramid builds the body's essential systems—cardiac, nervous, and hormonal—that help keep you young and vital. At the same time, it eliminates most of the toxins and harmful chemicals that create degenerative, chronic disease. But most important, you will simply feel better, with abundant energy, mentally and physically working at your peak.

Not surprisingly, it also helps with weight control. You may be one of those people who think about diet only when they want to lose weight for cosmetic reasons. You may not be used to thinking of a diet in terms of a lifetime choice for vital health. The principles built into the Nutritional Pyramid provide both benefits in one. Not only is its careful balance of elements a "one-stop shop" to lessen your risk for all the serious maladies that cut life short; it also helps you keep your weight down. When you are feeding your body the best possible balance of fuel, with the smallest percent of impurities, less of your food is left over to be turned into destructive, unsightly fat. And the better you look and feel.

As you make the Nutritional Pyramid a part of your life, you will notice significant psychological benefits as well. Eating more carbohydrates and no refined sugars means your blood sugar will stay more stable, so your moods and energy peaks and valleys will even out. You won't ride the roller coaster of dizzying highs and depressing lows. You'll be less anxious and better able to cope with that crippler of modern times—stress.

Let me emphasize that the Nutritional Pyramid dietary ratios are designed for people in ordinary good health, people with no special conditions or circumstances that might require a different dietary balance of carbohydrates, fiber, fats, and protein. If you are pregnant, nursing, an athlete, if you have diabetes or suffer from high cholesterol, make sure you read the special section that tailors this ideal diet to your individual needs.

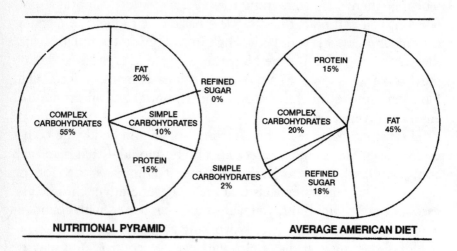

You may wonder why I haven't mentioned vitamins, minerals, and amino acids. It's not because they aren't important. They are vital. But your body needs these elements in much smaller amounts than the macronutrients I have just talked about. So they are called micronutrients. We'll be talking about them in detail in later chapters.

IF THIS SOUNDS FAMILIAR, IT SHOULD

Now that you have seen the basic balance of the Nutritional Pyramid, you may be thinking, "I've heard this before. Many health groups, from the American Heart Association to the American Cancer Society, promote high-carbohydrate, low-fat, low-protein diets."

If this sounds familiar, I can only say you should pat yourself on the back. Surveys show that more than half of American consumers think they should eat *less* starch, and our starch intake has actually decreased slightly in the last twenty years! Clearly, the message is not getting through very well.

The fact is, this program was not pioneered by the American Heart Association or the American Cancer Society. It was originated thirty years ago by the man whom I consider the most significant figure in twentieth-century medicine. In terms of saving lives, this person may have had a greater impact than anybody else.

He wasn't even a doctor, and he didn't see patients or perform transplants. His name was Nathan Pritikin, and he created the revolutionary idea of the high-carbohydrate, low-fat diet. When he came out with the idea—in the 1950s—he was laughed at. But today, after three decades of research, we now understand that this sort of regime is the single most critical factor in vital health and longevity. In terms of preserving human life and promoting more basic health, I believe Pritikin's contribution can only be compared to the discovery of antibiotics.

Almost all of the popular diets you have read or heard of in the last decade owe a debt to his original ideas and research. Several schools of nutrition have recycled those ideas, dressing them up in one way or another. Those concepts have also become the accepted wisdom of the most responsible voices in nutrition, including the American Heart Association, the Center for Science in the Public Interest, and the National Cancer Institute. I have drawn on these state-of-the-art principles for the backbone of this "survey course" of Nutrition 101.

SIGNS OF GOOD NEWS . . .

Because the medical establishment has now awakened to the nutritional truths represented in the Nutritional Pyramid, people are paying better attention to their diets. Instead of the usual doom-and-gloom statistics, let me present some very-good-news numbers that show how far consumers have come.

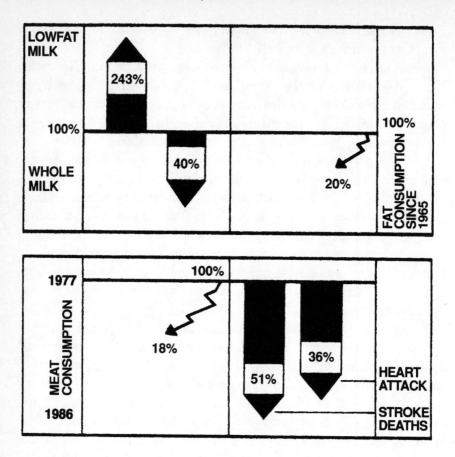

And the best statistics of all: Heart attack deaths DOWN 36%, stroke deaths DOWN 51%.

What's most remarkable is that all this good news has come not from wonder drugs or radical new surgical techniques but thanks to one vital new medical ingredient: public information, the prime ingredient in Nutrition 101!

Taking those ideas as a starting point, I have improved and expanded on these nutritional truths. In three ways, it adds up to the next step after the Pritikin breakthrough.

• First, I have incorporated new research findings about fish oils and essential fatty acids. We know much more about these elements than we did thirty years ago when Pritikin was making his basic discoveries. We now understand how vital these fats are for good health, and how they form an integral part of the membrane of all our cells. To maintain optimal health of those structures that have a fast turnover—like the white cells of your blood and immune system, and cells in your skin and gastrointestinal system—your body needs enough of these vital fats. We will discuss this more in the fats chapter.

- Second, it reduces intake of the health-damaging highly refined sugars more than most traditional regimens, simply because I have found that is what has worked best for thousands of patients in my practice.

- Third, it reduces still further the proportion of deadly, disease-causing saturated and polyunsaturated fats, in keeping with the newest epidemiologic and biostatistical findings on studies done with large populations. This will be common wisdom in a few years—I want you to be able to make use of it now, to build better health and longer life *today*. So join me—let's climb the Nutritional Pyramid together.

5.

On the Ground Floor of the Pyramid: Carbos and Fiber

"Thou shouldst eat to live, not live to eat."
—Cicero

At the base of the Pyramid, we start with the most important component of your diet, the macronutrient that should give you most of your calories—carbohydrates. There's one main thing to remember: In order to make yourself as healthy as possible, you need to make carbohydrates the backbone of your diet. Period.

Carbo Highs:
Time-Release Energy Boosters

Your body is a natural "carboholic," and it craves starches for one reason: *Energy.* Mental and physical. If you drive a car, you want peak performance at all times, right? You don't want the fuel to be watered down or the battery weak. So don't settle for anything less from your body. To get that superior performance, though, you have to fill up with high-octane fuel.

I'd be willing to bet that you want and need more energy. You may well feel dazed and foggy in midmorning, draggy by midafternoon and so wrung-out and grumpy by evening that your ritual run around the park seems more trouble than it's worth. If so, your body is probably crying out for a carbo fix—an energy boost that can come only from the most important macronutrient of them all, carbohydrates.

As I said before, 65 percent of your daily calories should be made up of carbohydrates. But that percentage is split between two different kinds—one known as complex carbohydrates and another called simple carbohydrates. Your body needs them in vastly different proportions.

This tends to confuse people. Well, I'll let you in on a secret: The distinction between complex and simple may be important for food chemists and biologists to understand, but not for you. As I tell my patients, the only thing complex about complex carbohydrates is their name. It's much easier to use the term our grandmothers did: starches. Plants are the original source of nearly all carbohydrates. Starch is their unique way of storing energy.

The other kind of carbohydrates, like their name, are "simple." They are, quite simply, natural sugars—the kind you get from fruit. We'll be talking about them in a later section called Super Sweets, but for now, the important thing to keep in mind is that they should provide only 10 percent of your calories whereas the starches should make up 55 percent.

Starches are storehouses of energy. They release 4 calories—our measure of energy potential—in each gram. In just one ounce of starch, there are 28 grams or 112 calories. That makes them incredibly densely packed high-octane bundles, efficiently concentrated by nature. As one patient put it, beaming, "Oh, I see. It's like eating lots of little batteries!" Not the most appetizing image, I thought to myself, but accurate.

When you eat these carbohydrates, they are broken down in your body into glucose, the prime source your body uses to fuel your muscles and brain. Then they are transported to cells throughout your body, bringing packets of glucose to enable the cells to do their work. In essence, starches stoke your body furnace, keeping you warm because they cause more calories to be burned as heat. If you're constantly cold, you might have circulation problems, or you might need to readjust your carbohydrate intake.

The special quality of starches is that they are digested, absorbed and assimilated by your body at a slow, steady rate. It is this slow-motion breakdown that helps you keep high and consistent energy levels. Starches are nature's time-release energy boosters.

There's something else wonderful about starches. *They are the only food category not linked to any leading killer diseases.* Even if you ate as many of 80 percent of your calories as starch, you would not undermine your health. That's one major reason why those people who eat a large percentage of their food-calorie intake in starches can look forward to a longer, healthier, more energetic life. If, on the other hand, you consumed 80 percent of your diet in fat, you could start digging your grave tomorrow—with your fork.

Starches And Staying Thin

We live in a country where obesity is our number-one health problem. That's because excess pounds are a stepping-stone to such potential killers as high blood pressure, heart disease, diabetes, and stroke. So, by losing weight, you do yourself not only a cosmetic favor but, more important, a health favor.

Happily, a diet high in starch is also a good weight-loss diet. Yet people persist in thinking that starches are fattening. Over a third of all Americans still believe that fable. Not surprisingly, when those people decide to diet, one of the first things they do is dump bread, spaghetti, and rice straight into the trash can. In fact, I tell my patients, these foods can become allies, not adversaries, in the anti-fat fight.

Of course, starches *can* be fattening. If you overdose, any food that contains calories is potentially an agent of weight gain. No, I am not granting you a license to indulge in pasta madness. You still need to keep portions conservative, not eat bread with your linguini and clam sauce, and devise toppings that don't add too many calories. But if you follow the rules, starches need not be fattening and can even help you stick to your diet. Where did the starches-make-you-fat myth come from? It's hard to say. At some point, it became fashionable gospel in this country that the best way to lose weight was with a high-protein, low-carbohydrate, low-fat diet. In the space of a few years, we saw a jumble of crash diets promising quick weight loss in dangerously short periods of time, the kind of diets popularized a decade ago. Judging by the numbers of these books still being sold, these regimens continue to capture the popular imagination—and I do mean imagination. With most of these diets, the goal is not to be slim forever, but to be slim overnight for the upcoming party, prom, or beach season.

Now that we know so much about nutrition, you would think we would have learned. But we haven't. The book that was at the top of the best-seller lists last season has been condemned by the American Dietetic Association as "not scientifically founded," by the National Council on Health Fraud as containing a "spectacular" amount of misinformation, and by nutritional scientists from Maine to Texas as dangerous and bizarre. Yet the book goes on selling.

With so many crazy fad diets around, people can get into real trouble. Not long ago, I had a patient who came to me after a stint on one such diet. A writer for popular magazines, Linda was pretty and had a charming way about her. But one look told me something was seriously out of balance. It all started, she said, because she wanted to lose fifteen pounds—and lose it fast. The first day of the diet, she told me, she felt incredibly fatigued, but not hungry. She had a pleasantly skinny feeling in her stomach. By the end of the second day, however, her euphoria had waned and she had become listless. She also felt irritable and spacy.

The third day was when she started getting scared. She was five pounds lighter, but her eyes felt "like they were wrapped around the back of my head," as she put it. She saw occasional red flashes, and had trouble telling how far away the floor was. Still, she bravely tried to stay strictly to the diet until a few days later, when she felt so weak that she finally kicked it with some strawberry ice cream and coconut macaroons, a quick but destructive source of energy. By the end of the week, she had gained back the five pounds she had lost, and had nothing to show for it except the memory of several days feeling awful and unproductive. She had come to me, she said with a sheepish smile, in hopes of "doing it right this time."

Linda's case illustrates perfectly the danger of high-protein, low-carbohydrate diets. I told her that her reaction is characteristic. First, she was not getting enough starches to produce glucose, which is not only essential for the nerves and brain to function properly but also for the retina of the eye. That's what caused her red flashes.

When you diet to this extreme—the almost total exclusion of starches—the deprivation depletes the brain of an important transmitter of nerve messages, serotonin. Researchers at MIT have found this chemical acts as a natural tranquilizer and sleep inducer. When brain levels of serotonin drop too low, cravings for starches get harder and harder to resist. It's a matter not of willpower but of biochemistry. Then you are likely to fall off your diet with a real explosive carbohydrate binge. There is a second grave danger to such drastic, ill-balanced diets. You may have heard about ketosis, an abnormal condition that occurs when the absence of starches prevents the complete breakdown of fats and proteins. Then your blood becomes "polluted" with a fat waste product called ketone bodies—toxic compounds that dull the brain and cause nausea, fatigue, and apathy. So much for depriving your body of starches when you diet.

The thing to remember about dieting is that it will work better if it works with, rather than against, your body's own biochemical needs and patterns. Drastic starvation diets, based on an imbalance of any kind—whether it is fats or proteins or starches—don't work. What *does* work is knowing enough to recruit your body's own exquisite health keeper to help you lose weight.

Enough diet myths! Here are the real facts to keep in mind about those "fattening" starches.

- First, up to a third of all starch calories are not digested and instead pass through you unabsorbed.
- Second, the calories you *do* get from starches are easier for the body to burn off than calories that come from fats or protein.
- Third, ounce for ounce, starches have the same number of calories as pure protein and less than half that of fat!

Where To Look For Starch

You will find your starches in any of a variety of appetizing sources. Try whole grains such as brown rice, and use whole-wheat flour to make muffins, bread, and even cakes. Or buy bread made from whole-wheat flour at the grocery store.

Notice I said "whole grain." You should get into the habit of using whole grains in your kitchen because they give you the extra nutrients and fiber that the milling and refining processes otherwise remove from foods. The bran—removed from rice and wheat in the milling process—is a sterling source of fiber and minerals, but you won't get it if you rely on white rice and flour. It's an easy habit to get into: When you're looking for carbohydrates in the market, stock up on whole-wheat flour instead of bleached white flour, steel-cut oats instead of oatmeal, brown rice instead of white. You may not usually think to include grains like buckwheat grouts, barley, and bulgur wheat, but they are super sources, too. If you try some of these different, whole-grain variations, not only will your meals taste richer and more interesting, you'll be getting the most health potential from your carbohydrate calories!

Pasta is another wonderful boon for the carbo-conscious eater. You can have a field day with it, in all its forms: spinach, tomato, artichoke, whole-wheat, durum-wheat semolina. Strangely enough, when most people think of pastas, they think of the one kind that isn't so good for you—egg noodles! Because they are made with a lot of eggs, they contain all the cholesterol of all those yolks, which raises your cholesterol dramatically. But if you can widen your tastes to include the many other interesting varieties of pasta, these versatile ingredients can be a major help to balancing your body's starch needs. Other good sources: potatoes, corn, peas, oats, buckwheat, rye, beans (preferably dried), bulgur, couscous, and millet. Nuts and seeds are rich in starch too, but they are also rich in calories.

THE CARBO QUIZ

1. Starches should make up the bulk of your diet—55 percent of your daily calories. True_____ False_____
2. Starches are your prime source of energy, both mental and physical. True_____ False_____
3. Starches and protein are the only food category not linked to any lethal diseases. True_____ False_____
4. Super Sweets are the destructive sugars. They are found in fruits and vegetables. True_____ False_____
5. A diet high in starch is a bad weight-loss diet. True_____ False_____
6. Ketosis occurs when you eat too many starches. True_____ False_____

Answers:

1. T   2. T   3. F   4. F   5. F   6. F

The Super Sweets

The second kind of carbohydrates, you remember, are the natural sugars. They should make up the smallest number of calories in your diet—only 10 percent. Like starches, they provide energy. Super Sweets give you quick surges rather than time-release boosts, simply because your body has to do less work to break them down into usable energy.

The best sources are fruits. To keep your consumption down to that 10 percent, you should eat no more than two or three small servings each day. Nonfat milk is another source of Super Sweets, including products made with skimmed or partially skimmed milk, buttermilk, or plain yogurt.

I've talked about two kinds of energy boosters that ought to be in your diet. Now here's one that should not. The dastardly "Sweet Nothings." They are sugary desserts, cookies, pastries, candy, ice cream, and the like. Unlike Super Sweets, which have been concentrated by nature, Sweet Nothings are concentrated artifically, and they add nothing to your diet. Except useless calories, that is, and they do that extraordinarily well, adding about 112 calories per ounce of refined sugar. That is, they add the same amount as starches but without the same benefits.

Sweet Nothings mostly come originally from plant sources, from which they are extracted, and then processed and refined. During that metamorphosis, they may be concentrated to thousands of times their original potency. Yet they lose their natural fiber along with vitamins, minerals, and other nutrients. *Voilà*—Sweet Nothings.

Not surprisingly, they can do your body significant harm. In your body, these demons of food technology are rapidly absorbed and work like drugs, stimulating your pancreas into a frantic effort to produce the hormone insulin to rebalance your blood sugar. This stresses the pancreas, which was never designed by Nature to deal with such sugar megadoses. As it scrambles to counteract the powerful refined sugar, it may lower your blood sugar down to unsafe levels, and at the same time your energy level plummets. If this weren't bad enough, new evidence has now confirmed that sugar can also be a key element in raising your blood pressure.

Sweet Nothings, stripped of their nutritive value and ferociously concentrated, are truly a one-way ticket to an emotional and physical roller coaster, stressing your body and its delicate chemical-regulating mechanisms. This is another way the Nutritional Pyramid expands on traditional regimes. I recommend a much stricter level of refined sugars. Now that you've seen the damage they do in your body, you'll understand why.

I won't deny the appeal and temptation of Sweet Nothings. The average American eats about 100 pounds of sugar a year, and more than 70 percent of that is sucrose—white table sugar! For many people, that is like eating 80 percent or more of their body weight in sugar every year! Think of a sugar sack that size: not very appetizing, is it?

But, you protest, there's no way I eat that much. I warn you, these dastardly Sweet Nothings are infinitely deceptive. They hide in soft drinks, thousands of prepared dressings and cake mixes, breads, molasses, honey, and various sweet syrups. Most of them are disguised in foods you would never dream contain sugar. That's also why I tell my patients to be very strict. If they get only the sugar in prepared foods, they are getting too much. If you don't believe me, take The Sugar Nobody Knows Test. How many hidden sources can you identify?

THE SUGAR NOBODY KNOWS TEST

Arrange the following food items in order from the least amount of sugar to the most.

1. One marshmallow
2. A small slice of angel-food cake
3. One piece regular chewing gum
4. One serving fruit sherbet
5. A wedge of home made apple pie
6. One glass (8 ounces) of unsweetened grapefruit juice
7. Four to six dried apricot halves

The real answers may surprise you:

1. One stick of chewing gum ($^1/_2$ teaspoon)
2. One marshmallow ($1^1/_2$ teaspoons)
3. Half a dozen dried apricot halves (5 teaspoons)
4. One cup unsweetened grapefruit juice (5 teaspoons)
5. One small slice angel-food cake (6 teaspoons)
6. One-sixth wedge of apple pie (12 teaspoons)
7. One cup sherbet (12–16 teaspoons)

Remember: If a sweet tooth strikes, reach for the Super Sweets and leave those Sweet Nothings behind.

Fiber: The Rolls-Royce of Nonnutrients

Even though fiber is technically a carbohydrate, there is one crucial distinction: You don't digest it. It moves all the way through your system practically intact, and never gets absorbed and broken down to feed your cells. That may not sound like much of a plus, but it is.

Even though fiber contributes nothing to your body in real nutritive value, it is a key player in your body's fight against disease, and one of the most effective players in the preventive-nutrition battle. That's why I call it the Rolls-Royce of nonnutrients.

If fiber brings to mind the image of something stringy, you're on the mark. Most sources of the Rolls-Royce of nonnutrients are actually coarse and stringy in composition. That's what makes the "crunch" you hear when you bite into a stick of celery, a raw carrot, or a fresh asparagus spear.

Surely you are not too sophisticated to remember the cartoon character Bugs Bunny? Sometimes you could hear the feisty little critter gnawing on his favorite food before he ever made his on-screen appearance. Bugs was doing what came naturally with little thought to nutrition. Perhaps Nature designed a high-fiber diet for rabbits to protect them from some of the most painful, debilitating diseases known to man. With all that fiber, no wonder Bugs is still alive and well and performing today!

The Benefits Of Fiber

Fiber performs its most essential service in one area of your body— your intestinal tract. Its job is to keep your digestive system running smoothly and eliminating wastes regularly. Fiber is nature's own laxative. It works by making your stool absorb more water. That increases its size, and makes it easier to pass your waste. As simple a change as changing from white to whole-wheat bread can increase your waste volume by 20 percent—as well as saving you calories!

Although there are several sorts of fiber, they all boil down to one of two basic kinds, and each plays a role in keeping you healthy. One kind, soluble fiber, dissolves in water, soaking up fluid in your stomach and small intestine. It works like a sponge, slowing the absorption of your food. That's what gives you that full, satisfied feeling after a meal. It's also what absorbs fats and cholesterol, so your body doesn't.

The other kind of fiber is not a sponge but a broom. It moves through your body fairly quickly, sweeping along with it substances you have eaten that may be harmful. Eating enough fiber gives you an army of pushbroom-wielding janitors, sweeping out toxins, poisons, and potential cancer-causing chemicals before your body can absorb them. It speeds up what is called transit time—the time it takes for food to get from the entrance to your digestive tract to the other end. By eating a correct balance of fiber, you can actually cut that time in half. Researchers in Britain compared transit time for average Britishers who eat a Western refined-food diet and African villagers eating traditional high-fiber diets. The "civilized" eaters took almost three times as long for their food to pass through, up to eighty-nine hours in some cases! Think what that means for a moment: The food those British men eat stays inside them three times as long—almost four whole days! That means three times as long for food to decompose, three times as long for impurities, chemicals, and toxins to be absorbed into their bodies. Ghastly, isn't it?

FIBER FORMS

I notice that many of my patients seem unduly confused about the various types of fiber—what each does, where they come from. For those of you who are true fiber freaks, here is as complete a list as you'll find anywhere.

Name Food Sources	Health Actions			
	Absorbs water	Speeds transit time	Absorbs fats and cholesterol	Slows stomach digestion
CELLULOSE AND HEMICELLU-LOSE Wheat flour, beans, bran, broccoli, bulgur, carrots, apples, beets, Brussels sprouts		√		
LIGNIN Cereals, eggplants, green beans		√	√	
PECTIN Apples, grapes, potatoes, squash, oranges, lemons, grapefruits	√		√	√
GUM Oats, oat bran, barley, lentils, chick-peas, black-eyed peas, pinto beans, navy beans, split peas	√		√	√
Mucilage Seeds	√		√	

But remember, whatever the name or source, all of it boils down to sponges and brooms!

Now that you know what fiber does inside your body, look at the tremendous benefits it has for your overall health:

Fiber helps protect you from cancer of the colon and rectum—the second most common cancer in men and third in women. This year alone, 60,000 Americans will die from this lethal cancer. Because of our fiber-poor diet, our country has a rate of colon cancer eight times that of many developing countries. In many "primitive" areas of Africa, where fiber consumption and stool bulk are high, colon cancer is virtually unknown.

The tragedy is that a good number of the deaths in the United States could be avoided if only people paid more attention to this component of their diets. Even the National Cancer Institute agrees that you can substantially reduce your chances of developing cancer of the colon by eating more fiber. The proof comes from studies where scientists have tracked people who migrate from parts of the world where colon cancer is high. When they relocate to a land where the rate is low and fiber intake high, their own rates become the same as those of their new environment.

Researchers are still working to find out just how fiber performs its miracles. Part of the answer, of course, is that fiber moves toxins out of your system in such a hurry that they never have a chance to do their dirty work. But there is intriguing evidence that fiber may in fact neutralize cancer-causing toxins, in effect, defusing those biochemical time bombs.

The most recent dispatches from the research laboratories suggest that fiber itself may not be the key ingredient, or only part of it. We are now finding other substances contained in certain kinds of fiber that seem to have strong anticancer properties.

Indoles are chemical compounds found in vegetables of the cruciferous family—including cauliflower, broccoli, and Brussels sprouts. We have long known that these vegetables help reduce colon cancer in animals. Researchers now believe this protective effect may relate to the content of indoles.

Another prime anticancer ingredient of fiber was discovered only last year. Some fiber contains a substance called **phytic acid.** It is particularly abundant in cereal grains: Whole wheat, bran, and many kinds of seeds are good sources. Research from the prestigious journal *Cancer* suggests phytic acid may deserve credit for some of the anticancer action of fiber. The researchers came to this conclusion after looking at a curious phenomenon in Scandinavia. Danes, they saw, have a much higher rate of colorectal cancer than their neighbors in nearby Finland—yet they eat almost twice as much fiber. When the two peoples' diets were carefully analyzed, the scientists found that the Finns eat foods that contain 20 percent to 40 percent more phytic acid. It may well be, say researchers, that it is phytic acid, not fiber, that helps prevent colon cancer.

If you have heard of phytic acid, you may also share a common misconception. There is some research showing that the substance can impair your absorption of key minerals like calcium, iron, magnesium, and zinc. I had one patient, Elma, read me the riot act for suggesting she eat more cereals containing phytic acid. "As a woman, I need extra iron and zinc," she said. "Won't eating too much phytic acid deplete my resources?"

Well, Elma was half right. What she didn't know about was some recent research that puts phytic acid back on the "acceptable" list. Two researchers, from MIT and the University of Texas Health Science Center, found that even though wheat fiber may block your body from absorbing a few micronutrients, it brings along so many of its own that it puts you back in balance. Even the Mayo Clinic now advises that you can offset whatever minerals you may lose by eating a balanced diet and raising your fiber intake moderately.

Colon cancer is not the only intestinal disorder that fiber wards off. It works wonders for constipation, a major problem for Americans. Sales of laxatives and stool softeners in the United States amount to a colossal $400 million every year! Although you may think of constipation as an occasional and simply annoying problem, it can lead to hemorrhoids—varicose veins of the intestine— and diverticular disease of the colon, where pockets form in the large intestine. These outpouchings can become painfully inflamed and infected. Irritable bowel syndrome is a well-known problem to millions of Americans. They suffer cramps, diarrhea, spasms, constipation, and flatulence. And most of that is preventable: Diets high in fiber have been shown to reduce the risks of developing these serious and painful diseases. The beneficial effects of fiber extend to many other systems of the body:

• **Heart disease.** Around the world, people who eat a lot of fiber have much lower rates of heart disease than those who don't. Japan has the highest estimated fiber intake of any country in the world, and only 88 deaths from heart attack per 100,000 people. In the United States, where we have the lowest fiber intake of any country, the rate of heart-attack death is seven times higher!

Even in our own country, vegetarians who eat a lot of fiber have less fat in their blood, and lower average blood pressure, than people with low-fiber intake. That doesn't mean you have to drop all meat and become a strict vegetarian. But it does mean that a reasonable increase of fiber in your diet may help you control fats and blood pressure.

Fiber helps your heart by absorbing fats in your gut, so your body can push it out as waste. That means less fat is free in your bloodstream, gumming up the pipes. Fiber also reduces the amount of artery-damaging cholesterol molecules, produced when your body tries to process fats. Wheat fiber lowers not only cholesterol but also your triglycerides—the amount of fat in your blood plasma.

When it comes to clearing out fat, not all fiber is created equal. Soybean fiber has been shown to significantly decrease cholesterol in people with moderately high cholesterol; wheat cereals are also highly effective, as are oats and rice.

Another effective fiber is guar gum. You may recognize the name from reading food labels—it is often used as a thickening additive in processed foods. The small amounts of guar in these foods aren't enough to significantly affect your digestion process. But a recent report from Stanford University shows that concentrated guar-gum supplements can reduce both overall cholesterol and the specific type of cholesterol (LDL) most implicated in cardiovascular disease. The researchers conclude that this fiber may be a promising tool to help people lower their high cholesterol, blood fats, and so reduce heart disease.

• **Blood pressure.** Fiber is also a natural way to control your blood pressure. That's what British researchers found when they compared fiber consumption and blood pressure for ninety-four healthy people. Those who ate more fiber had significantly lower blood pressure than those on low-fiber diets. But even better, when they then increased the fiber for the low-fiber group, their blood pressure dropped significantly after only one month!

Fiber can be particularly important if you are older. In America, people's blood pressure rises as they age. Yet that's not true for people in less industrialized societies. The difference? Their diets provide many times more plant fiber than ours does.

• **Blood sugar.** Some fiber foods slow the absorption of the energy-giving sugar, glucose, in your body. That means a more stable energy thermostat, leveling out the sugar boom/bust cycle, more consistent high energy and fewer destructive mood swings. This is particularly important for diabetics because it helps keep their blood sugar even. Several studies have shown that, when used in a careful balance, high-fiber foods can even reduce the need for insulin or other antidiabetic drugs.

One of the most dramatic of these studies took place in Australia. The subjects were ten aborigines living in cities, and suffering from diabetes. The men agreed to return to their traditional country in the outback and live as their ancestors had for seven weeks—trapping animals, hunting, and living off the land. After seven weeks away from their citified diets, the men were much healthier than when they began the study: They had dropped their extra weight, their blood-sugar levels had returned to normal, and their symptoms had either greatly reduced or completely disappeared! That doesn't mean that you have to move to the outback and trap kangaroos. But it does indicate that traditional high-fiber, low-fat diets can help stabilize and improve diabetic control.

Recently, a new kind of fiber substance, Xanthan gum, has been shown to help diabetes. It works by slowing stomach emptying, like other fibers, but it seems to have an added effect of making the stomach process sugar and fat at the same time, instead of dumping a sugar flood into the intestines and so destabilizing blood-sugar levels. Patients taking Xanthan gum reported feeling satisfied, and blood tests showed they had improved glucose response and lower cholesterol after several weeks.

Foods that are particularly useful for diabetics to help smooth out the ups and downs of sugar responses include: beans, peas, lentils, and whole-grain cereals.

• **Weight control.** Fiber can also act as a natural, safe appetite suppressant. As any dieter knows, the hardest part about many diets is that you rarely feel satisfied—so it's always easy to fall off the diet, eating "just this one" snack in a guilty effort to feel satisfied.

Now research from UCLA suggests that there is a clear biological reason for this. The stomachs of obese people empty out much faster than those of thin people—so they feel hungry again. That's where fiber can really help. Although it supplies few or no calories—how can it when you don't digest it?—it does give you "roughage." That bulk makes you feel full and so you eat less.

Several experiments with guar gum have demonstrated how well this works. Guar gum is a highly water-soluble kind of fiber. Inside your stomach, it absorbs water and swells into a viscous gel. That gel has been shown to significantly delay stomach emptying in obese patients. Thus they feel fuller longer—and eat less. I have used a concentrated form of guar gum with some of my overweight patients with tremendous weight-loss results.

But this benefit is not limited to this one kind of fiber. The same principle holds true for all people who eat high-fiber diets—fiber fills you up, not out! My patients consistently report that when they increase the fiber in their diets, they find themselves eating much less—for the simple reason that it takes them longer to chew their way through fibrous foods. One of my patients, a young man who makes his living illustrating medical textbooks, told me he had clocked his meals, and it took him 35 percent more time to eat the same amount. The result, of course, is that people end up eating much less—sometimes only half as much as they would otherwise wolf down.

The second way fiber helps control your appetite is by stabilizing your blood sugar. With no fiber in your diet, your blood sugar fluctuates widely as the sugars from your food are immediately absorbed into your blood. The result? You feel hungry, jumpy, irritable, and low in energy. But fiber added to your meals slows the absorption of the starches and sugars you eat, so your blood-sugar levels don't peak and fall quickly. Your mood is more even, the need to go on food binges reduced. In both these ways, fiber makes it easier to stick to your diet and lose more weight.

FIBER FLOW—
HOW FAST YOU ELIMINATE FOODS

You can get a rough gauge of how efficiently your digestive system is working by measuring your own transit time.

1. Without changing your regular diet, observe how long it takes from when you eat a food to when you eliminate it. To be sure, I suggest you eat a meal including corn kernels. They will pass through largely undigested, so you can use them as a marker. If you prefer, you can eat fresh (not canned) beets, using their red color as a marker. You may be surprised at how long it takes your "food processor" to fully process your foods.

2. For one day, eat three high-fiber meals in a row, again using a marker food. Note the length of time from intake to elimination. This number is probably better than your first, but not yet to your optimal—when you are regularly eating more fiber, the time will get even shorter. But it does give you an idea of the significant difference you can make easily. As you look back on this chapter in several weeks, I think you will be amazed at how much progress you have made in speeding and streamlining your digestive process.

Where to Get the Best Fiber

By now, you're probably thoroughly convinced that you should load up on fiber. With sound reason. Even the National Cancer Institute, known for its conservative policies, recommends that we all double our daily fiber intake from 10 to 20 grams to 25 to 30 grams.

Once my patients "get religion" about fiber, many of them are tempted to run out and buy popular dietary supplements like wheat bran to boost their fiber intake. I counsel them not to. Although these supplements do improve your bowel function, they don't offer the full range of health benefits available in natural forms of fiber. Combinations of naturally occurring fibers—each with its own actions and properties—offer the very best results. That way, you are eating according to what Nature designed.

Fortunately, you don't have to follow Bugs Bunny's example and stuff yourself with carrots to get plenty of fiber in your diet. There are lots of sources to choose from. The best way, recommended by the National Research Council, is simply to eat more fruit, vegetables, and whole-grain products. The good news is that these are also all starches—because starches are the only source of this critical layer of the Nutritional Pyramid. In fact, if you eat the right proportion and kinds of carbohydrates, you will also give yourself all the fiber you need—automatically. That's why they are combined in the Nutritional Pyramid.

Where can you get good fiber? That's easy. The very best source of insoluble fiber—the kind that passes through your digestive tract more or less intact—is wheat bran. Wheat foods are the major source of dietary fiber in the United States, providing about a third of the fiber our nation eats. Oat bran is also an excellent fiber source. If you haven't eaten oatmeal since childhood, now's the time to get used to it again. A breakfast that includes fresh citrus fruit, oatmeal or a bran cereal, and a whole-grain bread is a perfect fiber-full way to start the day. In addition to their mechanical fiber action, cereals are the best source of phytic acid.

SAMPLE HIGH-FIBER BREAKFAST MENU

Medium serving puffed
wheat, corn, or rice cereal
Skimmed milk   2 slices whole-wheat toast
1 sliced banana   Herbal tea

POPULAR CEREAL FIBER RATINGS

Find your favorite here. If it is not among the fiber "A" group, see if you can find a cereal you like that is. For my patients, I suggest that their breakfast should provide at least 9 grams of fiber.

Food	Serving Size	Fiber Content (in grams)
Cereals		
All-Bran (with extra fiber)	1 ounce	13
Fiber One	1 ounce	12
100% Bran	1 ounce	9
All-Bran	1 ounce	9
Bran Buds	1 ounce	8
Corn Bran	1 ounce	6
Bran Chex	1 ounce	5
Natural Bran Flakes	1 ounce	5
40% Bran Flakes	1 ounce	4
Cracklin' Oat Bran	1 ounce	4
Fruit 'n' Fiber	1 ounce	4
Fruitful Bran	1 ounce	4
Shredded Wheat & Bran	1 ounce	4
Wheatena	1 ounce	4
Ralston Instant	1 ounce	3
Shredded Wheat	1 ounce	3
Frosted Mini-Wheats	1 ounce	3
Raisin Bran	1 ounce	3
Total	1 ounce	2.5
Wheat Chex	1 ounce	2.5
Wheaties	1 ounce	2.5
Grapenuts	1 ounce	2.2

For lunch, look to fruits and vegetables. The pectin they contain makes them a good fiber source, especially when you eat them with their skins. Paring fruits and vegetables reduces their fiber, so get in the habit of leaving your peeler and paring knife in the drawer. Citrus-fruit skins are, of course, an exception. But with oranges, grapefruits, tangerines, tangelos, and other citrus fruits, remember that you get considerably more bulk from eating the segments than from the juice alone.

For dinner, other good sources are broccoli, Brussels sprouts, carrots, corn, parsnips, potatoes, squash, and yams. Legumes like dried beans and peas are an excellent source of fiber, and can make wonderful casseroles, soups, and salads. You may be daunted by the time needed for soaking and cooking and reach for the canned chickpeas, red beans, kidney beans, and pintos instead. In this, as in so many things, the extra time pays nutritional dividends. Unfortunately, cans may be convenient, but temperatures used in the canning process also cancel out some of the fiber benefits.

For those through-the-day snacks, try nuts, seeds, and dried fruits if you're not dieting. And that old standby, popcorn—minus the butter and salt—is a perfect high-fiber snack.

Ironically, the same fiber that brings such magnificent benefits to your digestive tract also brings some magnificent side effects. You may experience bloating, gas, diarrhea, or flatulence. That is your body's way of signaling that you have raised your fiber intake too quickly. When this happens to my patients, I tell them not to overdo it. It's best to add fiber to your diet gradually. After all, you are a unique individual and your dietary needs are totally distinct from anybody else's. Even with a slow increase, don't be surprised if you experience a few bothersome symptoms. Just take your time and let your body adjust to its new fiber load. It may take several weeks for your digestive system to get used to the added bulk. Then before you know it, the side effects will diminish.

FIBER EXERCISE

1. Make a list of the foods you think are high fiber, which you have eaten in the last three days.
2. Compare that list with the chart below, listing accurate fiber content of foods.
3. Now score your fiber intake according to the values listed next to each food, and total. Where do you fall on the Fiber Scale? FIBER GOAL: I tell my patients to try to get a minimum of 25 grams of fiber each day.

Food	Serving Size	Fiber Content (in grams)
Grains		
Wheat germ	⅓ cup	7
Wheat bran	⅓ cup	6.5
Oat bran	⅓ cup	4
Popcorn	2 cups	3
Brown rice	⅓ cup, cooked	1.5
Millet	⅓ cup, cooked	1
Whole-wheat bread	1 slice	1.5
Rye bread	1 slice	1
Spaghetti	⅓ cup, cooked	.5
White bread	1 slice	.5
White rice	⅓ cup, cooked	.1
Vegetables		
Spinach	½ cup, cooked	6
Sweet potato	½ cup, cooked	4
Brussels sprouts	½ cup, cooked	4
Corn	½ cup, cooked	4
Baked potato (med.)	½ cup, cooked	3.5
Turnips/rutabagas	½ cup, cooked	3
Carrots	½ cup, cooked	2
Asparagus	½ cup, cooked	2

Food	Serving Size	Fiber Content (in grams)
Green beans	½ cup, cooked	2
Broccoli	½ cup, cooked	2
Mushrooms	½ cup, raw	1
Tomato	1 medium size	2
Celery	2 large stalks, raw	3
Zucchini	½ cup, cooked	1.4
Squash	½ cup, cooked	.5

Legumes

Food	Serving Size	Fiber Content
Lentils	½ cup, uncooked	11
Kidney beans	½ cup, cooked	6
Pinto beans	½ cup, cooked	5
Split peas	½ cup, cooked	5
White beans	½ cup, cooked	5
Lima beans	½ cup, cooked	5
Peas (green)	½ cup, cooked	4

Fruits and Nuts

Food	Serving Size	Fiber Content
Apricots (dried)	½ cup	15
Prunes (stewed)	½ cup	15
Almonds	½ cup	10
Peanuts	½ cup	6
Blackberries	½ cup	4.5
Raspberries	½ cup	4.5
Prunes	4	4
Apple (with skin)	1 medium	3.5
Dates	4	3
Nectarine	1 medium	3
Figs (fresh)	1 medium	2.5
Pear	1 medium	2.5
Banana	½ cup	2
Orange	1 large	2
Grapefruit	½	2
Peach	1 medium	1.5
Melon	¼ average	1.5
Strawberries	½ cup	1.5

FIBER WRAP-UP

1. The major benefit of fiber is to protect you from cancer of the colon and rectum.
2. Fiber will also help protect you from heart disease, high blood pressure, and excess blood fats.
3. Fiber can help control appetite and help you lose weight.
4. Set a goal of increasing your fiber intake to twice your normal amount.
5. Always increase fiber gradually, over a month.

Carbos and Fiber Together: The High-Performance Pair

Why did I put starches and fiber together as the ground floor of the Nutritional Pyramid? Because they work as a team. From Harvard Medical School to the Mayo Clinic, there is a solid medical consensus that these two substances, one a macronutrient, the other an essential non-nutrient, are the two crucial ingredients of your diet. As I sat down to write this book, a gathering of nutritional experts drawn from all over the country reaffirmed these high-carbohydrate, high-fiber guidelines. Fiber and carbohydrates complement each other beautifully. Starches work chemically by supplying your cells with the vital fuel your body needs. Fiber works mechanically by cleaning out your system, ridding your body of fats and toxins that could gum up the works. Together, they don't just put you on the ground floor of the Nutritional Pyramid—they put you in on the ground floor for strong health and long life!

6.

Fats: The Moral of Jack Sprat

"Jack Sprat could eat no fat,
his wife could eat no lean;
And so between them both, you see,
They licked the platter clean."
—Nursery rhyme

It's too bad epidemiologists didn't write this nursery rhyme, or we would know which of the Sprat couple lived longer. But it's not hard to figure out. Fat is public-health enemy number one, and poor Mrs. Sprat might have died of any of a score of fat-related diseases, many of them as unpleasant as they are deadly.

However Mrs. Sprat met her fate, one thing is for sure. She was almost certainly obese. Fat is the most concentrated source of calories. You get 100 to a tablespoon no matter what kind of fat you eat. Gram for gram, Mrs. Sprat was gaining more than twice the number of calories she would have from protein or carbohydrates.

Why all this talk about Mrs. Sprat? Because she is the closest model for the way most Americans eat. In the typical diet in this country, some 40 percent of our daily calories come from fat. Nearly half is of the so-called saturated variety, and a third of that fat comes directly from the meat we eat.

The Costs of Fat

The link between fat and heart disease is so well documented and so well understood that it is one of our few absolute nutritional truths. The roster of scientists recommending a low-fat diet is a virtual *Who's Who* of nutrition: the Mayo Clinic, the University of California, Harvard University, the American Heart Association, the American Cancer Society, the National Cancer Institute, and the National Academy of Sciences.

In study after study, researchers have documented that no group of people in the world who eat a low-fat/low-cholesterol diet has a high rate of heart disease. The National Institutes of Health have established an absolute link between obesity and heart disease, and the rate of diabetes is three times higher in obese than in normal people. Obese males are more likely to get cancer of the colon, rectum, and prostate; overweight women are at risk for cancer of the breast, uterus, ovaries, cervix, and gallbladder. The evidence is so overwhelming that it is now recommended that anybody even 20 percent over his or her ideal body weight is well advised to diet.

But it is one thing to hear about studies, and another thing to have a clear image of what fats do in your body. I had one patient, a plumbing engineer, who just couldn't see why he should bother. "Hey, Doc," he protested, "coming home to a sirloin-steak dinner after a day on the job—that's what life is about!" It was clear he wasn't about to be convinced by the lab results of his blood-fat levels. So I told him I needed some of his professional advice. I asked him what would happen if after tomorrow's breakfast, I went around my house and dumped a cup of library paste mixed with axle grease into each sink, toilet, and shower. His eyes widened in a look of pure horror. Then I told him I would do the same thing after tomorrow's lunch, and dinner, and every day this week. After every meal, I would get up and flush another cup of sludge down every drain in the house. "So, Frank," I asked, "what do you think would happen?"

His response was loud and immediate: "What are you, crazy or something? You'd have a holy mess! You'd clog up your pipes, valves, tubes and . . ." he stopped spluttering, and a sheepish grin crept over his face. I saw I had made my point: That is exactly what happens when you eat fatty, greasy foods.

Of course, there is one crucial difference: You can call someone like Frank to come ream out your house's pipes. But in your body, these fats can accumulate to the point where all of a sudden, your arteries clog or your heart stops in mid-beat. So while that may look like a sizzling, juicy steak, or a rich creamy butter sauce, remember: To your arteries, it is exactly like a cup of library paste and axle grease. Oh, I should mention this: When Frank came back four months later, now eating according to the Nutritional Pyramid, his blood fats were reduced 45 percent and his cholesterol 20 percent.

It's not just your heart that fats damage. Fats are also clearly implicated in high blood pressure. You may have heard that people with high blood pressure should watch how much salt they eat. Recent studies indicate that, for most people, fat has more to do with hypertension than salt does. Fat stored as excess weight increases your risk for high blood pressure—in some cases by more than five times—and scientists have found that less saturated fat in the diet leads to lower blood pressure.

There's more bad news about fats. Fat has the strongest link to cancer of any dietary component, according to the National Academy of Sciences Committee on Diet, Nutrition and Cancer. We have long known this was true for cancers of the breast, colon, and prostate. We know now that colon cancer is associated with high cholesterol levels. It appears that the more fat you eat, the more cholesterol your liver manufactures. As that cholesterol collects in your colon, it raises your chances of getting colon cancer.

Now we are finding out that fat plays a highly suspicious role in malignancies of the endometrium (the lining of the uterus), the pancreas, the lung, and even the ovary. Recent evidence strengthens the link to ovarian cancer. In a massive study of sixteen thousand women, researchers found that women who eat fat in any of several forms, such as fried potatoes, pork, or eggs—are at greater risk. Women who eat fatty foods five or more times a week are almost three times as likely to die from ovarian cancer than those who eat them fewer than three times a week.

Interestingly, in one study, fried eggs have the single strongest association with ovarian cancer deaths. Women who eat eggs three or more times a week have a three times greater risk of developing fatal ovarian malignancies than those who eat them less than once a week. That's really not too surprising. After all, fried eggs have a double whammy: their own cholesterol, plus the fats added in frying.

Every month, we learn more about how fat promotes cancer. Researchers now believe that during the metabolism of fats and cholesterol, substances are formed that are cancer promoting, including some chemicals that mimic the action of sex hormones. These hormones are notorious for their ability to stimulate the growth of cancers. Other researchers believe that dietary fats enhance the cancer-causing potential of other chemicals.

Still, even in the face of all the evidence, some of my patients have strange misconceptions about the fat they eat. Robert, a speechwriter for a well-known politician, asked me if cutting down on fats wouldn't rob his body of precious micronutrients. "I need fat-soluble vitamins, right?" he asked. "If I cut out all cheeseburgers, milk, and ice cream, I don't see how I'll get enough vitamins A, D, E, and K."

Again, it's a case of a half-truth being more confusing than no information. The fact is that while these vitamins do depend on fat to push them through your intestinal wall and out into your bloodstream, you will not reduce your levels of them significantly by going on a low-fat diet. It takes only a minuscule amount of fat, I told Robert, to meet all your nutritional needs. Believe it or not, you can get by on only three teaspoons of vegetable oil a day. If you just pour a couple of thimblefuls into a saucer, you'll get a good idea of just how little your body requires.

Low-Fat, Not No-Fat

After such a litany of fat woes, you may conclude that it would be more prudent to adopt Sprat's no-fat diet. Not so. First of all, you can't. Small amounts of fats are everywhere in our foods, and the totally nonfat diet would be as unappetizing as it is unhealthy.

But second, a small amount of fat is essential for your good health. You won't read that very many places, certainly not in the popular press, but it's true. I said earlier that this book takes up where

Pritikin leaves off. That's because we now know much more about fats—good and bad—than we did only a few years ago. Yes, if you reduce your fats to my recommended level of only 20 percent, you will be well protected against the legions of bad-fat diseases. But, equally important, you will get the essential mono- and un-saturated fats that are crucial in trace amounts for vibrant growth and health.

The fact is, your body needs fat. Fat plays a role in many of the complex biochemical processes that keep you alive, it helps you conserve precious body heat, and, most important, it is your body's critical energy reserve. That's why Nature equipped you with some 35 billion fat cells. But the trick is to get enough fat—and of the most healthy kinds—without getting too much.

BODY MASS WORKSHEET

The first step to figuring out how much fat you need is to set an accurate goal for your overall weight. You've already seen how much the height-weight charts vary. Here, from a recent report by the National Institutes of Health, is a new, more personalized method to find out if you are at the right weight. It's called the Body Mass Method. (It may look complex, but it's not. Most of the arithmetic is based on the fact that we have to convert to metric numbers in this worksheet. With a calculator, it's easy.)

1. How much do you weigh nude?   ―――――――
   To get metric equivalent in kilos, divide by 2.2.   ―――――――
2. How many inches tall are you?   ―――――――
   To get metric equivalent in cm, divide by 39.4.   ―――――――
3. Multiply that number by itself.   ―――――――
4. Divide (1) by (3). This is your Body Mass.   ―――――――

BODY MASS

Women	Men	
B.M. less than 20	Underweight	B.M. less than 21
B.M. 21–23	Optimal weight	B.M. 22–24
B.M. 27–31	Overweight	B.M. 28–32
B.M. over 31	Obese	B.M. over 31

If you are in the Optimal range, congratulations! Only one American in five falls in the correct weight range.

If you fall in the Overweight or Obese category, the bad news is you have a lot of company: fully three Americans out of five fall into these groups. The good news, though, is that you have room for improvement. By being your own nutritionist, you are learning things those other people don't know—by balancing your diet according to the Nutritional Pyramid, you can join the (much more exclusive!) Optimal Weight Club.

When they first come to see me, many of my patients tell me they are totally confused about what kinds of fats they should eat. Maybe they have read terms like saturated and polyunsaturated, HDLs and triglycerides, but they are confused about the differences, and about the right proportions of one kind to the other.

All fats are made up of fatty acids. Some of these acids, according to the most recent findings, can actually help guard *against* artery-clogging fat deposits. Fats *preventing* artery disease? Sounds unlikely, doesn't it? To really understand the fat story, you need to know the players.

The fat that has gotten the most attention is, surely, cholesterol. It has gotten such terrifically bad press that many people don't know it is a vital chemical for your well-being—in moderation, that is. Your body could not build cells, or nerves, without it. It makes up several essential hormones, and is used to help break down fats in your food so they can be absorbed in your intestine. In fact, cholesterol is so vital to your body's existence that your liver actually produces it.

Ah, but there's the rub. Left alone, your diligent liver is set to make all the cholesterol you need, even if you eat absolutely none. But we don't leave it alone: Most Americans eat an extra 500 milligrams each day. Added to the liver's already sufficient production, that adds up to a chronic cholesterol overdose. To make matters worse, new findings suggest that the cholesterol we eat is actually more likely to lead to artery-clogging deposits than the cholesterol we produce. You would think the prescription would be clear, but the fact is, as recently as this year, studies show only one American in four actively takes steps to reduce cholesterol!

Once inside your body, cholesterol takes one of two forms, either "HDLs" (high-density lipoproteins) or "LDLs" (low-density lipoproteins). Both are formed from fats and both account for most of the cholesterol in your blood. But there the difference ends.

LDLs are the black-hat villains most people think of when they hear the word *cholesterol*. They deliver cholesterol to all of your body cells, including those in your artery walls. As your body tries to dispose of the excess cholesterol deposits, the fatty gunk begins to accumulate on the walls of your arteries, thickening them, hardening them, and eventually perhaps clogging them entirely.

HDLs, on the other hand, are the white-hat cholesterol. They do their moving in reverse, carrying away some of the accumulated sludge before it can harden into dangerous plaques inside your blood vessels. The HDLs also move the excess cholesterol to your liver, which then passes it out through the digestive system as bile acids. They also transport those fat-soluble vitamins I talked about before into your bloodstream. Your body can even use HDLs for energy.

That means the optimal fat profile is high in HDLs, low in LDLs, with a diet low in cholesterol. The newest research indicates that when it comes to protecting against disease, having the right HDL/LDL combination matters more than your total cholesterol level. That combination is what I prescribe for my patients, and it is what you will achieve as you follow the rules in these pages.

BAD EGGS

Quick, name the most cholesterol-rich food! Did you guess red meat? The fact is that eggs, all by themselves, account for more than one third of all the cholesterol Americans eat! Foods like steaks and roasts account for only one-fourth that much.

8.7%   35.9%

The Fat Family: The Good, the Bad and the Borderline

Dietary fats stretch across a broad spectrum from bad to good with one shady character that straddles the dividing line. We've already met cholesterol. Here are the other members of the Fat Family.

First, the infamous. The black sheep of the fat family is saturated fats. "Sat-fats" are the worst kind because they raise your cholesterol level. Meat is the major source of this biochemical ne'er-do-well, accounting for fully one third of the deadly sat-fats we eat. They also hang out in butter, suet, lard, and products made of butterfat like milk, cheese, and ice cream. These last three may look innocuous, but don't underestimate them. Researchers at Harvard recently compared a group of vegetarians who allow themselves dairy products—up to 29 percent of their calories—with strict vegetarians who get only 15 percent of their diet from fat. The dairy set's cholesterol levels were 21 percent higher than their more pure counterparts'. Worse yet, most of the dairy eaters' cholesterol was the bad kind—LDLs.

The infamous sat-fats don't come just from animals. They also hide in three vegetable oils: coconut oil, palm oil, and palm-kernel oil. Unfortunately, these three are among the most popular fats used in processed foods. They're disguised in such substances as nondairy creamers, cookies, crackers, and cocoa butter (found in chocolate). These gremlins rev up the cholesterol-manufacturing plant in your liver just as much as red meat does. The bottom line on saturated fats is simple: Avoid them. Your body has no known need for them. Some people insist that they make meat taste wonderful. But when that taste is the taste of death-dealing fats, your health is too high a price to pay.

Since you're trying, though, I'll make you a deal. If you stay away from them most of the time, and stick to less toxic kinds of fat, there is no reason you can't enjoy a sizzling, juicy, fat-marbled steak, say, once a month. But I expect that, if you are like most of my patients, you'll find that you soon lose your taste for those fatty meals.

You don't have to become a dietary despot, ruling over your nutrition with an unforgiving hand. The main thing is balance. With saturated fats, as with all nutritional truths, it's what you do every day that counts. No, occasional excess won't hurt, but the operative term here is "occasional." In the meantime, remember: The less saturated fat you eat, the better off you'll be. Your heart, and your arteries, and all your other organs, will thank you. And then, when you're ninety-two and still clearheaded and full of energy, you'll thank me!

Polly, the Borderline Child

The middle child of the Fat Family, the polyunsaturated, or poly-fats, is a chameleon. It can change from good to bad, depending on the circumstances. The good side is simple: These fats, such as corn, soybean, safflower, sunflower, and cottonseed oils, have become popular because they are a lot less dangerous than saturated fats. Studies have shown that where saturated fats raise blood pressure, polyunsaturated fats (specifically those called linoleic acid) actually can help lower it. So it seems a reasonable, and easy, way to cut down on sat-fats: Switch to polyunsaturated margarine. Today, margarine eaters outnumber butter eaters by more than two to one.

But this is where we see polyunsaturated fats turn chameleon, because these poly-sat margarines contain extra ingredients—stabilizers, emulsifiers, and preservatives. You may wonder if they aren't more dangerous to your health than the saturated fat in butter.

The truth is, the real danger of margarine comes not just from such artificial ingredients, but from its heat processing. When vegetable fats are heated to make margarine, they undergo a chemical transformation called *hydrogenation*, and some of them become what are called trans-fatty acids. Unfortunately, there is good evidence that fatty acids in this form have a significant cancer-causing potential.

The more we learn, the more we understand that the wholesale substitution of polyunsaturates for saturated fats is not enough. Poly-unsaturates and trans-fatty acids have recently been linked to cancer. The kind of fatty acid found in polyunsaturates, called Omega-6, seems to promote tumor formation in animals.

It is the dilemma of the chameleon: The fats of butter lead to cardiovascular disease, but the fats of margarine lead to cancer. What's the best solution? There are as many answers to this as there are experts, but when my patients ask me whether to use butter over margarine, I tell them that it boils down to a question of which diseases you want to put yourself at risk for.

At present, we know better how to assess, monitor, and reduce the risk of heart disease than we do of cancer. So, if you have to eat one or the other, it makes sense to eat butter. After all, it is a naturally occurring food, with fewer chemicals, and you can better monitor your status in the areas it puts you at risk for.

I tell my patients it is better to use a small amount of butter rather than margarine—but the operative word here is "small." As the slogan says, it's better with butter—but what the slogan doesn't tell you is that it's best of all when you use butter very sparingly indeed. While research is continuing, and until we know more, you would do best to limit your use of polyunsaturates.

The Best Child

But if you can't eat the sat-fats, and you have to watch the polys, what's left? I'm glad you asked. Meet the one member of the Fat Family with a record any mother could be proud of: the monoun-saturates. They're the popular member of the family, and no wonder: They include olive oil, almost oil (as well as olives, almonds, avoca-dos) . . . even peanut butter! You'll also find mono-fats in many plant foods, like beans, grains, vegetables, nuts, and seeds, where they come mixed with polyunsaturates.

The mono-fats bring great benefits. In a very recent study, re-ported in the *New England Journal of Medicine*, researchers gave a group of volunteers a high-fat diet where two thirds of the fat came from mono-fats. They fed another group a diet with *half as much overall fat* but with equal amounts of sat-fats, poly-fats, and mono-fats. Surprisingly, it was the high-fat diet—*with all those monofats*—that lowered cholesterol 50 percent more!

The difference clearly shows the magic of the mono-fats. These fatty acids seem to equal or exceed carbohydrates in their ability to lower LDL levels. (Think about that for one second: If mono-fats did so much in a *high*-fat diet, think of what they can do when you combine them in a low-fat diet *along with* the added benefits of starches. You begin to understand the powerful synergy of the Nutritional Pyramid!)

But while they lower LDLs, mono-fats do not seem to lower the "good" cholesterol, HDL. That means that they help maintain the crucial ratio that protects you against heart disease.

Such studies suggest that we should use olive oil—much more tasty than bland vegetable oils—to season salad dressings, pasta, and stir-fry concoctions. As you probably know, in countries such as Greece and Italy, the traditional diet is high in olive oil, and the total intake of fat is relatively high. Yet rates of heart disease are low. Medical science has now caught up to what generations of *paisans* have long known—that judicious Mediterranean cooking can actually help keep your cholesterol levels low over a long period of time. Of course, it's not just olive oil, but delicacies like peanuts, avocados, and almonds as well. It was the kind of news that made gourmets across America say: *Mama mia,* bring on the main course!

The Child Prodigy

If you think that was good news, wait until you meet the last, and most gifted, member of the Fat Family—fish oils. I call them the child prodigy because they are very new and they do wonderful things. That is, they are new to us. We are only beginning to understand the potential of this *Wunderkind.* It began back in the 1970s when researchers looked at the Japanese and Eskimos in Greenland. Although their diet of raw-fish sushi, walrus, and whale gives them about 40 percent of their calories in fat—as high as most Americans—they have a drastically lower rate of heart attack. Moreover, they have lower triglycerides and cholesterol and higher HDL levels than Americans, as well as lower rates of cancer of the colon and breast.

What is their secret? Scientists think it is fish oils, and the high levels of certain fatty acids, the Omega-3 group, in their foods. The

Omega-3 group may sound like a new John Le Carré novel, but it's not. It *is* equally exciting, however, because it represents some of the newest, and most intriguing, facts now coming out of our research laboratories.

Most of the attention has centered on one element, a chemical with the tongue-twisting name of *eicosapentaenoic acid*—or EPA. In fact, early findings have been so promising that ten institutes at the National Institutes of Health are moving full speed ahead with fish-oil research.

Look at some of the recent findings about these newly understood fish-oil substances:

- People with **high triglycerides** can benefit enormously from fish oils. Studies have shown drops of as much as 64 percent in their triglycerides and 27 percent in their cholesterol on a high-fish-oil diet—after only one month!
- Fish oils may help retard **thrombosis,** the deadly blood clots that cause strokes. The result can be fewer lethal blood clots. In addition, researchers at Harvard have documented that these same fish oils reduce blood pressure. That's important because high blood pressure puts you at greater risk for both heart attack and stroke.

We do not yet fully understand how fish oil achieves such impressive results. Scientists now believe that the EPA in fish oils blocks the production of a body chemical, *thromboxane,* involved in the chemical cycle of blood clotting. Essentially, EPA makes your blood-platelet cells less sticky, so they clump together less and are less likely to form a clot that would choke off an artery. New evidence suggests that the fish-oil fatty-acid EPA can actually disrupt the process of atherosclerosis at such an early stage that their action is truly preventive.

- These versatile substances may also be a particular boon for **migraine** sufferers, according to new evidence from the University of Cincinnati College of Medicine. Doctors there have found that severe migraine sufferers have a deficiency of Omega 3-group fatty acids in their blood. After only six weeks of treatment with fish-oil capsules, severe migraineurs recorded fewer, and less severe, attacks. The researchers theorize that low fatty acids may promote the release of the nerve chemical serotonin in the brain. This neurotransmitter constricts blood vessels and clamps down on them during a migraine. The more serotonin released, the more painful the attack. But when the migraine sufferers take the capsules, the excess release of serotonin is blocked.

- Fish oil may also provide relief for **arthritis.** Preliminary research indicates that the fatty acids found in fish oils may act as anti-inflammatory agents. They reduce joint inflammation in rheumatoid arthritis and weaken those white blood cells that contribute to inflammation.

- **Psoriasis** may be helped by these same oils, reducing the itching, caking, and flaking of skin that mark this painful and disfiguring disease. Researchers think the O-3 fats in fish oils may slow down the overproduction of skin cells that leads to psoriasis. Similar fatty acids have also been used to treat dermatitis and excessive facial-skin oiliness.

While scientists are beginning to understand how fish oil works to relieve arthritis, migraines, and skin problems, the heart-disease connection remains something of a mystery. Every day new findings about these substances appear.

Fortunately, you don't have to wait for the definitive answers to benefit from these breakthrough findings. A twenty-year study of Dutch men, reported in the *New England Journal of Medicine*, finds that if you eat one or two fish dishes each week, you will cut your risk of heart-attack death *by more than half.* No wonder the prestigious medical journal *Lancet* recently ran a letter suggesting that a diet high in fish oils could be the optimal diet for everyone.

The best sources for fish oil are fatty fishes like tuna, salmon, sardines, mackerel, sable, whitefish, bluefish, swordfish, rainbow trout, eel, herring, squid, and shellfish. It even turns out that that dreadful cod-liver oil your mother forced you to drink so many years ago is a good source. But not, probably, the best—in addition to its strong taste, it is so high in vitamins D and A, you can overdose if you down more than about one to two tablespoons a day.

I have had patients ask if they can't just eat the fish filet sandwiches at the fast-food emporiums. The answer is "Definitely not!" Not only is it fried in a variety of unhealthy fats, but it is almost completely depleted of the essential fish oils. A recent spot check by a scientist from the National Institutes of Health found that fast-food fish sandwiches have fewer beneficial O-3 fatty acids than a pepperoni pizza, and one *tenth* as much as a four-ounce can of Chinook salmon!

Whatever your source of fish oil, remember: Although it is a "good" fat, it is still a fat. It should *substitute for*, *not add to*, the other fats in your diet.

FAT FACTS TO REMEMBER

1. The sat-fats are unequivocally bad—cut out as many as you can.
2. Poly-fats are less harmful, but not harmless. Use butter instead of margarine, but sparingly.
3. Mono-fats are relatively beneficial, so get in the habit of using oils like olive and avocado for cooking and salad dressings.
4. Make fatty fish a part of your diet at least once a week, but use it to replace, not augment, your total fat intake.

Protein: The Most Versatile Nutrient

Even though protein makes up the smallest layer of macronutrients in the Nutritional Pyramid—I recommend it provide no more than 15 percent of your daily calories—don't underestimate its power! Its very name comes from the ancient Greek meaning "of prime importance."

Every cell in your body is built from protein. This thin layer of the pyramid makes up about half your body's dry weight. Protein is not one but literally tens of thousands of different substances, each serving its own purpose. Protein makes up the essential building blocks of your muscle, bone, cartilage, skin, blood, and lymph. Your hair and fingernails consist of fibers of a protein called *keratin*. You've probably heard of the protein *collagen*, which strengthens your skin, blood vessels, bones, and teeth and provides the glue that binds the cells in your various organs and tissues together. Your muscles are composed of fibers of the proteins *myosin* and *actin*.

Other proteins serve very specialized functions. *Hemoglobin,* for example, a protein in the red cells of your blood, carries molecules of oxygen from your lungs to every corner of your body, where it is used to burn molecules of food to give you energy. Protein helps regulate the balance of water and acids in your body and transport nutrients in and out of your cells. It is an integral part of the antibodies you need to fight disease, and even plays a role in the clotting of blood and the formation of scar tissue. In fact, virtually nothing goes on in your body that doesn't need protein.

Because tissues are in a constant battle of destruction and rebirth, and because your body has no way to store proteins, you need enough of this macronutrient to keep your vital processes well stocked.

Vital Nutrient Necklaces

Protein is composed of chains of amino acids—nitrogen-containing chemicals—strung together in ever-larger units. It usually takes 100 to 300 separate amino acids to form a protein molecule—the kind of protein we talk about in foods. But therein lies a great biological paradox. Proteins are big, complex molecules, far too complex to be absorbed through the fine mesh walls of our intestines. So how can we get all of them we need?

Fortunately, Nature gave proteins the ability to be master smugglers. It's as though you wanted to smuggle a diamond-studded necklace across a checkpoint. You could unstring the diamonds, bring them through unnoticed one by one, and reassemble the necklace inside. That's what proteins do. When these complex proteins pass through the stomach and intestine, they are broken down into their component amino acids. Once they have been reduced to a batch of loose amino acids, they pass quickly into your blood, where they are carried to your tissues and easily slip into your cells. Then, once smuggled into the cells, the amino acids regroup into their original long chains. *Voilà*, the great biological smuggling act is complete. It is the order in which the amino acid "jewels" fit together on each chain that determines how that protein will work, and what it will do. No wonder that protein has been called the most versatile nutrient.

TOO MUCH OF A GOOD THING

If proteins are so necessary, you may wonder why I am telling you to keep your consumption down to a scant 15 percent. The fact is, too much protein is not good for you either. Even though protein performs such amazing feats in your body, you don't need all that much. Most adults consume two to three times the amount they actually require. That can be dangerous. The excess nitrogen wastes from protein are excreted into your urine, making your kidneys work overtime to cope with the excess. The rest is used for energy. But as protein levels rise, it is stored as fat, and that means weight gain.

But that's not all. Excess nitrogen may also cause your body to flush out the vital micronutrient calcium that builds your bones and teeth.

Eating too much protein has been linked to shorter life expectancy, increased risk of cancer and heart disease, loss of calcium, stress on the kidneys, obesity, and even osteoporosis.

GETTING THE PRIME FROM PROTEIN

So the trick is to get enough protein to keep your body supplied with the matériel it needs to keep itself running, but not so much as to disrupt your body's fine-tuned chemical-regulating mechanisms. Unfortunately, this is a delicate balance because your body cannot store this vital macronutrient—not even for a few hours. Since your body uses protein so quickly, you need to replenish your supply regularly. Your body, remember, is a master scavenger. If it can't get enough protein through your food, it will turn to the next most easily available source: your muscles. After just one day, it will begin to break down the protein in your muscles to reconstruct those precious protein chains your organs need to survive.

WHAT'S YOUR PROTEIN QUOTA?

Part of being your own nutritionist is tailoring this part of the Nutritional Pyramid to your own body. By doing this Protein Worksheet, you can determine your own optimal protein quota. Think of it as a biological tax return, and get those calculators ready!

1. Multiply your body weight by .36   _____
2. Are you younger than 19? If so, add 10 percent   _____
3. I try to get most of my protein from:
   a. Vegetable sources (add 10 percent) *or*   _____
   b. Meats, poultry, and fish (subtract 10 percent)   _____

If you are a man, your final number is the number of grams of protein you should aim for every day. If you are a woman, you have two more questions. (You know what they say . . . a woman's work . . .)

Are you pregnant?
If so, add 6 grams to your Daily Quota   _____
Are you lactating?
If you have been lactating for six months or less,
add 16 grams to your Daily Quota   _____
If you have been lactating for more than six
months, add 13 grams to your Daily Quota   _____

Done! (If only taxes were so easy)

But not all protein is created equal. You need to eat *complete* protein. What is complete? Remember those amino-acid "jewels"? There are twenty-two different amino acids. Of those, your body can manufacture thirteen. But there are nine that it can't make on its own—the "essential" amino acids. Since you can't make them, you have to get them from the food you eat. So a complete protein is one containing all nine essential amino acids plus some of the other, "nonessential," ones.

Meats, fish, poultry, dairy products, and eggs all have reasonable amounts of all the essential amino acids plus others. But they all come with a walloping dose of—you guessed it, those deadly saturated fats. In fact, animal protein contains far more fat than protein —the Allens' T-bone steak contains only one fifth of its calories as protein, and a walloping 80 percent in fat calories.

But if the animal proteins come laced with fat, most of the vegetable proteins are incomplete. So what's the solution? It's called combining, completing those incomplete proteins by combining them with other foods in your meals.

The richest sources of vegetable protein are legumes—dried peas and beans, lentils, black-eyed peas, chick-peas, kidney beans, pinto beans, and black beans. But because vegetable sources are incomplete, you have to eat two or more together to give your body all the amino acids you need. For example, you can complete the amino-acid balance of peas and beans (legumes) by eating them along with rice, corn, or any grain or cereal food.

PROTEIN MATCHING CHART

WITH THESE FOODS

Legumes

Beans, lentils, peas, soybeans

Examples:
Black beans and rice
Cornbread with soy flour
Bean or lentil soup with
whole-wheat bread/rice
crackers
Split-pea soup with rice
Rice and lentil stew

Grains

Wheat, rice, corn, barley

Examples:
Whole-wheat pasta Alfredo

MATCH WITH

Grains

Rice, wheat, corn

Dairy Products

Milk, cheese, yogurt

WITH THESE FOODS   *MATCH WITH*

Rice pudding
Grilled cheese sandwich
(low-fat)
Cereals with milk
Corn chowder

Seeds   *Legumes*

Sunflower, sesame, coriander   Beans, lentils, peas, soybeans

Examples:
Humus (chick-peas and sesame
seeds)
Sesame-seed garnish on lentil
casserole
Gorp (raisins, peanuts, sunflower
seeds)
Sunflower seeds in bean soup

One vegetable protein closely resembles the complete animal proteins. Like them, it is a "one-stop shop" for all the amino acids you need. Tofu, or soybean curd, is a gummy white substance you have no doubt seen in the vegetable section of the local supermarket. It can be stir-fried with vegetables or combined with greens and vegetables in salads. Recent studies both in the United States and Italy show that soy protein helps lower cholesterol and may protect against heart disease—while giving you all the protein you need.

But whether you get proteins from tofu or from complementary vegetable proteins, they are every bit as good as protein from fatty meat and dairy sources. Vegetarians can live entirely on vegetable protein without ever eating a cheeseburger or a can of tuna fish.

This may seem as if I am calling for a drastic upheaval in how you eat, asking you to swear off all hamburgers and steaks and eat only tofu and sprouts. Nonsense! It is really only a question of degree. What I *am* saying is that, in the interest of preventive nutrition, you may want to put more emphasis on low-fat vegetable sources of protein and less on fattier animal proteins. You should start thinking of animal protein as an infrequent treat, or a condiment to your meal, rather than the centerpiece of a heavy, fatty meal.

Throughout most of the world, this is how people eat, not out of choice, but from necessity. Look at Ho Si Ping's table: His family's tiny amount of meat is simply a garnish for rice and vegetables. Americans could do themselves a big favor by taking a leaf from their book—exactly the principle of the Nutritional Pyramid.

PROTEIN REVIEW

1. Eat small amounts of complete or complementary protein frequently throughout the day.
2. Reduce your dependence on fatty animal proteins.
3. Get most of your proteins from vegetable sources, but make sure they are balanced.

Graduation from Nutrition 101!

It seems like a long time ago that we sat down at the Allens' dinner table. But now you've passed Nutrition 101. You now know all the basics you need to design a maximally healthy, perfectly balanced diet. If you still feel insecure, that's understandable. You're taking your first few steps into a brand-new world. Take your time. Don't rush. You may well want to review this section before going on.

Look back at all we've covered in these three chapters. I hope it's reassuring to you. You can be proud that you have now a solid grounding in the crucial macronutrients—starches, fats, protein, simple sugars, and the critical nonnutrient, fiber—that make up the Nutritional Pyramid. You know what proportion of each should make up your daily diet. If you forget, keep in mind the diagram of the Nutritional Pyramid: 55 percent starches, which will give you all the fiber you need; 20 percent fat, chosen sparingly from polyunsaturates and liberally from monounsaturates and fish oils; 15 percent protein, selected primarily from vegetable sources with a garnish of animal protein; and 10 percent natural sugars from fruits.

Real-Life Menu Planning

If you feel that you would benefit from a review, try this simple, real-life exercise. I have put together some sample meals. First are shown typical meals you might eat for breakfast, lunch, and dinner. Unfortunately, each is seriously out of balance with the correct Nutritional Pyramid.

Then come eight more sample meals—each balanced according to the optimal percentages of the Nutritional Pyramid. Study these until you get a feel for what combinations work together. Not only are these models for well-balanced Nutritional Pyramid meals—you may even want to use them as sample meals at home!

BAD MEALS

Breakfast:

Bowl of Frosted Flakes with whole milk
2 Fried eggs
2 Slices white toast with butter
Coffee with sugar and cream
    Calories: 730
    Protein: 13%
    Carbohydrate: 42%
    (13% refined)
    Fat: 45%

Pancakes with maple syrup and butter
2 Sausages
Coffee with sugar and cream
    Calories: 809
    Protein: 9%
    Carbohydrate: 43%
    (18% refined)
    Fat: 48%

Lunch:

Corned beef sandwich on rye bread
Pickle
Potato salad
Fruit yogurt
    Calories: 600
    Protein: 28%
    Carbohydrate: 35%
    (7% refined)
    Fat: 37%

Pepperoni pizza ($^1\!/_2$ pizza)
Coke
Chocolate cupcake
    Calories: 1117
    Protein: 17%
    Carbohydrate: 37%
    (20% refined)
    Fat: 46%

Quarter-pound hamburger
French fries
Chocolate milk shake
Chocolate-chip cookie
    Calories: 1248
    Protein: 13%
    Carbohydrate: 45%
    (18% refined)
    Fat: 42%

Dinner:

Fried chicken
Mashed potato and gravy
Biscuit
Apple Pie
    Calories: 1360
    Protein: 16%

Carbohydrate: 34%
(15% refined)
Fat: 50%

Lasagne with meat
Salad with creamy Italian dressing
Chocolate ice cream
Calories: 916
Protein: 15%
Carbohydrate: 44%
(15% refined)
Fat: 41%

Fried steak
Fried onion rings
Baked potato with butter and sour cream
Cheesecake
Calories: 1385
Protein: 18%
Carbohydrates: 33%
(15% refined)
Fat: 49%

GOOD MEALS

Breakfast:

Puffed corn cereal with skimmed milk
Sliced banana
2 slices whole-wheat toast
Herbal tea
Calories: 368
Protein: 13%
Carbohydrate: 82%
Fat: 5%

Buckwheat pancakes with Sliced fresh fruit
Coffee substitute with skimmed milk

Calories: 280
Protein: 14%
Carbohydrate: 73%
Fat: 13%

Lunch:

Turkey breast with mustard
Whole-wheat bread
Salad
Unsweetened applesauce and cinnamon
Calories: 300
Protein: 22%
Carbohydrate: 65%
Fat: 13%

Pizza with 2-oz. skim mozzarella and whole-wheat crust
Salad with oil-free dressing
Pear
Calories: 460
Protein: 17%
Carbohydrate: 63%
Fat: 20%

Tuna, water-packed
Salad
Rice cakes
Peach
Calories: 370
Protein: 19%
Carbohydrate: 68%
Fat: 13%

Dinner:

Chicken kabob with onion, pepper and tomato
Brown rice
Carrots
Baked apple with raisins

Calories: 678
Protein: 17%
Carbohydrate: 66%
Fat: 17%

Vegetarian lasagna with beans, vegetables, and whole-wheat
noodles
Steamed zucchini
Salad with oil-free dressing
Fruit salad
    Calories: 548
    Protein: 15%
    Carbohydrate: 75%
    Fat: 10%

Shrimp in tomato and herb sauce
Baked Potato with plain yogurt and chives
Broccoli
Whole-wheat roll
Peach
    Calories: 522
    Protein: 20%
    Carbohydrate: 65%
    Fat: 15%

The Nutritional Pyramid may still seem confusing. I don't expect
that you are yet ready to go out tomorrow and stock your grocery
cart and cupboards with the right proportion of each layer. But you
will be amazed how you have already started to internalize the right
habits. Before you know it, the process will seem second nature.

You may want to make a trial run of your supermarket at this
point to see how well you do. I have no doubt that, armed with the
new information you've gained in this section, you will do better
than ever before.

Now that we have covered the basics, you have a solid foundation
from which to start. In the following chapters, you will learn how to
tailor your diet for the specific micronutrients—the vitamins and
minerals—you need most in your own life-style. As you read further,

you will put the other pieces in place until you have your own, individualized, ideal regimen. Soon you will develop the same unerring instinct that guided generations of Ho Si Ping's ancestors. The same instinct that Bugs Bunny relies on. For you, as for them, preventive nutrition will become doing what comes naturally!

7.

Your Personal Prescription

"I should not talk so much about myself if there were anybody else whom I knew as well."
—Henry David Thoreau

By mastering the Nutritional Pyramid, you have already put in place the most fundamental aspect of your nutritional program—the macronutrients. These are the basics for you to assure yourself a healthy nutritional balance.

Now the time has come to tailor those basics to your own individual needs and life-style. Because of special needs in your life, you may need more of certain macronutrients, or may need different balances of specific vitamins and minerals. It all depends on your Personal Prescription—tailored to the special, individualized elements that make you, *you*.

This is the prescription I follow with my patients every day. Hank is a sixty-one-year-old labor negotiator and father of three. Marianne, a young advertising representative, diets frequently and is in training for a competitive women's decathlon. Tory, a twenty-two-year-old paralegal secretary, takes frequent doses of aspirin to relieve her headaches. And Damon, a poet, is a strict vegetarian, but he joins friends for drinks every night in an artists' café in Greenwich Village.

All these patients have one thing in common: at least one risk factor that changes their needs for micronutrients away from the standard Micronutrient Composite. In fact, I can't think of any patient who doesn't fall into at least one of the special categories. These include my older patients (Hank wouldn't like that description, but at age sixty-one, he has special nutritional considerations), athletes and dieters like Marianne, others, like Tory, who take medication regularly, and as for Damon, not only is he a vegetarian, but his nightly drinks affect his nutritional needs.

This list goes on and on. Who needs to pay special attention to micronutrient supplements? Look at the list below—are you, or any of your family, on it?

Are you:

An athlete?   _____
A smoker?   _____
Taking oral contraceptives?   _____
Taking blood-pressure medications?   _____
At high risk for heart disease?   _____
Overweight?   _____
Pregnant or nursing a baby?   _____
On a calorie-reducing diet?   _____
Under physical or emotional stress?   _____
Over sixty?   _____
A postmenopausal woman?   _____
Scheduled for or recovering from surgery? _____
A drinker of coffee or colas?   _____
A teenager?   _____
A man?   _____
A woman?   _____

Those last two give it away: The truth is, each of us has some specific, personalized micronutrient needs. Undoubtedly you recognize yourself in one or more of these groups.

This is where your Personal Prescription comes into action. Each special nutritional factor in the chart above is referenced to a page number in the Personal Prescription section. On each of these pages, you'll find all sorts of special information for each of these health groups, so you can find your own needs and tailor a standardized regime accordingly. Then your program will meet all your basic needs as well as the special considerations of your particular lifestyle. The basic composite plus the Personal Prescriptions: a complete formula for full, rounded micronutrient health.

In this section, you'll find eighteen Personal Prescription categories. I have listed them here, with their page numbers, for quick reference. Do you see yourself in any of these categories?

Do You See Yourself Here?

If you do not find yourself in any of these Personal Prescription pages, you may not need the extra advice in this section. For you, following the proportions of the Nutritional Pyramid and adhering to the basic Micronutrient Composite I list at the end of this chapter will assure you spectacular health, brimming energy, and better mental sharpness. Welcome to a fit and active long life! For you, your health equation looks like this:

$$\text{NUTRITIONAL PYRAMID} + \text{MICRONUTRIENT COMPOSITE} = \textbf{HEALTH}$$

You may want to read the next three chapters, which tell you in specific detail about the next leg of your personalized health regimen: the micronutrients, vitamins, minerals, and amino acids.

If you aren't so interested in the new research and the detailed information about micronutrients, that's fine, too. You may just want to finish your own personal nutrition plan. In that case, I suggest you skip to Chapter Eleven, where you can take the last step to tailor your new regimen to your own individual needs by diagnosing your own individual food sensitivities.

Do You Need a Personal Prescription?

On the other hand, you are more likely to be a person who sees yourself, your family, or friends in one or more of these categories above. If so, turn to those pages for special advice. They are your own nutritional prescription—selected by you. Each one contains valuable information on macronutrients, vitamins, minerals, and amino acids that you can use to compensate for your personal factors and build yourself into terrific health.

It is easy to use the advice in these pages, following a simple two-step process:

1. Find yourself on the pages of Personal Prescriptions, and note the doses of specific micronutrients listed there.

2. Write these in on the Personal Prescriptions Worksheet at the end of this section. Remember, the Micronutrient Composite is simply a good basic plan for everyone—by itself, it doesn't take into account any aspects of your Personal Prescription. But when you add the specific Personal Prescription from this section, you will be tailoring the basics to meet your own needs.

Don't be concerned if you find yourself in more than one of the Personal Prescription categories. In fact, that's very likely. You may be a young woman on the Pill who does strenuous aerobics five times a week and who suffers from migraines. Or perhaps you are an older man who smokes and has kidney problems. Not to worry—after all, tailoring your regime as closely as possible to your needs is the whole point of being your own nutritionist. *Simply take the highest level listed for that nutrient in your Personal Prescriptions,* and use that as your guide.

After you have written your own prescription, you may want to go on and get further, in-depth information about the vitamins, minerals, and amino acids. Part of being your own nutritionist means knowing what information you need, so I'll leave this decision up to you. What I can promise is that you will find complete information on our state-of-the-art knowledge about these health givers—as well as breaking research news—in the following chapters.

If you are eager to finish your own nutritional guide, however, you will want to skip to Chapter Eleven, where you can learn to diagnose your own individual food sensitivities—and take the final step to being your own nutritionist. For you, your health equation looks like this:

NUTRITIONAL PYRAMID +
MICRONUTRIENT COMPOSITE +
PERSONAL PRESCRIPTION DOSES

=   HEALTH

IMPORTANT NOTE:

IF YOU HAVE A PERSONAL PRESCRIPTION

By adding several Personal Prescriptions together, you may run the risk of overdosing. On the Personal Prescriptions Worksheet at the end of this section, I have also listed safe and allowable maximum doses. Make sure your combined dose does not exceed any of the maximums listed for any micronutrient. If it does, reduce your dosage to the maximums shown, so you don't get too much of any one vitamin, mineral, or amino acid.

That's it! Two simple steps and you have written your own prescription for solid preventive nutritional health. Easy, efficient—and effective.

Good luck in building your own prescription. I have included your worksheet—complete with the Micronutrient Composite levels—at the end of the chapter, to help you get started. The next step is up to you!

Arthritis

Arthritis can attack any joint in your body where two bones come together and, contrary to popular belief, it can strike at any age. If you suffer from osteo-, rheumatoid, or any of the other kinds of arthritis, you suffer much the same symptoms. You may experience pain or stiffness in the morning, or pain, tenderness, and swelling in one or more joints. Perhaps you find difficulty walking or being as active as you once were. But today, we know a tremendous amount about the role of proper nutrition in helping control, and cure, this debilitating disease.

Your Macronutrient Reminder

1. Steer clear of foods that can worsen the inflammation. Such foods may include: tomatoes, zucchini, eggplants, bell peppers, white onions, potatoes, squash, and paprika.

2. New research shows fish oils can act as anti-inflammatory agents, so be sure your diet includes fatty fishes like tuna, salmon, sardines, mackerel, sable, whitefish, bluefish, swordfish, rainbow trout, eel, herring, and squid. If these aren't available locally, or if you simply don't like fish, take three capsules of 1 gram of fish oil, such as Max-EPA, each day.

ARTHRITICS' PERSONAL MICRONUTRIENT PRESCRIPTION

1. Vitamin B_3 (niacinamide)	100 mg
2. Vitamin B_{12}	150 mcg
3. Vitamin B_5 (pantothenic acid)	250 mg
4. Vitamin C	3 grams
5. Calcium	1,200 mg
6. Magnesium	800 mg

Athletes

With the current emphasis on aerobic exercise, walking, running, weight training, and other forms of fitness, many people may think they fit into this category. Working out—even if it's only two or three times a week—increases the physiological stress on your body. If you're a weekend golfer or swim occasional laps, this advice is not for you. You really don't have to compensate in your nutrition balance unless you engage in strenuous, aerobic exercise *at least three times a week*. But if that describes you, then it's essential to compensate, or your exercise may end up doing you as much harm as good.

Professional athletes have done this for a long time, dosing themselves with those elements that get depleted by sweating, running, batting, or simply playing hard to win. You can take a tip from them to keep yourself in prime athletic shape—and make sure your exercise is doing you the most possible good.

FOR SUPER-JOCKS ONLY

If you are a competitive athlete, in training, you may be trying to reduce your body-fat ratio with a very low-calorie diet. This is not a good idea because your athletic exertion actually increases your need for protein dramatically—up to 50 percent, according to one study. In addition, if your daily intake is less than 1,400 calories a day for women or 2,000 calories a day for men, it is likely that you are running a deficit of calcium and vitamin D. For women, these deficiencies, along with low levels of vitamin E, can lead to excess bone thinning and increased risk of injury. Also, in such super-athletes, whether men or women, pounding exercise can actually break down red blood cells and lead to iron-deficiency anemia.

YOUR MACRONUTRIENT REMINDER

If you are trying to reduce some of your body fat, it is doubly important for you to get enough protein. The newest research indicates that even thirty minutes of aerobic exercise three times a week increases your protein requirements by 25 percent. For you, it is crucial to get your full Pyramid quota of protein—15 percent, plus some extra. But make sure it comes from vegetable sources rather than animal. As you know, the last thing you need is extra, hidden fat!

ATHLETES' PERSONAL MICRONUTRIENT PRESCRIPTION

1. Vitamin B complex*   1 tablet
2. Vitamin B_2 (riboflavin)   150 mg
3. Vitamin C   1 gram
4. Vitamin E   600 I.U.
5. Potassium   50 mg
6. Magnesium   100 mg
7. Iron   20 mg
8. Chromium†   40 mcg

* May contain niacin. If you have a liver problem, consult your doctor before taking niacin.

† For heavy-duty exercise only—hard workouts more than five times a week.

Caffeine Consumers

- Do you drink more than three cups of coffee, or tea, a day?
- Do you drink several cans of Coke, Pepsi, Tab, or similar sodas throughout the day?
- Do you consistently eat a lot of chocolate (every day)?

If you answer yes to any of these, your body is absorbing dangerous levels of caffeine. Scientists at Johns Hopkins University have found that five cups of java a day increase your heart-attack risk almost three times over that of a non-coffee drinker. Coffee has also been linked to birth defects, bladder cancer, and heart disease.

Even moderate amounts of caffeine drinks can sap your micronutrients. The chemical limits your body's absorption of calcium, and makes your kidneys flush out essential vitamins and minerals. That loss, plus the direct effect of caffeine on your central nervous system, creates hypertense nerves, insomnia, poor concentration, and a weakened immune system.

However, you can help offset some side effects with a corrective dose of vitamins and minerals. Just don't take them with your coffee, tea, or soda!

CAFFEINE DRINKERS' PERSONAL MICRONUTRIENT PRESCRIPTION

1. Vitamin B complex*	300 mg
2. Vitamin C	3,000 mg
3. Calcium	1,200 mg

* May contain niacin. If you have a liver problem, consult your doctor before taking niacin.

4. Magnesium   800 mg
5. Zinc   75 mg

Cardiac Problems

If you have heart problems, no doubt your doctor has already told
you to watch very carefully what you eat. Even in its healthy state,
this dynamo muscle needs tender, loving nutritional care. But when
it is damaged, or you have recurrent chest pain, a family history of
heart disease, or perhaps you've had a coronary bypass, you need to
be even more conscious of the heart nutrients you take. With an
extra boost from these supplements for a hardy heart, you can rest
assured that you are giving your heart the very best nutritional
support.

YOUR MACRONUTRIENT REMINDER

First, balance your fats:

- Avoid all saturated fats, found in meat, cheese, and butter.
- Polyunsaturated fats, like those in vegetable oils, are borderline.
  They may lower your risk for heart disease, but they increase your
  risk for cancer. Eat them only in moderation.
- Monosaturated fats are the best, from olive oil, almonds, peanuts,
  and avocados. They can help lower your cholesterol levels, but are
  fairly high in calories.
- There are also two guardian fatty acids—linolenic and gamma-
  linolenic—that help protect you from artery-clogging fat deposits.
- **Fish is your dish.** There's evidence that fish oils protect against
  heart attack, so eat one or two fish items a week—research shows
  it may cut your chances of a fatal heart attack by more than half!
  The oils in the fatty fish—tuna, salmon, sardines, mackerel, sable,
  whitefish, bluefish, swordfish, rainbow trout, eel, herring, squid—
  can even reduce your triglycerides and cholesterol.

- **Keep fiber high,** especially oats, as it lowers triglycerides. Soybean fiber and wheat cereals, oats, and rice are also good.

CARDIAC PATIENTS' PERSONAL MICRONUTRIENT PRESCRIPTION

1. Vitamin B_3 (niacin)*   50 mg
   Lowers cholesterol, triglycerides; may help reverse atherosclerosis. **CAUTION:** May disrupt heart rhythm. Doses from 2,000–6,000 milligrams can lower cholesterol and heart disease, but should be taken only under your doctor's supervision.
2. Vitamin B complex   200 mg
3. Vitamin C   3 grams
   Increases HDL levels, reduces cholesterol.
4. Vitamin E   600 mg
   Increases HDL cholesterol. Doses above 800 I.U. a day may cause blood clots.
5. Selenium   200 mcg
6. Chromium   200 mcg
   May prevent hardening of the arteries.
7. Manganese   50 mg
   Deficiency linked to atherosclerosis.
8. Inositol   400 mg twice a day
   May reduce cholesterol.
9. Choline   400 mg twice a day
   Helps prevent atherosclerosis.
10. IodineBalances cholesterol/prevents athero-   From diet
    sclerosis. Get it from dietary sources: fish, shellfish, kelp (seaweed), mushrooms, and plenty of water.

* If you have liver problems, talk with your physician before taking niacin.

MICRONUTRIENT CAUTIONS

Calcium ensures the steady functioning of your cardiovascular system. But you need a delicate balance. DO NOT TAKE MORE THAN 1,500 MG WITHOUT SUPERVISION OF YOUR DOCTOR.

Likewise, do not take more than 600 I.U. of vitamin D, as it can lead to calcified coronary-artery lesions.

Magnesium can be a problem for you, as it can produce arrythmias—irregular heartbeats. DO NOT TAKE WITHOUT SUPERVISION OF YOUR DOCTOR.

Diabetics

Diabetes is a failure in the way your body metabolizes three major levels of the Nutritional Pyramid: carbohydrates, fat, and protein. It often tends to occur as you age and your body naturally loses its ability to remove excess sugar from your blood.

If you are a diabetic—Type I or Type II—you surely know your diet is the best way to control your blood-sugar levels. If you have Type II diabetes, you may be able to control your blood sugar through diet and exercise alone without taking any medications. Since 40 percent to 80 percent of all diabetics are hypertensive, you'll also want to watch what you eat to keep your blood pressure even.

If you are not diagnosed a diabetic you should likewise be alert to your diet if you fall into any of these high-risk groups:

- Do you have a family history of diabetes?
- Are you overweight?
- Are you over forty?
- Are you a female? (twice as much risk as men)
- If so, have you given birth to a baby who weighs nine pounds or more?

If you see yourself in this profile, paying strict attention to your macronutrients can lower your chances of developing diabetes.

YOUR MACRONUTRIENT REMINDER

Since diabetes is a breakdown of the Nutritional Pyramid, it means you must pay special attention to reestablishing a correct balance of macronutrients. If you don't have diabetes yet, this can help prevent it; if you do, it can help control the symptoms of the disease. As a diabetic, you have a slightly different Nutritional Pyramid to follow than the one we saw earlier.

Sixty-five percent of your calories should come from carbohydrates—preferably whole-grain breads, cereals and grains, fresh fruits and vegetables, dried beans and legumes; 10 to 15 percent from fats—keep high on the mono-and polyunsaturated fats, remember—and 20 percent from protein. In general, you should use low-fat products such as skimmed milk, low-fat yogurt and cheese, lean meats, fish, poultry, and meat-substitute dishes with beans, grains, and complementary proteins. It's also important to keep your salt intake moderate.

In your case, it is particularly important to keep your fiber high—especially beans, peas, lentils, and whole-grain cereals. These fibers slow the absorption of glucose, and may even reduce the need for insulin and antidiabetic drugs. Studies show that if you eat between 30 and 70 grams of fiber a day, you can improve your glucose tolerance. Of course, eating so much fiber means you have to pay special attention to getting adequate vitamins and minerals.

Iodine can be helpful for you because it helps stimulate your metabolism, burn off extra fat, regulate your body's production of energy, synthesize protein, and absorb carbohydrates from your intestine. I have included it in the macronutrient section because you should make sure to get it from your diet, instead of taking supplements. (See Iodine, page 341.)

Avoid **sugar.** You may have read that ice cream and other Sweet Nothings are permissible on a diabetic diet because they don't raise your blood sugar any more than complex carbohydrates. But now research from Stanford University School of Medicine finds that sugar raises triglycerides and cholesterol levels in diabetics, and with it heart disease—a particular concern, since diabetes itself doubles the risk of cardiovascular problems. These increases showed up in as little as two weeks of eating an average intake of table sugar. We don't yet know if these changes will prove to be permanent, or if your body adapts to increased sugar over time, but for the moment, there is not enough evidence to allow sugar as a regular item on your diet list.

Alcohol poses special risks, as you may know.

MANY DIABETICS CANNOT TOLERATE ANY ALCOHOL WHATSOEVER, SO DO NOT CONSUME ANY ALCOHOL WITHOUT CONSULTING YOUR OWN PHYSICIAN.

Even if your doctor says it is allowable for you, one drink a day should be your upper limit, whether beer, wine, or hard liquor. Otherwise, the alcohol will interfere with your blood-sugar metabolism, and raise your triglycerides.

If you do drink, you should count alcohol like fat in your diet. Some alcohol also has added carbohydrate—a beer, for example, contains not just the alcohol calories, but the carbohydrates of a slice of bread. Since many diabetics also need to lose weight, you should be aware that each drink you take adds 100 calories to your diet.

Although your special Nutritional Pyramid applies to you whether you are Type I or Type II, there are special considerations depending on which form of the disease you have.

If you developed diabetes as a child (Type I), these are your special considerations:

- Time your eating schedule so meals come when your insulin peaks.
- Try to keep the level of calories you eat relatively consistent from day to day.
- You have special needs for exercise and for hypoglycemia. In general, avoid sugar except before strenuous exercise or for correcting hypoglycemia.
- When you are ill, try to eat normally, even though you don't feel like it. Your illness may increase your requirements for insulin and consequently for extra carbohydrates to balance the medication.

If you become diabetic as an adult (Type II), you are more than likely trying to control your weight. (Over 80 percent of Type II diabetics are overweight.) So cutting calories is your first priority, and timing of meals is less important. Your doctor can help you work out a weight-loss plan that is best for you. Regular exercise is also crucial, and I include that in your Personal Prescription.

If you are a Type II diabetic on medication, even small amounts of alcohol may interact with your oral medication and can make you nauseated and flushed, impair your speech, and speed up your heartbeat.

DIABETICS' PERSONAL MICRONUTRIENT PRESCRIPTION

Correct doses of supplements may help you reduce your medication. BEFORE TAKING ANY SUPPLEMENTS, ALWAYS CONSULT YOUR OWN PHYSICIAN.

1. Vitamin B_1*   200 mg
   Helps your body squeeze the most out of starches and natural sugars.
2. Vitamin B_2 150 mg
   Helps convert proteins, fats, starches, and natural sugars into energy.
3. Vitamin B_5 500 mg
   Required to absorb proteins, fats, and carbohydrates.
4. Biotin   150 mg
5. Magnesium   300 mg
   Necessary for proper metabolism of foods.
6. Zinc   75 mg
   Helps form insulin to keep your energy stable and strong.
7. Chromium   400 mg
   Helps with natural loss of ability to take sugar from blood that occurs with aging.
8. Manganese   50 mg
   Increases glucose tolerance. Low levels can affect how you remove sugar from the blood and set the stage for diabetes.

MICRONUTRIENT CAUTION

*DIABETICS SHOULD NOT TAKE large doses of vitamins B_1, C, and the amino acid L-cysteine, EXCEPT UNDER THE SUPERVISION OF A DOCTOR. THE COMBINATION MAY INACTIVATE INSULIN. Also consult your physician before taking niacin (vitamin B_3).

Dieters

Approximately one in three American women, and one in six men, follows some kind of diet to lose weight. If you are one of them, you know how hard it is to resist a diet that radically slashes your calories and promises quick weight loss in return. Unfortunately, as they cut down on your food, many of them also slash your micronutrients. Studies of eleven popular diets found that none provides the recommended dosages for the thirteen major vitamins and minerals.

The general rule of thumb is that if you eat less than 1,800 calories a day, the only way you can get proper levels of micronutrients is to cut way back on your alcohol, sugars, and fats. If you eat less than 1,200 calories, there is virtually no chance that you will get sufficient micronutrients from your food alone—not even enough to meet the scanty RDAs. Most often, these diets put you at risk for deficiencies of B_1, B_6, B_{12}, calcium, iron, zinc, potassium, and magnesium.

Any diet that tries to sell you an excess of one of the macronutrients—most often protein—at the cost of another—frequently carbohydrates—can produce significant nutrient deficiencies in as short a time as two weeks. So if you're dieting, you need to hedge your losses. Here's how:

YOUR MACRONUTRIENT REMINDER

Fiber is your best friend. Review Nutrition 101 and you'll find that fiber:

- acts as an appetite suppressant
- has few or no calories
- makes you feel full because of its bulk
- stabilizes your blood sugar so your moods don't swing wildly between highs and lows
- slows the absorption of your carbohydrates

Starches also fill you up, give you ample energy—and if you keep your portions small, they won't add significant extra calories.

DIETERS' PERSONAL MICRONUTRIENT PRESCRIPTION

This regimen will not only help rebalance your micronutrients, but can even help control your appetite.

1. Vitamin B_1	300 mg
2. Vitamin B_6	200 mg
3. Vitamin B_{12}	200 mg
4. Vitamin C	3,000 mg
5. L-phenylalanine*	500 mg
6. Calcium	1,200 mg
7. Iron	15 mg
8. Zinc	75 mg
9. Magnesium	800 mg

* DO NOT TAKE phenylalanine if you have been diagnosed a phenylketonuric (PKU) or have high blood pressure.

Drinkers

Alcohol is a robber baron when it comes to nutrients. Even drinking only one or two drinks a day can significantly deplete your micronutrient stores. Some people try to lessen the biologic cost of liquor by drinking beer or wine. In general, it's not helpful—there is as much alcohol in a glass of wine or bottle of beer as there is in one and a half ounces of hard liquor.

If you are a man who consumes more than three drinks a day, or a woman who consumes one and a half a day, your alcohol may interfere with your body's vitamin and mineral levels. The most common and serious deficiency caused by heavy drinking is a marked loss of B vitamins. This decline has been linked to polyneuritis, painful nerve inflammation, and liver disease. Likewise, it hinders your ability to use vitamin D, and so can contribute to osteoporosis.

SPECIAL CONSIDERATIONS FOR WOMEN

If you're taking oral contraceptives—which contain female hormones—your body is much less able to eliminate alcohol from your body. Likewise, when the hormones shift just before your menstrual period, alcohol metabolism slows down—and you are much more vulnerable to the effects of liquor.

Pregnant and nursing women should avoid alcohol altogether. You put yourself and your unborn baby at risk for fetal alcohol syndrome, miscarriage, stillbirth, and low birth weight.

GOOD NEWS ABOUT BOOZE

There are a few good things to be said for alcohol from a preventive-nutrition standpoint. There is some evidence that people who drink no more than two drinks a day are actually healthier than people who either drink more or don't drink at all. A massive study at Johns Hopkins Medical School of the drinking habits of seventeen thousand people found that moderate beer drinkers reported infrequent sickness, went to the doctor less often, and missed fewer days from school or work than control groups.

Those who drank one beer or more a day reported the lowest incidence of sickness. When they reached thirty-five beers a week, however, the health benefits turned around.

The landmark Framingham study followed five thousand adults for twenty-two years and found that men who drank one or two drinks a week had a lower mortality rate than those who drank heavily or not at all.

How does it work? We know that alcohol can boost your HDL-cholesterol levels that protect against heart disease. But we also know that there is more than one type of HDL-cholesterol, and the kind that is elevated by drinking, unfortunately, does not guard against cardiac problems. Again, it could be that people who drink moderately have personalities or life-styles that promote longevity.

On the other hand, there is evidence that alcohol is implicated in other health problems. Drinking beer can lead to heart problems and having even one drink can cause acute liver inflammation.

For now, we don't know enough to predict whether having a moderate two drinks a day will make you healthier than being a teetotaler. Until further research resolves this question, only your nutritionist knows for sure—and that, of course, means you.

YOUR MACRONUTRIENT REMINDER

In general, pay special attention to your full Nutritional Pyramid quota for protein. It helps vitamin C combat alcohol's harmful effects on your body, including counteracting the poison acetaldehyde, produced when the liver processes alcohol.

Specifically, try to make sure you have eaten some fiber-rich carbohydrates before you lift a glass. It will smooth the absorption of alcohol into your system.

YOUR PERSONAL MICRONUTRIENT COCKTAIL

Even if you drink moderately, this special mix will keep your nutrients high and reduce the toll alcohol takes on your body's systems.

1. Beta-carotene   20,000 I.U.
2. Vitamin B complex   1 tablet a day
3. Vitamin B_1 100 mg
4. Folic acid   400 mcg
5. Choline   500 mg three times a day
6. Inositol   500 mg three times a day
7. Vitamin C   3 grams
8. Zinc   100 mg
9. Octacosanol   3 mg

MICRONUTRIENT WARNING

If long-term alcohol intake has impaired your liver functioning, your liver may be less able to store vitamin A. That means you must be very careful not to get too much. It could build up to toxic levels in your blood. Neither the Micronutrient Composite nor the Personal Prescription includes this vitamin, using safe beta-carotene instead. But most commercial multivitamins do include vitamin A. If you have severe liver disease, it is important that you avoid overdosing. Also, B complex contains niacin. Because drinkers usually have liver problems, this vitamin can spell trouble for you. Consult your doctor before taking any combination containing niacin.

High Blood Pressure

This is one of the most "popular" of the Personal Prescriptions— and I wish it weren't. Today, one American in six has high blood pressure. Those at highest risk include blacks, those who are twenty pounds or more overweight, and those with a family history of hypertension. If you are one of the 38 million people with high blood pressure, your diet can be one of your most potent, positive allies for better health and longer life. Without dietary help, you leave yourself wide open to potentially lethal consequences—heart disease, kidney disease, and stroke.

Alcohol is a particular concern for you. We do not know what percentage of high blood pressure is directly caused by alcohol, but it is clear that for millions of people, alcohol can greatly aggravate— and even cause—high blood pressure. For all of us, drinking increases our chances of developing blood-pressure problems. Research shows that as alcohol intake goes up, so does blood pressure, particularly if you are older than fifty.

YOUR MACRONUTRIENT REMINDER

Consider fiber your good friend. Enough of it in your diet can help bring about a significant blood-pressure drop.

Keep your fat consumption down to my recommended 20 percent.

Fat is now thought to play a larger role in blood pressure for most people than salt. There is still much we don't understand about the fat-hypertension link. We do know that when fatty cholesterol is deposited in the walls of the branches of your arteries, it constricts them. The blood must flow through the smaller-diameter opening, which causes the pressure to rise.

Stored as excess weight, fat increases blood pressure. If you keep your weight where it belongs, it will help lower blood pressure.

HYPERTENSIVES' PERSONAL MICRONUTRIENT PRESCRIPTION

1. Vitamin D   400 I.U.
   Helps calcium stabilize blood pressure.
2. Vitamin E   600 I.U.
3. Calcium   1,500 mg
   Can help vitamin D stabilize blood pressure;
   take under doctor's supervision, as some people
   actually have a *rise* in blood pressure with calcium.
4. Magnesium   1,000 mg
5. Potassium   100 mg
6. Vitamin C   3,000 mg
7. Vitamin B$_6$ (pyridoxine)   75 mg
8. Taurine   50 mg three times a day

WARNING:

REMOVE THE AMINO ACID L-PHENYLALANINE FROM YOUR MICRONUTRIENT COMPOSITE. DO NOT TAKE IT WITHOUT CONSULTING YOUR DOCTOR, AS IT CAN RAISE YOUR BLOOD PRESSURE.

IF YOU HAVE A HISTORY OF KIDNEY STONES, CALCIUM AND VITAMIN D CAN LEAD TO KIDNEY-STONE PROBLEMS— TAKE ONLY UNDER PHYSICIAN'S SUPERVISION.

Hypoglycemics

You may well have hypoglycemia and not even know it. This disease (the medical term is *reactive hypoglycemia*) is caused by periods of very low blood sugar. It is the exact opposite of diabetes, which is caused by high blood sugar. But in hypoglycemia, the levels of glucose in your blood don't stay uniformly low. They swing, sometimes so rapidly that within the course of one day, you may find that your energy goes from manic peaks to lethargic, depressed valleys. Hypoglycemia may make you often feel vaguely depressed for no apparent reason, have difficulty concentrating just before lunch or in the late afternoon, get severe headaches or feel lightheaded or faint if you haven't eaten for a while, and become tense and irritable for no good cause.

YOUR MACRONUTRIENT REMINDER

Just as diabetics have different macronutrient needs than healthy people, so do you.

Because it breaks down more slowly than carbohydrate, protein offers a way to help stabilize your energy levels. Make sure you get the correct 15 percent Nutritional Pyramid proportion of time-release proteins. The level of dietary fat can stay the same—20 percent.

• Eat enough to prevent hunger, but not so much that you feel stuffed.

• Try to spread out your calories over the day—eating more often to keep a constant glucose level in your blood and brain. You should eat three small meals a day plus frequent snacks in between. They should be timed by the clock, not by when you feel hungry. Just how often is determined by a glucose-tolerance test. If you suspect that you might be hypoglycemic, you should consult your own physician.

WATCH WHAT YOU EAT

1. Meats: any unprocessed fish, fowl, or other animal protein.
2. Liquids: vegetable juices, herbal teas, decaffeinated coffee, plain soda, all mineral waters or other bottled waters.
3. Vegetables: preferably fresh, steamed or raw:

Artichokes	Celery	Parsley
Asparagus	Chives	Peppers
Avocado	Cucumber	Pimiento
Bean sprouts	Eggplant	Pumpkin
Beets	Lettuce	Sauerkraut
Broccoli	Mushrooms	Spinach
Brussels sprouts	Okra	Squash
Cabbage	Olives	String beans
Carrots	Onions	Tomatoes
Cauliflower		

4. Fruits: two servings daily, eaten in the fresh, raw state:

Boysenberries	Lemon/lime	Rhubarb
Cantaloupe	Melons	Strawberries
Cranberries	Papayas	Tangerines
Grapefruit	Peaches	

5. Nuts and seeds: preferably raw, unsalted, and unprocessed.
6. Dairy products: including plain, low-fat yogurt.
7. Bread: whole-grain only.
8. Avoid caffeine, alcohol, and foods high in refined sugars.

Kidney Problems

Your kidneys are among the most crucial organs underpinning your nutritional well-being. They keep track of what vitamins and minerals you need, and constantly rebalance your body's reserves.

Your kidneys flush out excess water-soluble vitamins and minerals, as well as waste material from the body's processes. If they aren't working properly, your nutritional health can be seriously compromised.

One of the most common problems is kidney stones—accumulations of mineral salts, mostly calcium—which can occur in the bladder or anywhere else in the intricate piping of your urinary tract. As any kidney-stone sufferer knows, they can cause excruciating, debilitating pain.

YOUR MACRONUTRIENT REMINDER

The more protein you eat, the more work and stress on your kidneys, as they try to eliminate the excess nitrogen from protein. If you have kidney problems, research suggests that moving to a more vegetarian diet, and supplementing with amino acids instead of protein, can help. In one study, at Harvard University, such a diet even eliminated the need for dialysis for two thirds of the patients tested.

As we age, our kidney function declines, so eating a lot of protein puts an unnecessary load on these vital organs. Keep a careful eye on this proportion of your Nutritional Pyramid, and don't overdo the protein. As always, try to get your protein from vegetable, not fat-laden animal, sources.

YOUR PERSONAL MICRONUTRIENT PRESCRIPTION

1. Beta-carotene	25,000 I.U.
2. Vitamin B$_6$	150mg
3. Inositol	250 mg
4. Vitamin C	2 mg
5. Vitamin E	600 I.U.
6. Folic acid	400 mcg

MICRONUTRIENT WARNING

DISREGARD THE MINIMUM TOXIC DOSE LEVELS IN THE TABLE ON PAGE 401. YOUR KIDNEY DISEASE REQUIRES SPECIAL—LOWER—MAXIMUMS. DO NOT TAKE CALCIUM, MAGNESIUM, OR MORE THAN 500 MG OF VITAMIN C A DAY WITHOUT CONSULTING YOUR DOCTOR.

Medications

You probably know that it's unwise to take certain drugs—prescribed medications—together because the combination may make one drug work faster, or less well, or the combo may produce serious side effects. Although it has received very little attention, exactly the same is true of vitamins and minerals. As bioactive substances, they can interact with medications in complex ways. Even if the only medication you take is aspirin, you may need to be alert for changes in your micronutrients.

Certain vitamins and minerals make your drugs less effective. Sometimes the reverse happens: Medications may deplete your vitamin and mineral reserves, so you need to take more to make up for the loss. We still have much to learn about drug-nutrient interactions, so if your medication is not listed in the table below, that does not necessarily mean that no micronutrient interaction will occur. Here are a few of the common interactions. But each case can vary, so the best rule of all is: If you are taking any medication, be alert to changes in your body.

MEDICATION	MICRONUTRIENT EFFECTS
1. Antacids (magnesium-containing)	Calcium 1,500 mg
2. Antibiotics	Folic acid 100 mcg
If your doctor has put you on a	Vitamin B_{12} 50 mcg
prescribed course of antibiotics, take:	Vitamin C 500 mg
Neomycin	Beta-carotene 20,000 I.U.
Reduces absorption of vitamins A, E,	Vitamin D 400 I.U.
D, K. When taking neomycin, take:	Vitamin E 600 I.U.
3. Anticoagulants (oral)	
Drug action increased by vitamins	
A, D, E, K.	
Drug may be less effective in	
combination with Vitamin C.	
	Magnesium 100 mg
	Zinc 20 mg

MEDICATION	MICRONUTRIENT EFFECTS

4. Barbiturates
   B$_6$ reduces drug action.
5. Chemotherapy
   Drugs may reduce magnesium
   absorption.

   Folate interferes with methotrexate
   chemotherapy. If taking folate,
   discontinue during chemotherapy
   (including folate-containing B
   complex).

   Adriamycin   Vitamin E 600 I.U.
6. Cholesterol drugs: Beta-carotene 20,000 I.U.
   Cholestyramine, Colestipol
   Reduce uptake of Vitamins A, E, D, K.   Vitamin D 400 I.U.
   When taking these drugs, take: Vitamin E 600 I.U.
7. Cortisone   Calcium 1,500 mg
                                                                 Vitamin C 200 mg
                                                                 Vitamin D 400 I.U.
                                                                    Zinc 75 mg
                                                    Sodium—reduce dietary
                                                                           level
8. Diuretics   Magnesium 100 mg
                                                                    Zinc 20 mg

9. Antipsychotic drugs:
   Hydralazine, Isoniazid
   May increase vitamin B$_6$ requirement.   Vitamin B$_6$ 100 mg
   Isoniazid may also increase B$_3$ Vitamin B$_3$ 50 mg
   requirement.
10. Levodopa (L-dopa)
    Reduced drug action when taking B$_6$
    If you are taking this drug for
    Parkinson's disease, don't take B$_6$
    without consulting your doctor. It can
    interfere with the action of L-dopa-type
    drugs in the brain, and worsen your
    symptoms.
11. Phenobarbital
    VITAMIN B$_6$ CAN INTERFERE WITH PHENOBARBITAL'S
    ACTION

MEDICATION	MICRONUTRIENT EFFECTS
12. Phenytoin	
Decreases activity of Vitamin D.	Vitamin D 400 I.U.
Reduces absorption of folic acid from foods.	Folic acid 600 mcg
13. Mineral oil laxatives deplete vitamins A, D, E, and K. When taking mineral oil, take:	Beta-carotene 20,000 I.U. Vitamin D 400 I.U. Vitamin E 600 I.U.
14. Oral contraceptives	
Increase B vitamin needs (B_2, B_6, B_{12}, folic acid) Take additional:	B complex 1 capsule/daily
Increases zinc needs.	Zinc 100 mg
Reduces levels of C.	Vitamin C 1 gram
Too much Vitamin C can concentrate estrogen in the blood, leading to adverse effects.	
15. Penicillamine	
Increases B_6 requirement.	Vitamin B_6 50 mg
16. Sulfasalazine	
Reduces absorption of folic acid.	Folic acid 600 mcg
17. Triamterene	Folic acid 600 mcg Calcium 1,200 mg
18. Aspirin	
Interacts with many micronutrients. Reduces vitamins C and K, iron.	
Vitamin C slows aspirin metabolism, so a toxic buildup can occur with even moderate aspirin doses.	

Men

Men are almost twice as likely as women to eat whatever they want, according to food-preference surveys. The problem is that what many men want is red meat—which brings along an overdose of fats, chemicals, and salt. It also can lead to some chronic micromineral deficiencies—almost half of all men get less than even the minimal RDA for vitamin A, and most men are short of selenium, zinc, potassium, and magnesium.

To keep your reproductive organs healthy and functioning normally, and for sexual vitality, you need those vitamins and minerals. If you're a teenaged male, going through the normal adolescent growth spurt, you have special needs for certain micronutrients that your diet is almost certainly not providing, including vitamins A, B_6, and C, zinc, calcium, and iron.

As a man, you need different nutrients throughout your lifetime —not just to keep your sexual system healthy, but to protect all the organ systems of your body. As a senior, you need to make sure you have enough vitamin D, calcium, and phosphorus to protect you against bone-wasting.

YOUR PERSONAL MICRONUTRIENT PRESCRIPTION

FOR ADOLESCENT MEN

1. Beta-carotene	20,000 mg
2. Vitamin B_6	200 mg
3. Vitamin C	3 grams
4. Zinc	100 mg

FOR MEN 18 TO 60

1. Vitamin E	600 I.U.
2. Zinc	100 mg

Keeps prostate healthy, prevents cancer.
May raise testosterone levels, sperm count, improve potency.

3. Selenium	150 mcg

Helps regulate sexual functioning.
Lost through ejaculate.

FOR MEN ABOVE AGE 60

Same as above, but add:

1. Vitamin D	400 mg
2. Calcium	1 gram
3. Magnesium	750 mg

Migraine Sufferers

It's hard for anyone who hasn't experienced a migraine to appreciate just how incapacitating one of these attacks can be. But 20 million Americans know how these killer headaches can put you flat on your back, out of commission, and radically alter your personality. As you probably know, migraines come with a whole assortment of side effects, including nausea, dizziness, and head-splitting pain that can —almost literally—knock you out of your social and professional life.

YOUR MACRONUTRIENT REMINDER

Many migraineurs are sensitive to the amino acid tyramine, which can trigger an acute migraine episode. Those people should avoid tyramine-containing foods such as avocados, aged cheese, bananas, beer, red wine, and pickled herring.

New research shows fish oil can help alleviate migraines in some people, so it is probably a good idea for you to make sure you get enough fresh fish in your diet to take advantage of this anti-head-ache effect. Or you may want to take fish-oil capsules, such as Max-EPA, available in any health-food store.

MIGRAINEURS' PERSONAL MICRONUTRIENT PRESCRIPTION

The bulk mineral magnesium has recently been found to have a positive effect against these headaches. (See page 210.) In order to see if it works for you, I suggest you try the following combination.

1. Fish-oil capsules   1,000 mg three times daily
2. Magnesium   850 mg

Discontinue if headaches do not improve.

Seniors

As you get older, all the systems in your body undergo changes. Since you metabolize foods differently, your cells may have a difficult time getting enough of the crucial vitamins and minerals. Recent research from the University of Illinois indicates that the immune systems and blood of older people are weaker, and that nutrition plays an important role in this cycle. Because your body does not absorb micronutrients as efficiently as it used to, you are also put at risk for deficiency of one or more vitamins. One study found that one half of those older people surveyed had seriously low vitamin C. You also may have a significant lack of iron, calcium, and zinc. Inadequate calcium has been proved to be the most serious nutritional problem for older people, due to its link with osteoporosis. Also, because your kidneys and liver may be less efficient than they once were, they can take longer to clear substances out of your body, and this has an effect on your nutrient status. All in all, your special needs require a special prescription—and here it is!

YOUR MACRONUTRIENT REMINDER

Be sure to get lots of fresh vegetables and fruits with beta-carotene and vitamins A and C. These will help lower your risk of cancer, fight biological damage to your cells as you age, and decrease the rate of age-linked diseases. For all these reasons, I suggest you eat at least one three-ounce serving of green, red, or yellow vegetables each day.

SENIORS' MICRONUTRIENT PRESCRIPTION

1. Vitamin B complex   1 capsule daily
2. Vitamin C   3 grams
3. Vitamin E   600 I.U.
4. Selenium   150 mcg
   Retards hardening of tissues.
   May increase alertness, elevate mood.
5. Chromium   40 mcg
   improves body's use of sugar fuel.

6. Calcium   1,500 mg
7. Magnesium   1,000 mg

Smokers

You don't need me to tell you not to. You've heard all the reasons. But you may not know the nutritional ones. Smoking uses up many vitamins and minerals: B_1 (thiamine), B_6 (pyridoxine), and particularly vitamin C. Each cigarette destroys an average of 25 mg of C. So if you smoke, you have much less C in your blood than non-smokers do. So your first task is to replace what the smoke has depleted from your body.

But micronutrient supplements may also provide you with some protection—and I emphasize "some"—against several dangerous substances in cigarettes. One is the toxic metal cadmium. The mineral zinc and vitamins C and E can make cadmium less toxic and slow its absorption. Other antioxidant minerals and vitamins work against other constituents of cigarette smoke, to make them less destructive in your body.

MARIJUANA

Marijuana has a higher concentration of carcinogens than tobacco smoke. Since you inhale more deeply, you get more exposure to poisonous chemicals with each puff. Marijuana may have a debilitating effect on your reproductive system, sperm and hormone levels. While there is little good research yet, we think various vitamins, like C, may offer some protection.

So if you do smoke—anything—here are some steps you can take to begin compensating.

YOUR MACRONUTRIENT REMINDER

Eat generous helpings of green and yellow vegetables. They contain beta-carotene. Studies have found that smokers who boost their consumption of these foods are much less likely to develop lung cancer than those who don't. So load up at the vegetable stand.

SMOKERS' PERSONAL MICRONUTRIENT PRESCRIPTION

1. Beta-carotene   25,000 I.U.
   Helps protect smokers against cancers of lung,
   bronchial tubes, and mouth.
2. Vitamin B_1 100 mg
3. Vitamin B_2 100 mg
4. Vitamin B_6 200 mg
5. Vitamin B_{12} 200 mcg
6. Folic acid   400 mcg
   May help protect against lung cancer.
7. Vitamin C   3 grams
   May be particularly useful for marijuana smoke.
8. Vitamin E   600 I.U.
   Start with 200 I.U., build up gradually to 600.
9. Zinc   100 mg
10. Selenium   150 mcg

Stress

There are a number of different kinds of stress, but each can change your needs for certain micronutrients. The one we're most familiar with is psychological stress—the countless demands of coping with work, relationships, crises, and life in general that can make us anxious, tense, depressed, or sleepless. Maybe it's studying for a big exam, meeting a project deadline, or going through a difficult period with mate, family, or friends. But no matter the cause, each takes a real micronutrient toll.

Less obvious, but equally important, is the physiological stress caused by illness, infection, injury, burns, even surgery. Any time your body needs to draw on its micronutrient reserves to heal you, it depletes your stores.

Finally, there is a subtle kind of stress that comes from the environment. Some of this comes when your body has to deal with cell-toxic elements like air, food, and water pollutants and radiation.

Each of these can damage your cells, increasing the body's workload as it tries to repair them, and in the process depleting vital micronutrients. Another—often ignored—type of environmental stress comes from extremes of temperature—either hot or cold—which force your body's thermal-conservation systems to do extra work to keep you purring along at a steady 98.6 degrees.

Whether you suffer from one, two, or all three of these types of stress, you need to boost your vitamins and minerals to keep yourself in optimum shape, to give your body the necessary nutritional material it needs to keep you well.

Psychological Stress

PERSONAL MICRONUTRIENT PRESCRIPTION

1. Vitamin B complex	1 capsule daily
2. Pantothenic acid	500 mg three times daily
3. Biotin	100 mcg
4. Inositol	300 mg
5. Vitamin C	3 grams
6. Vitamin E	600 I.U.
7. Calcium	1,200 mg
8. Magnesium	800 mg
9. Zinc	100 mg

ARE YOU AN INSOMNIAC?

Sleep is the body's "downtime," when it repairs itself and rids itself of the damage created by the day's stresses. Yet when we are most stressed we often can't sleep, depriving ourselves of the rest we need. To break this vicious cycle, here is a safe, natural prescription to help you sleep:

L-tryptophan	1,000 mg

Take 500 mg six hours after getting up and another 500 mg one hour before bed.

Works best when taken on an empty stomach.

Sweet dreams!

Physiological Stress

As your body goes through physiological stress, your metabolism moves into high gear, drawing on vitamins and minerals to help keep your energy high, heal wounds, synthesize hormones, repair tissue damage, and aid your many types of cells to function properly. Consequently, your needs for micronutrients increase radically.

INJURY/SURGERY/SEVERE BURNS/INFECTION

Reduces stores and changes metabolism of several minerals and vitamins. Take these levels for two weeks before surgery, and a month after surgery, injuries, severe burns, or infection.

YOUR DAILY MICRONUTRIENT PRESCRIPTION

1. Beta-carotene   20,000 I.U.
2. Vitamin B complex* (with inositol)   1 tablet a day
3. Pantothenic acid   500 mg
4. Vitamin C   6 grams
5. Vitamin D   400 I.U.
6. Vitamin E   600 I.U.
7. Potassium   200 mg
8. Zinc   100 mg

*May contain niacin. If you have a liver problem, consult your doctor before taking niacin.

Environmental Stress

Nitrite Preservatives

In spite of the clear cancer-causing effects of nitrite preservatives, many people continue to eat processed meats—salami, pastrami, bologna, ham, and smoke-cured meats of all kinds. If you are one of those people, you may be absorbing a walloping dose of nitrites into your body, which can then be converted into highly carcinogenic substances. To offset this process, I recommend you take:

1. Beta-carotene   20,000 I.U.
2. Vitamin C   4 grams
3. Vitamin E   600 I.U.
4. Zinc   100 mg

The combination can help break down sodium nitrite and block the formation of the carcinogenic substances.

RADIATION (NATURAL OR FROM X RAYS) AND POLLUTANTS

If you are exposed—in your work or home life—to an excessive level of environmental pollutants, take the supplements listed under nitrites as well as:

1. Increase your food sources of Vitamin K: cauliflower, cabbage, leafy green vegetables, fruits, cereals, kelp, fish oils.
2. Calcium   1,200 mg
3. Magnesium   800 mg

CLIMATE—EXTREME HEAT OR COLD

1. Vitamin C   3 grams
   Reduces perspiration rate, improves skin blood circulation for more efficient control of body temperature.

Vegetarians

Your Macronutrient Reminder

If you're one of the millions who have removed meat from their diets, you have already taken a big step toward ensuring longer, healthier life. However, just as eating vegetarian removes some risks from your food, it can add others if you are not careful.

Protein is probably your largest concern—make sure that you get enough of it by carefully matching complementary proteins in your food.

If you are a strict vegan vegetarian—that is, you don't even eat dairy products—you are at risk for B_{12} deficiency, which can lead to serious anemia. Make sure to take a supplement of this crucial B vitamin to balance your diet.

Because fiber probably makes up an important part of your diet, you'll be glad to know that research has recently put to rest a concern about eating too much fiber. It had been believed that a high-fiber intake could retard absorption of certain minerals like iron, copper, and zinc. It now appears that after several weeks on a high-fiber diet, your body adapts and becomes more efficient about absorbing, and conserving, these minerals from your food. Unless you are in a particular risk group that needs an extra dose of these minerals, you probably don't need to be too concerned.

FOR STRICT LACTO-OVO VEGETARIANS, REMEMBER:

1. Vitamin B_{12} 100 mcg
   To prevent anemia.

Women

If you're female, all the special things about your reproductive system—menstruation, contraception, pregnancy, nursing, and menopause—mean special needs for particular vitamins and minerals. Every month you lose iron when you menstruate, making iron second only to calcium as the major mineral deficiency among women. Because of poor attention to micronutrient balance, one third of all young women have low iron stores, and as many as eight out of ten teenage girls are actually iron-deficient. Among other problems, women with very low iron are more vulnerable to the vaginal yeast infection known as Candida.

The same is true for calcium, which plays such an important role in keeping your bones solid and strong, and preventing the wasting disease of osteoporosis. The most recent findings reported by the

American Society for Clinical Nutrition point to a serious calcium problem: Fully one half of middle-aged women in this country absorb *less than one quarter* of the minimal RDA for this vital micronutrient. That means they are overdrawing their calcium accounts at an alarming rate. The answer is a complex of supplements, geared to rebalancing their bones' mineral accounts: calcium, phosphorous, and vitamin D.

Because one third of American women diet, you may want to take a look at the section for dieters as well. You may be getting too few calories to supply all the nourishment you need, especially during your childbearing years, and that calls for special nutritional support.

Women's special needs begin in your teen years.

YOUR PERSONAL MICRONUTRIENT PRESCRIPTION

FOR ADOLESCENT WOMEN

1. Beta-carotene	20,000 I.U.
2. Vitamin B$_6$	200 mg
3. Vitamin C	3 grams
4. Iron	20 mg
5. Zinc	100 mg

FOR NONPREGNANT, NONNURSING WOMEN—IF YOU ARE OVER 18

1. Folic acid	400 mcg
2. Calcium	1,000 mg
3. Iron	18 mg
4. Magnesium	750 mg

EXERCISE   If you have been inactive, and then you begin an exercise program, expect your iron reserves to drop. But after about six weeks, your body will adapt and the stores will return to normal.

PREMENSTRUAL SYNDROME

Just before your period, you may experience a specific set of symptoms that can only be blamed on the shifting levels of your hormones. These include anxiety, irritability, headaches, dizziness, sweet cravings, weakness, painful, tender breasts, depression, confusion, fatigue, and lethargy. B$_6$ has become a popular antidote, but megadoses—2,000 to 6,000 mg a day—have been linked to serious side effects, including sensations of burning, pain in your limbs, numb skin, clumsiness, and loss of balance. **If B₆ doesn't help you after a month, you should stop taking it.**

Instead, I prefer to treat each set of symptoms with a different vitamin-mineral supplement combination. For best results, take these combinations for the ten days before your period starts. If you have several of these symptoms, decide which is most severe, and take the supplements I recommend for that problem. Do not take supplements from more than one symptom category.

IF YOU SUFFER FROM . . .	TAKE THESE SUPPLEMENTS	
Anxiety, irritability	Vitamin E	600 I.U. a day
	Vitamin B_1	250 mg a day
	Vitamin B_6	400 mg a day
	Magnesium	500 mg three times a day
Headaches, dizziness, sweet cravings, weakness	Vitamin E	800 I.U. a day
	Vitamin B_1	250 mg a day
	Vitamin B_6	400 mg a day
	Vitamin C	2 grams three times a day
	L-glutamine	500 mg three times a day
	Tryptophan	200 mg before meals
Depression, confusion, fatigue, lethargy	Vitamin E	800 I.U. a day
	Vitamin B_1	250 mg a day
	Vitamin B_6	400 mg a day
	Zinc	100 mg a day
	*L-tryptophan	1,000 mg a day

* If you feel no response, or get headaches, switch to the same dose of another amino acid, L-phenylalanine.

MENSTRUATION

If you suffer from excessive menstrual flow and severe cramps, Vitamin K may help. I don't recommend supplements, but you can get your K from foods like leafy green vegetables, fruits, cauliflower, cabbage, kelp, dairy products, and fish oils.

ORAL-CONTRACEPTIVE USERS

The powerful hormones in these medications are associated with significant changes in several micronutrients. For example, low levels of B_6 in women on the Pill have been associated with mood changes and depression. I suggest the following combination to off-set the use of these drugs—especially if you have symptoms like headache, fatigue, or nausea.

1. Vitamin B complex   1 capsule daily
2. Vitamin C   1 gram
3. Vitamin E   600 I.U.
4. Folic acid   600 mcg
5. Zinc   100 mg

PREGNANCY

As the old saying goes, you're eating for two now. Your swelling tummy is the outward sign of the additional nutritional burden that pregnancy puts on your body. At this time, your regular diet can't easily give you enough extra nutrients to adequately meet the demand, so you need extra supplements above and beyond the levels I've already given for women.

YOUR PERSONAL MICRONUTRIENT PRESCRIPTION

1. Beta-carotene   20,000 I.U.
2. Vitamin B complex*   1 capsule
3. Folic acid   600 mcg
4. Vitamin C   3 grams
5. Vitamin D   1,000 I.U.
6. Vitamin E   600 I.U.
7. Iron   30 mg
8. Calcium   2,000 mg
9. Magnesium   1,000 mg

*Contains niacin. If you have a liver problem, consult your doctor before taking niacin.

In addition, vitamin K can be helpful both before and after child-birth to prevent excess blood loss. (See "Menstruation" for the best food sources of this important vitamin.)

CAUTION FOR PREGNANT WOMEN

If you're pregnant—whatever your age—don't take more than 50 mg of vitamin B_6 each day. Also avoid overly high doses of vitamin C because, ironically, it may create an abnormally large need for C in your infant.

ALWAYS CONSULT YOUR OWN DOCTOR BEFORE TAKING ANY PREGNANCY VITAMIN OR MINERAL SUPPLEMENTS. YOUR OWN DOCTOR MAY HAVE A DIFFERENT SUPPLEMENT THAT (S)HE PREFERS.

NURSING MOTHERS

1. Vitamin B complex* (with inositol)	1 tablet a day
2. Folic acid	500 mcg
3. Vitamin C	2 grams
4. Vitamin D	1,000 I.U.
5. Iron	20 mg
6. Calcium	2,000 mg
7. Magnesium	1,000 mg

* Contains niacin. If you have a liver problem, consult your doctor before taking niacin.

CAUTION

Don't use vitamin E oil on your nipples to prevent soreness or cracks. Not only is there no evidence that it works, but it may harm your baby, leading to blood disorders.

MENOPAUSE

If you haven't started boosting your calcium before, you certainly should as you approach menopause. Eight times as many women as men get osteoporosis, mainly because of the winding down of their ovaries' production of estrogens at menopause. Those women at greatest risk are postmenopausal and those who have had their ovaries surgically removed.

YOUR PERSONAL MICRONUTRIENT PRESCRIPTION

1. Vitamin B complex*   1 tablet a day
2. Vitamin D   400 I.U.
3. Vitamin E   600 I.U.
4. Selenium   150 mcg
5. Calcium   1,500 mg
6. Magnesium   1,000 mg

*Contains niacin. If you have a liver problem, consult your doctor before taking niacin.

PERSONAL PRESCRIPTIONS WORKSHEET

MICRONUTRIENT	BASIC COMPOSITE DOSE	PERSONAL PRESCRIPTION	MINIMUM TOXIC DOSE
Beta-carotene	17,500 I.U.	_____ I.U.	25,000 I.U.
B$_1$ (thiamine)	100 mg	_____ mg	500 mg
B$_2$ (riboflavin)	50 mg	_____ mg	300 mg
B$_{3A}$ (niacinamide)	50 mg	_____ mg	800 mg
B$_5$ (pantothenic acid)	200 mg	_____ mg	1,000 mg
B$_6$ (pyridoxine)	150 mg	_____ mg	500 mg
B$_{12}$ (cobalamine)	100 mcg	_____ mcg	500 mcg
Folic acid	400 mcg	_____ mcg	800 mcg
Biotin	50 mcg	_____ mcg	500 mcg
Inositol	200 mg	_____ mg	500 mg
Vitamin C	2,000 mg	_____ mg	6,000 mg
Vitamin D	200 I.U.	_____ I.U.	1,000 I.U.
Vitamin E	400 I.U.	_____ I.U.	1,000 I.U.
Calcium	1,000 mg	_____ mg	2,000 mg
Magnesium	750 mg	_____ mg	1,000 mg
Zinc	75 mg	_____ mg	150 mg
Potassium	100 mg	_____ mg	600 mg
Selenium	150 mcg	_____ mcg	300 mcg
Iron	15 mg	_____ mg	25 mg

8.

Meet the Micronutrient Miracle Workers

"The physician heals,
Nature makes well."

—Aristotle

In the last section, you met the macronutrients—the bedrock elements that make up the foundation of the fight for wellness and vitality. Then, you tailored your macronutrients along with selected micronutrients for your own Personal Prescription.

Now, in these next three chapters, you are going to have the chance to really get to know the micronutrients: vitamins, minerals, and amino acids. If you are interested in what these can do to improve your health, what parts of the body they work in, and the latest findings on the preventive-nutrition benefits of these nutrients, these chapters have it all. If, on the other hand, you are impatient to finish tailoring your own nutritional plan, you can skip ahead to Chapter Eleven, where you learn about the final phase of tailoring your diet for your needs.

I do hope you will read these chapters, though. After all, being your own nutritionist means truly knowing the whole range of effects of a given element—not just how it affects you. To get the most out of this book, you'll want to know the details, and the late-breaking research bulletins, in these three chapters.

Vitamins, minerals, and amino acids are termed *micro*nutrients, but don't be fooled by the word *micro*. It doesn't mean either minis-cule or negligible. *Micro* means only that your body needs these substances in much smaller amounts than it needs carbohydrates, fiber, fat, protein, and natural sugars. But when it comes to powerful, individualized nutrition, these elements are no poor second cousins.

They are key players in your well-being. Each vitamin, mineral, and amino acid performs a specific function to keep you healthy and fight off disease, to keep you alive with energy and emotionally balanced.

There are certain basic amounts of micronutrients that everyone needs, a baseline that I call the Micronutrient Composite. These levels are based on the premise that you are an adult and you are in ordinary good health. The first thing you may notice is that the amounts I recommend in the Micronutrient Composite far exceed the government's RDA.

As we saw in Chapter Two, the Recommended Dietary Allow-ance (RDA) levels are defensive illness-avoiding prescriptions, rather than formulas to assure positive, forward-looking well-being. But you want to have optimum health, not just to be guarded against borderline malnutrition. So the level of each vitamin and mineral I've specified in the Micronutrient Composite is called "Optimal." They are the levels that will help guarantee you a long, illness-free life, full of vitality and energy—the Optimal state of health. Taken together, they create the Micronutrient Composite, which is the baseline levels.

Beyond this composite, you may need to boost your intake of one or another of the micronutrients, or several, to meet the needs of your individual life-style. That is what you have already done in the Personal Prescription section. This section now fills in the gaps, with state-of-the-art information about all the rest of the basic micronu-trients you need.

The Myth of the Well-Balanced Diet

I have had several patients ask me why I prescribe extra micronutrient supplements for them. After all, they protest, they eat a balanced diet, so don't they get enough of the crucial nutrients they need? It's a hard question to answer simply, because the honest answer is: Yes, No, and Maybe.

"Yes," to some extent, they are right. If you eat the proper proportions of the Nutritional Pyramid, you will automatically get a good baseline supply of vitamins, minerals, and amino acids. But that is not enough. The well-balanced diet approach to micronutrients is actually a throwback to the nutritional Dark Ages—the RDA, Illness-Avoiders school.

The "No" part comes in because very few people do eat a truly well-balanced diet. Thanks to the wonders of food processing, with its added fats and sugars and chemicals, and its depleted minerals and vitamins, unless you make a consistent and dedicated effort to eat fresh foods, the chances are you don't get as much of certain vital elements as you might think. Beyond that, the standards used to define "well-balanced" are the impoverished RDAs—not the more comprehensive levels of preventive nutrition.

Even with these problems, such a balanced-diet approach could still work—if we were all alike. But we're not. There would have to be as many different balanced diets as there are different categories of people who need special help: a substantially different diet for women and men, children and grandparents, runners and accountants, and so on down the line. It just doesn't make sense.

Let me give you just two examples. It is quite clear that smokers need higher levels of certain vitamins—including the antioxidants A, C, and E—to restore levels of vitamins lost by smoking, and to help decrease their risk of cancer. Yet vitamin A can be toxic if too much of it builds up in the body. Clearly, this smoker would be advised to eat differently from her health-food-addict boyfriend, who already gets a whopping amount of vitamin A in his fresh vegetables.

It is the same story for minerals. Report after report has documented the fact that women—beginning as early as their teen years —need at least 1,000 milligrams of calcium a day to prevent the fractures of the hip and back and the "dowager's hump" that often occur after menopause as a direct result of low calcium. The best dietary source of calcium is milk, which supplies 300 milligrams per cup. Yet how many adults do you know who drink milk? Moreover, a single cup of whole milk contains 8 grams of fat—a big chunk of your daily 20 percent maximum. Clearly, it makes no sense that the same balanced diet would work for a calcium-deficient woman and her overweight husband who needs to restrict his fats. The answer is calcium supplements to round out her diet and give her an adequate, *preventive* supply of this micronutrient.

The Micronutrient Debate

If you want to take full advantage of the newest research showing how we can use nutrition to prevent cancer, heart disease, and many other chronic illnesses, you need to take your micronutrients into account. But that is more easily said than accomplished. There is no other area of nutrition research that arouses such discord, conflict, and confusion as vitamins and minerals.

As you saw, there is clear consensus in the medical community about the low-fat, high-carbohydrate, high-fiber diet. But micronutrients are still the nutritional Wild West. The field is fraught with conflicting opinions: Some experts call for megadoses of every vitamin and mineral. Their promises are seductive, but they may not be sound. Others say we should do nothing, keep our vitamin bottles locked up, follow habit and tradition, until every last scrap of data is in. Still others, myself included, are greatly excited by the potential of certain micronutrients to prevent cancer and many chronic, debilitating diseases, and are ready to apply some of those promising findings now. For the hapless person who is concerned about maximizing health and minimizing disease, the result can be a real nutritional gridlock, where you feel frozen in place, not sure of which way to go.

Now is the time to break through that gridlock. Every week in my professional life, I sort through the piles of medical journals and newsletters that come across my desk. I confer with researchers and medical specialists. I've carefully evaluated which researchers I believe are on the track of a genuine breakthrough and doing a responsible job of testing their hypotheses. I've discarded those studies that lead people astray with false starts, faulty conclusions, and specious methodology or logic. In researching this book, I have culled the latest, most reliable information on vitamins and minerals. Let's look at it together, beginning with the vitamins.

The Most Abused Drug

You may not think you know any serious drug abusers. I'll bet you do, because if you know people taking vitamins and minerals, chances are they are not doing it right—and that's abuse! When people talk about the drug problem, they usually don't have vitamins in mind. But the fact is that these substances are far more abused than heroin or cocaine. Sounds impossible, doesn't it? Yet one half of all Americans are "hooked" on these legal drugs, taking them either regularly or occasionally. Vitamins alone account for an astounding $3 billion in sales every year—all in the name of health!

Yet few of those people understand that micronutrients like vitamins and minerals, are, indeed, drugs of a sort. They tend to think of them as innocuous. But each vitamin tablet or capsule contains a potent bioactive substance, capable of altering your body and perhaps your mind as well. Vitamins have the potential to do you considerable harm. So, too, can the wild enthusiasms and outrageous claims surrounding them. Vitamin abuse is insidious because the dealers operate within the bounds of legal sanction. They are subject to no repercussions, no midnight raids, no fines or imprisonment. And, believe me, they have no scruples. You've heard how hard drug pushers will often substitute a fake for the real thing. The same is true of vitamin dealers. They even promote nonvitamins, labeling them as newly discovered vitamins.

For example, the mythical vitamin B_{17}, laetrile, contains 6 percent cyanide and, not surprisingly, has caused fatal poisonings. There is simply no proof it is useful as a cancer cure. Likewise, some brands of so-called vitamin B_{15} (pangamic acid) actually contain

cancer-causing ingredients. Or perhaps you have seen advertise-
ments for "vitamin P." In truth, there is no such thing. But the
pushers would have you believe it exists. The so-called vitamin P
(bioflavonoids, including rutin and herperidine) is technically not a
vitamin at all. It is a growth factor required by certain organisms—
but not, as far as we know, by human beings. Some people have even
classified PABA as a vitamin. This substance—the scientific term is
para-amino-benzoic acid—is best known for being an effective sun
block for your skin, but if you take it in any significant amount
internally, it reduces the number of your essential immune-system
white blood cells and creates fatty changes in your heart, liver, and
kidney. Believe me, that's not the action of a health-promoting
vitamin!

The Supplement Pushers have gotten a free ride on the health-
food movement. Under the guise of such seductive labels as "natural," "pure," and "organic," they get away with all sorts of nonsense.
The truth is that "natural" vitamin and mineral supplements are
chemically exactly the same as synthetic ones. There is one crucial
difference: "Natural" vitamins cost more. In the case of certain
minerals, naturally derived substances can even be worse for you.
Natural calcium supplements from bone meal, dolomite, or oyster
shell could contain contaminating impurities, toxic heavy metals
like lead and aluminum.

Another common misconception involves the multivitamins,
hawked by the big-name pharmaceutical companies. The sales pitch
is attractive: "Get your complete daily fix by popping only one of our
super-formula pills." That magic bullet is supposed to meet all of
your requirements without the fuss and bother of taking one of the
white pills, four of the green ones, and two of the orange each day.
There's only one problem. The magic-bullet theory is as unfounded
as the myth of the well-balanced diet. There's no way any prepackaged formula can really meet your individual needs. Yes, they can be
a good starting point to build on—that's the idea behind the Micronutrient Composite we build in these next two chapters. But beyond
that, you have to tailor them to your own specific needs.

Another reason I counsel patients not to rely on multivitamins is
the increasing evidence that some of these combinations aren't even
well balanced. You would think that if somebody is selling a one-

stop supplement tablet, they would have carefully formulated it so that it was adequate, right? Guess again. A researcher at Yale analyzed 257 popular multivitamin/mineral supplements and found many contained levels more than 200 percent over the Recommended Dietary Allowance for ten major vitamins and selected minerals. Only one in six formulas, said the study, had even appropriate levels of vitamins. When it came to minerals, only eight of the combination pills contained enough iron to meet the rock-bottom RDA. It isn't just the contents of these pills that creates problems: Very few of these brands have expiration dates or are certified for potency. The result is that many such formulations are of dubious value if you rely on them for a one-stop nutritional boost.

I have seen these factors at work more times than I care to recall. Recently, a patient of mine, Edward, showed me the multivitamin he was taking. The label revealed that they contained, indeed, an adequate level of most necessary nutrients. But buried among the other elements, my eye caught one figure that was astronomically out of proportion: the B_6 level was 3,750 percent *over* the RDA! Recent research has shown that of all the B vitamins, B_6 is the one with the most acute, and frequent, reported toxicity. So, while Edward had been doing himself a "favor" by taking these vitamins in most ways, he was also giving himself a potentially dangerous overdose of a vitamin with proven toxic effects—thanks to the sloppiness of the multivitamin manufacturers!

The truth is that often multivitamins are compounded with an eye less on the health of the consumers than on the producers' wallet. They know that megadosing means megabucks, and unfortunately, they have won many converts. Though the absolute numbers are still small, more and more people are taking vitamins and minerals many times over safe limits. No wonder we are seeing increasing reports of toxicity. Vitamin B_3 (niacin) produces tingling or flushing after large doses of 75 milligrams. Much higher doses cause not only flushing but itching, skin rash, heartburn, and nausea. As for vitamin A, 25,000 I.U.s, a dosage often recommended by health-food enthusiasts, can produce liver damage. There have even been several deaths reported from people taking excessive doses of vitamins A and D!

Vitamin abuse has reached such serious proportions that the FDA has issued overdose warnings. The agency has called on the nation's doctors to record their patients' vitamin use in medical records and to report side effects. It is an ironic turn of things, indeed, that vitamins, which exist to improve our health and well-being, have actually become a source of illness and overdose.

Overdosing is bad enough, but it is only half the story of vitamin misuse. The other problem is the exact opposite. For believe it or not, today, in 1987, there are people in our country who do not get enough vitamins. A lot of them.

Deficiency states of vitamins are alive and well in the United States—not only in Third World countries. You probably believe— so do many "experts"—that scurvy—caused by a gross lack of vitamin C—is a disease that has long since gone the way of smallpox. But as recently as 1985, the *Journal of the American Medical Association* reported three cases, found at just one hospital in Portland, Oregon. That number suggests there may be hundreds of other hidden cases across the country. Recently a nutritional abstract stated that *fully one half of elderly people in institutions* may have classic scurvy—in 1986! Another study, completed last year, showed that three quarters of the people it examined had levels well below even the insufficient RDA for this most common of vitamins, and so are vulnerable to this "old-fashioned" (and absolutely unnecessary!) disease.

This story has a tragic corollary. Because doctors aren't used to seeing scurvy symptoms, they may often diagnose them as other ailments. In happens that scurvy can mimic many serious disorders like blood clots deep in the veins and systemic bleeding disorders. How would you like to be given the drastic treatments necessary for such a harrowing diagnosis when your real problem could be cured by eating two oranges each day?

In another classic study, reported in the *American Journal of Clinical Nutrition*, researchers selected 120 patients admitted to U.S. hospitals and tested their vitamin levels. In our most affluent culture, *only 12 percent had proper levels of all vitamins*. Eighty-eight percent lacked at least one essential vitamin, and 67 percent came up short in two essential vitamins. Yet most of these people were consuming what appeared to be a normal U.S. diet. Even more disturbing was the fact that two thirds of them showed no overt signs of vitamin deficiencies, suggesting that *people who appear healthy can actually have subclinical deficiencies.* When you consider that the researchers used the minimal RDA standards, rather than the more stringent standards we now have adopted for preventive nutrition, the findings are even more alarming.

I treat dozens of such patients every week—people who aren't sick, but aren't well, either. People who know they could feel better, look better, have more energy, more stable moods and emotions.

ON A DIET?

If you are on a weight-loss diet, take special note. You may never have stopped to think about it, but the very same diet that restricts your intake in the form of calories—fats, protein, or carbohydrates —also greatly restricts your intake of vital micronutrients. Because you are subjecting your body to a sort of voluntary malnutrition, your diet almost certainly is not giving you even the scanty RDA levels for essential micronutrients. And I guarantee *absolutely* that it won't give you the vitamins and minerals you need for the glowing health of preventive nutrition. If this describes you, then being your own nutritionist means taking extra care to get an adequate micronutrient dose!

Now you see why I am so concerned about Vitamin Confusion. Whether the problem is too much or too little, it is clear that people are not getting the most from their micronutrients. Happily, there is a way you can outwit the dealers and the pushers and come out on the side of vitamin virtue. Here's how.

The Simple Truth About Vitamins

First and foremost, remember that vitamins are potent bioactive substances. Think of them like drugs. But unlike the illegal kind, they are absolutely essential to life. Among their many tasks, they ensure proper functioning of your nervous system and heart, promote good vision, create strong bones and teeth, and form normal blood cells. While they do not directly supply energy, without them your body could not convert the food we eat into energy. Since your body cannot manufacture its own vitamins, you must get them either from your food and/or from supplements, depending on your individual needs.

In spite of what the newest fad diets may tell you, there are really only fourteen vitamins: A, C, D, E, K, and the nine B vitamins. (I call them the B Team because they work together in your body. You may know them as B complex.) They include thiamine, riboflavin, niacin, B_6, pantothenic acid, biotin, folacin, and B_{12}.

You probably know by now that there are principally two kinds of vitamins. The fat-soluble vitamins, A, D, E, and K, are stored in your body fat and liver, so you do not need to consume them every day in order to maintain adequate levels. The water-soluble vitamins, on the other hand—the nine B-complex vitamins and C—dissolve in the water of your body, and your body generally stores them less well. In some cases, it can't store them at all, so you should consume them every day. (Vitamin B_{12} is the one exception. Your liver stores enough B_{12} to meet your body's needs for three to five years!)

But "every day" doesn't mean huge doses. For both kinds of vitamins, your body's cells require relatively tiny amounts to function well—tiny, that is, compared to the requirements for the macronutrients of the Nutritional Pyramid. Think of micros as measured in teaspoons and macros as measured in dump-truck loads and you'll get an idea of the relative proportions!

With most vitamins, your body can absorb only a finite amount. This is because vitamins, in order to do your body any good, must work hand in hand with certain proteins, called apoenzymes. Since your body produces only limited amounts of these proteins, the excess vitamins can't find protein partners, so they get stored (in the case of fat-soluble vitamins) or flushed out in your urine (in the case of water-soluble vitamins).

Deficiency states occur when a particular vitamin is either grossly lacking or is improperly absorbed by your body. As we age, all of our physiological systems change, and our vitamin needs are partly tied to the aging changes in our bodies. This has an impact on how well our body uses vitamins and therefore on how much we require to stay in good health. In older age, our risk of vitamin deficiency for one or more vitamins increases.

Armed with this knowledge, it's time for you to push aside the pill pushers. Let's look now at each vitamin, one by one. We'll start with the micronutrient I call the King.

Vitamin C:
The King of Vitamins

No other vitamin does as much for as many systems in your body as vitamin C, also known as ascorbic acid. Without this micronutrient, our bodies would (quite literally) fall apart. C helps produce collagen, the intercellular "cement" that gives structure to your muscles and the tissues of your blood-vessel system, as well as your cartilage and bones. Vitamin C also contributes to the health of your teeth and gums, and aids in the absorption of the essential mineral, iron. Deprived of this substance, imagine what would happen! We would probably disintegrate segment by segment. Whew—it's enough to make you want to go eat an orange, isn't it?

That's only the beginning of King C's claim to the crown. Of all the vitamins, ascorbic acid has the strongest positive effects on your immune system. The more C in your diet, the greater the weight of your vital immune-system tissues such as your thymus and lymph nodes, and the more efficiently your thymus works preparing your blood cells to fight bacteria and viruses. C also helps your body produce antibodies, the fighter proteins that patrol your system looking for foreign infectious invaders and doing battle with them.

Because of its immune-boosting action, vitamin C has long enjoyed the reputation of "preventing" the common cold. Actually, that is not quite accurate. Researchers have only been able to document that C lessens cold symptoms. As early as 1979, it was shown that C supplements can reduce cold symptoms by 14 to 21 percent. That relief is directly due to the immune-enhancing power of the King of Vitamins. C also plays a crucial role in healing by helping the body rebuild the skin and tissues that are damaged in a wound, in the process sealing out infectious germs.

VITAMIN C AND CANCER

This most regal of vitamins also appears to ward off a variety of cancers. Recent studies in several countries confirm a clear and provocative pattern: In areas where people get little vitamin C, the overall cancer rate is high. In this country, researchers have shown that men with the lowest intake of vitamin C have twice the risk of certain cancers as men with a much higher intake of the vitamin. And new findings show that women who have cervical dysplasia—a condition we believe is a precursor to cancer of the cervix—have markedly low levels of C. The evidence is overwhelming that C can reduce several kinds of cancers, including cancers of the stomach, esophagus, and cervix.

THE KING VERSUS THE RADICALS

King C seems to prevent cancer in several ways. First, it disables the biological renegades known as free radicals—highly unstable chemicals that attack, infiltrate, and injure vital cell structures. Most stable chemical compounds in the body possess a pair of electrons. But sometimes one member of the electron pair gets stripped away and a free radical—or oxidation product—is born. Then the remaining electron goes on the prowl, careening around your body's cells to find a mate. Sometimes, in desperation, it will steal an electron mate from another stable compound, breaking up that contented couple and creating another unstable radical. It is, as one of my younger patients ruefully observed, not unlike what happens at the singles bars she visits every Friday night.

Unfortunately, while they are on the prowl, these oxidation radicals can do tremendous damage to the delicate machinery of your cells, altering their DNA coding. The result can be a first push on the road to potentially lethal cancer.

Your body forms these radicals constantly, as a natural byproduct of body chemistry. But they also come from a number of very unnatural substances: Environmental pollutants, radiation, cigarette smoke, chemicals, and herbicides can all work within your body to unleash free radicals.

The good news is that Nature has thoughtfully provided a powerful antidote to the oxidation radicals in the form of the antioxidants. Like a persuasive bouncer, the antioxidants deactivate potentially dangerous free radicals before they can damage a cell's machinery. Among the most effective and dedicated antioxidants are the vitamins A, C, and E—the ACE Trio against cancer. Of the trio members, none is more powerful than the most versatile vitamin, King C.

In addition to its potent antioxidant powers, vitamin C can work against cancer in another way. It appears to block the formation of nitrosamines, highly carcinogenic substances that can be formed from nitrites in our diet. One common source of nitrites is sodium nitrite, used as a food preservative and in cured and prepared meats. Of course, I tell my patients to avoid such foods, but if they do eat them, it is vital that they increase their levels of the antioxidant vitamins like C.

VITAMIN C AND STRESS

A peaceful kingdom, as any good monarch knows, must be free of turmoil and stress. Again, that is a key element in the reign of the King of Vitamins. Your body has two powerful systems that help it cope with physiological and psychological stress: the nervous system and the endocrine system. In simplest terms, your nervous system controls rapid body changes in response to the environment, while the endocrine system regulates longer-term patterns of response through the release of hormones into your bloodstream. In fact, they work together in close teamwork. These two systems meet in the hypothalamus, the area of your brain that coordinates with the master endocrine gland, the pituitary. We now have good evidence to suggest that most stress-related diseases occur when the hypothalamus orders up an improper balance of stress hormones. These hormones are helpful when we need to react quickly to a stressful event, but they can create real problems when we have a chronic oversupply revving our body's stress-reaction systems into perpetual—and deadly—high gear. C seems to play a direct role in the stress response. Your body's highest concentration of this vitamin is found in the adrenal cortex, smack in the middle of the endocrine system. Your body uses this vitamin C to chemically regulate the levels of your stress hormones. Not surprisingly, you need more C when you are under stress, and the more severe the stress, the greater the drain of vitamin C. In studies of burn patients, of people recovering from surgery, injury, illness, or infection, we know that the body's need for vitamin C increases.

C also seems to help your body adapt to the stress of extreme temperatures, both heat and cold. Researchers studying mine workers found that although miners got adequate amounts of vitamin C in their diets, they had very low levels in their blood. When scientists supplemented the workers' diets, they found that the workers were better able to withstand the heat. C appeared actually to reduce the perspiration rate and improve blood circulation close to the skin, which resulted in more efficient control of body temperature. While most of us don't work in a mine, we can still use this benefit to our advantage. If you live in a part of the country where there are tremendous temperature extremes—in Minnesota's winters, say, or Florida's summers—this benefit may be important to you. As for myself, in the sweltering New York summers, I make sure to keep a good supply of vitamin C to alleviate the discomfort.

Vitamin C helps not just with physiological stress but with emotional stress as well. There is a dramatic study demonstrating this link. A researcher had been studying vitamin C in prison volunteers. During the study, two prisoners managed to escape and another, still in custody, turned informer. Then he realized with sudden clarity that, as an informer, he might very well be killed by some of the other convicts. Talk about stress! Suddenly, the researcher noted he was burning two or three times as much C as normal. As soon as he was assured safe conduct into civilian life, however, his rate returned to average.

Stress, anxiety, and excitement all accelerate the depletion of vitamin C. Vitamin C status has also been found to be poorer in psychiatric patients who have high levels of anxiety. Low C levels are related to a number of psychological symptoms—including fatigue, lassitude, depression, and in some cases, paranoia. The high concentration of C in your brain suggests a possible crucial role for the vitamin in mental function and behavior. In short, if you are under psychological stress, C may stand for: cool, calm, and collected.

KIND HEARTS AND CORONARIES

The King of Vitamins is also the king of hearts, according to two intriguing new studies. The first, from the Human Nutritional Research Center on Aging at Tufts University, shows the vitamin lowers our risk of coronary heart disease by increasing our levels of "good" cholesterol, HDL. Doctors studied five hundred elderly, healthy volunteers and found a strong positive link between C levels in blood plasma and higher HDL. This is a side of this versatile vitamin that we have never known about before, and it may open terrifically exciting prevention possibilities. Another study suggests that proper amounts of C could actually help reduce elevated cholesterol.

PROCLAMATIONS FROM THE KING

If this were all, vitamin C would have earned its title as the King of Vitamins. But in addition, King C has declared war on a host of other diseases:

- C supplements have restored fertility in some males with low levels of the vitamin who suffer from a condition called sperm agglutination—excessive amounts of sperm cells clumping helplessly together rather than rushing to unite with an egg.
- The vitamin has been shown to alleviate iron deficiency anemia in children.
- C also prevents the buildup of heavy metals in the body. These toxic substances—such as lead, mercury, and aluminum—can lead to a variety of serious problems, including Alzheimer's disease, mental retardation, hemorrhage, anemia, and a variety of blood diseases.

But although King C is a benevolent monarch, he can also mete out punishment if he is crossed—that is, if you don't respect his limits. So in the interests of a peaceful, healthful reign, keep these points in mind:

- Vitamin C causes your body to process aspirin more slowly. As a result, it can cause a toxic buildup of this drug after several doses.
- Many people feel that it won't hurt if they take too much C— after all, their body will just flush out the excess it doesn't need. Unfortunately, though, if you are a person with existing or hidden kidney problems, massive doses of the vitamin—10 grams a day —are likely to block up your kidneys, causing agonizing kidney stones. Massive megadoses of C—say, 10 grams or more a day— can trigger anemia by lowering the levels of the mineral copper in your blood.
- *During pregnancy*, high doses of C could cause symptoms of scurvy and an abnormally large need for the vitamin in infants.

If too much C creates dangerous side effects, too little is an equal problem. As we saw earlier, contrary to popular opinion, scurvy was not left behind in the eighteenth century. It can occur when your body's normal reserves of vitamin C—about 1,500 milligrams— drop below 350 milligrams. Then you may develop the telltale symptoms—swelling, pain, and discoloration of your legs. If you were to eat no vitamin C at all, these signs would show up in two to three months.

Scurvy, of course, occurs when your C reserves are very seriously depleted. But low C affects many other body systems long before these telltale signs appear, compromising your immune system, weakening your blood, nerves, skin, digestion, hormones, and even your mental capacity.

Happily, there is no reason why you should ever suffer from vitamin-C deficiency. Simply by including fresh fruits and vegetables, such as broccoli, Brussels sprouts, cabbage, cauliflower, lemons, oranges, and potatoes, you don't have to worry.

One other thing about C: Though powerful, it is also fragile, and easily diminished by the heat of the cooking process. That means you should steam—never boil—C-containing vegetables, and do so briefly. New research from the American Dietetic Association shows that one way to help fresh foods retain their full quota of heat-sensitive vitamin C is to cook them in a microwave. This space-age cooking technology—which you may have in your kitchen—cooks from the inside out, so fast that many more nutrients are kept intact.

Because of the tremendous potential of this powerhouse of vitamins, you should not rely on your diet alone to top off your stores of this vital vitamin. I recommend your Optimal Daily Dose should be a strong 2 grams.

Vitamin A: The Antiaging and Anticancer Vitamin

If C is the King of Vitamins, A is certainly the Prince. As members of the ACE Trio, they are an unbeatable combination. Recent discoveries about a precursor form of A—known as beta-carotene—are already revolutionizing our ideas about preventive nutrition for cancer and aging. But before I tell you about this promising research, let's talk about your body's basic needs for this vitamin, and where it is found. Vitamin A occurs in nature in two forms. Ready-made vitamin A, called retinol, is found only in foods of animal origin. The other form, the carotenoids, come from both animal and plant food sources, and they are converted into vitamin A by the body. By far the most well known, and the most potent, of these is beta-carotene.

From whatever source, vitamin A is crucial to form the compound *rhodopsin*—also known as visual purple—necessary for strong eyesight, particularly at night. If you have trouble seeing road signs, traffic lights, or crosswalks after dusk, it may be a sign that you need more of this vitamin. In fact, deficiencies of this micronutrient have been linked to blindness.

Vitamin A is also important for keeping your skin, eyes, and the inner linings of your body healthy. Your bones, nails, glands, hair, and teeth need A for their optimum upkeep and growth.

Moreover, A also plays a key role in keeping you free of infection. Not only does it energize many of your immune cells, it actually works with your immune system to inhibit cells transformed by viruses. Not surprisingly, scientists have linked low levels of vitamin A with increased susceptibility to measles, diarrhea, and diseases of the respiratory tract, particularly in children. We are even now zeroing in on the effects of low vitamin A on cancer.

This vitamin is fat-soluble, meaning that it is stored away in your body fat and liver so you don't need to get it every day. That is lucky, because studies show that approximately half of American women —and an almost equal proportion of men—get less than the RDA for this vitamin. If you are either black or Hispanic, you should pay particular attention, because these are the most commonly affected groups.

Your body's storage of this vitamin may turn out to be a mixed blessing, however: Because you stockpile vitamin A, you need to watch your intake so it doesn't build up to dangerous levels. Overdosing on vitamin A is serious business, because this vitamin can have profound toxicity. Although some fad programs recommend levels up to 25,000 I.U.s daily, such a heavy dose can lead to severe complications, including anemia and agonizing gout—a form of arthritis.

As another strong member of the ACE Trio, A has been shown to help prevent several kinds of cancer, including tumors of the bladder, throat, and even the lung. Studies from Minnesota and Norway show that people who get colon cancer consume far less of the vitamin than similar people who don't have cancer.

Vitamin A and many of the retinoids—found in liver, milk, butter, and eggs—have been shown to be effective at suppressing tumors in laboratory animals. But many of these sources are also high in fats—which actually help promote cancer. Because of that, it is crucial that you get a balance of this important vitamin in supplement form. But I don't recommend you take it. Why? Read on!

THE BOUNTY OF BETA-CAROTENE

Beta-carotene, the substance that gives carrots and other orange or yellow vegetables their distinctive color, is a first-stage form of vitamin A. In biochemistry, it is known as a "precursor," a primary chemical that your body converts into usable vitamin A once it gets inside your tissues. That means you can take it *instead* of vitamin A —getting all the benefits without risking the toxicity that can be associated with taking the vitamin itself.

I don't want to suggest that beta-carotene is a mere assistant to the ACE Trio. Only recently, in fact, has the medical establishment truly awakened to the tremendous potential of beta-carotene. To prove this, guess what the National Cancer Institute, Harvard Medical School, and 20,000 doctors know that you don't? They know—or they suspect—that beta-carotene may have a very powerful anti-cancer effect—more powerful, perhaps, than even vitamin A itself. So the NCI has begun a monumental study involving highly unusual subjects—22,000 physicians. In this specialized "physician, heal thyself" research study, conducted by Harvard Medical School, 11,000 of the doctors receive daily doses of 50 milligrams of beta-carotene, while the other half of the doctors get placebo. The project will follow the physicians for twenty years, to determine which group gets the most cancers. At the end, they will have a long-term answer to one of the hottest questions in all of preventive nutrition: how we can use the powers of beta-carotene to fight cancer.

The doctors are taking what—on the face of it—looks like a hefty dose. But I think you can pretty much trust that—in this case at least—22,000 doctors can't be wrong. Not, at least, when they are the ones swallowing the pills!

Even if you took massive amounts of beta-carotene—enough to turn your skin orange—you probably wouldn't suffer side effects. That is one of the terrific "features" about this versatile substance: Your body converts only the amount it needs to make usable vitamin A, so you are naturally protected against a toxic vitamin-A overdose by taking beta-carotene.

Of course, I don't recommend such massive doses—you'd have a hard time explaining your new pumpkin color to your friends, at the very least. But it is a hopeful sign that such a promising health agent seems to have such benign side effects.

One of the most exciting research topics in preventive nutrition today is this agent's proven ability to protect us against deadly lung cancer. Studies by researchers in Norway found that cigarette smokers who eat lots of yellow and green vegetables—prime sources of beta-carotene—are three times less likely to develop lung cancer than those who don't eat these vegetables. A study in Chicago found men who consumed significant amounts of beta-carotene foods were seven times less likely to get lung cancer. Results have been so promising that a study is now going on among 30,000 smokers to compare the relative benefits of beta-carotene and preformed vitamin A against lung cancer.

Just as it's good for your lungs, it also appears to have strong benefits for other systems of the body:

- At Harvard, researchers studied over 1,200 elderly men and women, finding that those who eat a lot of beta-carotene-containing vegetables are far less likely to get cancer than those who don't.
- Also at Harvard, researchers have done work showing that beta-carotene may prevent or slow the development of skin cancer.
- From Japan, a study of 250,000 people shows beta-carotene clearly helps prevent cancer of the stomach, colon, prostate, and cervix.

Beta-carotene and vitamin A are such good cancer fighters because they are powerful antioxidants—like all the members of the ACE Trio. Like vitamin C, they fight free radicals. Beta-carotene is particularly effective at trapping free radicals in your cell membranes.

But it brings an additional weapon to the cancer fight. Beta-carotene also disables another kind of chemical saboteur—called singlet oxygen. Like the free radicals, this kind of oxygen is highly volatile, and can unleash even more free radicals into your cells. Although not technically a member of the free-radical gang, it is every big as dangerous for your cells. We now think cancer promoters work through these oxygen radicals. We also know they can produce eye damage.

The offspring of these two electrons are even more dastardly. Specifically, singlet oxygen can spawn the superoxide radical. This is one of the worst offenders, responsible for lung damage and many other severe breakdowns of your body systems.

If you are beginning to wonder how our poor cells survive at all, don't: because beta-carotene is galloping to the rescue. It can prevent renegade superoxides and singlet oxygen from ever seeing the light of day. In fact, this orange substance is quite simply the most effective, naturally occurring singlet-oxygen quencher around. As a partner in the ACE Trio, beta-carotene also helps fight the biological damage to our cells as we age. It not only decreases the rate of age-linked illnesses, but can even extend life expectancy in animals. While vitamin A itself is completely unrelated to long life, beta-carotene has been found to have a one-to-one relationship, lengthening healthy life all the way up the evolutionary ladder from mice to men.

The research news about beta-carotene is breaking as this book goes to press, and the year ahead will clearly bring much fascinating —and promising—news. To take advantage of that research now, I recommend that you eat at least one three-ounce serving of green, red, or yellow vegetables a day.

New research from Cornell Medical School indicates that too much sun can also deplete your body's stores of beta-carotene, so if you work outside—or are a sun worshiper—make sure to get enough of the beta bounty in your food and supplements.

There is really no excuse not to get enough beta-carotene, because there are so many good sources to choose from: spinach, kale, broccoli, sweet potatoes, tomatoes, pumpkins, parsnips, butternut squash, carrots, beets. One of my favorite sources is the greens— chickory, collard greens, watercress, dandelion, mustard, and radish greens. Fruits like cantaloupes and papayas are also rich. But not all beta-carotene comes from fresh produce. Often overlooked sources include vegetable soups, milk, cold cereals.

In short, there is simply no excuse not to get enough of this vital nutrient. Not only will it help protect you from cancer, infectious diseases, and aging, and keep your vitamin accounts full, it may be the easiest—and tastiest—way to assure a long healthy life.

Even with so many great dietary sources to choose from, you should include a supplement of beta-carotene in your life. I recommend an Optimal Daily Dose of 17,500 units.

The B Team

Even though each B vitamin occupies its own position on the nutritional playing field, it can't perform right without the rest of the team. That's why I call the nine B vitamins the B Team. You must take them together rather than individually because they function as catalysts and magnifiers for each other. Moreover, each B must be in a precise balance and relationship to the others, like the carefully crafted relationship of a baseball team. And believe me—it is a B Team in name only—in their biological action they are major-league players.

The other main thing to remember about this vitamin team is that most of them have short-lived careers. Because they are water-soluble, they are easily, well, rained out—flushed out of your body in your liquid wastes. Your body has no way to store most of these vitamins, with the exception of B_{12}. That means you should make sure to get a good dose of them every day.

FIRST BASE: VITAMIN B_1 (THIAMINE)

Thiamine's key role is to help your body squeeze the most out of your major source of energy—the starches and natural sugars you eat. This vitamin—found in grain, pork, cold cereals, breakfast bars, and breakfast drinks—is also essential for your proper muscle coordination, and for maintaining nerves throughout your body. It has a mild diuretic effect, helping to keep your body's water balance in check and flush out excess water from your system. When you are sick, under stress, or undergoing surgery, you need more B_1. In short, you need B_1 just to get to first base with the B Team.

For that reason, my Optimal Daily Dose for this first player on the B Team is a daily dose of 100 milligrams.

VITAMIN B_2 (RIBOFLAVIN)

B_2 is important in helping your body convert proteins, fats, and starches and natural sugars into energy. It is also necessary for building and maintaining your body's tissues, particularly your mucous membranes such as the lining of your nose. B_2 also helps protect your body from skin and eye disorders. Because it is one of the vitamins that help you deal with stress, you need to make sure that in these tense and active times you have adequate levels of B_2.

Research has shown riboflavin is a very common vitamin deficiency. Yet it is plentiful in such familiar foods as milk, eggs, leafy green vegetables, whole grains, liver, and other meat. Unlike some of the other vitamins, B_2 is not associated with any instances of toxicity.

Because of its wide range of strong biological effects, I recommend a basic Optimal Dose of 50 milligrams daily.

VITAMIN B_3 (NIACIN)

B_3—also known as niacin—is essential to convert your food into energy, and also for fat synthesis and protein metabolism. One of its special talents is to help your body deal with stress. After any injury to your body, your metabolic state goes into overdrive as your cells call for extra B vitamins to repair the damage. Niacin is prime on the list, along with its B Team partners riboflavin and thiamine. You need to increase your intake to make up for these losses.

For a long time, we have known niacin prevents the skin disease pellagra. But the newest, most exciting research about this vitamin is now centering around its magnificent effects for cardiac disease. A recent study in the *Journal of the American Medical Association* reports that patients taking B_3 reduced their recurrence of heart attacks by 29 percent. There is, however, a potentially serious side effect, as the vitamin may make your heart beat with an irregular rhythm. For this reason, it is wise to use it in carefully moderated doses.

Niacin also helps your cardiovascular health by lowering your cholesterol and triglycerides. (Although, if you are following the Nutritional Pyramid, you have already made big progress in those areas!) Some physician-researchers report their patients have seen their cholesterol drop by almost one quarter and their triglycerides drop by more than 50 percent! A pivotal study in *The New England Journal of Medicine* offers the encouraging finding that niacin seems to boost the action of certain cholesterol-lowering drugs by as much as 25 percent, and can actually help *reverse* atherosclerosis. Where your heart is concerned, B_3 is truly a Most Valuable Player on the B Team.

There is one problem with this helpful B vitamin. Taking niacin directly can give you a hot, uncomfortable flush. To avoid that, I recommend you take another form of the vitamin, niacinamide, which does not give you that flush. (However, niacinamide also does not have the cardiac and cholesterol-lowering properties of regular niacin, so if you need those, you should make sure to see the page on cardiac problems in the Personal Prescription section.)

For the rest of us, I suggest a basic Optimal Dose of 50 milligrams daily.

VITAMIN B₅ (PANTOTHENIC ACID)

Like most of the other players on the B Team, pantothenic acid is required for your body's metabolism of proteins, fats, and carbohydrates. But it is also necessary for your body's use of amino acids and the formation of certain proteins. B_5 is essential for the manufacture of many kinds of hormones and vital nerve-regulating substances.

B_5 could join the ACE Trio, because it works as an antioxidant. This powerhouse takes a swing at free radicals whenever they come up to bat, disabling them before they can do real damage to your cells.

In some ways you could call B_5 the shortstop of the B Team— because it stops short some of the effects of aging by attacking cell-destroying free radicals. Because it helps neutralize pollutants and toxins in our tissues, some researchers have reported that pantothenic acid can be used to improve the appearance of your skin.

The Optimal Dose I recommend for your Micronutrient Composite is 200 milligrams daily.

ON THE MOUND: VITAMIN B₆ (PYRIDOXINE)

Just as a pitcher is the key player of a baseball team, B_6 may be the most crucial member of the B Team. This central vitamin works throughout your body. In your blood, it helps produce antibodies and the crucial red blood cells that bring oxygen to your body's tissues. Patients with the fatal blood disorder sickle-cell anemia have been found to be deficient in B_6, and increasing their intake has reduced symptoms of the disease. In your nervous system, B_6 helps your nerve impulses transmit properly. It also plays a key role in your immune system: Without enough B_6, your immune tissues can actually shrink. Your thymus and spleen, two of your most critical immune organs, need pyridoxine for normal activity. Researchers find that some patients with asthma are deficient in B_6, and that B_6 supplements have reduced shortness-of-breath symptoms.

B_6 also helps keep our sexual organs healthy. In men, it helps reduce the inflammation of the prostate gland known as prostatitis. For women, this vitamin is especially helpful in relieving premenstrual fluid retention.

The lack of B_6 may also play a role in depression, according to recent research from Columbia Medical School. There, doctors studied patients admitted to a depression-treatment program, and found that one fifth of them had much lower than average levels of this vitamin.

One of the most encouraging findings about B_6 involves the rare disease called carpal tunnel syndrome. Until recently, surgery was the best treatment for this painful and often debilitating disease, which affects the major nerve running through the wrist into the hand. However, physicians have had such success with B_6 supplements in these patients that it is fast becoming recognized as an effective—and low-risk—alternative to surgery. This new research is a perfect example of the powerful role correct preventive nutrition can play in our lives.

Other people who benefit from increased B_6 levels are smokers. Not surprisingly, the stress of dealing with the added carcinogens that cigarette smoke brings into your body depletes this vitamin, and smokers need to increase their intake accordingly.

However, like many stellar performers, B_6 has a short career. It is excreted from your body—through the urine—a brief eight hours after you consume it. Obviously, you need to keep an adequate supply of B_6 coming in so you don't run short. And if you eat a diet very high in wheat, rice, or corn bran—or whole grains—that can reduce your B_6 levels, so you need to compensate accordingly.

But don't go overboard. More than with any other member of the B Team, you have to be careful not to overdose on B_6. Megadoses of pyridoxine—in some cases up to 6,000 milligrams per day!—used to relieve symptoms of premenstrual syndrome, have been associated with some serious side effects. Writing in the respected British journal *The Lancet*, a British researcher reported that 40 percent of a group of women taking B_6 for PMS reported a variety of symptoms: headache, bloating, irritability, and serious nerve impairment including burning, pain in the limbs, numb skin, clumsiness, and loss of balance. When they stopped taking the vitamin for two months, they reported a tremendous health improvement.

Of course, the problem isn't confined to PMS women. *The New England Journal of Medicine* reported several cases of men and women showing similar nerve-disorder symptoms when they took large amounts of B_6—and all improved when they stopped. Other research even suggests that the vitamin may have contributed to thalidomidelike birth defects in children whose mothers took excessive B_6 doses.

Clearly, this vital vitamin works best in a carefully controlled dose range. For that reason, you should take a basic Optimal Dose of 150 milligrams daily.

VITAMIN B_{12} (COBALAMINE)

Now we are starting to get into the far outfield of the B Team—not because these vitamins aren't essential, but because their wide-ranging health effects have been less thoroughly studied. Chief among these is vitamin B_{12}, also known as cobalamine.

It is no exaggeration to say you wouldn't be here without B_{12}, because it is essential to the production of the basic genetic coding, DNA and RNA, that you carry around in every one of your cells. If you have great hair, or gorgeous eyes, or, most likely, an inherited tendency to be witty, charming, and *terrifically* intelligent, at least some part of the thanks has to go to B_{12}—because without it your cells could never have coded the genetic instructions for making you so fantastic!

B_{12} also helps keep your blood healthy and oxygen-rich. Not only does your body use it to make healthy red blood cells, but it is also a key element in synthesizing hemoglobin, the molecule that transports oxygen to your tissues. Because of this blood-boosting action, physicians have long known that monthly injections of B_{12} can actually help make pernicious anemia essentially harmless in many people. It is also why the vitamin can increase your energy and promote growth.

Cobalamine works in your nervous system as well, by maintaining and repairing vital nerve structures. It also seems to have a profound effect on certain psychological disorders. Researchers have reported it can be helpful in treating memory loss, depression, and insomnia, and a lack of the vitamin can even create severe psychotic symptoms and brain damage resembling schizophrenia.

You need only a little bit of B_{12}, but if you don't get it, the results can be serious: Nerve disorders, problems in walking and balancing, and nervousness are often signs of a B_{12} deficiency. People who have to pay special attention to B_{12} are strict vegetarians, and those people regularly taking laxatives. (Believe me, after you climb the Nutritional Pyramid, with all that healthy fiber, the last thing you will want will be laxatives!)

Unfortunately, the best sources of B_{12} are not always the best foods for you in other ways: Fat-laden beef, pork, and eggs are prime sources. So are organ meats like kidneys and liver. On the healthier side, fish and yeast are also rich sources.

In order to be absorbed properly, B_{12} needs to pair up with calcium in the body, and it works best when you take it in several doses, with meals, rather than all at once. For that reason, I have included an ample amount of both nutrients in the Micronutrient Composite, but you should also make sure to get it in your diet.

While I do recommend you take it, you should know one comforting thing about B_{12}. Although it is a water-soluble vitamin, it is the only member of the water-soluble family that your body stores in bulk. If everything is working right inside, there is enough B_{12} in your liver right now to meet your body's needs for three to five years! But to keep up those stores, and give your body the B_{12} it needs, your basic Optimal Dose of B_{12} should be 100 micrograms each day. (Note: This B Team player is measured differently from its teammates—in micrograms, not in milligrams!)

FOLATE

Although it does not have a number, folate (also known as folacin or folic acid) is a crucial member of the B Team. In fact, it is absolutely essential to life itself. Like B_{12}, folate is needed by your cells to manufacture their DNA coding. It is also required for the formation of certain proteins in your body, including hemoglobin, the essential molecule that carries oxygen in your blood.

In spite of the fact this is a vital B Team member, it is an easy one to overlook. In one recent study, reported from the Institute for Human Nutrition at Columbia University, experts estimated that up to half of all women have some degree of folic-acid deficiency, which may cause bleeding gums.

A chronic and serious lack of folic acid in your diet may leave you open to a serious disease, one with the tongue-twisting name of megaloblastic folic-acid-deficiency anemia. Beyond that complex name is a fairly simple problem: Because of a lack of folate, your vital red blood cells don't develop properly.

The story behind our understanding of this disease is truly one of the fascinating sidelights of modern medicine. When I was born, doctors didn't even know that this disease was related to diet. But one physician, the eminent research hematologist Victor Herbert, had a hunch it might be. Because there was nothing in the medical literature, he decided to prove it by the most persuasive guinea pig possible: himself. For three months, he ate a special diet formulated to remove as thoroughly as possible any folate. He noticed he became increasingly forgetful and irritable. Then, on Christmas morning, he awoke to find he couldn't move his legs enough to get out of bed! Tests established the culprit: a lack of folate, the vitamin he had so scrupulously avoided for three months. The results of Dr. Herbert's noble self-experiment opened the door to a whole new understanding of the importance of that essential B Team vitamin.

In the two decades since, we have learned a lot about Dr. Herbert's vitamin. We now know that a lack of folate can give you a sore tongue and throat, sporadic diarrhea or constipation, gas and abdominal pains, weight loss, even make you infertile.

Alcoholics and elderly people are particularly susceptible to this devastating condition because they may not get enough folate in their diets or may be unable to absorb what they do get. The deficiency sometimes also occurs in pregnant women and infants. Certain medical conditions can also create problems: If you have chronic liver disease or are an epileptic taking the drug sodium phenytoin, you are vulnerable to folate deficiency. If you are undergoing cancer chemotherapy using the anticancer drug methotrexate, you should not be taking folate, because the vitamin interferes with the action of the drug.

But for the rest of us, the clue to getting enough folate lies in the word itself: It comes from the same Latin root as the word *foliage*. Think of green leafy things—those vegetables are great sources. But if you aren't in the habit of reciting Latin in the supermarket, don't despair; there are lots of other good sources, including whole wheat, mushrooms, liver, beans, avocados, carrots, apricots, even yeast. In order to provide your body with the folate it needs to keep your DNA and blood healthy, I recommend a basic Optimal Dose of 400 micrograms daily.

BIOTIN

This is one of the most recently discovered members of the B Team. Because of that, we don't know as much as we should about it. We do know, however, that biotin seems to perform at least one vital function on the inside, and one on the outside.

In your body, it lends itself to several important biological chemical reactions. Mainly, it helps your body break down all kinds of food—fats, starches, and proteins—into vital fuel for your cells. Preliminary research indicates it may help muscle pains and depression.

On the outside, it clearly plays a key role in keeping your skin healthy. Physicians have had good results using it to treat a variety of skin disorders like eczema and the inflammation of the skin known as dermatitis. While we are on the subject of outward appearances, there are even some who claim that biotin can help both gray hair and balding, but those claims seem to involve as much wishful thinking as hard science!

Biotin deficiencies don't usually occur, but when scientists have created a biotin deficiency experimentally, volunteers have shown the very symptoms that the vitamin normally helps cure: skin eruptions, depression, anemia, insomnia, and muscle pain.

The two reasons biotin deficiencies almost never occur is that, like vitamin K, biotin is actually synthesized by bacteria that live in the intestines. The second reason is that sources of biotin are readily available: Brewers' yeast, liver and kidney, mushrooms, milk, and brown rice are some of the best. Egg yolks are also good, although you should generally avoid this most concentrated source of cholesterol. While we're on the subject, note that raw egg white can block your absorption of biotin.

While deficiencies are uncommon, I still recommend that you include a modest amount of biotin along with your daily B Team vitamins, in a basic Optimal Dose of 50 micrograms daily.

LEFT FIELD: INOSITOL

You might say the last member of the B Team, inositol, is a bit out in left field. There is some dispute over whether this can properly be termed a B vitamin at all, but I include it here because it works along with the team members like biotin, B_5, and B_6 in important ways.

Though there has been little good research done on inositol, we are already seeing some of its promising effects in a wide variety of body systems:

- Cholesterol can be reduced with inositol.
- Along with the substance choline, it works to prevent atherosclerosis, or hardening of the arteries. It also seems to have beneficial effects on your kidneys, heart, and liver.
- On the outside, inositol prevents the flaking skin condition of eczema and plays a vital role in hair growth.
- Constipation may be helped by inositol because of its effect on the gastrointestinal tract.
- Psychological symptoms, including insomnia, may be relieved by moderate doses of this B Team player. In my New York practice, it is not uncommon that my patients confide in me that they have trouble sleeping. For those patients, I recommend a special mix that includes inositol and the amino acid tryptophan. Physicians have even used inositol to treat more serious psychiatric disorders of chronic anxiety and schizophrenia.

We don't yet know enough about the benefits of this substance, but it is clear that the more we learn, the more obvious place it has in our nutritional arsenal. Happily, according to the FDA, it is perfectly safe used at reasonable levels.

Some factors put you at special risk for low inositol:

- Are you a diabetic?
- Are you under heavy stress?
- Are you on a high-protein or low-calorie diet?
- Are you taking antibiotics?

If you answered yes to any of these, make sure to check the Personal Prescriptions section.

You could make an interesting meal out of the sources of inositol: dried lima beans, liver, beef heart and brains, wheat germ, brown rice, molasses, peanuts, cabbage, even fruits like raisins, cantaloupe, and grapefruit. Because it appears to be a helpful all-purpose B Teamer, I suggest a basic Optimal Dose of 200 milligrams daily.

Vitamin D: Here Comes the Sun

Just walk outdoors and let the sun shine in, and you'll start boosting your vitamin D. This is the only vitamin that comes to you directly from the environment as well as through foods. When the sun's ultraviolet rays interact with the oils of your skin, they produce vitamin D, which then perfuses through your pores into your bloodstream. That doesn't mean you should fry yourself in the sun and risk developing skin cancer. In fact, once you get a suntan, vitamin D production through your skin is blocked.

We are only now beginning to understand all that this Sunshine Vitamin can do for us. Its main power comes in its interactions with the vital micronutrient calcium, which I discuss in detail later in this chapter.

Unlike the general vitamin helpers like C and A, vitamin D is a great specialist. It works to keep important minerals calcium and phosphorus in balance in our bodies.

New findings published in *The New England Journal of Medicine* within the last year suggest that the team of vitamin D and calcium can significantly lower your risk of deadly colorectal cancer. Researchers report that people who get the least amount of sunshine—read vitamin D—are more susceptible to this often fatal malignancy.

Whether you get your D from sun, supplements, or diet—or better yet, a combination of all three—your body needs enough of this fat-soluble vitamin for several reasons. It helps keep your teeth and bones strong and hard. Inside your body, vitamin D actually converts into the hormone that keeps your calcium balance in check, calcitriol.

This same cooperation between vitamin D and calcium does far more than protect against cancer. It also seems to help keep your blood pressure even by maintaining constant levels of calcium in your blood.

The fast-breaking news about this vitamin comes in relation to a disease we have all heard a lot about, osteoporosis. There has been an awful lot of ink spilled over the osteoporosis epidemic affecting women—and men—in this country. But as they look more closely at the problem, scientists are coming to believe that it is not just calcium—as we once believed—but vitamin D that may hold the key to this tragic, and unnecessary, bone-wasting syndrome.

Recall that in your body, D "activates"—that is, it turns into—the hormone calcitriol. Among its other tasks, this hormone controls how well you absorb and distribute calcium throughout your body—how much of the vital bone-building mineral you absorb through digestion, and how much we put into—or *take from*—our bones. That means the ultimate controller of calcium is vitamin D, for without enough of this vitamin-D-created hormone, even the best calcium-rich diet won't do you any good!

Unfortunately, as we age, our bodies get less able to convert D to calcitriol, and we get less vitamin D. (When was the last time *you* drank a big glass of cold milk?) The result: a startling calcium deficiency, leading to a run on our bone banks of calcium and the wasting of osteoporosis. New findings published by the American Society for Clinical Nutrition suggest that vitamin D may be the real key to preventing and treating dangerous bone-wasting.

Research now going on at four major medical centers supports the idea that we can fight osteoporosis by giving people the vital D-vitamin hormone. In fact, by the time you read this, there is a good chance that the FDA will have licensed this as a treatment for victims of osteoporosis. But part of being your own nutritionist means guarding your health *before* you get disease—and that means making sure you get enough vitamin D to help your body make its vital calcium hormone.

In your enthusiasm, though, don't overdose. Too much of this calcium-helper vitamin means your body will store calcium where it doesn't belong. Tests show that both humans and animals who eat too much D develop excess calcium deposits throughout the cardiovascular system, which can lead to coronary-artery problems. But, scientists found, when the excess D was removed from the diet, the incidence of heart disease dropped.

For all its actions—for cancer, bones, and general health—there is no doubt this is a crucial micronutrient. I prescribe a basic Optimal Dose of 200 I.U. daily.

Vitamin E: The Sexy Vitamin

The last few years have brought an explosion in our knowledge about the tremendous benefits of vitamin E. Like its partners in the ACE team, A and C, E is an important antioxidant. It is the single most effective antidote to free-radical damage in your cell membranes. It also works its antioxidant action in the fatty tissues of your body.

Research at the University of California at Berkeley found that test animals who lacked vitamin E had a greater number of deadly free radicals loose in their bodies, and much greater cellular damage, than did animals who had enough vitamin E. Hand in hand with C, E breaks down sodium nitrite, a substance in many processed foods linked to increased cancer risk. This team also helps prevent the formation of carcinogenic nitrosamine compounds. There is evidence that the combination of E and C may protect you from the lung damage produced by nitrogen oxides. An equal-opportunity cooperator, E also works to help your body get the most out of its supply of vitamin A.

Not only does it help in the fight against cancer, but in many ways, E is the single best vitamin for its tremendous effects on many aspects of your blood. It aids your cardiovascular system by producing higher levels of HDLs, the "good" cholesterol in your blood. Studies show that it helps prolong the life of red blood cells in your circulatory system, dilates your blood vessels, and keeps your blood thin. This powerful vitamin is even being used to treat premature infants, to reduce the possibility of hemorrhage.

We now know that E can also improve your body's ability to fight off infection by strengthening the cells of your immune system. That, in turn, makes them more able to attack invading microorganisms—and keep you healthy.

Probably the effect for which E is best known is its action on our sexual organs and functioning. In fact, this idea has so inspired the popular imagination that E has been dubbed the "sex vitamin." An exciting reputation to be sure, but not absolutely accurate. Although these claims have often been exaggerated in the popular press, the reputation has a grain—in fact, several grains—of truth. E does seem to increase fertility in some cases in both men and women. The vitamin can be a boon to women, as it helps regulate uneven menstrual flow and relieves menopausal symptoms of hot flashes and headaches. In men, it helps prevent and relieve inflammation of the prostate.

For both sexes, its most touted quality is that it is reported to increase sex drive. This is largely subjective evidence, difficult to substantiate, and research suggests that the changes, if they occur at all, are short-lived. So don't count on it to be an aphrodisiac and you won't be disappointed. Of course, if you *do* notice a slight change for the better, well . . . lucky you.

There is one other popular use for E that has little grounding—but this one can actually have dangerous side effects. Some new and nursing mothers apply vitamin E in a salve on their nipples to prevent soreness or cracks. Unfortunately, not only is there no evidence that vitamin E actually helps this condition, but there is clear evidence that it can in fact harm the new infant. An unwitting dose of vitamin E with every feeding can create excessively high levels of the vitamin in the infant's system which can lead to significant blood disorders.

Hardly a month goes by that researchers from laboratories all over the world don't add a new page to our understanding of this multifaceted vitamin. The most interesting new finding comes from British scientists who have treated patients suffering from neurological disorders. Many were the result of nerve damage caused by other diseases, like cystic fibrosis and chronic liver disease. These researchers find that E supplements can actually arrest—and in some cases even reverse—these conditions.

The more we find out about this promising vitamin, the more benefits it seems to have. E is found in all your body tissues and is important for their health and proper functioning. It is stored in your liver, fatty tissues, heart, muscles, testes, uterus, blood, and adrenal and pituitary glands. Although it is a fat-soluble vitamin, in one way it behaves more like the water-soluble members of the B Team and vitamin C: It is stored in your body for relatively short periods of time. In fact, one half to three quarters of the E you consume is excreted in your feces.

For some people, that means they have to take extra care to make sure to get enough of this hard-working vitamin. If you are a regular jogger or runner or participate in other strenuous physical activity you may need more E. Biochemists of the University of California found that during physical exercise, animals consume greater amounts of E, and animals with enough E had far more endurance than those who lacked the vitamin.

But enough is not too much: Like many micronutrients, E works best in a fairly prescribed range. In too large doses—above 800 International Units a day—E may contribute to or cause dangerous blood clots. For that reason, I suggest a basic Optimal Dose for your daily Micronutrient Composite of 400 I.U.

Vitamin K

This may be a little-known micronutrient, but you should be very glad it's there. Unlike many of the other vitamins, it is not known for a wide range of effects—but you should be thankful for the one thing it does do, because you could not live without it. Also called the antihemmorrhage vitamin, it is crucial for your liver to produce a blood-clotting factor called *prothrombin*.

This chemical is a crucial link in the body's arsenal to stop excess blood flow. Thanks to vitamin K, prothrombin can help prevent internal bleeding and hemorrhages, protects you when you are cut or injured, and even aids in reducing excessive menstrual flow. Researchers report that it can be useful to reduce severe menstrual cramps.

Because it is a natural way to control bleeding, some doctors use it before and after childbirth and other operations to prevent excessive blood loss.

Infant formulas contain vitamin K because in the early weeks of life, babies do not have the intestinal bacteria to make enough of it.

Although rare, deficiency of vitamin K is serious because it can create excessive—and sometimes dangerous—bleeding. A number of factors can cut down on your vitamin K levels: Aspirin is the most common, but also radiation (natural or from X rays), some common air pollutants, even mineral oil. A deficiency can be aggravated by taking vitamin E, which thins your blood. If you don't have enough K, even a reasonable dose of E may thin your blood too much and make you bleed easily.

Very new research, done in conjunction with my alma mater, Tufts Medical School, and the New England Medical Center, suggests that chronic deficiencies of this vitamin may play an altogether unsuspected role in a whole range of diseases of the gastrointestinal tract. If this exciting lead proves true, this little-known vitamin may help treat such life-threatening conditions as Crohn's disease and ulcerative colitis.

Most of us do not need to worry about getting an adequate supply of K, however. Because it is so vital to our health, Nature built in an almost foolproof supply of vitamin K. Half we get from our diet— eating rich K sources like cauliflower, cabbage, leafy green vegetables, fruits, cereals, kelp, dairy products, even fish oils.

The other half—a slightly different form, but with the same benefits—is made by a species of bacteria that live deep in our intestines. Thanks to this two-tiered system, it is rare that we need to take supplements of vitamin K.

9.

Minerals: The Mighty Micronutrients

The minerals are mighty in their ability to stave off disease. The more we learn about them through the latest-breaking research, the more we understand their key roles in preventing cancer, heart disease, high blood pressure, osteoporosis, and many other chronic, degenerative diseases—as well as how we can use them to increase our vitality and strength.

Minerals, like vitamins, are micronutrients because you need them in relatively small amounts. Unlike vitamins, however, these substances come from nonliving, naturally occurring elements. The ultimate source of minerals is, of course, Planet Earth—usually in the form of mineral salts in the soil that find their way into the chemical makeup of foods or, in the case of seafood, dissolved minerals in ocean water. You may have heard about "bulk" and "trace" minerals. Those terms are a shorthand way to categorize how much of a mineral your body needs. If you require a significant amount per day of a given mineral, it is a bulk mineral. Calcium, magnesium, sodium, phosphorus, potassium, and sulfur are all bulk minerals.

Trace minerals, sometimes called trace elements, are those you need much less of: copper, zinc, iron, manganese, chromium, selenium, iodine, and molybdenum.

THE MICROMINERAL FAMILY

BULK	*TRACE*
Calcium	Copper
Magnesium	Zinc
Sodium	Iron
Phosphorus	Manganese
Potassium	Chromium
Sulfur	Selenium
	Iodine
	Molybdenum

In the last few years, minerals have taken their place in the nutrition spotlight; when *Newsweek* features calcium on its cover, you know it's become a celebrity. Unfortunately, this new public interest in minerals has also spawned some of the same distortions that have so long affected vitamins—and inspired some new ones. You may have seen ads for mail-order laboratories that promise to analyze your mineral needs by examining a lock of your hair. It's an appealing idea, and based on a sound principle. Hair analysis is used in sophisticated nutrition and medical research. But this is probably not the same test you get when you send off your ten dollars, because the laboratories that can perform this delicate test are generally not available to the public. In short, most commercial hair-analysis offers are useless. In our developed society, the chemical content of hair is so drastically altered by pollutants—shampoo, conditioners, mousses, dyes, and rinses, even elements in our water and air—that the real nutritional effects of your diet are buried. So if you are tempted the next time you see such an ad, do yourself a favor—turn the page and keep your hair.

Minding Your Minerals

Since those schemes aren't reliable, you'll have to figure out your mineral needs on your own. While the Nutritional Pyramid can almost certainly guarantee you a minimal baseline of vitamins, the same is not at all true for minerals. This is because the mineral content of your food is highly dependent on the soil where the crops were raised. If you live, say, in South Dakota, the selenium content of the ground is very high. Just by eating locally grown foods like onions and tomatoes you'll get all of this vital antioxidant mineral that you need. But if you live in Ohio, you might get very little selenium because the soil content of the trace element is so low.

In addition to these regional differences, a host of other factors influence your mineral nutrition. The widespread refining of foods can destroy fragile minerals. Acid rain can chemically block the availability of minerals in the soil. Modern fertilizers can disrupt the mineral balance of foods. In short, there is no easy way to balance your diet to ensure a 100 percent adequate intake of bulk and trace minerals.

We have already seen how frequent hidden vitamin deficiencies are. But the fact is, low levels of certain crucial minerals are even more widespread. For one thing, minerals are water-soluble, and so can get flushed out of the body regularly, increasing your need for them. They are also depleted by a wide range of biological functions, including stress, menstruation, childbearing, strenuous physical exercise, and simply the physiological changes of aging. Look at the table of groups at risk for mineral deficiencies: Are you on it?

ARE YOU:

Taking diuretic medication? _____
An athlete? _____
A smoker? _____
A heavy drinker? _____
Over 60 years old? _____

A vegetarian?   _____

On a low-calorie diet?   _____

A woman between 13 and 45?   _____

A postmenopausal woman?   _____

Pregnant?   _____

On the Pill?   _____

Taking laxatives regularly?   _____

Current research indicates that borderline mineral deficiencies are more common than we once believed.

- A significant number of older Americans lack iron, calcium, and zinc, says the USDA Center for Human Nutrition. Current research is now expanding that list.
- Calcium deficiency is now recognized to be taking a tremendous toll on older women. Yet despite the recent findings about the crucial need for calcium, three quarters of women over thirty-five consume less than the minimal RDA of this important nutrient.
- Iron deficiency appears to be disturbingly common among children and infants. The consequences of even a mild insufficiency can be quite profound, as it can retard the intellectual development of babies and preschool children.
- Even a marginal deficiency of magnesium can predispose you to cardiac-rhythm abnormalities, a potentially life-threatening condition.
- Research shows that people living in areas with low mineral levels in the water—that is, with very soft water—are much more likely to die from heart disease than people who get adequate minerals in their drinking water.

This list goes on and on. The rest of this chapter looks at the minerals one by one to help you determine your own needs for these vital micronutrients.

Bulk Minerals

CALCIUM

There's more calcium in your body than any other mineral—about two and a half pounds of it. Calcium ensures the steady functioning of your cardiovascular system, and even a minor imbalance can lead to potentially fatal disturbances in heart rhythms. But that's not all this mineral does. It also helps your nerves conduct impulses, allows your muscles to contract, and aids your blood to coagulate properly so wounds heal quickly.

But most people know calcium not for its benefits in the heart, muscles, and blood but for its crucial role in the bones. Ninety-nine percent of this white powdery mineral is found in your bones and teeth where it works with its mineral partner, phosphorus, to make them strong.

HOW'S YOUR CALCIUM RISK?

These groups can be at special risk for low calcium. Do these categories describe you, or your family members?

I am a woman over 45   _____
I am a man over 65   _____
I drink a lot of alcohol   _____
I have an inactive life-style   _____
I am on a low-calorie diet   _____
I am on a high-protein diet   _____
I am on a high-fiber diet   _____
I am pregnant   _____
I am a smoker   _____
I have lactose intolerance   _____
I take magnesium-containing antacids frequently   _____
I rarely get sunlight   _____
I have had a hysterectomy or my ovaries removed   _____

We now know that a lack of dietary calcium has become the single most serious nutritional problem of older Americans—more than with any other vitamin or mineral. Many of our seniors get far below even the minimal RDA for this crucial nutrient. Yet at the same time, we have learned that calcium supplements can help ward off one of the curses of aging, the most common metabolic disease of the bones—osteoporosis.

OSTEOPOROSIS

Behind that long Latin name is a simple, and serious, affliction. *Osteo* refers to bone; *porosis* means "being porous." Combine them, and you get just what it sounds like: porous bones. You also get the crippling, often fatal, disease that touches one in every eleven Americans.

How old are you? Anywhere near thirty-five years old? If so, your calcium stores are at the highest point of your whole life. In about your thirty-fifth year, the density of your bones is at its peak—they are the strongest, most calcium-rich, that they will ever be. But around that time, the ability of your body to absorb calcium through your digestive tract starts to drop. So your body, eager to keep things in balance, compensates for the lack from your intestines by borrowing against its richest calcium accounts—your bones. Year after year this overdraft continues, leaching out this vital mineral from your bones, reducing their mass and strength. It's like taking the mortar from a brick wall, little by little.

Soon, instead of the firm structural supports Nature designed, you are left with a lacy, brittle structure. As the process continues, the vertebrae of the back begin to collapse, creating the classic dowager's hump so common in older women. In this condition, even a minor fall can create fractures of those spinal vertabrae and of the hip—very serious injuries. Every one of us knows older people who have been hospitalized for just such fractures. It doesn't even take a fall—a hard bump, even a severe sneezing or coughing spell, can fracture the fragile bones of the osteoporosis victim.

Although men aren't immune to this disease—more than two million men suffer from it—osteoporosis is definitely not an equal-opportunity affliction. Fully eight times as many women develop this crippling disease as do men. It is estimated that one woman in four has or will have this disease. This is because the profound hormonal changes of menopause drastically change the body's reserves of calcium, and so open them up to the calcium-borrowing syndrome.

Those at highest risk are women who have had their ovaries removed, who have a one-in-two chance of developing the disease. Also, all postmenopausal women are at increased risk, particularly those who are small-boned, fair-skinned, and of Northern European, Japanese, or Chinese background. By the time they reach the age of sixty, one third of all women over the age of sixty show some signs of osteoporosis, making it more common than rheumatoid arthritis, diabetes, strokes, heart attacks, or breast cancer. To make matters worse, as you age and you need calcium more, your body also becomes less able to absorb it efficiently.

If you are an athlete, you have special cause for concern. New research indicates that young female runners and other highly competitive athletes are also prone to significant bone loss. We have long known that strenuous physical exercise can disrupt menstruation in these women. But now research from the University of Washington suggests that women twenty-four to twenty-seven years old who run twenty-five miles a week have the same mineral loss in their vertebrae as women twice their age! The finding applies only to serious, consistent athletes, but it is ironic that these women, so dedicated to increasing their aerobic health and longevity, may actually be doing real harm to their skeletal systems. But whether you are a fifty-two-year-old postmenopausal mother of three, or a twenty-five-year-old graduate-student runner, the end result of this calcium loss can be pathetic. When the calcium-depleted vertebrae in her back collapse, a woman can lose two inches of her height in as little as thirty days! Every year there are over a million and a half such osteoporosis fractures, and forty thousand older women are left permanently crippled. With bone-wasting can come excruciating, chronic pain. But it's not just uncomfortable, it can be lethal: One in five women dies from complications of hip fractures, making osteoporosis a leading cause of death among older women.

Yet such tragedy is absolutely unnecessary. For though we cannot change the body's need for calcium, we *can* do a better job of meeting it. In one study in rural Yugoslavia, researchers found that the residents of this goat-herding region, where milk and cheese were the backbone of the diet, had a much lower incidence of hip fractures than did members of another community who consumed only half as much calcium. There's no reason we can't take a lesson from those goatherds.

By taking calcium early and consistently, beginning even in their teen years, women can largely protect themselves against the bone damage of osteoporosis. If you fit into special risk groups—like those women runners—you should adjust your calcium intake accordingly.

In order to fend off bone-wasting, the National Institutes of Health recommend that women take far more calcium than they get now. The fact is, most Americans consume less than two thirds of their daily requirement for this vital mineral. The newest studies show most American women run a significant calcium deficit. Fully one half of middle-aged women get *less than a quarter of even the scant RDA requirement* for calcium.

Happily, this is starting to change. The number of women who take special care to get enough calcium has risen 15 percent in the last three years. That has made sales of supplements skyrocket from $47 million in 1983 to $125 million today and a projected $200 million next year. Calcium is beating out vitamin C as the "Supplement Most Likely to Succeed" in the nutritional marketplace. It's about time we started attending to this aspect of our nutritional needs!

But in all the hoopla, one fact is often overlooked: By itself, calcium is not a cure-all for osteoporosis. To keep your bones from thinning and cracking, you have to combine such supplements with enough vitamin D to help you absorb the calcium you do get, either from supplements or from your food. In fact, new research from the American Society of Clinical Nutrition indicates that vitamin-D deficiency plays a key role in our nation's calcium problems, and that the answer will lie with both these crucial micronutrients.

In addition, to rebuild your bones' calcium reserves, you need to give yourself some kind of regular exercise that puts stress on your bones. Making those bones work to carry weight is Nature's way of making sure they will absorb enough calcium to remain strong. Tennis, running, bowling, working out with weights, even some forms of aerobics can help. You don't, obviously, want to go out and run twenty-five miles a week, as that will only exacerbate your calcium loss. But some kind of regular, consistent exercise will help your body put the mineral back into your bones where it belongs.

THE CALCIUM-CANCER CONNECTION

The newest, most exciting findings about calcium suggest it has a significant ability to protect us against colorectal cancer. Researchers at New York's prestigious Memorial Sloan-Kettering Cancer Center have found that dietary calcium can actually prevent the development of familial colon cancer. They gave calcium to ten patients who were genetically at high risk for colon cancer. These patients had an abnormally high rate of growth in the cells lining the colon, considered a warning sign for cancer. But in three months, the patients' cell growth had, in fact, returned to normal. Researchers theorized that the mineral works by blocking bile and fatty acids, which stimulate the growth of cells in the colon and can lead to cancer.

And at Harvard Medical School, researchers found that calcium works in tandem with vitamin D to protect against colorectal malignancies. In a nineteen-year prospective study, researchers found that these elements are inversely related to the risk of colorectal cancer. While research continues on this exciting calcium-cancer breakthrough, you can put it to work for your own health right now.

NEW: A NATURAL TREATMENT FOR HIGH BLOOD PRESSURE

Hypertension is the third area where biochemists are proving the tremendous health-promoting potential of this vital micronutrient. This is truly at the frontier of medicine: These late-breaking findings were continuing to come out as this book went to press. What they suggest is that calcium has a real role in helping control blood pressure, and so lowering your risk of heart attack and stroke.

In a massive study at the University of Oregon, the diets of more than ten thousand people were carefully analyzed for seventeen vital nutrients. They found that those with high blood pressure got less calcium than healthy people. Other scientists have reported that calcium supplements actually helped lower blood pressure among women with high blood pressure.

It appears that when you eat too little calcium, the balance between calcium and sodium is disrupted. Instead of staying outside your cells where it usually belongs, the calcium is forced inside the cells lining your blood vessels. That sets off chemical reactions that contract the blood vessels, increase your heart rate, and send your blood pressure through the roof. The trick is to keep calcium in adequate supply so that it stays outside the cells and the contraction cycle is never unleashed.

This new therapy doesn't work equally well for everybody. There are even some hypertensives for whom calcium raises blood pressure. But for one person in three with high blood pressure, it seems to work well. The people most likely to be helped by calcium therapy are older people—especially women—blacks, women with pregnancy-related hypertension, and those who respond to diuretics. Supplements of 1,000 milligrams a day for only two months have proved both safe and effective in lowering blood pressure among forty-eight patients with moderate hypertension. Even among perfectly healthy people, there is some evidence that supplementation with calcium reduces blood pressure. Clearly, we need to broaden our understanding of the calcium-hypertension link, and the new and exciting ways that calcium can help maintain stable, healthy blood pressure.

WHERE TO FIND YOUR CALCIUM

It's no secret that milk—and dairy products like yogurt, cheeses, and ice cream—are the primary calcium source. One cup of milk contains 300 milligrams of calcium. But that means you would have to drink at least three glasses—up to five for some women—to meet your calcium needs. And, as you know, those dairy products often come laden with too much fat. Drinking that much milk—even the 99 percent fat-free variety—would give you several grams of needless fat. Besides, most of my patients, like many adults, have lost their taste for milk.

Fortunately, there are other good sources. Try canned sardines and salmon (which I hope you recognize as the same foods that gave you those wondrous fish oils we talked about in the last chapter). And don't scrape aside those soft bones. You can digest them easily, and that's where most of the calcium is found. (Of course, to avoid extra fat, buy these products packed in water.) You can also get your calcium from yogurt, buttermilk, green leafy vegetables like broccoli, kale, and collard greens, kidney beans, oysters, and the soy protein, tofu. Even such unlikely foods as spaghetti and pizza supply a reasonable dose of calcium!

But in order to be absolutely sure, most people need to rely on some kind of calcium supplements. Given the bewildering supply of products on the market, that is not always as easy it is appears.

BE A SMART CALCIUM CONSUMER

1. There are a number of different forms of calcium in the supplements—carbonate, phosphate, gluconate, lactate. The cheapest and the best source is calcium carbonate. It is "best" because it has the highest percentage of usable calcium—40 percent. (Some other forms have less than 10 percent—yet cost more!) That means that a single 1,000-milligram tablet gives your body only 400 milligrams of usable calcium.

2. If you take calcium carbonate with meals, you will absorb it better.

3. Stay away from supplements that contain dolomite, bone meal, or oyster shells. Yes, they are full of calcium, but they may also contain toxic minerals like lead, mercury, and arsenic. Such heavy metals can be very dangerous. Because these supplements come from natural sources, they can also contain a host of other minerals, like sodium, you may not want to add to your intake.

4. With calcium, as with all supplements, what counts is not just what they contain, but what they don't. Many pills are sold with sealers, fillers, artificial coloring, or, in the case of the chewable supplements, flavors and sugar. Go for the basics—calcium carbonate—and you'll be better off.

5. If you do take calcium, it is important to balance it with the mineral magnesium, which helps your body make the best use of calcium. Again, your best bet is calcium carbonate.

CALCIUM CAUTIONS

As with almost every vitamin and mineral, excessive doses of calcium can spell trouble. Overdose can lead to complications like constipation, nausea, a hyperactive stomach, and bloating. If you have kidney problems or are prone to kidney stones, you should not take calcium without consulting your doctor first—it may increase your risk of getting these painful stones. Even for people with no such problems, taking too much calcium over a long time could eventually result in kidney failure. In one laboratory study, animals fed calcium megadoses actually had *less* bone strength, severe internal bleeding, and lower absorption of vitamin K.

Calcium also has the potential to interfere with medications you may be taking, and to affect absorption of minerals like iron, zinc, and magnesium. So while calcium is necessary, it is important you take this mineral in correct amounts.

For example, too much calcium can damage your cardiovascular health. Research indicates that both humans and animals who overindulge in this nutrient may develop excess calcium deposits throughout the cardiovascular system. When these deposits grow on our artery walls, they can lead to blockages and heart attacks. For calcium, as for many other minerals, the correct level depends on your own personalized health status.

CALCIUM CALCULATOR

In order to determine your Optimum Calcium Dose, find yourself on this chart:

IF YOU ARE A . . .	DAILY DOSE (IN MILLIGRAMS)
Woman before menopause	1,000
Woman after menopause	1,500
Woman after menopause, taking replacement estrogens	1,000
Man	1,000
Serious aerobic athlete (woman)	1,500

Phosphorus

While it may not win the "most famous" award from its mineral partner calcium, phosphorus easily wins an award for the most versatile. No other mineral reaches so deeply into every one of your cells and biological processes. With all this work to do, it's not surprising that, next to calcium, you have more phosphorus in your body than any other mineral.

For its most obvious task—keeping your bones strong and resilient—phosphorus works hand in hand with calcium. Together, they combine into a tough, hard mortar, one part phosphorus and two parts calcium. But outside the bones, throughout the soft tissues of your body, phosphorus outweighs calcium substantially.

When you fracture a bone, phosphorus comes to the rescue, speeding up the healing process and putting a stop to the calcium loss from the injury. Not surprisingly, phosphorus has been found useful to help treat osteoporosis. It also helps treat or forestall bone diseases like rickets and it prevents stunted growth in children.

As important as this mineral is to your bones, it doesn't stop there. It permeates every one of your trillions of body cells, helping them absorb life-giving substances through their membrane walls. There is hardly a single one of the tens of thousands of chemical reactions in your body where this phosphorus does not lend its power. To name just a few, this mineral:

- Helps metabolize protein, fats, and carbohydrates for optimum growth and upkeep of your cells.
- Helps break up and carry away fats and fatty acids in your blood, keeping your blood chemically balanced.
- Works to keep your nerves from feeling frazzled, and your mind alert and sharp.
- Helps stimulate your glands to secrete hormones.
- Keeps your muscles—including the special one thumping away in the middle of your chest—contracting regularly and smoothly.
- Lets you digest two members of the B vitamin team, riboflavin and niacin.

- Assures smooth transmission of impulses from one nerve to another.
- Keeps your kidneys effectively excreting wastes.
- Gives you stable and plentiful energy.
- Keeps your smile attractive, by helping your teeth develop well and keeping them white and hard.

In fact, the whole human race owes a huge debt to phosphorus, because it forms our reproductive proteins. Without it, your parents could not have passed along all those *wonderful* traits that make you who you are!

I could go on, but I think you get the point: the catalog of the offerings of phosphorus is exhaustive, and impressive.

WHERE DO YOU GET IT?

Now that you've begun to appreciate phosphorus for all its wonder-working properties, you may be eager to run out and stock up. Well, the very best news is that you probably don't have to. You probably already have enough—and if you don't now, you will soon, just by eating according to the well-rounded Nutritional Pyramid.

Where do we get our phosphorus? First of all, thanks to modern food processing, you probably get a good deal more of this mineral in your diet than your grandparents got in theirs. Many of the common food additives contain phosphates, a form of the mineral. Do you often eat fish, poultry, or cheese? If the answer is yes, your phosphorus level may, in fact, be quite sufficient.

Also, if you eat a diet rich in calcium, you can be fairly certain that you will also get enough phosphorus. But unlike calcium, which your body has a hard time absorbing, about three quarters of the phosphorus you eat finds its way into your bloodstream, and from there to your body's major repositories in the teeth and bones. In order to get the best mileage from the phosphorus you eat, you should make sure to get the optimal levels of calcium and vitamin D in the Micronutrient Composite.

Unfortunately, a number of mineral interlopers can block your phosphorus. Excess aluminum, magnesium, or iron can block storage. Even white sugar—remember those deadly Sweet Nothings?—

can throw your phosphorus-calcium balance out of whack, as can high-fat diets. When you consider the average American diet—rich in both these substances—you see why it is so important to eat to boost our phosphorus levels.

Some people are at particularly high risk for deficiency:

- Are you on a weight-loss diet of 1,000 calories a day or less?
- Are you a pregnant or nursing woman? If so, see the Personal Prescriptions section.
- Do you consume large amounts of antacids? (They can deplete your bones' phosphorus supply.)

In general, phosphorus allowances are the same for men and women throughout our adult lives. In childhood, we often need a little extra, because of growing bones and tissues—but again, it's best for children to get the mineral from their diets, in balanced combination with calcium.

It is never a good idea to give infants phosphorus supplements, unless under a doctor's orders. During the first year, they need little phosphorus, and the balance of calcium and phosphorus is particularly delicate. Careless phosphorus dosing can upset the balance, creating a serious muscular condition called hypocalcemic tetany. As with all mineral supplements, I strongly suggest you avoid them with young children.

Look for your phosphorus in seeds, whole-grain flour and cereals, nuts, eggs, fish, and poultry.

Magnesium: The Forgotten Mineral

I call magnesium the forgotten mineral because it is only now getting the credit it deserves. Until recently, scientists have not fully appreciated the crucial role of magnesium in your body's well-being. It is one of the most abundant minerals in the body, one half of it found in your bones. The rest of it is in the fluids of your cells—there is virtually none floating free in the body.

This mineral plays a lead role in giving you vital, vibrant energy. It takes part in the chemical reactions of some 325 vital enzymes, the chemical controllers of almost all your vital life processes. When you consider that the failure of even a single one of these enzymes can result in serious, even fatal, metabolic disorders, you begin to appreciate all the work magnesium does to keep 300 of them running smoothly—and you feeling healthy.

It's hard to think of any part of your body where magnesium doesn't play a key role. Your cells? The mineral is essential for the manufacture of the DNA and RNA coding in each and every one of your trillions of cells. And the membranes of all those cells depend on magnesium. Your bones? Magnesium helps them form and grow. For nerves, muscles, and even heart action, this mineral is key.

As important as it is to so many body systems, many people neglect magnesium. The U.S. Department of Agriculture—hardly known for its radical positions—reports that the average American gets barely three quarters of the minimal RDA for this mineral. And that, remember, is just the level needed to prevent serious deficiencies.

Certain people are particularly vulnerable.

HOW IS YOUR MAGNESIUM RISK?

I am . . .

Taking diuretic medication   _____
Undergoing cancer chemotherapy   _____
Taking digitalis drugs   _____
An alcoholic   _____
A survivor of a heart attack   _____
Suffering from kidney problems   _____

If you find yourself on this list, you are at increased risk. If you appear here more than once, you should definitely be increasing your magnesium intake. See your own Personal Prescription later in this book.

To give you an idea of its many positive health actions, look at this sampling of recent magnesium findings:

TAKING MAGNESIUM TO HEART

Medical science has found few cures for broken hearts, but magnesium may well be one of the best. If you live in an area where the drinking water is hard—that means a high magnesium content— you are very fortunate. In these regions, the incidence of deaths related to heart disease has been found to be lower than in similar soft-water communities. Around the world, studies have shown that the less magnesium in the local water supply, the more people get heart disease. I suggest you make such heart-guarding water a part of your daily diet.

We do not understand fully how magnesium mends broken hearts, but an intriguing clue was found recently by researchers in Copenhagen, who found that patients who have suffered acute heart attacks have lower magnesium levels. We think that too-little magnesium may also play a role in hardening of the arteries. What is clear, even now, is that magnesium has a strong protective action against heart disease. A glass of water, anyone?

High blood pressure is also helped by magnesium, specifically high blood pressure in the arteries. As with heart attacks, there is a clear correlation between low levels of magnesium and high rates of blood pressure and stroke. Elsewhere in the cardiovascular system, it seems also to protect against toxic reactions for people taking the strong heart drug digitalis.

MAGNESIUM MAGIC FOR HEALTH

This mineral brings wide-ranging health benefits elsewhere throughout your body:

Migraines may be curbed by magnesium. Fifteen million Americans—two thirds of them women—suffer from these head-splitting, incapacitating headaches. A current finding from Tennessee reports that when doctors gave a group of five-hundred migraine sufferers 100 to 200 milligrams of magnesium each day, 65 percent of the group reported complete relief. For pregnant women, who cannot take standard migraine drugs because of their risk to the fetus, this is a watershed finding.

Exercise is also related to magnesium. If you are an athlete, a runner, or even get reasonably strenuous weekend exercise, you need to mind your magnesium. Physical exercise depletes the body of its magnesium reserves. This makes your muscle contractions weak and lowers your endurance to prolonged exercise. Laboratory animals deprived of magnesium lose up to 50 percent of their muscle functioning. On the other hand, the capacity of animals to withstand prolonged exercise and all activities of endurance improves dramatically when they get extra magnesium.

The new field of sports medicine has shown us that athletes are often lacking in magnesium. A patient of mine is in training for the U.S. Olympic track team. Needless to say, he is a spectacular athlete, doing everything he can to stay at his prime. When I mentioned his need for extra magnesium, a knowing smile crept across his face. He told me that he has heard a rumor in athletic circles that coaches in some of the Iron Curtain countries counsel athletes to increase their magnesium for several weeks before competitions. "The next time I hear that rumor," he smiled, "I'll know what they're talking about." So if you are a runner, a jogger, or simply planning to play a vigorous tennis match, you may want to make sure you have enough of this mineral.

Diabetes may be related to magnesium. Low levels of the mineral can disturb your body's ability to tolerate glucose, so you become less able to remove sugar from your blood—which, in turn, can lead to diabetes.

Kidney stones and gallstones may also be helped with magnesium. Most people know that these stones can be excruciatingly painful, but not everybody knows they can kill. About one million Americans will succumb to complications related to these agonizing stones. Several studies have now reported that magnesium supplements can help prevent recurrent kidney stones. In one, reported in the *Journal of Urology*, magnesium and vitamin B$_6$ proved highly effective in reducing these painful and dangerous attacks.

For women, magnesium may work with calcium to protect against postmenopausal bone loss. Belgian scientists have documented a significant lack of magnesium among women with osteoporosis. The mineral may even be helpful in relieving the tension of premenstrual syndrome. Some physicians are already using it for treatment. For pregnant women, magnesium also enhances general health, and for nursing women, it is a must, because your body needs extra magnesium at that time.

To get enough of this vital micronutrient, make an effort to include magnesium-rich foods in your diet. Some of the best are green leafy vegetables, seafood, nuts, dairy products, and cereal grains.

WHEN SUPPLIES ARE LOW . . .

Unfortunately, you can have a long-term magnesium deficiency and not know it. The signs are not highly specific, so they may be hard to recognize as being linked to magnesium deficiency. Signs of severe deficiency include loss of coordination, loss of appetite, confusion, diarrhea, nausea, vomiting, tremors, and occasionally fatal convulsions. A chronic deficiency of this mineral over time can lead to cardiovascular problems. In fact, evidence suggests that if magnesium deficiency goes on for long enough, say twenty years, your body may get to the point where vigorous exercise may actually hurt your heart more than help it.

This mineral should be a part of your Micronutrient Composite, in an Optimal Daily Dose of 750 milligrams.

DO YOU HAVE KIDNEY OR HEART PROBLEMS?

If so, DO NOT TAKE magnesium supplements without consulting your doctor. People with severely decreased kidney function, or certain kinds of heart rhythm abnormalities, should not take magnesium without a physician's supervision.

Sodium

Of all the minerals, sodium suffers from a real P.R. problem. Everybody has by now heard about the mineral's effect on blood pressure, so much so that in the last three years, our nation's sodium consumption has dropped almost one third. But what people haven't heard are the many good things that sodium does for us.

We should be a little more accepting of this mineral because we wouldn't get very far without it. Without enough sodium, your heart would stop beating in a strong, steady rhythm and would lapse into spasmodic, uncoordinated beats—useless for pumping blood and supplying your tissues with oxygen.

The same would happen to all the other muscles and nerves in your body, which are kept in condition by your sodium balance. Sodium is found in the fluid that surrounds all of your cells, where it is the prime regulator of your body's water balance, keeping your other vital minerals in proper concentration in your blood and tissues. It is also the one bulk mineral that everybody gets more than enough of—most of us consume three to five times the amount we need for optimum health.

Of course, what most people know about sodium concerns its effect on blood pressure. There has been so much publicity about sodium that I rarely see a patient who doesn't ask me about the sodium-hypertension link. The simple fact is that, along with alcohol and fat, sodium has one of the strongest links to high blood pressure of anything we eat.

But what most people think about sodium is out of date, based on yesterday's research. We have grown so used to hearing nothing except bad news about sodium that it's time for some—unaccustomed—good news.

New findings show that the sodium picture is quite a bit more complex than we once believed. Contrary to popular belief, sodium does not automatically lead to high blood pressure for most people. If you look at all the Americans with high blood pressure—about 40 million people—sodium appears to be the culprit for only about half. That is still a huge number, but that means that *there are ten times as many Americans for whom sodium does not create high blood pressure as there are those for whom it does.* Even the broadest estimates indicate that only one in ten of us has the genetic hypersensitivity to sodium that makes it raise our blood pressure to dangerous levels. For the rest of us, there is little relation between the salt we eat and our blood pressure.

BEYOND SODIUM:
AT THE HYPERTENSION HORIZON

Until recently, researchers had not given their full attention to the potential role of other nutrients in hypertension. Today, contemporary research is focusing more on other factors that enter into the cycle. There is early evidence that foods like fats, proteins, and sugars may bear some of the responsibility.

The spotlight is even moving beyond our diet, as we look at factors like age, weight, and race that affect blood pressure. Even psychological stress may compound the problem for those with a family history or with borderline hypertension. When a group of such young men was subjected to stress, they had a more severe blood-pressure response, and their bodies were less able to flush out sodium through their kidneys, than normal young men.

Until the answer is in, it seems wise to take the draconian hypertension advice with, well, a grain of salt. But that doesn't mean it's okay to upend the salt shaker over your food again. We know enough about the damaging effects of sodium in other body systems like kidneys and heart to recommend that you use it with respect and caution.

Let me suggest to you what I tell my patients: Most of us would do well to learn to appreciate the natural flavors of food without the aid of salt.

Interestingly, Nature puts very little sodium in whole, unprocessed food. In fact, that's part of the problem. Because the human animal—that's you, dear reader—evolved eating low-sodium foods, we developed highly effective means to retain the scant sodium we got. But then Man, with dubious wisdom, started adding sodium to foods to preserve them—but our bodies still hoarded it in the same efficient way. The result? A toxic sodium overload. One of the benefits of eating by the Nutritional Pyramid is that, as we increase our proportion of natural, unprocessed foods, we decrease our massive sodium overdose.

I counsel my patients to get in the habit of looking at the sodium content on food labels when they shop. Even their best intentions about sodium cutting can be sabotaged by the hidden sodium content in so much of our processed food. Some food sources, all by themselves, are full of sodium: shellfish and kelp, bacon, and organ meats like brains, liver, and kidneys.

Another hidden sodium source is in your kitchen right now—the kitchen faucet. New findings suggest that some local water supplies can give you up to one quarter of your daily sodium ration when you use water merely for cooking and drinking.

If you use certain types of water softeners, they add an additional dose of sodium. The solution? If you are on a sodium-restricted diet, you can check with local authorities to be sure your water is not sabotaging your diet. You may also want to use bottled water for drinking and cooking, or install a line in the kitchen that bypasses the water softener.

Most of us still get far more sodium than we need, and there's no chance we'll be running low anytime soon. So the recommendation for sodium is different from that for other micronutrients: On this one, keep your daily intake as low as possible.

The Potassium Powerhouse

Potassium is sodium's partner. They work in tandem to regulate your body's water balance and keep your heart muscle beating in a steady, normal rhythm. Potassium works almost entirely inside your cells, while its partner, sodium, works outside. Potassium also regulates nerve and muscle functions throughout the body, and helps keep your sharp by making sure your brain gets enough oxygen. This multipurpose mineral even helps rid your body of wastes.

Yet for all its health benefits, Americans don't pay enough attention to this vital mineral: Research shows 38 percent of men—and an astounding 65 percent of women—*get less than 70 percent of the minimal RDA of this mineral.*

The biggest late-breaking research news about potassium concerns its positive effect on high blood pressure. Scientists studying hypertensive laboratory animals found that the animals had fewer fatal strokes when potassium was added to their diet. Apparently, this also works for the human animal. We know that people with dangerously high blood pressure tend to consume less potassium than normal, healthy people, while people who eat diets higher in potassium have little hypertension.

The problem is, of course, that this low-potassium diet is exactly what is most common in affluent, developed cultures. Medical anthropologists have looked at vegetarians in rural areas of the South Pacific who eat exactly the opposite combination, low sodium and high potassium. Not surprisingly, they are far less likely to develop hypertension than their relatives who migrate to urban areas where processed and animal foods are abundant—and where "rural" potassium gives way to "citified" sodium in their diets. For South Sea Islanders, as for American heartlanders, when a low-potassium, high-sodium diet interacts with genetic susceptibility to hypertension, it spells trouble in paradise.

It may be that potassium prevents sodium from raising blood pressure. We have seen that when hypertensive patients go on a low salt diet and take extra potassium, they get better, their blood pressure goes down, and they feel better. But even more interesting is that they get much better than if they were just on the low-salt diet itself! The only problem is one of human nature—they start missing salt, and sneaking it on the side! Researchers solved that problem by giving them a blend of half salt (sodium chloride) and half potassium chloride—not unlike the butter-margarine blends. That way, people got the salty taste they wanted, but not the high blood pressure. You can buy that same blend in many health-food stores.

However, the potassium finding is so new that it is still very controversial. Some researchers maintain that potassium does not lower blood pressure in people who do not have high blood pressure, and that for some people with high blood pressure, potassium is not even very safe. Although the final research is not yet in, this area is being examined exhaustively. If you are one of the almost 40 million Americans with high blood pressure, you should know that potassium may be a very promising lead for a new, safer treatment for this serious disease.

Given its extensive range of important biological activities, we all need to make sure we stock our potassium reserves.

For all of us, the best dietary sources include green leafy vegetables, bananas, dates, raisins, apricots, cantaloupes, oranges and orange juice, prune juice, turkey, potatoes, tomatoes, sunflower seeds, buckwheat, and wheat germ.

POTASSIUM CHECK

You may need to pay special attention to potassium if you:

Take certain diuretics (thiazide type)   _____
Regularly take cortisone medications   _____
Have chronic liver disease   _____
Drink more than three cups of coffee daily   _____
Have more than two alcoholic drinks daily   _____

To avoid trouble, you should include potassium in your Micronutrient Composite. I recommend an Optimal Daily Dose of 100 milligrams.

Sulfur: Nature's Beauty Mineral

The last of the bulk minerals is something of a surprise—sulfur. Most of my patients are curious when I mention sulfur. After all, isn't that the stinky, dirty-yellow stuff? Instead, I tell them, they should think of it as Nature's Beauty Mineral. Sulfur helps keep your hair full, and your skin clear and youthful.

You need sulfur to build the protein keratin, a tough substance that helps maintain your hair, nails, and skin. But it's not just for vanity—without sulfur, you would simply fall apart, because it helps synthesize the glue that holds your body's parts together, the protein collagen.

Sulfur plays a number of other behind-the-scenes roles in your body. Found in insulin, it keeps your energy levels stable. It also works in heparin, a vital blood-thinning factor found in your liver and tissues. Sulfur also helps build the vital amino acids cysteine, cystine, taurine, and methionine, present in almost all your body's cells.

In combination with large doses of zinc, small doses of sulfur may help the skin disease psoriasis. There is even hope that this element could help sufferers from painful and debilitating arthritis. We know that levels of cystine, one of the sulfur-rich amino acids, is lower in arthritis patients, and some researchers believe that by augmenting levels of this yellow mineral, we may be able to reduce the agony of severe arthritis sufferers.

For most of us, by eating according to the Nutritional Pyramid, we will automatically get our sulfur quota. Unfortunately, the very best source for this is cholesterol-laden eggs. In fact, some people, such as strict vegetarians, who eat no eggs at all, risk not getting enough sulfur. In addition, since the soil in many areas is deficient in sulfur, plant foods may not have ample amounts of the mineral.

If you don't eat eggs, you can also get sulfur from meat, fish, cheese, and milk, and underground-growing bulbs like garlic and onions. Although this is a mineral we need in bulk, it is one we usually get enough of, so I don't recommend a special daily dose.

Trace Minerals and Your Health

In addition to the six bulk minerals, there are nine trace minerals that your body uses in lesser amounts. But just because you need less doesn't mean they are less important. You could not live without them, and each plays a role in the careful balance that assures spectacular health, radiant energy and appearance, and maximum longevity. Some of them—like zinc, iron, and molybdenum, appear throughout many of the body's systems. Others, like iodine, are highly specialized. But in all cases, you have to make sure that you have adequate levels or your whole body will feel the effects.

Copper

Just as potassium and sodium work as a pair, copper does its work with a partner, iron. But its job is very different. It is required to convert your body's iron into hemoglobin—the protein that carries most of the oxygen in your blood. Without copper, your cells would soon suffocate, robbed of the oxygen fuel they need. Copper also keeps your energy level up by helping you absorb the iron you eat. Copper is also involved in the production of the protein collagen, the mortar that holds your bones, cartilage, skin, and tendons together. If it weren't for copper, your skin, lungs, and blood vessels would lose much of their elasticity because copper helps form the stretching protein elastin. The last reason to be grateful for copper is a cosmetic one: It allows the amino acid tyrosine to color your hair and skin. Without it, you would be very strange and pasty-looking, indeed!

Despite its wide-ranging actions, doctors estimate that we get significantly less of this vital orange mineral than we should. In fact, dietary levels are even far below the minimal RDA levels! While this may not show up as overt clinical disease, it is very likely that it contributes to a higher cancer rate, more extensive cell damage and aging, and even a shorter lifespan.

OF MICE AND MEN:
COPPER AND YOUR HEART

We are now learning that this versatile nutrient may also help your cardiovascular health in several ways. New findings suggest that copper may have unsuspected benefits for your heart. Researchers at the USDA Human Nutrition Research Center put mice on a high-fat diet—giving some copper, and others none. The mice with copper showed none of the heart problems that usually come with such a diet. In fact, they lived *five times longer* than their unfortunate counterparts who ate less copper. Other animal studies confirm that an imbalance of copper in the diet throws cholesterol levels off, lowering HDL, the good cholesterol that protects you against heart disease.

What works in mice also works in men: Studies at the USDA Human Nutrition Center and in the *Journal of the American Medical Association* have confirmed the copper-cholesterol link. Again and again, the pattern is the same: An imbalance in your body's copper levels raises cholesterol significantly and lowers the proportion of HDL cholesterol. Copper is important to keep your body strong in another way. It is necessary for your body to build hemoglobin, and without enough of it in your food, you may be susceptible to debilitating anemia.

For pregnant women, we now think copper may also play a significant role. Research suggests that pregnant women need copper supplements because their bodies don't seem to be able to retain the element as well as they should. Another tantalizing clue is that some women who suffer frequent miscarriages early in pregnancy have very low copper levels.

THE COPPER-CANCER CONNECTION

After reading the above, you might think it's a great idea to run out and start gnawing on pennies to get more copper. Not so fast. The copper story is not over yet—this mineral that does so much good for our hearts may have a less welcome relation—to cancer.

High levels of copper have been detected in the blood of victims of several kinds of malignancy, including tumors of the digestive system, lung, and breast, Hodgkin's disease, and systemic cancers like leukemia, lymphoma, and multiple myeloma. We don't yet know whether the excess copper is a cause or a consequence of the disease process. But when researchers matched up the per person intake of copper with death from cancer in twenty-seven countries, they found direct links between the mineral and malignancies of the skin, breast, and intestine. It may be that copper is not dangerous in and of itself, but blocks the trace element selenium, which has a profound cancer-protective role. By doing so, some researchers believe, it leaves us open to cancer.

The research on copper is still so new that we clearly have much to learn. In the meantime, I recommend to patients that they stick to a middle road. As with any micronutrient, the first step is always to try to get it from your diet. With copper, that's not only easy, it's delicious, because prime sources include dark chocolate (not a bad prescription!), nuts, shellfish, and oysters—a gourmet's dream. Other good sources are liver, poultry, fruits, kidney, and dried legumes.

Zinc: The Vitality Nutrient

If the jury is out on copper, the word on zinc is clear: It is a powerful, terrifically beneficial mineral. If there is a Most Valuable Player on the trace-mineral team, zinc gets my vote. There is almost no part of the body where it doesn't have some beneficial effect:

- It helps form insulin, to keep your energy stable and strong.
- It helps synthesize protein in your body.
- It plays a part in the metabolism of carbohydrates.
- It is essential for the production of several key enzymes that your body uses to digest food.
- It helps your muscles contract smoothly.
- It boosts every area of your immune health.
- It helps you absorb your vitamins, particularly the B Team.
- It is crucial for the proper development of your reproductive organs.
- For men, it helps assure the normal functioning of the prostate.

In fact, not one of your body's cells could exist without zinc, because it helps build the cell membranes and even the genetic coding, DNA. Impressed?

Not surprisingly, there are many, many medical areas where we are finding zinc can play a key role:

Cancer. People with cancer of the esophagus and bronchial tubes have low blood levels of zinc, as do men suffering from cancer of the prostate.

Wound healing. Surgical wounds heal much faster when patients take zinc supplements. It has been definitively established that some postsurgical patients given a moderate dose of zinc daily completed healing almost twice as fast as untreated people.

Acne, that plague of adolescents and young adults. Zinc may hold the answer for you. We know of cases where zinc deficiency actually produces acne. But the real good news on this front comes from dermatologists in Sweden, where fresh, glowing skin is a national

treasure. They found that zinc, alone or in combination with vitamin A, decreased acne an astounding 84 percent in volunteers. It
doesn't work for everybody, but if you are one of the people whose
persistent acne is related to an underlying lack of this vital micronutrient, bringing your zinc levels back to normal may also help cure
your acne. And it may do it as effectively as the antibiotic tetracycline, the standard treatment you may now be on. Since tetracycline
can have significant side effects, a natural solution for some acne
sufferers is a real advantage.

If you are an acne sufferer who does not have an underlying zinc
deficiency, you can use the healing power of zinc in another way:
Zinc-oxide ointment applied to your skin can help tremendously,
especially if your dermatologist combines it with the use of antibiotics. The zinc seems to put a damper on the inflammation and reduces
the skin's production of oils that clog your pores, creating the ugly
red pustules.

Male potency and sex drive. Lots of miraculous claims have been
made for zinc's benefits for male sexuality. As with vitamin E, there
is often more fiction than fact in these reports, but they are based on
a foundation of truth. A mild zinc deficiency does lead to a low
sperm count, and a more severe lack can cause the male sex glands,
the testes, to atrophy. In one study of impotent men, it was found
they had low zinc levels in their blood. Giving them supplementary
zinc not only produced significant improvement in their impotency
problems, it also raised their testosterone levels. What is clear from
research is that, when males have a mild zinc deficiency, supplements can help raise both their sperm count and their testosterone.
But its effect on potency is less clear. The most dramatic response
appears to be confined to cases of impotence where there is also a
moderate to severe zinc deficiency.

New studies indicate that zinc may even protect against **herpes,**
the painful and emotionally stressful disease caused by the simplex
virus.

Rheumatoid arthritis sufferers can also benefit from zinc. We
know that these people often have low levels of zinc, and studies
have shown that patients—even those who had not been helped by
any other kind of treatment—improved dramatically on zinc supplements. Their joints were less swollen, they weren't as stiff in the

morning, and they walked more easily than another group of patients who didn't get zinc.

The common cold, that most persistent and irritating of medical
puzzles, may even be giving ground to the wonders of zinc. This was
discovered quite by accident. A three-year-old girl who had leukemia was found by her doctors to be deficient in zinc. They began
treating her with supplements to help boost her immune system
because she suffered from severe and frequent colds. When she
couldn't swallow the tablet, she let it dissolve in her mouth. Almost
miraculously, her cold symptoms disappeared. The doctors pursued
the clue, and in a study, gave 146 volunteers who were sneezing and
wheezing from colds either a 180-milligram zinc tablet or a placebo.
They were told to suck on the tablets for at least ten minutes every
two hours, so their mouths, tongues, and throats would be saturated
with zinc. In only twelve hours, 11 percent of the zinc-treated patients became well, and by twenty-four hours twice as many of these
volunteers reported their symptoms had abated! The zinc group got
over their colds a week before those who got nothing. The researchers believe that zinc may have the power to block the multiplication
of cold viruses. While you may want to try this trick next time you
get a cold, there is one warning: The dosage most of those patients
took, adding up to some 300 milligrams, is higher than you should
take over a prolonged length of time, so after you have given the
dosage a day to work, return to your usual dosage.

THE ZINC SINK

Because zinc has such strong benefits through so many of the body's
systems, it is vital that we get enough of this crucial health-giving
mineral. Unfortunately, USDA studies show that many people don't
get the zinc they need.

This seems particularly true in the stages of life when our bodies
are growing the fastest. In the womb, a zinc deficiency may slow the
natural growth of the fetus and make the newborn baby grow more
slowly. Infants and children need zinc's many strengths for body
systems to develop well. Doctors have found that children over four,
without enough zinc, grow more slowly and have a poorer appetite.

Later on, when these children enter their teen years, zinc is one of the elements most apt to be lacking in their diets.

The consequences can become serious in a short period of time. When six young men were depleted of zinc for only two months, their hair growth slowed dramatically, their red and white blood cells decreased, their sense of taste declined, and they got more infections.

As we age, we become more and more susceptible to zinc deficiency. Many of our senior citizens—even those in the middle and upper classes—don't eat enough zinc in their diets to meet their basic quotas.

There is one final group that has to be careful. "If you drink, mind your zinc" should be emblazoned in every bar in this country. As they are for many water-soluble vitamins and minerals, alcoholics are at risk. Their bodies absorb zinc at a reduced rate, and they would be well advised to boost their supply to make up for it.

All of us should get in the habit of getting enough of this important micronutrient in our diets. Prime sources include whole grains, poultry, legumes, nuts, seeds, seafood, wheat germ, and bran. An easy, delicious way to get enough zinc is to eat products made with whole-wheat flour—they have six times as much zinc as white flour. But in addition, because zinc is so important, I recommend a Daily Optimal Dose of 75 milligrams.

Iron

When we talk about someone with an "iron constitution," we usually mean somebody who is strong, tough, and resilient. There is no better description of what this vital mineral does for your body. Iron is the element for strong blood. It is essential for the synthesis and functioning of the protein hemoglobin in your red blood cells. These cells have one of the most vital functions in your body—they take the oxygen from your lungs and pump it throughout your respiratory system, and carry that same life-giving oxygen to your body's cells and tissues. Thanks to iron, they can give you powerful, exuberant energy. But when "iron-poor blood" weakens them, your whole body suffers. You feel tired, weak, listless, and dull. Although you need iron to feel red-blooded, it does as much for the other crucial component of your blood, the infection-fighting white cells I talked about in my *Immune Power Diet*. Those cells—the lymphocytes—are the prime guardians of your resistance, and they need iron to be strong.

Iron also helps in a myriad of other ways throughout the body. You need iron to metabolize the biological wonder-workers of the B Team vitamins. It even helps keep your skin tone lustrous and ensure your healthy growth.

Because low iron is so common, doctors have given it a name. Iron-deficiency anemia reduces the ranks of your vital red blood cells. It is an indiscriminate condition, hitting even the most vulnerable among us—infants and children. One reason iron deficiency occurs so often in infants is that babies are born with only a three-months' supply of iron—just enough to get them through the first few weeks of life. After that, they need to get it from their diet. That's where the problem comes in, because some physicians have found that as many as one third of the babies they examined have some degree of iron deficiency. For a civilized, developed country, that is an incredibly high percentage—and a serious one, when you consider that even a mild lack of this element can impair the intellectual development of both babies and preschool children.

Anemic infants are more fearful and tense, fussier and less active and responsive than healthy babies. If this lack continues into school age, the children's mental processes may be so slowed that they have to be exposed to the same information several times before they absorb it as well as their iron-rich classmates.

Happily, such a serious deficit can be easily cured with a short course of iron supplements and with proper attention to dietary sources of iron. Until recently, a major concern of pediatricians and nutritionists has been whether iron supplements could deplete a baby's supply of zinc. But the most recent data found no lack of zinc in healthy, well-nourished infants taking iron supplements—so there is no excuse not to give our infants healthy, iron constitutions.

IRON MAIDENS:
WHY WOMEN NEED TO PAY SPECIAL
ATTENTION

By now, it is well known that women require more iron than men. What you may not know, though, is that iron is second only to calcium as a major mineral deficiency among American women. Each month, new laboratory evidence reveals clues about women and iron that we have never suspected.

For example, *teenage girls* have to pay particular attention to iron. Even when they consume adequate levels of iron, researchers have found, they often do not store adequate iron reserves in their bodies. Not surprisingly, adolescent girls are at especially high risk of iron-deficiency anemia. First, like most teenagers, they rarely eat according to the Nutritional Pyramid. Second, they have one factor—menstruation—boys don't have, and the strain it puts on their iron reserves is a straight road to iron depletion. Starting in the teens, women need almost twice as much iron as men because of the blood they lose through menstrual flow. But because we often don't pay attention to this life-giving mineral, one third of all young women have low iron stores.

As they enter childbearing years, women also have to watch their iron intake. Then, not only is menstruation a factor, but pregnancy adds its own nutritional stresses. Also, iron-deficient women are particularly vulnerable to Candida, the common yeast infection. While this is the organism that causes the familiar "coated tongue" when we are sick, for millions of women, it can be far more than that. It can also cause difficult, and often painful, vaginal infections. For those women, it is particularly important to give their disease-fighting cells the extra strength of iron.

Researchers have recently uncovered another, hidden way women can lose iron. Scientists at the University of Illinois have documented that when inactive women first start a fitness routine, their iron reserves drop. This may be due in part to the fact that they lose iron through perspiration. The good news is that nature has taken this into account. Usually, there is no serious effect on the blood status, and after six weeks or so, your body adapts to the new demands of exercise and your iron stores go back to normal.

For men as well as women, if you are an athlete, iron is an important mineral for you. British studies show that iron supplements can help people exercise longer, harder, and even beneficially lower their heart rate during heavy exercise. In fact, people with anemic, iron-poor blood improved their exercise ability dramatically when given extra iron.

As important as they are, there are many ways we deplete our iron reserves. In adult men and women, iron deficiency can be caused by internal bleeding produced by such disorders as ulcers, intestinal polyps, or hemorrhoids. Taking too much aspirin, or drinking too much alcohol can also contribute to iron deficiency. Strict vegetarians may be at risk for low iron because many of the elements they eat frequently—soy and milk protein, fiber, and egg albumin—can inhibit iron utilization by the body. While they may not be frankly anemic, they may also have dangerously low iron reserves. If you are exposed to high levels of lead—by living next to a major highway, or through lead-based paint or industrial chemicals—you may also be at risk for low iron because this toxic mineral can impair your use of iron, depriving your tissues of vital oxygen.

When iron deficiency is present, whatever the cause, complications are likely to follow. Many infections are more common in people with low iron, including herpes simplex and Candida. Low iron has even been linked to learning, emotional, and social difficulties among adolescents and adults.

Even if you don't have clear-cut anemia, your iron stores may be below optimal. So how can you know if you may need to boost your iron? Try this quiz:

Do your muscles feel weak?_____
Do you poop out on a mild or accustomed exercise regimen? _____
Do you regularly feel fatigued and "bone-tired"?_____
Do you pick up infections easily?_____
Is your attention span briefer, or are you less alert than usual? _____

Fortunately, all these problems can be reversed by simply adding more iron to your diet or through supplements. Many of my patients are under the mistaken impression that dairy products are good sources of iron. I don't know where this myth got started, but it persists. And as to the food that gave Popeye superhuman strength, the one you may have loathed as a child—namely spinach—it, too, has low iron availability, as do most green vegetables.

Instead, look for it in fish and poultry, and in organ meats such as liver and kidneys. Other good sources are clams, peaches, soybean flour, and beans. To make sure you get enough, I also recommend to my patients that they take a supplement, at the Optimal Daily Dose of 15 milligrams.

Selenium: The Rising Star

If there is any one micromineral that is on the ascendant, it is selenium. Over the past six months, more medical reports on the wonders of selenium have crossed my desk than on any other mineral. Every week it seems we are finding out new, tantalizing facts about its ability to help protect against cancer, stroke, and heart disease. But before I tell you about these provocative new findings, let's look at the basic tasks selenium performs in your body.

Selenium is one of the strongest mineral antioxidants. Like its vitamin counterparts in the ACE Trio, selenium slows down some of the aging processes and the hardening of your tissues that occurs through oxidation. In good supply, the element is thought to help retain the youthful elasticity of your tissues. It also cooperates with E, enhancing its potency both as an antioxidant and in giving you more antibodies—the killer proteins that fight infection. Low selenium means a less aggressive immune system.

Selenium's teamwork with E also includes some psychological benefits, at least for our senior citizens. In a rest home in Finland, when researchers gave fifteen patients supplements of selenium and E, they found that after a year, the patients were better able to care for themselves, less hostile and anxious, and more alert. In other words, their outlook on life improved. For those older men and women, that's the work of a bright star indeed.

SELENIUM AND CANCER

This is where the rising star really shines. While we do not yet have solid conclusions about the ability of other minerals to ward off cancer, selenium offers genuine promise. Selenium helps build an enzyme, glutathione peroxidase, found in all our cells. The enzyme is a powerful antioxidant and helps deactivate deadly oxygen products in our cells before they produce damage leading to malignancy.

The evidence that it works is clear. Across the United States, there is a wide variation in the amount of selenium in the soil. In areas near Cheyenne, Wyoming, with plentiful selenium deposits, the cancer death rate is 25 percent lower than that of Muncie, Indiana, where the soils are poor in the mineral. In general, research shows, the states with the highest selenium concentrations have the lowest cancer mortality rates. The correlations are so uncanny that once upon a time, high-selenium South Dakota wheat and corn was shipped as cattle feed to selenium-poor areas in Ohio in order to boost the selenium content of beef! But it's a careful balance—feed cattle grain grown in soil too rich in selenium, and they die. But today, the Department of Agriculture has found a happy medium and allows the fortification of animal feeds with trace amounts of this element. Let me suggest that we can take a lesson from those healthy, long-lived cows, by adding some extra selenium in our "feed"!

These findings were broadened when scientists mapped the selenium and cancer patterns for more than twenty countries. Guess what they found? The lower the selenium intake, the higher the incidence of cancers of the prostate, pancreas, breast, ovary, skin, lungs, rectum, colon, and bladder and of leukemia. Another study documents increases for malignancies of the esophagus and a small increase in those of the pharynx, large intestine, and kidneys—where selenium was low or absent. With such overwhelming evidence, now do you see why I call selenium the rising star?

The good news is that you don't have to relocate to Cheyenne, Wyoming to avoid cancer. You can boost your own level of this important, perhaps crucial, micromineral. For starters, check the

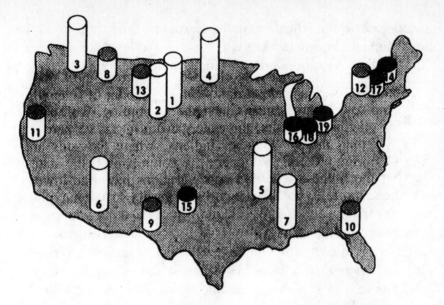

TOP SEVEN:
1 Rapid City, S.D.
2 Cheyenne, Wyo.
3 Spokane, Wash.
4 Fargo, N.D.
5 Little Rock, Ark.
6 Phoenix, Ariz.
7 Meridian, Miss.

MIDDLE SIX:
 8 Missoula, Mont.
 9 El Paso, Texas
10 Jacksonville, Fla.
11 Red Bluff, Calif.
12 Geneva, N.Y.
13 Billings, Mont.

LOWEST SIX:
14 Montpelier, Vt.
15 Lubbock, Texas
16 Lafayette, Ind.
17 Canadaique, N.Y.
18 Muncie, Ind.
19 Lima, Ohio

map above to see where your area ranks in selenium. Then you can adjust your selenium intake to fit your environment.

There is another environmental factor to consider: If you live in an area like the Northeast, which has significant acid-rain problems, that can affect your selenium. Even if the soil has good levels of selenium, the sulfur compounds in acid rain bind the selenium so that plants can't absorb it well—and it never gets to your dinner table.

GETTING TO THE HEART OF THE MATTER

Cancer prevention is not the only reason to watch your selenium intake. This shining star also casts its light throughout your cardio-vascular system. For one thing, it fortifies the heart's energy cells, making sure they get enough oxygen. And new research shows that the less selenium people get, the more heart disease they get.

A decade ago, medical researchers explained the then-mysterious heart ailment known as Keshan's disease—named for an area in Turkey where peasants were suffering from a mysterious disease that wasted and scarred the heart. It turned out that the soils in the area lack selenium, which we now understand to be the cause, and cure, for Keshan's disease.

Here in the United States, we have many spectacular natural wonders: the Grand Canyon, the Rocky Mountains, the Everglades. But there is one you may not know about, and it isn't so spectacular. It is the so-called "stroke belt," running through the Carolinas and in parts of Georgia, where strokes and heart disease are most prevalent. Not coincidentally, this is also a region where selenium content is very low. Again, the link has been borne out overseas: In Finland, where deaths from heart disease are extraordinarily high, scientists looked at eleven-thousand Finns. They found that those with a very low blood level of selenium—about one third of those studied—were more than three times as likely to die of heart disease than fellow Finns with more selenium in their blood. They also had more nonfatal heart attacks—twice as many as people with more selenium in their blood.

There is one other benefit of selenium that may be farther from our hearts, but is very dear to our hearts, if you know what I mean. I'm talking, of course, about sex. Listen up, men, because almost half of your body's supply of selenium is located in your testicles and the seminal ducts next to your prostate gland. Your sperm cells also include significant amounts of the mineral, so each time you ejaculate, you lose a quantity of selenium. That means you have to keep replacing it, to assure optimal sexual functioning.

If the researchers are right, there is hardly any part of you that isn't helped by selenium. They report it may improve your energy level, relieve arthritis and prevent cataracts from developing in your eyes, reduce symptoms of cystic fibrosis, protect against radiation and high levels of mercury, and along with its familiar partner, vitamin E, even help patients with muscular dystrophy.

OK, now that I have you convinced, where do you look for selenium? Good sources are celery, onions, brewers' yeast, radishes, broccoli, cucumbers, garlic, eggs, mushrooms, seafood, liver, meat, and kidneys. Again, it's a good idea to go for the whole grains:

Brown rice has fifteen times the selenium content of white rice, and whole-wheat bread contains twice as much of it as white bread. Just as refining of grains destroys this mineral, so does prolonged cooking —you lose almost half the selenium content of vegetables by boiling them.

SOME WARNINGS

At this point, you may well be ready to stock your refrigerator and vegetable bins full of selenium-rich foods, or start taking supplements tomorrow. But first, let me add a word of caution (you didn't *really* think such a wonderful mineral would come without strings attached, now did you?). Yes, you can overdose on selenium. In fact, in its natural state, selenium is highly poisonous (some string, huh?). Obviously, that is not true of the commercial supplements on the health-food-store shelves.

But indiscriminate use can lead to problems. If you notice a strange metallic taste in your mouth, dizziness and nausea that have no other apparent cause, lethargy, skin problems, progressive paralysis, fragile or black fingernails—even loss of nails as well as hair and teeth, or a persistent garlic smell on your breath and skin, you might be OD-ing on selenium. Acute poisoning causes fever, rapid breathing, gastrointestinal upset, inflammation of the spinal cord and bone marrow, anorexia, and even death.

Since copying machines use selenium plates and give off a form of selenium in the air, it's possible, if your job has you running a machine all day, you are getting enough—or too much—selenium.

I don't mean to make you overly concerned, but merely to emphasize that this mineral works best in specific doses. I recommend an Optimal Daily Dose of 150 micrograms.

Chromium

The last five essential minerals—chromium, manganese, molybdenum, iodine, and fluoride—are the ready-made minerals. Ready-made because you don't have to worry about taking special supplements. Yes, they are vital to your health, but since you need them only in trace amounts, you usually get enough of them in your diet. But though your need for them may be small, their range of health-promoting effects is not. Every week, new research is showing us surprising new ways these minerals work to keep us healthy, resilient, and full of energy.

Chromium serves many functions in your body. One of its main functions is to help in the breakdown and distribution of protein and carbohydrates, so your body can use those fuels. It has also been investigated as an aid to control high blood pressure and prevent diabetes. But its most important role is its direct link to your main source of mental and physical energy—glucose. By helping keep your blood-sugar level on an even keel, it helps you avoid depressions and mood swings and gives you strong, constant energy.

As you get older—and you will—your body naturally tends to lose its capacity to take sugar from the blood to nourish your cells. It is like what happens to diabetics, except that in that disease it happens very abruptly, and in aging it occurs gradually, over many years.

This is where chromium supplements may help. Researchers found that elderly people, who had trouble absorbing glucose fuel, improved when they took chromium supplements. In another study, ten out of twelve elderly people who took chromium supplements improved their bodies' ability to use their glucose fuel. This beneficial effect is not limited to seniors: Studies reported by the American Society for Clinical Nutrition report that chromium helps stabilize the body's ability to process sugar in people with abnormally high or low blood-sugar levels.

There is much we need to find out about this little-understood mineral. In one of the most interesting research avenues, some physicians now believe that enough chromium may help prevent hardening of the arteries.

There is no RDA for chromium because we don't know enough about it. But we do know that many people in other countries get a good deal more of this element than Americans do, and that most people in this country get less than one-half the level that many nutritionists recommend. We also know that chromium stores are depleted by strenuous exercise and physiological trauma, like injuries, burns, and surgery.

Clearly, older Americans have to pay special attention to chromium because our chromium supplies get lower and lower with age. That process suggests that our American diet may create a chronic chromium deficit. That may also be why older people are more likely to have problems with the body's sugar-regulating system, which chromium helps control. To reverse that trend, and guarantee that we reap the biological benefits of this nutrient, all of us should be sure to get enough of it in our diets. Chromium-rich foods include brewers' yeast, shellfish, meat, chicken, clams, mushrooms, whole grains, beer; even corn oil contains significant traces of chromium.

Manganese

Manganese is a nutritional jack-of-all-trades. It is best known as an essential element in the healthy structure of your bones. But it also plays a strong supporting role in your digestion, helping you properly digest and metabolize your food and vitamins like C, biotin, and thiamine. It also helps keep you from getting tired, keeps your muscles in good working order, and even maintains your levels of sex hormone.

Chemically, manganese performs a whole range of jobs. It helps build important compounds in your body, including thyrosin, the principal hormone of your thyroid gland, and cholesterol. Manganese plays an essential role in blood clotting. For nursing mothers, it is important in the manufacture of milk. Although it has a huge list of tasks, the manganese in your body adds up to only a minute amount—10 to 20 milligrams, stored in your kidneys, bones, liver, pancreas, and pituitary gland.

Did you get all that? If not, you may need some of this mineral, because it is also credited with improving memory, reducing nervous irritability, and generally helping keep things on an even balance upstairs. That can be useful in these stressful, harried times!

Not surprisingly, there are a number of diseases where manganese may help. We know it is useful for diabetics because it increases glucose tolerance. When combined with the B Team, this element has helped people with debilitating weakness by stimulating the transmission of impulses between the nerves and muscles. Manga-

nese also helps treat myasthenia gravis—failure of muscle coordination and loss of muscle strength. Researchers think it may even play
a role in the treatment of multiple sclerosis.

We need still more research on this micronutrient because we
know very little about all its health-giving effects. We do know,
though, that low manganese levels can affect how you remove sugar
from the blood, and set the stage for diabetes. Scientists also wonder
if low manganese may also be a factor in atherosclerosis and even in
triggering epileptic seizures.

The good news is that, fortunately, no studies have clearly shown
a deficiency in humans. As to overdose, you don't have to worry.
The most serious effect of too much manganese is probably the fact
that it can reduce the body's use of iron, so you don't want to
overdo. Other than that, there is really only one group at risk for
overdose: those who mine and refine manganese ore and breathe it
every day.

For the rest of us, who mine our manganese with our forks, look
for such "mother lodes" as shellfish, organ meats, nuts, green leafy
vegetables, seeds, and unrefined grains—particularly the bran.
Other vegetables and fruits contain moderate amounts, depending
on the soil in which they were raised. The other, very civilized,
source, is a simple cup of black tea. Because we tend to get enough in
our diet, you don't have to include it in your Micronutrient Composite.

Molybdenum

Molybdenum gets the prize for the "hardest to pronounce" mineral.
(It's "mohl-IB-du-num," if you want to impress the friends at your
next cocktail party!) If you haven't even heard of molybdenum,
don't feel embarrassed. Few of the people I treat have. And although
it sounds like some exotic metal they make rockets out of, in fact it is
a basic, essential mineral micronutrient throughout all the tissues of
your body. It helps you metabolize carbohydrates and fats for maximum energy. It also aids in preventing anemia and promotes your
general well-being. Without molybdenum, you wouldn't be able to

use iron, because molybdenum helps your body regulate its iron stores, and thus prevent anemia.

Some biochemists even report that a lack of molybdenum can lead to premature aging and impotence in older men.

LESSONS FROM THE EAST . . .

One interesting fact about the hard-to-say mineral comes from studies that show the states deficient in this element have exceedingly high rates of esophageal cancer. The same phenomenon has been documented in the Lin Xian province of China, where a lack of soil molybdenum had been linked to the highest incidence of esophageal cancer in the world. (Our friend Ho Si Ping doesn't have to worry, though—the provincial authorities in Lin Xian have now enriched the soil with molybdenum—and the rate of cancer seems to have dropped.) In South Africa, where they have a similar epidemic rate of esophageal cancer, they have found that local plants have almost no molybdenum. This connection has not been thoroughly studied, but these findings suggest molybdenum may have a tremendously important role to play in preventing cancers both of the esophagus and the stomach.

. . . AND CLOSER TO HOME

Molybdenum isn't helpful just in remote regions of Africa and China; it has a very special function for us here in our highly industrialized nation. Many of our foods are laced with sulfites, one of the most common food preservatives in developed countries. For some susceptible people, these preservatives can build up in the body and make real trouble. Reactions include diarrhea, acute asthma attacks, nausea, loss of consciousness—even fatal reactions have been reported. Ironically, one place these sulfites are particularly common is on fresh produce in salad bars used by the very health-conscious people who want to avoid preservatives. Again, molybdenum rides to the rescue because it helps create a body enzyme that can detoxify potentially hazardous sulfites. Thanks to that mineral, our salad bars are safe again!

SMILE POWER

Tooth cavities, that bane of our sweet-filled diet, may also be helped
by molybdenum. When U.S. Navy recruits from Ohio were found
surprisingly free of tooth decay, the reason was traced to the high
molybdenum content of the food they ate—straight out of that
same red Ohio soil that was so poor in selenium! Studies show that
people simply get fewer cavities with high-molybdenum diets. It's
not so surprising when you realize that tooth enamel contains a
significant amount of the mineral.

Like many other crucial trace micronutrients, molybdenum is best
taken in small doses—or better yet, gotten from your diet. If you
take too much—even a modest intake of 10 to 15 milligrams daily
—some people begin experiencing painful stiffness and swelling of
the joints, as though they had gout. That is because the mineral acts
on the same enzyme that raises the body's level of uric acid—and so
leads to gout.

Too much molybdenum can also inhibit growth of bones. One
possibility may be especially interesting to teenagers, who sometimes
experience runaway bone growth that is both physically and psychologically painful. Raising slightly their intake of molybdenum may
have the effect of decreasing growth.

For that reason, I counsel patients to stay away from supplements,
but to get their molybdenum from their diets by eating legumes,
particularly lima beans, canned beans and lentils, liver, and sunflower seeds. Whole grains are also a rich source, especially buckwheat, barley, and wheat germ.

Iodine: The Specialist Mineral

When most of us think of iodine, we think of the red stinging
solution mother put on our cuts when we were children—certainly
not something that sounds very health-giving. But if you want to
feel mentally alert and sharp, speak clearly and keep your nails, skin,
teeth, and hair in top condition, that same iodine is your ally.

Unlike many minerals, iodine is a real specialist. It performs its spectacular work in just one gland—your thyroid. Although your body contains only a minuscule amount—a mere 25 milligrams—you couldn't live without it. Iodine helps your thyroid's development and functioning, making up its principal hormone, thyroxine. Through that hormone, iodine helps regulate your body's production of energy, promotes growth and development, and stimulates your metabolism, helping you burn off excess fat.

By keeping thyroxine production optimal, iodine also helps convert beta-carotene to vitamin A, aids the synthesis of protein and the absorption of carbohydrates from your intestine—in other words, it keeps your body's energy furnace stoked with fuel.

Iodine indirectly helps your heart as well. Because it plays a role in the chemical synthesis of cholesterol, it can help head off atherosclerosis by making sure your body keeps its cholesterol within limits and preventing its buildup in your arteries. Some people believe it may help to relieve the chest pain caused by a lack of oxygen to your heart.

Without enough iodine, the thyroid, normally nestled invisibly at the base of your neck, swells to a lump the size of a baseball or even a melon. At the same time, it shuts down hormone production, throwing all your body's other systems off balance. Not surprisingly, the best treatment for the disease—now rare in our country—is iodine supplements.

The lack of this element may lead to slowed mental reactions, brittle hair, hardening of the arteries, obesity and lethargy, or intolerance to cold. Women who are pregnant or lactating need an extra dose of iodine. If they don't get enough, their children can be mentally or physically retarded. However, if these newborns are treated with iodine soon after birth, many of the symptoms are reversible.

Happily, iodine deficiencies are very rare today because most of the salt we eat in this country is iodized—fortified with this mineral. The most likely way people can have iodine problems is by eating large quantities of foods—such as cabbage and nuts—or taking drugs—such as lithium—which block thyroid hormone.

Japanese researchers have reported cases of toxicity resulting from too much iodine in the diet—in this case, people who ate iodine-rich seaweed. For most of us in this country, that's not a likely problem—at least, not until McDonald's comes out with a McKelp burger!

But there can be a problem when iodine is prescribed as medication. Then, the dosage must be carefully monitored because too much can create serious trouble. Abrupt large doses can damage a normal thyroid by diminishing the synthesis of the gland's hormones.

IODINE: THE NUCLEAR PROTECTIVE

Iodine has been in the headlines recently for its protective action against radiation, particularly after the tragic radiation-poisoning incident at the Chernobyl reactor. The way it works is simple. One of the dangerous elements in nuclear fallout is a radioactive form of iodine. Unfortunately, your thyroid gland has no way of recognizing its radioactivity, and would gladly absorb it, which could create a tumor later on. So doctors prescribe pills containing a form of iodine that is rapidly absorbed by your thyroid, filling its iodine reserves. That way, if you do absorb the lethal iodine, and it makes its way to the thyroid, it will be turned away unabsorbed, and your body will excrete it. For that reason, the U.S. government and hospitals keep a ready supply of iodide tablets, a prudent measure in case of public exposure to radiation.

After the Chernobyl disaster, my office phone lines lit up with patients asking: "Where can I get iodine to protect against the radiation?" The answer is: Don't. Unless you are exposed to a significant dose of radiation, many thousands of times the levels that were measured in our country after Chernobyl, taking iodine is likely to create worse problems than it solves. An iodine jolt can seriously disturb the thyroid gland, forcing it to close down, a much greater risk than the minuscule amount of radiation Americans could ever absorb from a faraway accident like Chernobyl.

The iodine we need in our diets comes from some delicious—and healthy—sources. Marine foods—fish, shellfish, and kelp—absorb the mineral from seawater, and are excellent sources. On dry land, mushrooms can be good sources, depending on the iodine content of the soil they are grown in. One of the other common sources is a long, cool glass of clear water—it brings iodine with it up from the earth.

Because we get most of the iodine we need, I don't prescribe an Optimal Daily Dose for this element—if you feel the need, I suggest a good seafood dinner!

Fluorine

Although fluorine may be a minor trace element, it has generated more than its share of hot controversy. Like iodine, it is a mineral specialist, doing much of its work in only one place—your mouth. About fifty years ago, it was found that fluorine—called fluoride in its normal chemical form—takes the bite out of tooth decay. It protects your teeth from cavities by making the enamel—the outer coating—tougher and more resistant to the insidious work of bacterial acids that bore into your teeth.

You may remember when dentists routinely gave fluoride treatments to your teeth. Nowadays, we get our fluoride not in the chair but from our water faucets, because most communities add fluoride to the water supply. For more than a decade, studies in many cities have proved that fluoridation cuts the rate of cavities in children by at least one half. The earlier you start drinking fluoridated water, the greater the benefits, and infants who drink the water get the best protection of all. If your community did not begin fluoridating its water until you were in grade school, your teeth were less well protected, but they still got a good head start against decay.

Today, in 1987, several hundred communities in the United States have added sodium fluoride to their water supplies as a preventive health measure. In the towns where this step has not been taken, the rate of dental decay remains high. Today, this treatment has passed from controversy to customary—in fact, what *should* be controversial is why every community does not *insist* on added fluoride—a simple, sure way to reduce cavities.

You should check to see whether your township has voted to add fluoride. If not, you have a sterling opportunity for strong nutritional action—not just for you, but for your friends and neighbors as well. But even if your community has taken steps, they may not be enough. One study of twelve cities with fluoridated water found that the fluoride content of the water varied by as much as a factor of two. In Durham, North Carolina, for example, the fluoride content of the water was only 42 percent as much as the water in Cleveland, Ohio. The total amount of fluoride you get each day depends not only on the degree of fluoridation in your locale but also on how much water you drink or use in cooking.

But water isn't the only fluoride source. We also get fluoride from food. How much depends on a whole rainbow of interlocking factors. The amount of this mineral in your diet depends on whether you consume the leaf, the root, or the fruit of plants, whether they were fertilized or sprayed with fluoride-containing mixtures, how they were processed—and, of course, whether the food was prepared using fluoridated or non-fluoridated water. All told, the amount of fluoride we get from our food can vary up to 100 percent!

BONING UP ON FLUORINE

But fluorine leaves you with more than a good smile. This mineral has a little-known attribute that hasn't received much press. Fluorine is readily absorbed, and stored in both your teeth and bones, where it enhances the deposit of calcium. The result: stronger, more solid bones. For women at risk for osteoporosis, putting fluorine on your side can be a significant help.

We now know that fluoride, along with calcium and vitamin D, can be tremendously helpful to prevent osteoporosis. Studies show many fewer cases of this bone-wasting disease in high-fluoride areas than in low-fluoride regions. Where water is fluoridated, elderly persons have much less osteoporosis. It seems that your bones grow more, and lose less calcium, if you get plenty of fluorine. People suffering from this bone-wasting condition have taken sodium fluoride and reported not only relief for their back pain but improved bone density and calcium balance. Doctors have also found that fluoride can help reduce the rate of bone fractures by almost two thirds in patients with osteoporosis. Because it is such a potent bone-growth stimulator, fluorides have also been used successfully to halt the loss of hearing that occurs in the disease known as otosclerosis, due to degeneration of a tiny bone in the middle ear.

JUST WHEN YOU THOUGHT IT WAS SAFE TO GO BACK IN THE WATER . . .

Now that you know how crucial this mineral is, I must caution you against getting too much. Deficiencies of fluorine are rare. But excessive amounts can produce some very alarming side effects. In levels of 50 parts per million—that's 2,500 times the recommended amount—fluorine can cause fatal poisoning. But don't worry. You couldn't overdose from drinking fluoridated water if you tried— you'd burst long before!

Too much fluorine unleashes a whole storm of unwanted effects. Ironically enough, when you get too much of this teeth-protecting mineral, the first place it shows is . . . your teeth. In some areas of the country, where natural fluoride water levels are very high, discoloration of the tooth enamel is a common problem. But this is only the outward sign of a more dangerous effect. In these areas, university researchers report, there are an uncommon number of babies born with Down's syndrome.

Excess levels can also disrupt your body's ability to use vitamins, retard growth, cause unwanted calcium deposits in your tendons and ligaments, even damage your reproductive organs, adrenal glands, central nervous system, brain, kidneys, and heart.

Because we get this mineral in abundant supply in seafoods, cheese, milk, tea, and cereal grains—and, of course, from the water tap—it's better to look for our fluorine at the water faucet than in the pill bottle.

The Heavies: Negative Minerals

By now, you have seen how to get your own optimal levels of bulk minerals like calcium and sodium, and trace minerals like molybdenum and manganese. Before we finish, there is one other group of minerals, the Heavy Metals.

No, I am not referring to a new type of rock music. These metals, including lead, mercury, aluminum, cadmium, and nickel, make up a class all by themselves. And for this group, the rule is simple: Avoid them at all costs.

Although they occur naturally, most of these metals we get come from toxic environmental pollutants. For some, like aluminum and lead, the amount we get in our daily lives can lead to serious problems.

Aluminum is clearly linked to the mental and psychological devastation of Alzheimer's disease. High concentrations of this toxic metal have been found in the brains of Alzheimer's disease sufferers *twelve times more often* than in healthy people. When you absorb this mineral, it makes its way to certain nerve fibers deep within the brain, and then slowly destroys them. Medical research has traced this overload to the corroding cheap aluminum pots used by many people—giving the syndrome the nickname "aluminum pot dementia."

Lead can build up over a long time because your body stores it in your bones and tissues. It has been a particular problem for children who live in houses where lead—from pipes, paint, and putty—is readily available. The symptoms of lead poisoning are tragic and insidious: The child may seem slow, tired, and listless, increasingly clumsy and unable to remember things, with a weak appetite. If it continues, lead overdose leads to vomiting, coma, even death. For adults, high lead levels can interfere with your body's oxygen transport mechanism, starving your cells of oxygen, making you fatigued, weak, and sickly.

Mercury has been implicated in serious blood-vessel disease, because it seems to erode the walls of our arteries. It also causes birth defects and a range of traumatic psychological symptoms.

Cadmium easily damages the immune system, as well as the digestive tract. Research suggests it is linked with diseases of the lungs and kidneys, and with high blood pressure. Like aluminum, it may affect your brain, causing severe memory loss.

WHERE DO THEY COME FROM?

Unfortunately, because we live in a developed country, we are widely exposed to toxic heavy-metal pollutants. That makes it all the more important to be aware of the sources of these metals in our own lives:

- If you have recurrent acid stomach, you may have gotten into the habit of swallowing over-the-counter antacids without even thinking about it. Well, think twice, because one of the main ingredients is **aluminum.** If you take them for a long time, you may open yourself up to an overdose of aluminum. And, while you have the medicine chest open, I suggest you look at the label for your anti-perspirant—it probably contains aluminum as its primary ingredient.

- Most of us cook with aluminum foil and use aluminum pots, pans, or implements somewhere in our kitchens. But if you put acidic foods—like tomato sauces, vinegars, or citrus juices—into contact with the metal, it can leach dangerous levels of **aluminum** into your food.

- Highly toxic **lead** is one of the most common pollutants. It is even added to automobile gasoline, then spewed by car exhaust into the air we breathe. Studies have shown that people living near major traffic arteries may have increased levels of lead—and an increased risk of cancer.

- Many people have favorite ceramic bowls, pitchers, or dishes, often passed down through the family. Unfortunately, certain of the glazes used in some kinds of pottery can leach **lead** and other toxic metals into acidic foods. Especially if your pottery is chipped, cracked, or otherwise blemished, it may be a good idea to replace it with new—and nonreactive—cookware.

- Do you have silver fillings in your mouth? It has been shown that these can leach **lead** and **mercury** into the body over a long period. A few experts believe that a quarter of the people with serious lead poisoning get it from dental fillings.

- Do you eat fresh-water fish more than once a week? If so, you may well be exposed to high levels of **mercury.** Mercury is a common, and deadly, byproduct of industrial processes, and too often finds its way into our water supplies—and into the fish that live in them.

- **Cadmium** is found in commercial herbicides, pesticides, and fungicides sprayed on the crops we eat. It is also found in cigarette smoke.

- When people think of **arsenic,** they think of old lace and Agatha Christie mysteries. We should just as well think of pesticides, smog, even tobacco smoke, because all contain levels of this lethal chemical.

MINERALS AND YOUR MEMORY

Because so many of the toxic heavy minerals end up in your brain, that's where some of the earliest signs of poisoning may occur. Often, those changes involve memory and retention. If you feel you are at risk, you may want to take this short memory quiz.

_____ Do you regularly have trouble recalling the names of acquaintances?

_____ When was the last time you went a whole week without misplacing something?

_____ Do you remember birthdays and anniversaries as well as you did a few years ago?

_____ If you look up a phone number, do you have to write it down before calling?

_____ Do you ever forget the name of a neighbor or family member?

_____ Has a friend, spouse, family member, or work associate pointed out memory problems to you in the last month?

_____ Have you recently felt that you are not quite as alert as you used to be?

_____ Have you had two embarrassing incidents where you forgot something important in the last month?

How many "yes" answers did you give? If you see quite a few, or if you are affected by several of the factors I listed earlier, your memory may be suffering from a toxic accumulation of heavy metals. You may want to consult your doctor. There are several methods of removing toxic metals from the body, and your own physician can help you assess if you need them, and if so, which is best suited to your situation.

Mineral Teamwork and Your Health

In these last two chapters, we have seen how each of the separate vitamins and minerals works to keep your body systems strong and vital. But I don't want to leave you with the idea that you have totally separate accounts for each vital nutrient—one for vitamin A, one for selenium, another for calcium. As you have seen all along, the micronutrient equation is far more subtle than that. Each element works in synchrony with many others, in an intricate chemical balance. For the best, and most spectacular, health and vigor, they must all work together. The next chapter will show you a glimpse into the far edge of the preventive nutrition frontier, as we look at the newest, least well-understood of all the micronutrients: the amino acids.

10.

Amino Acids:
The Nutritional Frontier

As the last two chapters have made clear, we have enjoyed a true Age of the Micronutrients in recent years. That research has been intensive and promising, and we have now begun to fill in many of the gaps in our knowledge of how these vital elements work.

But it seems appropriate to close this section with a look at the future of preventive nutrition. So in this chapter, I want to explore with you the amino acids, the substances in the forefront of current nutrition.

These essential acids are truly the outposts of the nutritional frontier. They are so poorly understood and so little researched that we have not yet established RDAs for them. Not all scientists even agree about just how many there are. Some that we have already identified have no known biological function. In short, they are largely uncharted territory, and as such, they are the most fertile field for new explorations.

Amino-acid research, now emerging from laboratories all over the world, is proving so provocative that it is clear these tiny molecules will become big-league nutritional players. Without any doubt, this will be *the* hottest field of preventive nutrition over the next few years. No other area in nutrition will open so many horizons, or promise so many hopeful avenues for safe, natural treatment as the amino acids.

Already, we know that these substances can:

- Alleviate chronic pain.
- Stabilize energy swings.
- Speed up recovery from genital herpes and prevent recurrences.
- Rebuild immune-fighting cells.
- Protect against cancer.
- Help control chronic renal (kidney) failure.
- Relieve arthritis.
- Reduce appetite.
- Help overcome jet lag.

Perhaps their most significant effect, though, comes in the psychological arena, where they can help cure depression, mood swings, insomnia, anxiety, even treat obsessive-compulsive disorders.

Vital Nutrient Necklaces Revisited

You need the diminutive amino-acid molecules to build the tens of thousands of proteins your systems need for various tasks. Carrying oxygen to your cells, building muscles, synthesizing hormones, digesting food, even thinking—all require proteins. And those proteins are made up of vital amino acids—twenty different ones in all.

You probably remember the story of the Vital Nutrient Necklaces from Nutrition 101. You saw how the large molecules of protein in our food are too big to squeeze through the fine sieve of the intestines and on to your bloodstream and cells. So these oversized molecules are broken down into strings of their component amino acids. There may be three hundred amino acids in a single molecule of food protein. Once unstrung from the protein "necklace," the tiny amino acid "beads" can move across the intestinal walls into your blood, and from there to your tissues and cells. Then, once at their destination, they regroup into their original long chains, making proteins. How they regroup determines just what that set of amino acids will do. They group one way to make the blood protein hemoglobin, another way for muscle cells, still a third to make the hormone insulin. There are thousands of such combinations, each making up a protein necessary to carry out one of the vital biological functions that keep you alert and alive.

Your proteins are constantly wearing out and need to be replaced. Your red blood cells, for example, live only about one month before their molecules are broken back down into their amino acids. Some kinds of white blood cells live only a few hours. Then their amino acids are used again, finding their way into new proteins, beginning the process all over.

A DELICATE BALANCE

With such complicated combinations and recombinations going on constantly, you can see why you must keep your amino acids balanced at all times. Only with such a balance can your body synthesize whatever proteins it needs. Since some amino acids are destroyed in the body, and others burned up for fuel, the only way you can maintain amino-acid balance is by continually adding more. That means eating regular portions of protein in your diet.

GETTING TO THE ESSENTIALS

Most of our amino acids can be manufactured by the body all on its own. But there are nine of them that your body has no way to make, so these must come from what you eat. These nine are the *essential* amino acids:

Histidine	Lysine	Threonine
Leucine	Methionine	Tryptophan
Isoleucine	Phenylalanine	Valine

Children may require one more—arginine—for their proper growth. The amounts required of each vary greatly—from half a gram of tryptophan daily for an adult man to 2.20 grams for leucine, methionine, and phenylalanine. Whatever the quotas, the Essential Amino Nine all come from the protein in your diet. To make sure of getting a correct balance, you should include at least some animal protein—a strict lacto-ovo vegetarian diet may be too low in lysine and methionine.

The rest of the amino acids—the majority of them—are the *nonessential* amino acids. The term is misleading. They are not dispensable in any way. But because your body can synthesize them, they are not an essential part of your diet.

The Mood Connection

You've seen what the amino acids are; now it's time to take a look at the wonderful things they do for you—to keep you feeling well, looking great, and enjoying bountiful, even energy. Clearly, the most significant effect of the amino acids occurs on your emotions, moods, and mental well-being.

One of the prime functions of the amino-acid beads is to build the crucial *neurotransmitters*, the chemicals that transmit messages through your brain and nerves. Research at MIT and elsewhere has quite clearly shown that the quantity and balance of these acids in the food you eat can actually determine the specific neurochemical balance of neurotransmitters in your brain. When you consider that each of these neurotransmitters plays a key role in mental states like depression, rage, boredom, attention, anxiety, sex drive, and sleep, you begin to understand the key role of these amino acids to your mental stability.

A WORD OF CAUTION . . .

Much of the excitement about amino acids is well warranted. But because this is such an uncharted area, there remains much we don't know. In general, you should proceed with caution before loading up on supplements. Along this new frontier, there are few markers or boundaries, and that has meant irresistible temptation for exploiters. They find it easiest to promote wild claims for substances where research is just beginning to break ground. And the tactic works. In

1985 alone, amino-acid supplements accounted for over a million dollars in sales.

To take one of the most obvious examples: It's no surprise, of course, that sex sells—at the health-food stores just like everywhere else. But when the aphrodisiacs being touted are the amino acids tyrosine or phenylalanine, the pitch is more marketing than medicine. The fact is, there is no clear-cut proof that either can increase sexual interest or arousal. Yet the claims continue to be made.

As unethical as the false advertising of some amino-acid pushers may be, the real worry is their megadose recommendations. In many cases, we simply know very little about long-term effects of large amino-acid doses. In excess, some of them may radically alter your brain's functioning. In one case, reported in *The American Journal of Psychiatry*, a patient took up to 4 grams a day of L-glutamine for only three weeks. He became psychotic, experiencing hallucinations, grandiose delusions, total insomnia, and an uncontrolled sex drive. Yet only one week after he stopped taking the supplements, his symptoms disappeared. Another patient taking glutamine complained of loss of sleep, hyperactivity, and highly vivid thoughts that made him feel intensely uncomfortable. Again, the symptoms went away as soon as the supplements were discontinued. Abnormally large doses of these substances, rather than helping, actually throw your amino-acid balance out of whack by increasing some amino acids at the expense of others—with serious results. The FDA has taken this collective evidence so seriously that in 1974 the agency removed amino acids from the list of substances generally recognized as safe.

So, until all the data has been collected on these newest members of the micronutrient family, I recommend that you stick very closely to what is proven and on the scientific record. In the rest of this chapter, we'll review my amino-acid files together.

This is not a complete listing of all the effects of amino acids. First of all, that would take a separate book. Second, research is moving so fast that it would be outdated before the book was a year old! But here I have selected just a few of the more exciting research bulletins. I hope it gives you an idea of the fascinating possibilities of these elements—and what further research may promise.

FOR YOUR OWN GOOD

One other safety note: For some people, keeping their amino acids in balance is not simply a matter of eating the Nutritional Pyramid quota for protein. Some people have a genetic inability to digest protein properly, or to absorb particular amino acids. The unfortunate amino-acid imbalance is called aciduriasis, and can create hypoglycemia and general suppression of the immune system. Happily, this condition can be treated by proper doses of amino-acid supplements, with very impressive results. If this sounds familiar, or you know you have some kind of protein digestive problem, *do not* take any of the amino-acid supplements I list in this book; doing so could seriously disrupt your amino balance. Instead, check with your physician before taking any dietary supplements.

Phenylalanine

Depression is more than the blues. It is a subtle, complex, and insidious disease, one that will affect one American in five at some point in their lives. Depression is a disease with a biological basis, which can ruin lives and careers, reducing smart, active people to silent, still shadows. At current estimates, it costs our nation over $6 billion each year.

Phenylalanine seems to offer some hope. In one study, 100 to 500 milligrams of this amino acid, taken each day for two weeks, completely eliminated patients' depression. These people had depression from a variety of causes—including drug abuse and schizophrenia, and some from no apparent cause. But the amino acid seemed to work equally well against the depression, lifting their mood and energy, no matter what the cause.

Pain relief. The new breed of pain medicine specialists, called *dolorologists*, have found that a form of phenylalanine, d-phenylalanine, has proved remarkably successful in the treatment of chronic pain, even when other drugs and physical therapy failed to produce relief. In one study of twenty-two patients who suffered from low-back pain, nerve pains, and postsurgical pain following back surgery,

250 milligrams of d-phenylalanine, taken three times a day for two weeks, gave significant relief and produced only minor side effects.

In another study, a man suffered from general pain in his arms, legs, and back as the result of a fracture of a particular vertebra. After five days of taking phenylalanine, he could roll over and get out of bed without feeling any discomfort. So long as he kept taking a dose of 750 milligrams a day, the relief continued. But when he tried to reduce the dosage, his pains returned. Staying on his phenylalanine regime, he has remained pain-free for a year.

Curiously, phenylalanine seems to have no effect on acute pain—the kind you feel right after you cut your finger, for example. But for chronic pain, the substance seems promising. Best of all, moderate doses of phenylalanine appear to be safe and nontoxic.

Appetite control. Have you ever found it difficult to stick to a diet because you were always hungry? If so, you may need phenylalanine. Along with another amino acid, tryptophan, phenylalanine governs the release of an intestinal hormone called cholecystokinin (CCK). This hormone signals your brain to feel satisfied after you eat. Usually, CCK starts sending its chemical "I am full" message about ten minutes after you first lift your fork to your mouth. But studies find that eaters given CCK stop eating sooner but feel just as satisfied. Because these amino acids trigger the release of CCK, having enough of them in your food may help activate your body's satiety mechanism. This could be your figure's finest ally!

Melanoma. One of the deadliest cancers known, this lethal form of skin cancer will kill almost two thousand Americans this year. For victims of this disease, it is not supplements of phenylalanine that help, but a reduction—along with reducing the amino acid tyrosine. In some way that we don't yet completely understand, these amino acids seem to nourish the malignant melanoma cells. Restricting phenylalanine helps starve the tumor. Some doctors have found that cutting back on these amino acids in their patients' diets has helped treat several forms of cancer, including malignant melanoma. They found that the tumors responded or the disease appeared to level off. However, this finding has been hard to replicate, and scientists are still exploring what dosage works best in such circumstances.

Jet lag. Following on the heels of malignant melanoma, jet lag may seem like a trifling concern. But it is an important consideration for thousands of travelers, particularly business people who must keep up a hectic schedule that takes them through a number of time zones, and remain alert for meetings and negotiations. Many resort to narcotics to ensure that they will be able to get their proper rest, and then to a stimulant to clear their minds for a hectic day. But both of these kinds of strong drugs take their toll.

Instead, amino acids may offer a safe, sane alternative. Phenylalanine converts in your brain to the neurotransmitter norepinephrine, important for alertness, memory, and learning. If you take this amino acid early in the morning or after a long dislocating flight, it may help you feel more alert and give you more energy. In order to help you regulate your body's clock when you change time zones, see the special advice under the section on tryptophan.

EASY DOES IT . . .

Though phenylalanine may be useful for a number of symptoms, be careful not to overdose. Too much of the helpful amino acid can raise your blood-pressure levels if you are sensitive. And if you are now taking any antidepressant containing MAO inhibitors, you should not take phenylalanine.

Whether you are on such medications or not, do not exceed the doses for phenylalanine that I give in this chapter.

SPECIAL NOTE: FOR PKU READERS ONLY

What is PKU? If you chose to read this note you probably already know. You, your child, or some other family member may have the genetic inability to metabolize phenylalanine properly, an inability known as PKU. If so, your doctor has probably told you to restrict your intake of phenylalanine. Obviously, you should avoid taking any amino-acid supplements until you have consulted with your doctor. As you may know, that also means you should watch out for the artificial sweetener Nutrasweet. Because it contains phenylalanine, it may raise your blood levels of this amino acid.

Tryptophan

Of all the essential amino acids, tryptophan is the least abundant in proteins, and it is also easily destroyed by your liver. But you need to make sure you have enough of it in your diet, because tryptophan is essential for your brain to manufacture the key neurotransmitter *serotonin*.

We are only beginning to appreciate all that this brain chemical does, but we know that research neurochemists have already linked low serotonin levels with such common psychological maladies as insomnia, anxiety, and depression. Among other things, serotonin regulates sleep.

AND NOW I LAY ME . . .

Sweet sleep! For some of us, it comes all too easily. And for others, tossing and turning, obsessing over a hundred worries is all too common. If that sounds familiar, tryptophan can be a terrific late-night friend. More than forty controlled studies have attested to the remarkable ability of this amino acid to help you fall asleep more quickly, to increase sleep time and reduce wakeful periods during the night. It works best for people with mild insomnia who take longer than average to leave worldly cares behind and drift off. Obviously, a natural, gently absorbed amino acid like tryptophan is a safer alternative than strong hypnotic drugs. If you have taken regular sleeping pills, you know that many of them give you a hangover, sometimes lasting all the next day. Your brain may feel cloudy and fuzzy; some people can even suffer memory loss. Research at MIT and Harvard, however, has found that tryptophan induces drowsiness at night but doesn't impair performance in the clear morning light.

Insomnia can be a special problem for older Americans, whose sleep patterns have changed as they age. Because their kidneys and livers may be less efficient than those of younger people, they cannot eliminate medications as quickly, so standard sleep medications can prove troublesome. Doctors have long been looking for better sleep aids for their older patients. For these people, again, tryptophan may be a safe, natural solution to what the French call *les nuits blanches*. One recent study showed that about a third of the patients tested were greatly helped by the amino acid—and over 90 percent of the patients suffered no side effects.

Even when insomnia comes from less natural causes, tryptophan can help. I know of a coronary bypass patient who was taking pain medication after her operation. An unfortunate side effect was severe insomnia—she got only two hours of sleep a night. Her doctors tried a number of standard tranquilizers, to no effect, and finally decided to use tryptophan as a last resort. After only a month of tryptophan she was able to get six hours of good, restful, uninterrupted sleep—the rest her heart needed to mend itself.

Tryptophan can be useful not only for insomnia but also for inducing sleep when you want to. You probably know the awful feeling when you travel to a far-off time zone and your biological clock keeps you awake and alert—even though it may be 4:00 A.M.! For those cases, and for any time when you need a safe, sure, natural sleep aid, try this formula:

Tryptophan	2 grams	(2,000 mg)
Vitamin B$_6$	100 mg	
Vitamin C	1 gram	(1,000 mg)

You should take this on an empty stomach, shortly before going to bed. The vitamins help your body convert the tryptophan to serotonin. This trick can help you reset your biological clock to any hour you please! So fasten your seat belt, and keep your tryptophan handy!

There is one note of caution, however: New research suggests that not everybody is sensitive to the sleep-producing effects of tryptophan. But for those who are, it seems a safe and benign remedy for those long, sleepness night.

Tryptophan is also proving useful in a wide range of other psychological problems:

Depression. If you are troubled by depression, and know the shadow it can throw over social activities and professional obligations, tryptophan may offer a ray of sunshine. Used in combination with drug therapy, tryptophan has helped previously unresponsive depressed patients.

Binge eating. If you are one of the people who suffers from the out-of-control binge eating known as bulimia, tryptophan may help curb your carbohydrate urges. By boosting serotonin, it resets your brain's thermostat and controls your body's craving for carbohydrate.

Unfortunately, few popular diets take this tryptophan effect into account. Ironically, most of them are designed exactly 180 degrees *wrong*. By encouraging carbohydrate-poor, protein-rich meals, these diets lower your brain serotonin levels unnaturally, and the resulting shift in brain chemistry can actually make you desire carbohydrates. When my patients show me these diets and complain that they have a hard time staying on them, I am not surprised—it's not a matter of willpower, but of biochemical programming! A far saner and more balanced way to keep your eating in check is to take a dose of appetite-suppressing tryptophan instead of binge-eating on ice cream and cookies.

OUT, OUT DAMNED SPOT!

When Shakespeare's Lady Macbeth uttered this famous lament, she wasn't referring to her pet dog or a dry-cleaning oversight. She was haunted by an obsession that she had too much blood on her hands. But any psychiatrist could see that Ms. Macbeth suffered from the classic symptoms of obsessive-compulsive disorder. No matter how many times she washed her hands, she could not feel they were clean. The hallmark is such repeated, ritual behavior. For most people, it's not a question of daggers or blood—but perhaps they take showers five times a day, or check ten times to see if they have the car keys, or return home repeatedly to make sure the stove is off. When this disorder takes its most extreme form, such people must be hospitalized. Unfortunately, the only real treatment is a variety of medications, which work with varying degrees of effectiveness.

But as we become more sophisticated in our understanding of the biologic origins of mental illness, we are learning that "natural" drugs can play a crucial role for these troubled people. It seems that obsessive-compulsive patients suffer from some deficiency in serotonin neurotransmission. The standard treatment, in fact, is to use drugs that block serotonin in the brain. But these drugs don't always work, sometimes produce side effects—and some people are resistant to their beneficial effects.

For those people, tryptophan may represent a hopeful answer. Two researchers from Brown University found that when they added tryptophan to these standard drugs, their patient improved significantly. The amino acid seems to help restore the balance of serotonin. While this was only the first hopeful glimmer for a more natural solution to this baffling disease, it was enough encouragement for the scientists to call for double-blind trials of tryptophan. If the Bard were alive today, perhaps he would have Lady Macbeth call the royal doctor and ask for some tryptophan!

FEELING NO PAIN

People suffering from chronic, unremitting pain may often have heard from doctors that "there's nothing we can find wrong—maybe it's all in your head." It now appears that there may be a germ of truth in that answer after all—and the truth is tryptophan. Preliminary evidence suggests this amino acid may be a useful friend for people suffering from chronic pain. Your sensitivity to pain is partly affected by the serotonin in your brain. When people take tryptophan in addition to their standard pain medications, they feel fewer painful, debilitating symptoms than when they use the pain drugs alone.

WHERE DO I GET IT?

The more we learn about the many health-giving effects of this amino acid, the clearer it is that we should get enough of it in our diets—in foods that provide a good dose of tryptophan in every forkful. Some of the best sources are pineapple, turkey, chicken, bananas, yogurt, and unripened cheese.

To make sure the tryptophan you eat makes it into your brain, where it is used to manufacture serotonin, it's a good idea to combine these foods with some carbohydrates (like pasta, bread, or potatoes) and keep your protein consumption relatively low—the perfect Pyramid balance. That's because carbohydrates have an effect in your body that "opens up" the brain to absorb tryptophan, whereas protein has the reverse effect.

You don't need to understand the biochemistry behind this to make good use of it. Just make sure your breakfast and lunch contain most of your daily protein, and your dinner or evening snack is heavy on carbohydrates. That will help you stay alert in the daytime, and relax and fall asleep at night—by opening your brain to the tryptophan that helps you sleep.

Your body's natural production of the hormone insulin also helps increase tryptophan absorption. If you have a weakness for Sweet Nothings—those sugar-laden confections—your insulin can careen wildly, and with it, the levels of tryptophan you absorb. That helps account for the sleepy, drugged-out feeling that follows a sugar rush. Staying away from those Sweet Nothings will help you avoid the boom-bust cycle—and keep your body's systems on a happier, healthier balance.

Lysine

Where tryptophan affects your head, lysine has received most of its popular attention for its effects on a more private part of your body. It has been shown, in some studies at least, to relieve genital herpes, that painful and difficult sexually transmitted disease. In a study of forty-five patients conducted at UCLA, daily doses of lysine not only speeded recovery, but suppressed recurrence. It seems to work by blocking the viruses' multiplication. Other researchers have not confirmed these optimistic results, but research is still going on to expand on and verify these hopeful beginnings.

It's easy to get enough lysine in an American diet. Some of the best sources are the national staples: lean meat, potatoes, and milk —low-fat, of course!

Tyrosine

Inside your brain right now are two crucial neurotransmitters that couldn't function without this amino acid. One is *adrenaline*, and the other is *dopamine*. Adrenaline is well known as the "fight-or-flight" chemical that regulates anxiety, alarm, and excitement. Dopamine, though less famous, may be the most important neurotransmitter of all in keeping your mental functions—like alertness, learning, and memory—healthy. It also seems to play a role in your sex drive. How your body uses each of these vital chemical messengers is directly linked to the tyrosine in your food. Medical explorers are finding more and more promising ways tyrosine can help us.

A research team headed by research physician A. J. Gellenberg at Harvard Medical School has used tyrosine successfully to treat chronic depression. Substantial improvements in the patients' moods were achieved simply by raising the levels of this chemical in their diets. In another report, two long-depressed patients who had not responded to antidepressants or electric-shock treatments were given tyrosine supplements of 100 milligrams once a day before breakfast. Both improved dramatically. One was able to be removed from amphetamine therapy, and the other could greatly reduce his dose of this dangerous drug. Tyrosine appears to be both effective and free of serious side effects. If further research bears this out, tyrosine may become a new, natural alternative to today's potent antidepressant drugs. When you consider the lives that could be turned around, this is no small tribute for this amino acid.

Again, because research is preliminary, you don't want to run out and start taking—or recommending—tyrosine. We know, for example, that it can affect blood pressure under some circumstances. That may be helpful, and several medical centers are now researching to find out whether the amino acid can help people suffering from abnormally high, or abnormally low, blood pressure. But until we know more, you may get yourself into trouble by using this amino acid carelessly.

NOTE:

If you are now taking MAO-inhibiting antidepressants, DO NOT TAKE tyrosine, as it can have serious effects on your blood pressure.

Cysteine

When Ponce de Leon went looking for the fountain of youth, he might have saved himself a lot of trouble if he had only had a bottle of this amino acid. Research from Eastern Europe suggests that when mice and guinea pigs get extra doses of cysteine, they live longer. This may be because cysteine contains sulfur that inactivates free radicals. Since animal research is the first step in scientific experimentation, these discoveries may be the first step to some very interesting results.

There is also some tantalizing research suggesting that this amino acid may help guard our bodies against the ravages of chemical pollutants: smog, fumes, chemicals, and additives in our food and water. Again, this effect may be due to the fact that cysteine is an antioxidant and strengthens our own body's line of defense against toxic substances.

Other research is being conducted on several fronts: cysteine to promote hair growth, to boost the immune system, to decrease the health risks of drinking and smoking and even block the symptoms of reactive hypoglycemia.

AND NOW FOR A DOSE OF REALITY . . .

Such a supposedly wonder-working amino acid *must* have some side effects, right? Indeed: It can contribute to kidney stones. Vitamin C should be taken along with cysteine to help prevent bladder and/or kidney stones. This amino acid is also risky for diabetics because it may interfere with insulin production and absorption. Some physicians warn, too, that cysteine may increase some peoples' sensitivity to MSG, the food additive often found in Oriental cuisine.

To be safe, since our information on cysteine is so new, it's best to take it only under a doctor's supervision. But keep your eyes open—

I predict we can look forward to some very interesting findings to come for this one!

Valine

You may never have heard of this amino acid, but your healthy growth depends on it to some degree. We know that lab animals—rats, to be specific—absorb much more valine when they are babies and growing fast than when they are grown. Scientists think valine may work this way in the human animal as well. Malnourished babies who do not grow normally often have a weak, underdeveloped digestive tract, which makes it hard for them to absorb amino acids. Valine seems to be of critical importance to these infants, especially during periods of rapid growth.

Methionine

There are some early claims being made that this essential amino acid can help wash out fatty substances from your system. If this research proves true, we may someday be able to use methionine to reduce fatty deposits that would otherwise clog arteries and produce heart disease.

Clearly, methionine does have some beneficial effects on fats. For one thing, we know that it can help prevent fatty infiltration of the liver. One of the other things we know about methionine is that it can be destroyed by overuse of alcohol.

Until we know more, I suggest you get your methionine from safe dietary sources: liver, milk, fish, and eggs.

Taurine

There is increasing evidence that taurine is an important regulator of various nerve and muscle systems, and it may be essential for proper growth. Early research indicates that it naturally regulates calcium, helps protect the heart, and can even balance cardiac-muscle chemistry. Taurine may also reduce the risk of bile stones.

Perhaps the most exciting finding about taurine has already been put to work helping epileptics. Since taurine reduces electrical activity in the brain, it can help prevent the seizures and convulsions that plague these patients. Several researchers have already predicted that taurine can significantly decrease epileptic seizures, and may even help in other brain disorders, including the tragic disease Huntington's chorea.

Arginine

This hot item on the food-supplement market has had all sorts of claims made on its behalf. Let's take them one by one. **Arginine burns fat while building muscle.** This claim has made arginine the darling of body-builders, athletes, and dieters, who are swallowing it like crazy. This seems to be based on a half-truth. One study found that arginine in combination with lysine did cause the release of growth hormone—but arginine alone did not do the job. And although arginine does have a stimulating effect on human growth hormone, there is little evidence that it significantly reduces fat stores.

Anticancer and immune-system stimulator. It appears that the growth hormone affected by arginine not only stimulates the thymus but has also been found to produce a significant antitumor effect in laboratory animals. A study in mice has shown that arginine supplements stimulate the thymus gland, one of the primary immune-system organs and various processes of this gland that are linked to enhanced immunity. They found that when cancer-prone mice were fed arginine in their water, they took longer to develop tumors, had fewer, smaller tumors, and were better able to fight off the cancers they got. Ironically, the same substance that is necessary for optimal growth of normal tissue may also be capable of holding back tumor development.

A study in humans taking arginine for only a week showed dramatically increased activity of the lymphocytes, the immune fighting cells that respond to infections. They found arginine nontoxic, with no serious side effects. Clearly, this amino acid may be able to help people who need an extra immune boost: those after surgery, with infections, even victims of AIDS and other immune-deficiency diseases.

Wound healing. Arginine has been shown to speed up wound healing in rats. Researchers from Albert Einstein College of Medicine suggest that patients hospitalized for various injuries might well benefit from increased levels of arginine in intravenous feedings.

Increased fertility in men. Men need arginine for normal sperm production. Research suggests that daily doses of this amino acid can help men with low sperm counts. In one study, 80 percent of the men had moderate to marked increases in sperm count and motility —and with clear results: When the study was published, twenty-eight pregnancies were confirmed!

A WORD TO THE WISE

Arginine is plentiful in various nuts, chocolate, and raw cereals. But taking too large a pure dose in supplement form can give you diarrhea, make you nauseated, and may even promote herpes. Children should not take supplements at all because these supplements may affect normal growth and development. Although children need arginine to grow, it should come from their diet, not from supplements. And adults should not experiment with the large doses used in these studies. They were considered safe for only short periods of time in extremely sick people who were under the constant supervision of doctors. We have not yet established safe supplement levels for healthy people. As with so many amino acids, we are eagerly awaiting the latest bulletins from the research frontier.

Tyramine

Often the problem is not too little of an amino acid but too much— specifically, of the wrong ones. Tyramine is one amino acid it's easy to overdose on. Found in large quantities in foods like avocados, sour cream, aged cheese, beef, Chianti wine, pickled herring, and beer, this chemical competes in your brain with beneficial *tyrosine*, which helps create serotonin. The more tyramine you eat, the lower fall your levels of vital serotonin. If you are susceptible to migraines, overgenerous consumption could trigger an attack. That is why migraine patients should avoid the trouble foods listed above.

The Micronutrients of Tomorrow

I have included much of this information in order to give you a glimpse of the exciting discoveries now being made in the laboratories of preventive nutrition. But while I may have convinced you that amino acids are the next generation of micronutrient superstars, don't rush to become a groupie.

I've included them here to give you an idea of the exciting things to come, not to encourage you to self-dose. Watch for further developments in responsible sources. You might want to start a special file for the clippings you find, or jot notes in this book next to each amino acid. That way you can keep pace with groundbreaking developments. Stay tuned! There's so much more to come. . . .

11.

Eating Your Way to Health

===

"All I ask of my food is that it doesn't harm me."
—Michael Palin,
Monty Python

You can now take your new-found knowledge about nutrition and start applying it in your own life. In fact, if you didn't read one page farther, and just put into action what we have discussed so far, I know that you would observe tremendous, positive changes in your health and well-being. In just a few weeks' time, not only will you feel lighter and more energetic, not only will you feel your body coming back into tone, but your mental state will be clearer, sharper, more relaxed. It's an easy guarantee to make, because it is backed by Mother Nature's own flawless biological engineering!

But now there is one final phase to creating the most individualized possible nutrition plan, and that is understanding your own food sensitivities. If you read my *Immune Power Diet*, you may already know the terrific improvement that this change can bring to your health and energy. For you, this chapter is a chance to review these important ideas, and learn about new research developments that have appeared since I wrote that book.

Eating for Health, Not Harm

The basic idea of food sensitivities, or intolerances, is really quite simple. Each of us has a group of foods that react with our own unique biological makeup in specific, negative ways. In the *Immune Power Diet*, I talked mostly about those reactions in terms of your white blood cells, which can self-destruct when they come into contact with your own particular set of "trigger" foods.

Through most of this book so far, we have talked about a variety of wonderful, nutrient-rich foods: wheat, fish, green leafy vegetables, beans and peas, fruits of all sorts, nuts—the list is as wide as your nearest supermarket. They are just the kinds of foods our mothers always told us: "Eat, eat, it will make you strong!" Intuitively, our mothers knew what they were talking about. After all, those foods are wholesome, balanced, and nutritious.

But the hidden key factor—one our mothers definitely didn't know about—is that all of those same foods can, for a given person, unleash physiological and psychological symptoms in the form of allergic or food-sensitivity reactions. In fact, according to a report from the Institute of Food Technologists, reactions "have been linked to virtually every food in the American diet." This is one case where what Mom *didn't* know can definitely hurt you.

Each time you eat one of your hidden trigger foods, it can react with elements in your blood. It may release histamines, the body's own protectors, in a classic allergic reaction. Or the reaction may be more subtle, setting off a chain of unwelcome side effects. No matter the kind of reaction, it can have wide-reaching results.

Food-sensitivity responses are the biological equivalent of dropping a pebble into a pond—the ripples that are sent out from the initial food reaction can unbalance all the major systems of your body, unleashing all sorts of unpleasant, painful, and debilitating symptoms, in virtually every area of the body. The truth is that when we sit down to what looks like a perfectly nutritious repast, we may be unleashing powerful negative effects for our body's myriad cells— all in the name of health!

What's *Your* Food Fingerprint?

The main thing to keep in mind is that your particular set of food reactions is 100 percent unique—like everything about you. One person may respond to wheat, dairy, beets, and beans, another to barley, mustard, legumes, and soy products. A third may react to none of these, but have a terrible time with cabbage, almonds, and celery.

We do not know just *why* a food may cause a severe reaction in one person, yet be harmless for someone else. But the fact that it does happen is quite indisputable. Studies show that even children raised in the same homes, eating the same food, develop distinctly different food sensitivities. The way I explain it to my patients is that your own constellation of food sensitivities makes up a sort of molecular fingerprint, distinctive and all your own.

NO TWO SNOWFLAKES

It's not too surprising, when you think about it. Science has repeatedly proved the infinite variation in human biology. The DNA coding in each of our cells that makes us who we are is ours alone. You all know that your fingerprints are so individualized that there is no set anywhere in the world that matches yours. So, too, your voiceprints and teethprints are all unique to you and you alone. The more we learn, the more we see that such individuality extends through every corner of your body. In a new discovery last year, researchers found that the pattern formed by the tiny network of blood capillaries at the back of each human eye is absolutely one-of-a-kind. They are now putting this space-age discovery to use as a means of identification in top-security military inspections.

In short, in every expression of our biological systems that we know about, each of us is a wholly different, wholly unique entity. So is it any surprise that our cell biochemistry—that unbelievably complex interaction of scores of biological organ systems—is also highly individual?

But unlike our fingerprints, our food-sensitivity patterns shift over time. We seem to acquire, and lose, sensitivities depending on the dose we get of a given food—that is, how often we eat it. Once upon a time, in the prehistoric age before the supermarket was invented, nature regulated this automatically, simply because most foods were available only in certain limited growing seasons. That way, we simply couldn't overdose—the food supply wouldn't let us. But today, mass industrial food production has made most foods available 365 days a year, and we eat whatever we please. But what pleases your palate may not be so good for your body, and the result is a devastating set of shifting, often elusive, symptoms. Researchers believe that this fundamental change in our patterns of eating may account for the rising numbers of people reporting food-sensitivity symptoms today.

The range of symptoms that these reactions can trigger is truly monumental. Among my thousands of patients, I have observed every one of the following symptoms. More important, I have seen every one of them disappear when the trigger food was eliminated.

Dizziness

Headaches

Feeling faint

Watery/scratchy eyes

Persistent runny nose

Ringing/throbbing in ears

Frequent ear, nose, throat, or eye infections

Bleeding gums

Irritability

Confusion

Anxiety

Crying fits

Low alertness/trouble concentrating

Abrupt mood swings

Asthma

Congested "rattling" chest

Persistent cough

Palpitations

Rapid heart rate

Nausea

Flatulence

Intestinal/stomach cramps

Heartburn

Constipation

Diarrhea

Bloated/heavy feeling in stomach

Sore muscles in arms and legs

Muscle weakness

Joint pains

Swelling in hands, feet, and ankles

Hives

Itching

Rashes

Irritated areas on skin

Excessively dry, flaky, or horny skin

Low appetite

Chronic fatigue

Difficulty falling asleep/frequent
 waking
Major weight gain in short period

Do any of these sound familiar? If you are routinely troubled by
any of these symptoms, and there doesn't seem to be a clear-cut
cause, there is a good chance that you are suffering from the telltale
mark of food sensitivities at work. Often, these reactions, though
profound at a cellular level, go unrecognized for what they are.
Often they show up as "not feeling quite right"—slightly low on
energy, a "draggy" feeling, an extra edge of anxiety or irritability. Do
you recognize yourself in that description?

The reactions are not limited just to physical signs. They can also
create emotional turmoil. In my patients, I have seen food allergies
cause debilitating headaches, insomnia, depression, profound fatigue, lethargy, irritability, raging hyperactive outbursts, seizures,
forgetfulness, inattention, anxiety, and loss of appetite or sex drive.

GULP—IS HE TALKING TO ME?

In a word—absolutely. I am virtually certain that you have several
major food intolerances, *even though you may not recognize them.*
How can I be so sure? In my years of practicing medicine, I have seen
only a tiny handful of patients who did *not* have several clear,
measurable reactions to specific trigger foods. All of the rest of them
—over 99 percent—tested positive. Yet most of those men and
women had never before dreamed that food intolerance was the root
of their medical woes.

We have no way of knowing how many thousands of people have
found themselves tagged as hypochondriacs and neurotics because
they suffer from hidden food responses that their doctors do not
know how to diagnose. I do know, however, that as a practicing
physician, I have seen patients who have been bounced among as
many as twenty doctors without success. My office waiting room is
full of people who have been referred with a variety of diagnoses that
could fill a medical text. They have gone on a fruitless quest, making
the rounds of the most prestigious clinics, the most eminent special-

ists, and been told the same thing: "There's nothing wrong with you."

Yet once they identify their own allergy foods and carefully eliminate them from their diets, these men and women often find themselves transformed. Their symptoms dissipate, their mood lifts, their mind clears, and they regain a strength and energy they had long-since forgotten.

WHAT'S ALL THE FUSS ABOUT?

It is strange to me that the subject of food intolerance generates such heated controversy in medical circles. After all, we have long known that there is a core of adults—about 5 percent—who suffer from classic food-allergic responses. These people usually know it—they may break out in hives when they eat salmon, or get violently ill if their dinner has beets in it. As I said, these allergies are a different phenomenon from food intolerance or sensitivity. Because they are mediated through the allergic branch of the immune system, their results are usually acute; sometimes, even fatal.

But these most severe reactions are simply the tip of the allergy iceberg. The kind of intolerance responses I am talking about here are not the violent, gut-wrenching, acute kind. They are the next step down the sensitivity ladder. For every one full-blown allergy that we *do* recognize in our diet, I believe there are several other hidden ones.

Because they occur along a different biological pathway, they are more likely to result in chronic, ongoing symptoms that do not take their toll in dramatic emergency-room events, but creep up insidiously over weeks, months, even years. These cumulative, chronic food intolerances can undermine our health and sap our well-being. You only have to glance at the symptoms I listed above to see what I mean.

Not one month ago, I read a report prepared by the experts' panel of the Institute of Food Technologists. Their conclusion: "True food allergies represent only a fraction of the individual adverse reactions to foods."

Yet many physicians still don't accept the overwhelming evidence. The same doctors who easily accept the idea of allergies, because they learned about them in medical school, seem unable to grasp the wide-ranging effects of the more subtle food intolerances. They refuse to believe these represent a real, and significant, problem. I just wish these people could sit for a week in my waiting room, seeing the steady line of patients who know from their own lives just how real, and crippling, these food reactions can be.

Such medical skeptics point out that since we can't explain how food intolerance works, it can't be real. Using that logic, we'd have to throw out an awful lot of modern medicine! The fact is, we don't really understand how aspirin does all it does, and we have yet to fully comprehend the mechanism behind the anesthetic you get during surgery. But still we know how to use them, and do so routinely, helping millions of people every year.

In much the same way, there is much we still have to understand about food intolerance. I am the first to admit that more research must be done. As you will see, there are some very promising leads now coming out of very eminent laboratories, as biologists and doctors explore these complex responses. If you ask me, that research can't happen soon enough—it is high time to separate the hard science from the hoopla, and quiet the critics who have not seen the wonders this treatment can mean for people. That would certainly make *my* job a lot easier!

But all this controversy over how it works is far less important than the fact *that* it works—with clear and stunning results. What is crucial, and unmistakable, are the dramatic improvements patients experience every day in my office. Can we guarantee that it will help absolutely everybody? No, nothing in medicine comes with such guarantees. But has it given an awful lot of relief to an awful lot of people? Judge for yourself:

One of the most dramatic cases I ever saw was Jeannine. A general nurse at one of the finest hospitals in Ohio, Jeannine had suffered from extremely painful, debilitating arthritis in her arms and legs for two years. Because of her job, she had access to some of the nation's finest medical and rehabilitation services, but they could do nothing for her. She was only in her mid-thirties, but was seeing hands, once deft and firm, grow gnarled, puffy, and frozen with the increasing pain of her progressive disease. The pain in her legs had become so severe that she had been forced to give up her job. When it rained, she couldn't even get out of bed.

When she came to me, she needed leg braces to walk. Every one of her joints was bulbous and red with painful swelling, and hot to the touch. To control her agony, she was taking a massive dose of potent painkillers every day.

Her symptoms were so widespread, and so severe, that I immediately suspected food sensitivities. A series of blood tests confirmed my hunch. Jeannine was extremely reactive to a wide range of foods she was eating almost every day. Wheat, eggs, certain beans, chocolate, and dairy products. In her case, her diet meant the kind of agonizing symptoms that had brought her, on the verge of despair, into my office. Her treatment was clear: a diet designed to remove those hidden harmful foods from her plate and substitute for them foods that she didn't react to.

I put her on a strict food-sensitivity diet. Within ten days of starting the regime, she called to tell me her symptoms had completely disappeared. The swelling was diminishing, her limbs were again regaining their mobility, and best of all, she was able to stop taking the painkillers entirely. When I last heard from her, she had gone back to work in the children's ward of the hospital.

NEWS FROM THE RESEARCH HORIZON

Happily, we don't have to rely simply on these success stories. Since I researched and wrote the *Immune Power Diet*, a raft of new and promising studies has appeared. Slowly we are beginning to fill in the gaps in our knowledge about the subtle—and not-so-subtle—links between hidden food reactions and our physical well-being.

What we are now finding in the research laboratories is completely changing our traditional thinking. To take only one example, look at the new research on migraine headaches. This field, more than any other, demonstrates the fast-breaking discoveries now coming from the food-intolerance frontier.

- In a hallmark British study from the Hospital for Sick Children, physicians tested eighty-eight children with severe migraine problems. When they put them on special diets, taking food sensitivities into account, the results were little short of remarkable: *Eighty-two out of the eighty-eight children* had no further symptoms whatsoever—a diet success rate of 93 percent!

- At the University of Chicago Medical Center, John Crayton, M.D., associate professor of psychiatry, compared forty-five psychiatric patients with a history of food-linked symptoms with a group of twenty healthy volunteers. Over an eight-day trial 70 percent of the patients showed highly significant mood changes correlated with what they ate. These patients became anxious, fatigued, irritable, depressed; they even had trouble thinking clearly. The worst reactions occurred when they ate the trigger foods wheat and milk. Further tests on the patients' blood showed significant changes in the patients' immune systems when they ate the trigger foods.

- California's prestigious Langley Porter Psychiatric Institute is often in the research vangard. There, psychologist David King is mapping the relationships between food and mood. His preliminary findings indicate that when people eat minute portions of certain foods, they show a definite emotional response: Sometimes their moods go up, but often they report feeling dulled, irritable, or depressed.

- At the Texas University Health Sciences Center in El Paso, a study of over forty migraine sufferers reported that one third of them improved dramatically when they went on special, allergen-free diets.

- Finally, a joint study from premier headache clinics at the Chicago Medical School and the National Hospital in London went straight to the top. They polled over three hundred leading headache specialists to find out what they thought about the connection between diet and migraines. The answer was clear: Dietary factors *do* play a role. How big a role? The answers varied. Most of the doctors said it was a factor for one migraine sufferer out of every five—but some experts felt that as many as *four out of five* of their patients' attacks could be traced to diet.

The doctors even agreed on the most common trouble foods: chocolate, alcohol, cheese, monosodium glutamate (MSG), nuts, citrus fruit, meat, coffee, nitrates, fish. Lower down on the list came dairy products, onions, hot dogs, pizza, wheat products, bananas, tomatoes, apples, and various vegetables. You may already know that list—many of them are foods I cite in my earlier book.

Migraines aren't the only area where we are making progress. Researchers from the Royal Postgraduate Medical School in London report a case study of a patient who had an eleven-year history of progressive, crippling rheumatoid arthritis. A mother of three, she had watched her life fall apart as she tried every drug and cure, all to no avail. The physicians investigated her diet and found a strong response to cheese and dairy products—foods she craved and ate daily. (We don't know why such cravings are so common with food sensitivities. One theory, from Swiss research, suggests that intense carbohydrate cravings, especially in obese people, may be due to low levels of a brain protein, 5-HT, which is in turn caused by low tryptophan in the blood.) Whatever the exact mechanism, many of my patients crave just the foods to which they have powerful sensitivity reactions.

When she stopped eating those foods, her symptoms abated markedly. After ten months, she tried eating them again—and the painful joint symptoms returned. Blood tests showed highly elevated levels of allergic elements in her blood, and high levels of red-blood-cell damage. Since then, she has been put on a diet to eliminate these trigger foods once and for all, and she reports being well and fully mobile, leading an active life, free of pain and medication.

- At the University of Melbourne, Australia, researchers tested a group of women arthritis sufferers. When they fed them certain challenge foods—including eggs, wheat, potatoes, and beef—the patients' joints became inflamed, swollen, and very painful to move. Blood tests showed a radical change in blood levels of certain inflammatory agents. The researchers hypothesize that for some people, these trigger foods signal blood-platelet cells to release a chemical that strongly increases inflammation.

- Just two months ago, the prestigious British journal The Lancet reported a blind trial where forty-nine subjects with severe rheumatoid arthritis were put on dietary restrictions. They found that on a special diet, controlling for common trigger foods, the people reported fewer stiff joints, shorter periods of morning stiffness, and a general improvement. Statistically, the results were very impressive: Forty percent of the patients reported less pain, day and night, on the controlled diet!

These are just a few examples from my research files. Rarely does a week go by that I don't hear of some new intriguing study, some promising link being drawn. In a very real way, academic researchers are just now catching up to what those of us on the front lines of medicine—the doctors who see large numbers of private patients— have long acknowledged: What you eat can have profound effects on virtually every system of your body.

Putting This to Work for You

Now that you know the facts, it's clear what the next—and final— step is in becoming your own nutritionist. You need to determine *and eliminate* your own trigger foods. There are many complex scientific tests physicians use to determine allergies, and which one works best is the subject of a heated, ongoing debate.

The real truth is that each test has its own set of assets and liabilities. Over time, more and more sophisticated and reliable tests are being perfected, and there is no question that we are far from having the ideal test for the full range of food allergies and sensitivities. The chart below lists the various popular kinds of tests now available. But all of them, from the simplest to the most sophisticated, have one thing in common: They are done in laboratories, clinics, doctors' offices, and hospitals. That means they are of tremendous help to physicians and their patients, but they can't help you be your own nutritionist.

TYPE OF TEST	ADVANTAGES	DISADVANTAGES
Scratch-type skin tests (given on arm or back)	Easily available Standardized interpretation	Long, time-consuming Expensive Inaccurate, may miss hidden sensitivities Reactions can block each other

TYPE OF TEST	ADVANTAGES	DISADVANTAGES
Sublingual test (under the tongue)	Symptom-specific Highly reliable	Time-consuming May miss some hidden food sensitivities
IgG RAST (radioimmunoassay)	Highly sensitive Very reproducible Measures antibody reaction	Very specialized Expensive Requires sophisticated laboratory
Cytotoxic (blood sample)	Rapid results No unnecessary patient reactions Sensitive to subtle reactions	Not highly reproducible
Isolation Test (in hospital)	Best in severe cases Symptom-specific	In-hospital Time-consuming Very disruptive Expensive

Happily, there is one very effective means by which you can determine for yourself very precisely which foods may cause trouble for you. It is similar to the last test on the list, the isolation method, and relies on two simple, scientific principles.

First, that the best test is your own body, so the idea is to allow your body to show you which are the foods it reacts to.

Second, that to see your reactions clearly, you must eliminate the confusing variables, and then look closely at each factor alone. That means changing your diet to eliminate common food-allergy trigger foods for a period, then reintroducing them one by one, so you can clearly identify which food has which effects.

Not long ago, this was the accepted way for doctors to test people with severe food allergies. The people would check into a hospital for three weeks, during which time everything that they ate, drank, breathed and contacted was carefully controlled. The idea was to wipe the body's slate clean, removing everything from the environment that could possibly cause allergic reactions. Then, by reintroducing foods one by one, the doctor could pinpoint the cause of the problems.

Unfortunately, most of us don't have a spare three weeks to shut ourselves off in a controlled hospital environment. Even if we did, few of us could afford the expense of such exhaustive tests. But the good news is, you don't have to. You can easily create a very similar sort of test on your own terms—at home, at work, during the course of your daily life.

It follows exactly the same three-step principle:

The first is the **Avoidance Phase,** when you stop eating the likely danger foods altogether. A three-week avoidance diet is optimal. That length of time gives your system a chance to clean itself out, and plenty of time for any residual intolerance symptoms to die down. At the end of this chapter, you will find my suggested three-week avoidance-phase diet plan, which uses the perfect balance of the Nutritional pyramid as well as removing the most common food-intolerance trigger foods.

The seven most common foods, and the ones that this diet builds out of your life, are:

Cow's milk products
Wheat
Brewers' and bakers' yeast
Eggs
Corn
Soy products
Cane sugar

SOUND FAMILIAR? EXPERIMENT!

If you read the *Immune Power Diet*, much of this will sound familiar. But there are several crucial differences.

- Unlike my earlier book, this plan has been formulated in exact accordance with the Nutritional Pyramid percentages, so it represents a perfectly optimal balance of macronutrients. That way, you can use it not only as a guide to help you during the Avoidance Phase but as a general model for a well-balanced nutritional regimen.

- It also relies on some of the more current research I cited earlier in this chapter, confirming the role of the principal food-sensitivity trigger foods.
- If you have already gone through the Avoidance Phase, you can use this time to broaden your testing, going beyond the seven basic trigger foods.
- Try experimenting beyond the original list. Do you notice any other foods that you feel may be triggering problems? Below is a list of other common foods that often trigger sensitivity responses. I have not pinpointed these foods by reading laboratory research reports—because there aren't very many. Instead, the results have been validated again and again over my years of clinical experience. From treating so many patients, I have learned that these represent the next set of common foods that seem to cause a wide range of sensitivity problems. If you see foods here that you think may be affecting you, try tailoring your *own* elimination regime, building these out of your life—and seeing what changes you enjoy in your health, attitude, and energy.

EXPANDED LIST OF FOOD-SENSITIVITY TRIGGER FOODS

chocolate	soybeans	pizza
cocoa	meat, especially beef	potatoes
alcohol	coffee	paprika
cheese	tomatoes	zucchini
nuts	apples	cottonseed oil
citrus fruits:	fish	squash
lemons	white onions	bananas
limes	eggplant	
oranges	bell peppers	
tangerines	hot dogs	
grapefruit		

Foods containing additives like sodium nitrate, sodium nitrite, monosodium glutamate (MSG), sulfur dioxide, sodium bisulfite

A Word About Yeast

Yeast is such a common, and powerful, food-sensitivity culprit that it merits a moment's special discussion. Yeast is an animal—a tiny organism that multiplies, making things rise and bread smell wonderful—but it can create all sorts of problems in the body. Because all of us are exposed to yeast all the time; it actually lives in our bodies—one of our myriad of microorganism hitchhikers. Normally this is not a problem, but it can get out of control, causing all sorts of problems. Many women know this because they are prone to yeast infections in the vagina, which occur when the body's normal balance is disrupted and the yeast organisms multiply out of control. This is the same thing that happens in certain mouth infections—the "coating of the tongue," or thrush—which can occur in everything from a common cold infection to AIDS.

While nobody ever sits down to eat a handful of yeast, it is present in a huge range of the foods and drinks we consume every day: baked goods of all sorts (yes, bread and cookies, too!), all sorts of alcohol, vinegar, pickled or fermented foods, most cheese, mushrooms, dried fruit—the list of yeast foods goes on and on.

Yeast needn't cause problems in moderation, but we get such large quantities of it in our modern diet that it can create a wide range of emotional and physical problems. I find that many of my patients who complain of depression, irritability, or fatigue are in fact intolerant of yeast. Often, when they alter their diets, the emotional cloud that has been hanging over their lives seems to lift. The range of physical symptoms includes every part of the body: headaches, indigestion, aching joints, fatigue, and vaginal infections, to name but a few. I strongly suggest that you make yeast—in all its forms—one of your test foods, and see if you aren't surprised by the results! For your health's sake, it's well, the *yeast* you can do!

If you are new to the Avoidance Phase, there is one caution. In the first few days you may feel somewhat worse. You may find yourself wondering: "What kind of a strange plan is this?" All I can tell you is, don't worry, that's natural. It happens with every kind of addiction we know about—coffee, heroin, tobacco, even pharmaceutical drugs. In this case, it is due to the fact that your body has gotten accustomed to "fighting" foods to which you are sensitive. When, all of a sudden, they are no longer there, it takes your body awhile to adapt and turn off your defensive response. In short, it's doing exactly what it should be doing.

However, that may be scant comfort at the time, because withdrawal symptoms can be unpleasant. They may show up as worse versions of exactly the same problems you noticed at first: Headaches may worsen, you may have increased nausea, stomach or joint pains, irritability, or trouble sleeping. You should take those as confirmation that the Avoidance Phase is working. In a few days, your body will adjust, the symptoms will pass—once and for all. Remember: This "withdrawal" is really a "deposit" on a lifetime of better health!

Step Two: Challenge Phase

In the second step you introduce, one at a time, a series of these same trigger foods back into your diet—and watch what happens. Whether you are reintroducing foods from the seven frequent trigger foods, or from the expanded list, or whether they are completely different foods that you chose to test your own reaction, the key is to monitor your reactions very carefully. If you're like most people, you will notice a sharp recurrence of symptoms upon reintroducing certain foods. It may be wheat or dairy products or squash or chocolate, but whichever food pushes your sensitivity buttons will become obvious—just by the symptoms it creates.

For the seven frequent trigger foods, I suggest a two-week reintroduction period, reintroducing a new food every two days. That gives your body enough time to react—and you enough time to be sure the reaction is caused by the specific food. Keep a reintroduction log like this:

Food-Sensitivity Reaction Log

Avoidance Phase	Symptoms

Challenge Phase Day Trigger Food	Symptoms
1 2	
3 4	
5 6	
7 8	
9 10	
11 12	
13 14	

Of course, you aren't limited to these foods. If you suspect you have other reactions, or just want to broaden the program, you can test any seven food substances this way. For accuracy and simplicity's sake, though, I suggest you try no more than seven foods in any one test cycle.

The tricky thing about being your own nutritionist is that you will be both scientist and guinea pig. Earlier in this book, you may recall I said that nobody else knows you as well as you do. That is the basic theory behind being your own nutritionist. This testing process is where you really put that idea to work.

Nobody else can know how you're feeling, the little twinges and subtle signals your body is sending you, and how they make you feel compared to your usual state. Only you know that. *You* are the one recording your symptoms; *you* are the one monitoring your progress.

At one and the same time, you are the laboratory in which this experiment will be conducted and the one doing the measuring. At no other stage in this book are you so completely "being your own nutritionist"!

TRY THE BUDDY SYSTEM

This doesn't mean you can't enlist the aid of a friend or family member to help you. Some people find that easier, for two reasons. First, for some symptoms, especially the psychological ones, outside observers can be helpful. They may notice when you are being irritable, or anxious, or lethargic, even before you do—because you, by definition, are in the middle of it.

The second reason is more social, but equally important. Many people simply find it more fun to go through the process with a buddy, sharing observations and goals. That way, you help each other out, and you both get the practice of being your own nutrition-ist.

Put Yourself on Maintenance

This is the final stage of keeping yourself free from food-sensitivity symptoms. You have now cleaned your system out and identified which are your own, personalized trigger foods. You have, in short, designed an absolutely personalized regimen, made by you, from you, and for you. And, if you're like most of my patients, you'll find you are feeling better, more whole and vibrant, than you can remember for a long time.

Now the trick is to keep it that way. That sounds daunting—after all, if you felt better only when you didn't eat those foods, doesn't that mean you'll have to avoid them for the rest of your life?

No, it doesn't. You should avoid them for a long enough period— I usually counsel patients six months—that your body's chronic sensitivity response can calm down. After that, many patients find that they can reintroduce the particular trigger food—*but only if they eat it in great moderation.*

My patients know it as the "four-day rule": That is, you can eat a given food no more often than once every four days, interspersed with other foods. This gives the body a low enough chronic "dose" that you can maintain yourself without symptoms, yet still eat many of the foods you enjoy. It even has a side benefit—because you can't rely on a small range of foods, it broadens your eating, makes your tastes more cosmopolitan, and assures that you are getting a wide range of naturally occurring nutrients like vitamins and minerals. But best of all, it awards you a life free of the chronic, painful, nagging symptoms that you may be suffering now.

Food Sensitivity Review

1. **AVOIDANCE PHASE**—For three weeks, remove all likely food triggers from your diet, and let your food sensitivity abate.
2. **CHALLENGE PHASE**—Reintroduce trigger foods one by one, observing reactions.
3. **MAINTENANCE PHASE**—Eat none of the trigger foods for six months, then try reintroducing them, one every four days. If symptoms return, eliminate the problem foods again.

That's it—by completing this simple, three-step program, you will do as thousands of my patients have done: build food sensitivities and the troublesome symptoms they cause *out* of your life, and build *in* health, energy, and vitality.

THREE-WEEK AVOIDANCE PHASE DIET PLAN

DAY 1

Breakfast

Oatmeal (1 cup)
Sliced apple (1)

Lunch

Flaked crabmeat (2 oz)
Endive (2 cups)
Alfalfa sprouts (1 cup)
Rice cakes (3)
Apple (1)

Dinner

Broiled salmon steak (4 oz)
Brown rice (1 cup)
Asparagus spears (1 cup)
Endive (2 cups)
Baked apple (1)

DAY 2

Breakfast

All-rye crackers (4)
Sliced banana (1)

Lunch

Sardines (2 oz)
Romaine lettuce (2 cups)
Raw zucchini (1 cup)
Rye crackers (4)
Banana (1)

Dinner

Broiled halibut (4 oz)
Boiled potato (1)
Green beans (1 cup)
Romaine lettuce (2 cups)
Banana (1)

DAY 3

Breakfast

Cream of barley cereal
  (1 cup)
Prune juice (1/2 cup)
Honeydew melon (1/4)

Lunch

Cold scallop salad:
  Scallops (2 oz)
  Peppers, red and
  green (1/2 each)
  Boiled barley (1/2 cup)
  Celery (1/2 cup)
  Boston lettuce (2 cups)
  Honeydew melon (1/4)

Dinner

Sliced turkey, white meat
  (3 oz)
Boiled barley (1 cup)
Brussels sprouts (1 cup)
Boston lettuce (2 cups)
Honeydew melon (1/4)

DAY 4

Breakfast

Cream of buckwheat
  cereal (1 cup)
Orange sections (1)

Lunch

Spinach salad:
  Spinach (2 cups)
  Feta cheese (2 oz)
  Garbanzo beans
    (²/₃ cup)
  Tomato (1)
  Onion, sliced (¹/₄ cup)
Orange (1)

Dinner

Broiled chicken breast (3 oz)
Buckwheat groats (kasha)
  (1 cup)
Steamed spinach (1 cup)
Bibb lettuce with tomato
  (2 cups)
Orange (1)

DAY 5

Breakfast

Puffed-rice cereal
  (1¹/₂ cups)
Sliced strawberries (1 cup)

Lunch

Steamed vegetable plate:
  Broccoli (1 cup)
  Brussels sprouts (1 cup)
  Butternut squash
    (¹/₂ med.)
Rice cakes (3)
Apple (1)

Dinner

Broiled sole (4 oz)
Brown rice (1 cup)
Steamed broccoli (1 cup)
Escarole (2 cups)
Apple (1)

DAY 6

Breakfast

Cream of rye cereal
    (1 cup)
Grapefruit (½)

Lunch

Tuna, water-packed (2 oz)
Artichoke heart (1)
Chopped red cabbage
    (1 cup)
Romaine lettuce (2 cups)
Rye crackers (3)
Grapefruit (½)

Dinner

Broiled shrimp (4 oz)
Steamed cabbage with dill
    (1 cup)
Steamed artichoke (1)
Romaine lettuce (2 cups)
Rye crackers (3)
Grapes (½ cup)

DAY 7

Breakfast

Boiled barley (1 cup)
Canteloupe (½)

Lunch

Turkey salad:
    White-meat turkey (2
    oz)
    Boiled potato (1)
    Green pepper (¼ cup)
    Red pepper (¼ cup)
    Celery (½ cup)
    Boston lettuce (2 cups)
Canteloupe (¼)

Dinner

Scallops and green pepper
    on skewer (4 oz)
Baked potato (1)
Sliced carrots (1 cup)
Boston lettuce (2 cups)
Canteloupe (¼)

DAY 8

Breakfast

Puffed millet (1½ cups)
Orange (1)

Lunch

Spinach salad:
    Spinach (2 cups)
    Feta cheese (2 oz)
    Garbanzo beans
        (⅔ cup)
    Tomato (1)
    Onion (¼ cup)
Papaya (¼)

Dinner

Roast chicken (4 oz)
Millet with onions (1 cup)
Beets (1 cup)
Steamed spinach (1 cup)
Papaya (½)

DAY 9

Breakfast

Cream of rice cereal
    (1 cup)
Strawberries (1 cup)

Lunch

Sardines (2 oz)
Kidney beans (½ cup)
Alfalfa sprouts (1 cup)
Escarole (2 cups)
Rice cakes (3)
Strawberries (1 cup)

Dinner

Poached salmon (4 oz)
Asparagus spears (1 cup)
Brown rice (1 cup)
Escarole (2 cups)
Strawberries (1 cup)

DAY 10

Breakfast

100% rye bread, toasted
   (1)
Sliced banana (1)

Lunch

Cold shrimp (2 oz)
Artichoke heart (1)
Chopped cabbage (1 cup)
Romaine lettuce (2 cups)
Rye crackers (3)
Banana (1)

Dinner

Chopped veal (3 oz)
Baked sweet potato (1 small)
Steamed cauliflower (1 cup)
Romaine lettuce (2 cups)
Grapes ($\frac{1}{2}$ cup)

DAY 11

Breakfast

Cream of barley cereal
   (1 cup)
Sliced peach (1 med.)

Lunch

Tuna, water-packed (2 oz)
Carrots ($\frac{1}{2}$ cup)
Boiled potato (1)
Celery ($\frac{1}{2}$ cup)
Red pepper ($\frac{1}{2}$ cup)
Boston lettuce (2 cups)
Peach (1 med.)

Dinner

Sliced turkey, white meat
   (3 oz)
Baked potato (1)
Steamed carrots (1 cup)
Boston lettuce (2 cups)
Sliced peach (1 med.)

DAY 12

Breakfast

Cream of buckwheat
   cereal (1 cup)
Blueberries (1 cup)

Lunch

Stuffed tomato:
   Tomato (1)
   Millet (1 cup)
   Diced chicken (2 oz)
   Onions (¼ cup)
   Bibb lettuce (2 cups)
Blueberries (½ cup)

Dinner

Broiled halibut (4 oz)
Millet (1 cup)
Broiled tomato with
   chopped onion (1)
Bibb lettuce (2 cups)
Blueberries (½ cup)

DAY 13

Breakfast

Oatmeal (1 cup)
Apple (1)

Lunch

Sardines (2 oz)
Cold green beans (1 cup)
Escarole (2 cups)
Rice cakes (3)
Apple (1)

Dinner

Baked filet of sole (4 oz)
Baked acorn squash (½)
Steamed zucchini (1 cup)
Escarole (2 cups)
Strawberries (½ cup)

DAY 14

Breakfast

Cream of rye cereal
(1 cup)
Grapefruit (½)

Lunch

Vegetable plate:
Baked potato (1)
Steamed cabbage (1
cup)
Steamed cauliflower
(1 cup)
Banana (1)

Dinner

Broiled shrimp (4 oz)
Steamed cauliflower (1 cup)
Baked potato (1)
Chopped cabbage (2 cups)
Grapefruit (½)

DAY 15

Breakfast

Cream of barley cereal
(1 cup)
Raspberries (½ cup)

Lunch

Tuna, water-packed (2 oz)
Kidney beans (⅔ cup)
Carrots (1)
Celery (2)
Red pepper (1)
Boston lettuce (2 cups)
Tangerine (1)

Dinner

Broiled scallops (4 oz)
Boiled barley (1 cup)
Brussels sprouts (1 cup)
Boston lettuce (2 cups)
Raspberries (½ cup)

DAY 16

Breakfast

Puffed-millet cereal
  (1½ cups)
Sliced orange (1) with
Blueberries (¼ cup)

Lunch

Spinach salad:
  Spinach (2 cups)
  Feta cheese (2 oz)
  Tomato (1)
  Garbanzo beans
   (⅔ cup)
  Onion (¼ cup)
Orange (1)

Dinner

Broiled chicken (3 oz)
Buckwheat groats (kasha)
  (1 cup)
Steamed broccoli (1 cup)
Sliced tomato (1)
Blueberries (½ cup)

DAY 17

Breakfast

Rice cakes (3)
Apple butter (2 Tb)
Strawberries (½ cup)

Lunch

Salmon (2 oz)
Cold asparagus (1 cup)
Alfalfa sprouts (1 cup)
Endive (2 cups)
Rice cakes (3)
Apple (1)

Dinner

Broiled veal chop (4 oz)
Brown rice (1 cup)
Butternut squash (1 cup)
Endive (2 cups)
Applesauce (½ cup)

DAY 18

Breakfast

Cream of rye cereal
    (1 cup)
Sliced banana (1)

Lunch

Cold shrimp plate:
    Shrimp (3 oz)
    Green beans (1 cup)
    Romaine lettuce
        (2 cups)
Rye toast (4)
Grapes ($^1/_2$ cup)

Dinner

Broiled red snapper (4 oz)
Baked potato (1)
Steamed cauliflower (1 cup)
Romaine lettuce (2 cups)
Banana (1)

DAY 19

Breakfast

Boiled barley (1 cup)
Papaya ($^1/_2$)

Lunch

Tuna, water-packed (2 oz)
Kidney beans ($^2/_3$ cup)
Carrots (2)
Green pepper (1)
Boston lettuce (2 cups)
Canteloupe ($^1/_4$)

Dinner

Roast turkey, white meat
    (3 oz)
Boiled barley (1 cup)
Steamed carrots (1 cup)
Boston lettuce (2 cups)
Papaya ($^1/_2$)

DAY 20

Breakfast

Cream of buckwheat
   cereal (1 cup)
Orange (1)

Lunch

Spinach and chicken
   salad:
   Spinach (2 cups)
   Chicken (2 oz)
   Millet (½ cup)
   Tomato (1)
   Onion (¼ cup)
Orange (1)

Dinner

Broiled halibut (4 oz)
Boiled millet (1 cup)
Steamed spinach (1 cup)
Sliced tomato (1)
Blueberries (1 cup)

12.

Your Good Health Contract

We've come a long way since the Nutritional Jungle! Or perhaps you've forgotten all about that confusing land where nutritional science fiction, mumbo jumbo and contradictions reign supreme. I certainly hope so. If you have, you have done your work well. The confusion of the Nutritional Jungle should feel as far away and foreign to you now as a South American rain forest.

Each chapter has marked a milestone in your progress. You've learned how your digestive system works from the first forkful of food to the final arrival of your nutrients in your body's trillions of cells.

You've conquered the heights of the Nutritional Pyramid. By now, you are no doubt eating very differently from when you began this book. Your body is getting just the right proportions of those macronutrient powerhouses—carbohydrates, fiber, fats, protein, and even the Super Sweets.

You know all about vitamins, and what each one can do for every system of your body. You've met and learned about the Mighty Minerals. You've reviewed what we know about the Micronutrients of Tomorrow, the amino acids.

But more than just imbibing information, you have actually written your own nutritional plan. First, you used the Personal Prescriptions section to design a micronutrient regimen that is just right for you, based on your age, sex, medical status, genes, and life-style. Then you tested your hidden food sensitivities and designed a diet to get them out of your life once and for all.

As you look back, you may be amazed at how far you have come. From page 1 until this page—in fact, every step of the way—you've given yourself a terrific nutritional workout. You may not have worked up a sweat, but believe me, in the long run the exercise in this book will be every bit as good for you—in fact, much *better* for you—than the toughest aerobics workout.

After you've been on your new regimen for several weeks, you may want to go back and retake the Body Systems Checkup in Chapter One. I think you'll be surprised at how far you've come, how much has changed in the original complaints you checked off. How do you feel? Proud? Elated? Surprised? Like an expert? You should feel all of that and more. You've given yourself a precious gift —one that will last you a lifetime.

Here are just some of the benefits you've gained:

- Greater resistance to cancer and heart diseases
- Stronger muscles, bones, and organs
- Increased energy and vitality
- Improved concentration, memory, and mental acuity
- Healthier fat to muscle ratio
- Fewer colds and flus
- Steadier and happier moods and emotions
- Heightened sexual energy and interest
- Clearer, more youthful skin and hair
- Better, deeper sleep
- Greater peace of mind
- Longer life

No small feat. Have your friends and loved ones remarked about the change? They will, believe me, unless they are too envious to own up to it! They, too, want what you have—health. You can anticipate a lot of questions, an excitement that you will generate. They may even come to see you as an expert. But don't get too carried away. As you have found, each person can design a health plan only for themselves. They can get what you have only by going through the same process.

How long has it taken you to bring about this revolution in your health? A week? A month? Get out your calendar. In Chapter One, I told you to circle the date you embarked on this journey. Today, I want you to do the same. It doesn't matter how long the trip has taken. I've given you a great deal of information to digest, if you'll pardon the expression. But today is also a red-letter day. And I'd venture to guess that this tour has taken a lot less time than you ever imagined. But it's not quite over. . . .

The Rest of Your Life

What's left? Just the rest of your life. Your Personal Prescription may work very well for you right now. But it could change tomorrow. This afternoon even, if you get positive results from a pregnancy test, decide to become a vegetarian or take up jogging, or make any of a hundred other changes in your life. You can—and you should— feel free to repeat the nutritional tailoring process I describe in your Personal Prescription throughout your life as your special needs change.

You may be twenty-three years old when you first read this book, active in sports and a smoker. In a few weeks, months, or years, perhaps you stop smoking (good for you!), quit eating meat, start taking various medications, become pregnant, in short, make any one of a number of changes that affect your nutritional status. Even if you don't opt for any of these life-style changes, your needs will evolve as you age. If you are a woman, you will eventually go through menopause. Your body's systems, such as those involving bones, heart, kidneys, and liver will change with age. Perhaps you will begin to take medications as you get older.

Whenever any of your special needs change, it is a good idea to rechart your Personal Prescription. Being your own nutritionist means going in for "checkups." At every stage, you will want to make sure you are being the best nutritionist you know how.

I've designed this book not just for today but to serve you well throughout your life. I hope you will keep it handy so you can refer to it often. In fact, I truly hope it will still be on your bookshelf in twenty years—well-thumbed and dog-eared. Then I'll know I did my job well!

Even so, I don't make claims that what is in these pages is the final word on all things nutritional. That would be foolhardy and misleading in such an expanding, ever-changing field. Even some of the latest findings that I've included will eventually and inevitably be updated. Today's truths will give way to tomorrow's discoveries, and those in turn will be superseded.

I have tried to write this book to take that into account. You have given yourself more than just a static set of facts. You have provided a dynamic foundation from which to learn, a solid basis to help you expand and explore areas of special concern to you.

Keeping track of new developments is your job. Remember, we talked about personal responsibility in the first chapter? That doesn't mean a weekly trip to the medical library, and poring over each issue of the leading biomedical journals. It does mean paying attention to responsible sources—any major daily newspaper, television or radio station will do—and filing away the information in your own Personal Nutrition file. Start one today. It's not as difficult as it sounds. Simply be alert to the reports that touch on your life, your own nutritional prescription.

One word of caution: Being your own nutritionist doesn't mean avoiding your doctor. It means working with whatever health professionals you see—family doctor, gynecologist, chiropractor, therapist—and joining in a conspiracy to create better health.

It is particularly important to let your doctor know if you are making any significant changes in your diet. Because you will be fine-tuning every organ system in your body, putting your nutritional reserves back in balance, you need to keep your physician informed. If you take medications or are under your doctor's care for chronic illness, these changes may mean that you need fewer drugs, or smaller doses, as your body comes back into tune. Your physicians will help you taper your medication regimen as you become healthier.

Your Good Health Contract

You may remember that in the first chapter, I made a promise. I said I would provide a contract, my guarantee to you that from now throughout the rest of your life you would experience better health and vitality than you ever had before. Well, here it is.

There is one "but." This contract is conditional. Since it's really a pact you are making with yourself, before signing it you must first promise yourself that you will use your newfound knowledge constructively every day of your life to improve your health. It's no small pledge, so if you have any qualms, I urge you to reread now any sections of the book that you feel unsure of, to make sure you understand all the principles and the effects of the various nutrients. Once you feel completely secure, read the contract carefully and then sign it.

YOUR GOOD HEALTH CONTRACT

I pledge my best effort to take responsibility for my own health and follow the health-giving principles of this book. I understand that by following the principles of the Nutritional Pyramid and my Personal Prescription for micronutrients, I am taking a positive step to ensure myself the personalized health program that I need. I agree to update my Personal Prescription as my special needs change throughout my life.

In return, I understand that I will enjoy bountiful well-being, stronger health, greater resistance to chronic diseases, enhanced alertness and energy throughout my life, and improved mood and psychological health.

Signed on this day of _____, 19___

_____
Your name here

Congratulations! You've just made what may be the most important commitment of your life—because it is a commitment *for* your life, a commitment to health.

I have no doubt that you will continue the good work you've started here for as long as you live. In a short time, you will look back and wonder how you ever lived without being your own nutritionist. You will look back on your vague symptoms, on creaking joints and puffy skin, on that tired, draggy feeling, on mood swings and psychological symptoms, and all the other symptoms of nutritional imbalance, and you'll wonder why you ever lived that way.

I want to close this book with a charge to you. You have before you a unique opportunity to be good to yourself, to enjoy strong health, abundant energy, clear thinking, and longer, more vital, life. You have taken a step to rid yourself of the ravages of heart disease, cancer, diabetes, osteoporosis, and other chronic, debilitating illnesses.

Being your own nutritionist means that you alone have the power to control your health. In offering you the chance to choose the empowerment of health over the frustration of bad habits, I also wish you the strength to choose wisely. I've done all I can to help you along the way. The rest is up to you. I wish you the very best that nutritional health has to offer. You deserve it!

Quick
Reference
Section

I.

Nutrients and Your Body's Systems

$\overline{\hspace{6cm}}$

You have already designed your own individual nutrition plan, using the Nutritional Pyramid and your personalized Micronutrient Prescription. But sometimes patients come to my office with a special interest in a particular body system. Perhaps it is their heart and blood vessels they are concerned about. Or maybe they have a problem in the reproductive system, such as infertility, and want to know what specific nutrients can help.

You may also have such concerns for one of your body's systems— or several. Your doctor may have cautioned you about your heart, or perhaps your family has a history of digestive tract problems. Or maybe you are a dedicated student of nutrition, or just curious to learn what nutrients act how throughout your body. If you recognize yourself in any of the above, this special organ-systems section is written for you.

I have designed this chapter as an easy, quick reference to tell you the major known effects of the nutrients for each of your body's primary systems. In the following pages, you'll find these vital systems:

Each section lists the nutrients we have talked about in this book that have specific and important effects on these organ systems. It does not list every single effect of every single nutrient—you'll find that elsewhere in these pages. Instead it shows only the key nutritional elements for each system—with the most important, clear-cut health-giving action.

As you read this section, I hope you will keep one point in mind. These systems are listed separately only for reference purposes. In reality, they are all tightly interwoven. You may think of your heart and circulatory system as separate, but they are controlled by the nervous and the endocrine systems. All of them are protected by your immune system, and nourished by your digestive and metabolic system. In short, these systems aren't soloists, they are cooperating members of an extraordinarily intricate symphony. And they can perform together only when each of them has the correct nutritional support it needs.

That cooperation, of course, is the basic principle of being your own nutritionist. The regimes you have tailored for yourself throughout this book—from your first steps up the Nutritional Pyramid to the sophisticated Micronutrient Prescriptions you tailored for your own health needs—are geared to giving *all* your body's systems *all* the nutrients they need.

Your Heart and Circulatory System

MACRONUTRIENT FACTORS

FIBER
Lower blood pressure
High fiber intake can lower rate of heart disease
Reduces cholesterol
Wheat fiber lowers triglycerides

FATS
Two fatty acids—linolenic and gamma-linolenic—help guard
   against artery-clogging fat deposits
Monounsaturated fats like olive oil, almonds, peanuts, and avo-
   cadoes lower cholesterol
Reducing percentage of overall fats lowers blood pressure

OMEGA-3 FISH OILS
Their EPA constituent helps:

- Reduce high triglycerides and cholesterol
- Lower high blood pressure
- Retard thrombosis, clots that cause strokes
- Relieve migraines
- Eating one or two fish dishes per week can cut your risk of fatal
  heart attack by half

KEY VITAMINS FOR YOUR HEART AND CIRCULATORY SYSTEM

B COMPLEX
Necessary to keep blood cells strong

VITAMIN B$_3$ (NIACIN)
Lowers cholesterol and triglycerides
May actually help reverse atherosclerosis

Reduces repeat heart attacks by 29 percent. Has potentially serious side effect—producing irregular rhythm

VITAMIN B$_6$
Can reduce symptoms in patients with the fatal blood disorder sickle-cell anemia

VITAMIN B$_{12}$
For pernicious anemia, monthly B$_{12}$ injections help make this blood disease harmless
Helps keep blood healthy and oxygen-rich
Key element in synthesizing hemoglobin, molecule that transports oxygen to your tissues

FOLACIN
Required for formation of certain proteins, including hemoglobin, essential molecule that transports oxygen in your blood
Deficiency may produce megaloblastic folic-acid-deficiency anemia —your vital red blood cells don't develop properly

INOSITOL
Can reduce cholesterol; along with choline works to prevent atherosclerosis

VITAMIN C
Helps produce collagen, giving structure to blood vessels
Lowers risk of cardiovascular disease by increasing HDL cholesterol

VITAMIN D
Excess vitamin D can form calcium deposits that can create coronary artery lesions
D and calcium together keep blood pressure even by maintaining constant levels of calcium in your blood

VITAMIN E
Raises levels of HDLs, the "good cholesterol"
Helps prolong life of red blood cells

Dilates blood vessels and keeps blood thin
Prolonged use of too much E—above 800 I.U. a day—may contribute to or cause dangerous blood clots

VITAMIN K
Crucial to blood-clotting mechanism prothrombin, prevents internal bleeding and hemorrhages, protects in cuts/injuries

KEY MINERALS FOR YOUR HEART AND CIRCULATORY SYSTEM

CALCIUM
Helps regulate normal blood pressure
Can lower blood pressure; works best for older people—especially
women—blacks, those with pregnancy-related hypertension,
and those who respond to diuretics
Ensures steady functioning of your heart and blood system
Keeps heart and blood vessels in muscular tone
Excess may produce deposits throughout your heart and circula-
tory system
Helps blood coagulate so wounds heal quickly

MAGNESIUM
Necessary for normal heart action; marginal deficiency can predis-
pose you to cardiac-rhythm disturbances
Heart-attack victims are at risk for low magnesium
Magnesium appears to be an important deterrent to heart disease
If you have an arrythmia—an irregular heartbeat—don't take
magnesium without your doctor's supervision
Helps reduce high blood pressure, specifically in arteries
May help prevent stroke
Protects against toxic reactions for people taking digitalis

SODIUM
Can raise blood pressure for one in five Americans with genetic
hypersensitivity to sodium

PHOSPHORUS

Helps break up and carry away fats and fatty acids in your blood and keep blood balanced

Keeps your heart contracting regularly and smoothly

POTASSIUM

Good for high blood pressure particularly when combined with low-sodium diet

SULFUR

Helps your vital blood-thinning factor, heparin

COPPER

Prevents anemia

Required to build hemoglobin—the protein that carries most of the oxygen in your blood

May protect against heart problems and help you live longer

Imbalance throws cholesterol off, lowering HDL ("good") cholesterol

IRON

Helps build strong blood

Prevents anemia

Essential for synthesis and functioning of hemoglobin

MANGANESE

Essential to blood clotting

Low levels may be a factor in atherosclerosis

CHROMIUM

May help prevent hardening of the arteries

SELENIUM

Protects against heart attacks

IODINE

Helps in cholesterol synthesis; can prevent excess cholesterol buildup in arteries

MOLYBDENUM
Helps prevent anemia

Your Brain and Central Nervous System

MACRONUTRIENT FACTORS

FATS
Need adequate fats to build healthy nerve fibers

PROTEIN
Need balanced protein and amino acids to build brain's neurotransmitters

KEY VITAMINS FOR YOUR BRAIN AND NERVOUS SYSTEM

BETA-CAROTENE/VITAMIN A
Play role in nerve chemistry, neurotransmitters
Essential role in the visual process of the retina

VITAMIN B_1
Helps maintain your nerves

VITAMIN B_3
Deficiency may impair recent memory, produce depression, apprehension, hyperirritability, emotional instability

VITAMIN B_5
Essential for manufacture of vital nerve-regulating substances

VITAMIN B_6
Helps nerve impulses transmit properly
Supplements are effective, low-risk alternative to surgery for car-
pal-tunnel syndrome (nerve disease affecting hand)
Megadoses of B_6—2,000 to 6,000 mg a day—can produce serious
complications of the nervous system: impairment of sensory
nerves, pain in limbs, numb skin, clumsiness, loss of balance

VITAMIN B₁₂
Maintains and repairs vital nerve structures
Helps in treating memory loss, depression, insomnia
Deficiency can create severe psychotic symptoms, nervousness, nerve disorders, problems in walking and balancing, nerve transmission problems

FOLACIN
Deficiency damages nerve transmission

BIOTIN
Helps treat depression

INOSITOL
Helps relieve insomnia
Helps treat chronic anxiety and schizophrenia

VITAMIN C
Possible crucial role for C in mental functioning and behavior
Can prevent buildup of heavy metals like lead, mercury, and aluminum that lead to mental retardation and Alzheimer's disease

VITAMIN E
Can arrest and reverse nerve damage caused by such diseases as cystic fibrosis and chronic liver disease

KEY MINERALS FOR YOUR BRAIN AND NERVOUS SYSTEM

CALCIUM
Helps nerves conduct impulses

MAGNESIUM
Necessary for the proper functioning of your nerves

PHOSPHORUS
Works to keep your nerves in balance, boost mental alertness
Assures transmission of impulses from one nerve to another

POTASSIUM
Helps nerves conduct impulses
Regulates nerve functions
Helps assure enough oxygen to brain

IRON
Low iron may create learning, emotional, and social difficulties
    among adolescents and adults

MANGANESE
Improves memory
Reduces nervous irritability

SELENIUM
Can reduce symptoms of cystic fibrosis

IODINE
Helps mental alertness and sharpness

Your Digestive and Metabolic System

MACRONUTRIENT FACTORS

STARCHES
Only macronutrient not linked to disease
Time-release energy, reduces stress on digestive process

FIBER
Slows absorption of glucose
Reduces absorption of fats and cholesterol
Helps prevent colon/rectum cancer
Helps prevent constipation, hemorrhoids, diverticular disease, and
    irritable bowel syndrome

THE SUPER SWEETS (NATURAL SUGARS)
Create unstable and destructive sugar highs
Strain pancreas and insulin system

FATS
High cholesterol may promote cancer of the colon

KEY VITAMINS FOR YOUR DIGESTIVE AND METABOLIC SYSTEM

BETA-CAROTENE/VITAMIN A
Essential to cells lining digestive tract

VITAMIN B_1
Helps your body best utilize starches and natural sugars

VITAMIN B_2
Helps body convert proteins, fats, starches, and natural sugars into
  energy

VITAMIN B_5
Required for metabolism of proteins, fats, and carbohydrates, use
  of amino acids and certain proteins

BIOTIN
Helps body break down fat, starches, and protein into fuel

INOSITOL
May help alleviate constipation

VITAMIN D
With calcium, helps protect against colon cancer

VITAMIN K
Helps treat such life-threatening conditions as Crohn's disease and
  ulcerative colitis

KEY MINERALS FOR YOUR DIGESTIVE AND METABOLIC SYSTEM

CALCIUM
Helps protect against colorectal cancer
Helps prevent the development of familial colon cancer, possibly
    by blocking the bile and fatty acids that stimulate abnormal
    growth of cells in the colon

MAGNESIUM
Essential for proper metabolism

PHOSPHORUS
Helps metabolize protein, fats, and carbohydrates for optimum
    growth and upkeep of your cells
Helps you digest two B vitamins—B_2 and B_3
Keeps your kidneys effectively excreting wastes

SULFUR
Necessary for insulin
Helps keep your energy levels stable

ZINC
Necessary for insulin to keep your energy consistent
Essential for the production of more than 15 key digestive en-
    zymes

MANGANESE
Helps metabolize food, absorb vitamins like C, biotin, thiamine
Low levels can disturb blood sugar and encourage diabetes
Helps you digest foods properly

CHROMIUM
Helps correct loss of blood-sugar regulation that occurs with
    aging

IODINE
Stimulates your metabolism, helps burn off extra fat
Helps regulate your body's production of energy
Aids in synthesis of protein and absorption of carbohydrates

MOLYBDENUM
Helps metabolize carbohydrates and fats for energy

Your Reproductive and Sexual System

MACRONUTRIENT FACTORS

FATS
Excess dietary fat promotes ovarian, cervical cancer

KEY VITAMINS FOR YOUR REPRODUCTIVE AND SEXUAL SYSTEM

VITAMIN B$_6$
Helps reduce the inflammation of the prostate (prostatitis)
Helps relieve premenstrual fluid retention and other symptoms in
   some women
Excess produces serious side effects

VITAMIN B$_{12}$
Necessary for sperm/egg cells to manufacture DNA coding

FOLACIN
Necessary for cells to manufacture DNA coding

VITAMIN C
Can restore fertility in some men suffering from sperm agglutination—excessive sperm-cell clumping

VITAMIN E
Improves fertility in men and women
Helps regulate scanty or excessive menstrual flow
Relieves menopausal symptoms of hot flashes and headaches

Helps prevent and relieve inflammation of the prostate
Possible short-term increase in sex drive

VITAMIN K
Aids in reducing excessive menstrual flow

KEY MINERALS FOR YOUR REPRODUCTIVE AND SEXUAL SYSTEM

CALCIUM
Essential for the manufacture of DNA and RNA coding in cells

PHOSPHORUS
Helps form the proteins that allow us to reproduce

ZINC
Crucial for proper development of reproductive organs
Helps assure normal functioning of the prostate
May help prevent cancer of the prostate
Mild deficiency can lead to low sperm count
Severe lack causes male sex glands, testes, to atrophy
May help raise sperm count
Helps correct impotence in cases when it's caused by zinc deficiency
Elevates testosterone levels
May protect against herpes
Helps build the genetic coding

IRON
May offer some protection against herpes and Candida, vaginal yeast infection

SELENIUM
Necessary for optimum sexual functioning in men
Helps alleviate hot flashes and menstrual distress in women

MOLYBDENUM
Deficiency may lead to impotence in older men

Your Endocrine System (Hormones)

MACRONUTRIENT FACTORS

FATS
Necessary to build and metabolize hormones

PROTEIN
Necessary to build hormones

KEY VITAMINS FOR YOUR ENDOCRINE SYSTEM

VITAMIN B$_5$
Essential for the manufacture of many hormones

VITAMIN C
Helps adrenal gland regulate levels of stress hormones

KEY MINERALS FOR YOUR ENDOCRINE SYSTEM

PHOSPHORUS
Helps stimulate your glands to secrete hormones

IODINE
Helps thyroid's development and functioning, making up its principal hormone, thyroxine
Keeps thyroxine production optimal
Deficiency produces goiter, shutting down of hormone production

Your Musculoskeletal System

MACRONUTRIENT FACTORS

STARCHES
Key source of minerals for strong bones (calcium, phosphorus, magnesium)

PROTEIN
Necessary for muscle building and repair

KEY VITAMINS FOR YOUR BONES AND MUSCLES

VITAMIN B_1
Essential for proper muscle coordination

BIOTIN
Helps relieve muscle pains

INOSITOL
VITAMIN C
Helps produce collagen, which gives structure to your muscles, cartilage, and bones
Contributes to the health of teeth and gums

VITAMIN D
Helps keep your teeth and bones hard
Controls the hormone calcitriol, which oversees your body's use of calcium for bone building

VITAMIN E
In combination with selenium, helps patients with muscular dystrophy

KEY MINERALS FOR YOUR BONES AND MUSCLES

CALCIUM
Aids muscle contraction
Crucial to good health of teeth and bones
Megadoses actually decrease bone strength

PHOSPHORUS
Keeps bones strong and resilient
Speeds up healing process when you fracture a bone
Prevents loss of calcium due to injury
Helps prevent and treat osteoporosis
Prevents bone diseases like rickets
Prevents stunted growth in children
Keeps muscles contracting regularly and smoothly

POTASSIUM
Regulates muscle functions

COPPER
Helps in production of collagen to hold your bones, cartilage,
    skin, and tendons together
Lack can lead to bone-wasting

ZINC
Helps muscles contract smoothly

FLUORINE
Enhances the deposit of calcium in your bones
Protects against osteoporosis
Improves bone density and calcium balance

MANGANESE
Essential for the normal structure of your bones
Helps treat myasthenia gravis—failure of muscle coordination and
    muscle strength
May help in the treatment of multiple sclerosis

SELENIUM
With vitamin E can help patients with muscular dystrophy

Your Immune System

MACRONUTRIENT FACTORS

FATS
Essential fats necessary for membranes of immune cells

PROTEIN
Necessary to build immune cells

KEY VITAMINS FOR YOUR IMMUNE SYSTEM

BETA-CAROTENE/VITAMIN A
Strong antioxidants, help protect against cancer
Prevent or slow the development of cancers of the skin, bladder,
    throat, and lung
Trap free radicals, particularly in cell membranes
Disable singlet oxygen that can produce eye damage
Energize many immune cells
Work with the immune system to inhibit cells transformed by
    viruses
Deficiency may increase susceptibility to measles, diarrhea, and
    diseases of the respiratory tract, especially in children

VITAMIN B$_6$
Helps produce antibodies
Necessary for thymus and spleen, two critical immune-system or-
    gans
Low levels may cause immune tissues to shrink

VITAMIN C
Necessary for antibody production
Increases weight of vital immune tissues—thymus, lymph nodes
Helps thymus prepare blood cells to fight bacteria and viruses
Helps body rebuild skin and tissues damaged by wounds

Helps protect against cancers of the stomach, esophagus, and cervix

Reduces symptoms of the common cold

VITAMIN E

Strengthens immune cells, makes them more able to fight micro-organisms

KEY MINERALS FOR YOUR IMMUNE SYSTEM

MAGNESIUM

Boosts immune cells' fighting actions

PHOSPHORUS

May help prevent cancer

ZINC

Even moderate depletion for only two months may decrease white blood cells and resistance to infections

Boosts every area of immune health

Helps surgical wounds heal almost twice as fast

Deficiency seems to contribute to cancer of the esophagus and bronchial tubes

May block multiplication of cold viruses so you recover more quickly

IRON

Helps strengthen infection-fighting white blood cells

SELENIUM

Potent antioxidant

Protects against cancers of the prostate, bladder, pancreas, breast, ovary, skin, lungs, rectum, colon, esophagus, pharynx, and large intestine and against leukemia

MOLYBDENUM

Deficiency can contribute to esophageal cancer

May prevent cancers of the esophagus and stomach

Your "Beauty" Systems—Skin, Tissues, Hair, Eyes

MACRONUTRIENT FACTORS

STARCHES
Best dietary source of major minerals and vitamins

THE SUPER SWEETS (NATURAL SUGARS)
Strong dietary source of vitamins for skin

FATS
Fish-oil supplements may help prevent and treat psoriasis

PROTEIN
Supplies amino acids to build elastin, keeps skin supple
Supplies amino acids to build keratin, for hair and nails

KEY VITAMINS FOR BEAUTY

BETA-CAROTENE/VITAMIN A
Vital to keep your nails, hair, and teeth in optimum health
Crucial to form the compound rhodopsin, necessary for strong
   eyesight, especially at night
Deficiencies of A have been linked to blindness
Quench oxygen radicals that can produce eye damage

VITAMIN B_2
Necessary for building and maintaining mucous membranes
Helps protect you from eye disorders
Helps protect you from skin disorders

VITAMIN B_3
Prevents the skin disease pellagra

VITAMIN B$_5$
Helps neutralize pollutants and toxins in your tissues
Improves appearance of your skin

BIOTIN
Keeps skin healthy and resilient
Helps prevent and treat eczema and skin inflammation

INOSITOL
Helps hair growth

VITAMIN C
Contributes to health of teeth and gums

VITAMIN D
Helps keep teeth hard

VITAMIN E
Vital for youthful, healthy skin

KEY MINERALS FOR BEAUTY

PHOSPHORUS
Helps your teeth develop well and keeps them white and hard

SULFUR
Keeps your skin clear and youthful
Helps build the protein, elastin, that works to maintain your skin
Helps keep hair glossy
Helps build the protein, keratin, that maintains your hair and
    nails

COPPER
Helps in the production of collagen that holds your skin together
Helps create pigment in hair and skin

ZINC
Deficiency may produce acne
Supplements can decrease acne pustules
Can reduce skin inflammation, and production of oils that clog
  pores

IRON
Helps keep skin tone lustrous

FLUORINE
Protects teeth from decay, makes enamel more resistant to
  bacterial acids

SELENIUM
May help retain elasticity of your tissues
Can help prevent cataracts

IODINE
Helps keep nails, skin, teeth, and hair in top condition

MOLYBDENUM
May protect against tooth decay

II.

The Vitamins and Their Effects

Vitamin A/Beta-Carotene

Vitamin A is fat-soluble, stored in body fat; you don't need to eat it every day in order to get enough. But it is vital for many body systems. It helps form a substance known as *rhodopsin*, necessary for good vision—particularly night vision—and plays a key role in the visual process of the retina. The vitamin helps keep the inner linings of your body, your mucous membranes, your skin, and your eyes in good health and resistant to infection. There is good evidence that it may energize the cells of your immune system. Vitamin A helps fight cancer and the degenerative diseases of aging by soaking up what are called "free radicals"—destructive molecules that interfere with normal cell activities, disrupt essential enzymes and damage the membranes of your cells, and lead to mutations and cell damage. It also aids the development of bones, glands, hair, nails, and teeth. Both Vitamin A and beta-carotene are essential for healthy development of the cells lining your digestive tract.

Vitamin A occurs in foods in two forms: *Retinol*, or preformed vitamin A, is found only in foods that come from animals; retinoids, like *beta-carotene*, occur in both animal and plant foods. Beta-carotene is called a "precursor" to vitamin A—that is, the body converts it into usable vitamin A. They both play a role in nerve chemistry, and neurotransmitters.

Vitamin A by itself can have significant toxicity if you overdose, but beta-carotene is not toxic even in large doses—because your body converts only what it needs, you can't easily overdose. For that reason, I recommend that instead of straight vitamin A, you take safe, effective beta-carotene.

GOOD FOR THESE SYMPTOMS

Poor night vision; dry or rough skin; respiratory infections.

SIGNS OF DEFICIENCY:

Drying of skin, eyes, and mucous membranes; poor night vision; defective tooth enamel and impaired bone growth. Blacks and Hispanics both at risk for deficiency.

SOURCES:

Found as *retinols* in animals and their products, particularly in liver, including fish-liver oil, milk, butter, and eggs; as *carotenes* in plants, especially spinach, kale, broccoli, sweet potatoes, tomatoes, pumpkins, parsnips, butternut squash, beets, chicory, collard greens, watercress, dandelion, mustard, and radish greens, carrots, cantaloupes and papayas, vegetable soups, milk, and cold cereals and margarine.

RDA: 1,000 I.U. vitamin A for men
        800 I.U. for women
Optimal Level: 17,500 I.U. beta-carotene
Maximum: 25,000 I.U. vitamin A; unknown for beta-carotene
Signs of Toxicity: Irregular periods, fatigue, liver enlargement, bone pain, hair loss, blurred vision, nausea, vomiting, headaches, and diarrhea. Anemia and gout—a form of arthritis. No known toxicity from beta-carotene.
Drug Interactions: Phenytoin (Reduces effectiveness)

Oral anticoagulants (High vitamin-A doses can increase drug effects)

Vitamin B₁ (Thiamine)

Vitamin B_1—like all B vitamins—is water-soluble, so it is not stored in your body. You should try to include B vitamins in your diet every day. Any excess will be excreted. You should take the entire family of B vitamins together because they function together, helping each other perform more efficiently than if you took any one alone. You have to get the Bs in the right balance and proportion to each other. That's why they are often taken as B-complex vitamins, so that they can work together.

Thiamine, or B_1, helps your body get maximum benefit from carbohydrates, our major source of mental and physical energy. It is also vital for adequate muscle coordination and the good functioning of your peripheral nerves, like those found in your hands and feet. Thiamine has a mild diuretic effect, which will help rid your body of excess fluid. During periods of sickness, surgery, and stress, you need more B_1.

GOOD FOR THESE SYMPTOMS:

Feeling of "low energy," irritability, headaches, loss of appetite, frequent indigestion.

SIGNS OF DEFICIENCY:

Beriberi: appetite loss, mental confusion, muscle weakness or paralysis, rapid heartbeat and enlarged heart. (Most common in heavy drinkers.)

SOURCES:

Enriched starches and whole grains like wheat, oatmeal, and bran; pork, liver, dried yeast, milk, peanuts, breakfast bars and breakfast drinks, and oysters.

RDA: 1.4 mg for men
       1 mg for women
Optimal Level: 70 mg
Maximum: 100 mg

Vitamin B$_2$ (Riboflavin)

Like B$_1$, riboflavin must be consumed every day to keep your body functioning at optimum level and increased during times of stress. This vitamin is crucial to help extract energy from the carbohydrates, proteins, and fats that you eat. It helps protect you from common eye and skin problems. Riboflavin is essential for maintaining and building body tissues like mucous membranes.

OTHER BENEFITS:

Helps you deal with stress.

GOOD FOR THESE SYMPTOMS

Inflammation of the tongue, insomnia, eye fatigue, blurred vision, bloodshot eyes.

SIGNS OF DEFICIENCY:

Dermatitis; cracks at corners of mouth; eye itching, burning, and sensitivity to light.

SOURCES:

Milk, eggs, leafy green vegetables, whole grains, liver and other meats, fish, cheese, and eggs.

RDA: None
Optimal Level: 50 mg
Maximum: 100 mg

Vitamin B₃ (Niacin, Niacinamide)

This vitamin helps transform food into energy in the body and is crucial to metabolize fat and protein. One of its special talents is to help your body deal with physiological stress after injury. You need more B₃ at that time. There are some differences in the two forms of the vitamin. The niacin form of this vitamin can reduce the risk of recurrent heart attack. It lowers your triglycerides and cholesterol and may actually help reverse atherosclerosis. Reduces repeat heart attacks by 29 percent. Has potentially serious side effect—producing irregular rhythm. Because it causes your blood vessels to dilate, too much niacin makes you look and feel flushed.

Neither the heart benefits nor the uncomfortable flush happens with the niacinamide form of the vitamin, also known as B₃ₐ, which is the one I prescribe.

GOOD FOR THESE SYMPTOMS:

Dermatitis, digestive problems, anxiety, fatigue, insomnia, headache, physiological stresses (injury, surgery), cardiac disease, high cholesterol and triglycerides.

SIGNS OF DEFICIENCY:

Pellagra, a skin disease: redness of the skin and inflammation caused by gastrointestinal disturbances. Impaired recent memory, depression, hyperirritability, apprehension, emotional instability.

SOURCES:

Meat, fish, green vegetables, whole grains like wheat, peas and beans.

RDA: Niacin: 18 mg for men
     1 mg for women
Optimal Level: Niacinamide 50 mg

Maximum: 250 mg
Drug Interactions: Zinc (Niacinamide blocks zinc in the body)
Isoniazid (Niacin requirement may be increased)

Vitamin B₅ (Pantothenic Acid)

Vitamin B_5 is important for forming particular nerve-regulating substances and hormones. Like the other Bs, it is needed for the metabolism of carbohydrates, fats, and proteins. Vitamin B_5 is needed in your body for the use of amino acids and the assembling of certain proteins. It is essential for the manufacture of many kinds of hormones and vital nerve-regulating substances. B_5 works as an antioxidant and stops short some of the effects of aging. It helps neutralize pollutants and toxins in your tissues.

GOOD FOR THESE SYMPTOMS:

Stress, low energy, wound healing, allergies, frequent colds or infections.

SIGNS OF DEFICIENCY:

Naturally occurring deficiency not observed.

SOURCES:

Yeast, liver, eggs, kidney, peanut products, rice bran, wheat bran.

RDA: 10 mg
Optimal Level: 75 mg
Maximum: 100 mg

Vitamin B₆ (Pyridoxine and Related Compounds)

Vitamin B_6 is actually a group of closely related substances—pyridoxine, pyridoxinal and pyridoxamine—that work together. They are excreted by your body about eight hours after you consume them, so you need to replace this vitamin regularly. B_6 acts as a natural, safe diuretic, flushing extra water and water-soluble wastes from your body. The B_6 trio helps your nervous system function properly. Helps nerve impulses transmit properly.

Pyridoxine and its related compounds are also essential for your immune system, and a lack of B_6 may even shrink your immune tissues. This vitamin helps the body produce antibodies—those proteins that fight off foreign infectious invaders—as well as red blood cells. Two of your immune system's most important elements, your thymus and spleen, need pyridoxine for their normal functioning.

OTHER BENEFITS:

Helps keep sexual organs healthy. In men, helps reduce the inflammation of the prostate gland known as prostatitis. For women, this vitamin is especially helpful in relieving premenstrual fluid retention. May help alleviate depression. Supplements are an effective and low-risk alternative to surgery for the nerve disease carpaltunnel syndrome. Can reduce symptoms in patients with the fatal blood disorder sickle-cell anemia.

GOOD FOR THESE SYMPTOMS:

Premenstrual tension, depression, sore mouth and gums, some skin problems.

SIGNS OF DEFICIENCY:

Mouth and tongue inflammation, convulsions, and depression. Deficiency most common among heavy drinkers and users of oral contraceptives.

SOURCES:

Herring, salmon, beef, pork, lamb, liver, kidney, poultry, whole grains including wheat germ, grapes, cantaloupe, bananas, nuts, brewers' yeast, blackstrap molasses, milk, eggs, carrots, peas, and potatoes.

RDA: 2.2 mg
Optimal Level: 150 mg
Maximum: 100 mg
Signs of Toxicity: In megadoses of 2,000 to 6,000 mg a day, B_6 can create serious side effects including impairment of the sensory nerves including burning sensation, pain in limbs, numb skin, clumsiness and loss of balance.
Drug Interactions: Barbiturates (B_6 may reduce the drugs' effect)
Oral contraceptives (May increase B_6 requirement)
Hydralazine (May increase B_6 requirement)
Isoniazid (May increase B_6 requirement)
Penicillamine (May increase B_6 requirement)
Levodopa (Reduces levodopa's effect)

Vitamin B_{12} (Cobalamine)

Vitamin B_{12} is the only B vitamin your body stores in quantity— enough for three to five years. It is vital for the production of healthy red blood cells, genetic DNA material, and for the proper function of the nervous system. It helps prevent anemia and increases your energy. To help your body get the most out of vitamin B_{12}, you need to combine it with the mineral calcium during absorption. This micronutrient promotes growth and increases appetite in children.

OTHER BENEFITS:

Essential to the production of the basic genetic coding, DNA and RNA. Helps keep your blood healthy and your oxygen rich. Works as a key element in synthesizing hemoglobin. Maintains and repairs vital nerve structures. Can be helpful in treating memory loss, depression, and insomnia.

GOOD FOR THESE SYMPTOMS:

Low energy, fatigue, vision problems, depression. For pernicious anemia, monthly B_{12} injections render this blood disease largely harmless.

SIGNS OF DEFICIENCY:

Deficiency generally results from inability to absorb B_{12}. Results in *pernicious anemia* and nervous system damage—may produce problems walking and balancing, and nervousness. Strict vegetarians may be at some risk for deficiency.

SOURCES:

Milk, pork, kidney, liver, shellfish, sardines, salmon, herring, cheese, and egg yolk.

RDA: 3 mcg
Optimal Level: 100 mcg (**Note:** dose in micrograms, not in milligrams like the other B vitamins)
Maximum: 100 mcg

Inositol (A B-Complex Vitamin)

Inositol is important in feeding your brain cells, and plays a key role in helping metabolize cholesterol and fats.

BENEFITS:

- Cholesterol can be reduced with inositol.
- Along with the substance choline, it works to prevent atherosclerosis, or hardening of the arteries. It also seems to have beneficial effects on your kidneys, heart, and liver.
- Prevents the flaking skin condition eczema and plays a vital role in hair growth.

- May help constipation.
- May relieve insomnia.

GOOD FOR THESE SYMPTOMS:

Insomnia, anxiety, high cholesterol.

SIGNS OF DEFICIENCY:

Eczema.

SOURCES:

Liver, beef brains and heart, whole grains, especially wheat gum, brewers' yeast, vegetables, especially dried lima beans and cabbage, cantaloupe, grapefruit, raisins, peanuts, unrefined molasses.

RDA: None
Optimal Level: 100 mg
Maximum: 1,000 mg

Folic Acid (Folate, Folacin) (A B-Complex Vitamin)

Your body needs folic acid, or folate, to form particular essential body proteins and genetic materials for the nucleus of the cell. It also helps prevent anemia and has the power to make blood cells grow larger than normal. Folic acid promotes the synthesis of the oxygen-carrying blood protein hemoglobin.

GOOD FOR THESE SYMPTOMS:

Frequent colds and viruses, fatigue, depression, irritability, indigestion, slow wound healing.

SIGNS OF DEFICIENCY:

Enlarged red blood cells—*megaloblastic anemia*—diarrhea, bleeding gums, fetal abnormalities in pregnant women. Most common deficiency in infants and children in the United States. Pregnant women and those on oral contraceptives, alcoholics, those with chronic liver disease, epileptics taking the drug sodium phenytoin, and the elderly are also at risk.

SOURCES:

Liver, kidney, leafy vegetables, especially kale, parsley, and spinach, whole wheat, mushrooms, avocados, carrots, apricots, yeast, wheat bran, fruit, dried beans, peas, almonds, peanuts, rye, and milk.

RDA: 400 mcg
Optimal Level: 400 mcg
Maximum: 2 mg
Drug Interactions: Phenytoin (Decreases drug's effect and decreases absorption of dietary folate)
Sulfasalazine (Decreases absorption of dietary folate)
Triamterene (Decreases body's ability to use dietary folate)

Vitamin C (Ascorbic Acid)

Since vitamin C is a water-soluble micronutrient and cannot be stored in your body, it should be included in your diet every day. It helps your adrenal gland regulate your levels of stress hormones. Under stress, you use up even more, so you need to increase your intake during those times. Ascorbic acid helps your body absorb the mineral iron. It also helps contribute to the health of your teeth and gums. The vitamin aids your body in producing the protein collagen, which gives structure to your muscles, the tissues of your blood-vessel system, your bones and cartilage, your teeth and gums. Vitamin C can also help lower blood cholesterol. Lowers risk of cardiovascular disease by increasing HDL cholesterol. Possible crucial role for C in mental functioning and behavior. Can prevent buildup of heavy metals like lead, mercury, and aluminum that lead to mental retardation and Alzheimer's disease.

Along with vitamins A and E, C is a potent antioxidant, chemically neutralizing oxidation products ("free radicals") before they can damage delicate cell DNA and membranes. As such, it has clear anticancer properties. It also seems to help neutralize many carcinogens before they damage body tissues.

Of all the vitamins, C has the most potent good effects on your immune system, increasing the weight of essential immune tissues like the thymus and lymph nodes. It also energizes your white blood cells that fight infection, and helps your body manufacture a chemical that promotes antibody production. C protects two other vitamins, A and E, from breakdown.

GOOD FOR THESE SYMPTOMS:

Stress, wound healing, frequent colds and viruses.

SIGNS OF DEFICIENCY:

Scurvy: bleeding gums and other hemorrhaging, loose teeth, emotional disturbances, and failure of wounds to heal.

SOURCES:

Citrus fruits like oranges and grapefruit, potatoes, tomatoes, melons, strawberries, and green vegetables like broccoli, kale, cabbage, and cauliflower and sweet peppers.

RDA: 60 mg for men and women
Optimal Level: 2 grams
Maximum: 4 grams
Signs of Toxicity: Massive doses—10 grams a day—may block your kidneys, causing agonizing kidney stones if you have existing or hidden kidney problems. Can also trigger anemia by lowering the levels of the mineral copper in your blood. During pregnancy, high

doses of C may cause symptoms of scurvy and an abnormally large need for the vitamin in infants.

Drug Interactions: Oral anticoagulants (May decrease drug's effect) Oral contraceptives and estrogens (Increased serum concentration and possibly adverse effects of estrogen with 1 gram a day of vitamin C)

C causes body to process aspirin more slowly. As a result, it can cause a toxic buildup of this drug after even moderate doses.

Vitamin D

Vitamin D is fat-soluble, so you need not eat it every day. The ultraviolet rays of the sun interact with the oils on your skin to produce this micronutrient, which is then absorbed into your body. But once you get a suntan, this source of the vitamin is blocked. It is important to have adequate levels of D to regulate your bones' supply of vital minerals calcium and phosphorus, essential for the healthy maintenance of your bones and teeth. It helps prevent osteoporosis. Vitamin D and calcium can significantly lower your risk of deadly colorectal cancer and keep your blood pressure even by maintaining constant levels of calcium in your blood.

GOOD FOR THESE SYMPTOMS:

Problems relating to bone growth and healing.

SIGNS OF DEFICIENCY:

In children: *rickets*—stunted bone growth, bowed legs, and poorly formed teeth. In adults: *osteomalacia*—softening of bones, causing deformity and fractures.

SOURCES:

Exposure of skin to sunlight converts body chemicals to Vitamin D. Dietary sources: milk fortified with vitamin D; egg yolk; tuna;

salmon and liver, fish-liver oil, sardines, herring; margarine and dairy products.

RDA: 400 I.U.
Optimal Level: 200 I.U.
Maximum: 1,000 I.U.
Signs of Toxicity: Abnormal calcium deposits in blood-vessel walls, liver, lungs, kidney, and stomach; itching skin, diarrhea, urgent need to urinate, sore eyes, and unusual thirst.
Drug Interactions: Phenytoin (Decreases effect of vitamin D)
Phenobarbital (Decreases effect of vitamin D)

Vitamin E

Unlike other fat-soluble vitamins, vitamin E is stored in your body for relatively short periods of time like some of the Bs and vitamin C. In fact, 70 percent of it is excreted in your feces. It plays a role in the formation of many body tissues, including muscles and red blood cells. This micronutrient helps protect cell membranes and prolongs the life of red blood cells. Vitamin E is stored in the uterus, testes, adrenal and pituitary glands, blood, muscles, heart, and liver.

It acts both as a vasodilator, opening up your blood vessels, and an anticoagulant, thinning your blood and helping prevent clots. It also helps raise the levels of HDLs, the "good" cholesterol in your blood. Vitamin E directly aids all components of your immune system. It is one of the most potent known antidotes to free radicals, deactivating them chemically before they can destroy cells. Moreover, it helps heal scars, scratches, and burns. This micronutrient may even increase fertility in both men and women. In men, it can help prevent and cure inflammation of the prostate gland; in women, it helps regulate menstrual flow and relieve menopausal symptoms. It may even produce short-term rises in sex drive.

GOOD FOR THESE SYMPTOMS:

Muscle cramps, muscle growth and strength; aids in healing; neurological disorders—nerve damage caused by diseases like cystic fibrosis and chronic liver disease.

SIGNS OF DEFICIENCY:

In newborns: hemolytic anemia.

SOURCES:

Vegetable oils, enriched flour, margarine, leafy green vegetables, especially broccoli, Brussels sprouts, and spinach, and whole-grain cereals and breads, especially whole wheat and wheat germ, soybeans, eggs, nuts, and fruits.

RDA: 30 I.U.
Optimal Level: 400 I.U.
Maximum: 1,000 I.U.
Signs of Toxicity: May produce significant blood disorders in newborns if nursing mothers apply E oil to their nipples to prevent soreness and cracks. In too large doses—800 I.U. a day—E may contribute to or cause dangerous blood clots.
Drug Interactions: Oral anticoagulants (May increase drug's effect)

Vitamin K

This fat-soluble vitamin helps prevent internal bleeding and hemorrhages and aids in reducing excessive menstrual flow. These benefits come from the micronutrient's vital role in forming prothrombin, a blood-clotting chemical. Protects in cuts and injuries.

GOOD FOR THESE SYMPTOMS:

Bruising, nosebleeds, excessive bleeding when cut or scratched. Helps treat such life-threatening conditions as Crohn's disease and ulcerative colitis.

SIGNS OF DEFICIENCY:

Defective blood clotting—occasionally seen in newborns, rare in others.

SOURCES:

Leafy green vegetables, cauliflower, peas, yogurt, kelp, fish-liver oils, safflower and soybean oils, egg yolk, cabbage, and meat. Intestinal bacteria produce vitamin K from foods.

RDA: None
Optimal Level: From dietary sources
Drug Interactions: Oral anticoagulants (K reduces these drugs' effects)

III.

The Minerals and Their Effects

Bulk Minerals

Needed in relatively large amounts by your body.

Calcium

Calcium helps form your bones and teeth. It is important to muscle contraction, blood clotting, and enzyme activity. There is more calcium in your body than any other mineral. Almost all of it—some two to three pounds—is found in your teeth and bones. Calcium works together with another mineral, phosphorus, to make your teeth and bones healthy. Along with the mineral magnesium, calcium works for cardiovascular health.

OTHER BENEFITS:
- Helps prevent osteoporosis.
- Helps protect against familial colorectal cancer.

- Works with vitamin D to protect against colorectal malignancies.
- Helps control your blood pressure.
- Lowers your risk of heart attack and stroke.
- Helps conduct nerve impulses.
- Speeds wound healing because it helps your blood coagulate.

GOOD FOR THESE SYMPTOMS:

Allergies, backaches, irritability, depression, insomnia, leg cramps.

SIGNS OF DEFICIENCY:

In children: *rickets*—stunted bone growth, bowed legs, and poorly formed teeth. In female adults: *osteoporosis*—loss of bone mass and increased fragility leading to breakage. Lack of calcium is the most serious nutritional problem of older Americans. Many get far below even the minimal RDA for this micronutrient. Three quarters of women over thirty-five consume less than the minimal RDA.

THOSE AT RISK FOR LOW CALCIUM:

- Women over forty-five
- Men over sixty-five
- People who drink a lot
- Those with an inactive life-style
- People on low-calorie diets
- Those on high-protein diets
- Pregnant women
- Smokers
- Those with lactose intolerance
- Those who take magnesium-containing antacids frequently
- Those who take cortisone medication

SOURCES:

Milk and milk products, yogurt, all cheeses, ice cream, buttermilk, canned salmon and sardines; citrus fruits, peas, beans, soybeans, peanuts, walnuts, sunflower seeds and leafy green vegetables such as broccoli, kale, and collard greens, kidney beans, oysters, and tofu. For supplements, the cheapest and best source is calcium carbonate. Take with meals. Stay away from supplements with dolomite, bone meal, and oyster shells; they contain toxic minerals. Balance calcium with the mineral magnesium so your body can make best use of the calcium.

RDA: 800 mg
Optimal Level: 800 mg for men
    1,000 mg for premenopausal women
    1,500 mg for postmenopausal women
Maximum: 1,500 mg
Signs of Toxicity: Extensive calcification in bones and tissues. Constipation, nausea, a hyperactive stomach, and bloating. Can increase your risk of developing kidney stones if you have kidney problems or are prone to kidney disease. Excessive supplements could eventually result in kidney failure even if you don't have kidney disease. Too much can damage your cardiovascular health by creating calcium deposits on blood-vessel walls, leading to blockages and heart attacks.
Drug Interactions: May affect absorption of minerals like iron, zinc, and magnesium.

Potassium

Potassium regulates the balance of your body acids and plays a role in nerve and muscle function. Together with sodium, potassium works to regulate your blood pressure and water balance and to keep your heart muscle beating in a steady, normal rhythm. Potassium helps sharp, clear thinking by assuring adequate oxygen transport to your brain. It even helps your body dispose of wastes.

GOOD FOR THESE SYMPTOMS:

Muscle weakness, fatigue, irritability, confusion, muscle cramps, constipation.

OTHER BENEFITS:

May lower high blood pressure and protect against the blood-pressure-boosting properties of sodium.

SIGNS OF DEFICIENCY:

Muscle fatigue; constipation; weak, slow, irregular pulse; muscle cramps while exercising; lack of appetite; mental apathy. Low potassium leads to altered heart rhythm and muscle weakness. It can occur with excessive fluid loss from sweating, diuretic medications, or diarrhea. Also, physical and mental stress can lead to a deficiency of potassium. About 38 percent of all men and 65 percent of all women get less than 70 percent of the minimal RDA for this mineral.

AT HIGH RISK FOR LOW POTASSIUM:

Are you taking thiazide-type diuretics?
Are you taking cortisone medications?
Do you have chronic liver disease?
Do you drink a lot of coffee?
Do you drink alcohol regularly?

SOURCES:

Bananas, potatoes, dates, raisins, apricots, cantaloupe, oranges and orange juice, prune juice, turkey, tomatoes, broccoli, watercress, mint leaves, lettuce, Brussels sprouts, green leafy vegetables, sunflower seeds, and wheat germ.

RDA: None
Optimal Level: 100 mg
Maximum: 5 grams
Signs of Toxicity: Lack of appetite, apathy, muscle fatigue.

Magnesium

Magnesium is essential for the transmission of nerve impulses and muscle contraction. It is required by your body to convert into energy the blood sugar stored as glycogen in your liver. This mineral is necessary for calcium and vitamin-C metabolism as well as that of phosphorus, sodium, and potassium. It also helps in bone building, and aids your body in dealing with physical and emotional stress.

OTHER BENEFITS:

- Essential for the manufacture of the DNA and RNA coding in your cells.
- Protects you from heart disease.
- Helps lower high blood pressure.
- Helps relieve migraines.
- Makes your exercising muscles stronger and increases your endurance to prolonged exercise.
- Supplements can help prevent recurrent kidney stones.
- Works with calcium to protect against postmenopausal bone loss.
- Enhances the health of pregnant and nursing women.
- May help relieve premenstrual tension.

GOOD FOR THESE SYMPTOMS:

Insomnia, anxiety, depression, irritability, muscle tremors and weakness, fatigue, poor memory, water retention.

SIGNS OF DEFICIENCY:

Loss of appetite, confusion, diarrhea, nausea, vomiting, tremors, uncontrolled muscle contractions, and in severe deficiency, convulsions. Even a marginal deficiency can predispose you to cardiac-rhythm abnormalities, a potentially life-threatening condition. Over time, a deficiency may create cardiovascular problems. The average American gets barely three quarters of the RDA for this mineral.

AT HIGH RISK FOR LOW MAGNESIUM:

Do you take diuretics?
Are you undergoing cancer chemotherapy?
Do you take digitalis drugs?
Are you taking antibiotics?
Are you a heavy drinker?
Have you had a heart attack?
Do you have kidney problems?

SOURCES:

Figs, lemons, grapefruit, corn, almonds, apples, nuts, seeds, whole grains, leafy green vegetables, and shellfish.

RDA: 350 mg
Optimal Level: 750 mg
Maximum: 1,000 mg
Signs of Toxicity: Drowsiness, lethargy, sluggishness, stupor, coma.
CAUTION: IF YOU HAVE KIDNEY OR HEART PROBLEMS, DO NOT TAKE MAGNESIUM SUPPLEMENTS WITHOUT CONSULTING YOUR DOCTOR.

Sodium

Sodium keeps your heart beating in a strong, steady rhythm. It also helps balance the functioning of all your muscles and nerves. Sodium is the major regulator of your body's water balance and keeps the other vital minerals in proper concentration in your tissues and blood.

WARNING:

Sodium has one of the strongest links to high blood pressure of anything we eat, although only one American in five has the genetic hypersensitivity to sodium that makes it raise our blood pressure to dangerous levels. Too much sodium can produce other damaging effects, however, in body systems like your kidneys and your heart.

SOURCES:

Salt, almost inevitable in processed foods. Also seafood, including shellfish and kelp, bacon, organ meats such as brains, liver, and kidneys; sometimes high levels of sodium present in the water supply.

RDA: None
Optimal Level: You can't help but get enough sodium without even trying, so make an effort to keep your daily intake as low as possible.
Maximum: 15 grams

Phosphorus

Along with the B vitamins, phosphorus is needed to extract energy from food, particularly fats and starches. It is a component of healthy bones, teeth, gums and many other tissues. Phosphorus also helps with kidney functioning and heart regularity. It lessens arthritis pain. But none of this would be possible without proper levels of vitamin D and calcium, which phosphorus needs to function properly.

OTHER BENEFITS:

- Speeds up the healing process and puts a stop to calcium loss from injury.
- Helps prevent and treat osteoporosis.
- Helps treat or forestall bone diseases like rickets.
- Prevents stunted growth in children.
- Helps break up and carry away fats and fatty acids in your blood, as well as keeping your blood balanced.
- Works to keep your nerves from feeling frazzled, and your mind alert and sharp.
- Helps stimulate your glands to secrete hormones.

- Keeps your muscles, including your heart, contracting regularly and smoothly.
- Lets you digest two members of the B-vitamin family, riboflavin and niacin.
- Assures transmission of impulses from one nerve to another.
- Keeps your kidneys effectively excreting wastes.
- Gives you stable and plentiful energy.
- Forms the proteins that help all of us reproduce.
- May help block cancer.

GOOD FOR THESE SYMPTOMS:

Muscle weakness, susceptibility to infections.

SIGNS OF DEFICIENCY:

Weakness, appetite loss, malaise, and pain in bones.

THOSE AT RISK FOR LOW PHOSPHORUS:

- Those on weight-loss diets of 1,000 calories a day or less
- Pregnant and nursing women
- Those who drink heavily
- Those who consume large amounts of antacids that deplete the bones' phosphorus supply

SOURCES:

Dairy products, meat, poultry, fish, whole grains including flour and cereals, nuts, seeds, eggs, dried beans, and peas. In order not to disturb your phosphorus-calcium balance, stay away from soft drinks, meat, and foods that contain phosphorus additives (phosphates).

RDA: 1,200 mg
Optimal Level: From dietary sources
Maximum: 800 mg
Signs of Toxicity: Too much can upset the balance, creating a serious muscular condition called hypocalcemic tetany.

Trace Minerals

Your body needs these in considerably smaller amounts than the bulk minerals. Scientists are still discovering new trace minerals, so the list of trace minerals is probably not yet complete.

Chromium

Chromium helps prevent and lower high blood pressure. It also works as a deterrent of diabetes because it works with insulin in the metabolism of blood sugar. This trace mineral helps transport protein where it is needed in your body.

OTHER BENEFITS:

- Helps improve glucose uptake in elderly people when loss comes as natural result of aging.
- May help prevent hardening of the arteries.

SIGNS OF DEFICIENCY:

Adult-onset diabetes. Most people get only about half the level of chromium that nutritionists recommend.

SOURCES:

Brewers' yeast, meat products, chicken, shellfish, especially clams, corn oil, and whole grains.

RDA: None
Optimal Level: From dietary sources

Fluorine

Fluorine works in the development and maintenance of healthy bones and teeth by enhancing the deposit of calcium. It decreases your chances of cavities and strengthens your bones.

OTHER BENEFITS:

- Helps prevent osteoporosis.
- Helps relieve back pain and improve bone density.
- Reduces fractures caused by osteoporosis.

GOOD FOR THESE SYMPTOMS:

Frequent dental cavities, tendency to bone fractures.

SIGNS OF DEFICIENCY:

Excessive dental decay and possible osteoporosis.

SOURCES:

Fluoridation of water supply; seafood, cheese, milk, tea, cereal grains, and animal products.

RDA: None
Optimal Level: Get it from water and diet.
Signs of Toxicity: Too much can disrupt your body's ability to use vitamins, also retard growth, cause unwanted calcium deposits in your tendons and ligaments, even damage your reproductive organs, adrenal glands, central nervous system, brain, kidneys, and heart.

Copper

This mineral keeps your energy level up by helping in effective iron absorption. It also helps the color of your hair and skin by making the amino acid tyrosine usable so it can work as a pigmenting factor. Copper is essential for your body's use of vitamin C. It also is vital for transforming your body's iron into hemoglobin. Too little and too much copper have a negative effect on your immune system, making you more prone to infections. Your thyroid gland must have just the right balance of copper to properly secrete hormones.

OTHER BENEFITS:

- In proper balance with zinc, helps protect your heart by keeping HDL, or good cholesterol, high.
- May extend life by protecting against heart disease.
- Helps keep tissues oxygen-rich.

POSSIBLE SIGNS OF DEFICIENCY:

Anemia with weakness, labored breathing, skin sores, puffiness or swelling around ankles and wrists, skin problems, including eczema, frequent infections and fatigue, loss of bone mass, and osteoporosis. Dietary levels are often far below the minimal RDA levels. Chronic deficiencies may contribute to higher cancer rate, increased cell damage and aging, and even a shorter lifespan. Pregnant women need supplements because their bodies can't retain copper as well as they should. Frequent miscarriage early in pregnancy may be due to very low copper levels.

SOURCES:

Calf and beef liver, dried beans, peas, shrimp, oysters and most seafood, whole wheat, prunes, margarine, dark chocolate, nuts, fruits, and many other unprocessed foods.

RDA: None
Optimal Level: Dietary sources
Maximum: 75 mg
Signs of Toxicity: High levels of copper have been detected in the blood of victims of several kinds of malignancy, including tumors of the digestive system, lung, and breast, Hodgkin's disease, and systemic cancers like leukemia, lymphoma, and multiple myeloma. Researchers don't know if it is a cause or a consequence.

Iodine

Two thirds of your body's iodine is found in your thyroid gland. It is an important component of thyroid hormones—essential for reproduction. Since your thyroid also controls your metabolism, a lack of this micronutrient may show up in weight gain, lack of energy, and sluggish mental reactions. On the other hand, proper levels of iodine will help you diet by burning off extra fat, give you more energy, and heighten your mental sharpness. Iodine also promotes healthy teeth, skin, nails, and hair.

OTHER BENEFITS:

- Helps convert beta-carotene into vitamin A.
- Can help head off atherosclerosis by making sure your body synthesizes cholesterol properly.
- Iodide tablets can help protect against radiation from nuclear fallout.

SIGNS OF DEFICIENCY:

In newborns: *cretinism*—delayed growth and swollen features. In others: *goiter*—enlarged thyroid gland. Lack may lead to slowed mental reactions, dry hair, hardening of the arteries, obesity and lethargy, and intolerance to cold. Deficiency during pregnancy and infancy can produce mental and physical retardation. Reversible with iodine supplements. Deficiencies rare today.

SOURCES:

Seafoods, iodized and sea salts, seaweed (kelp), vegetables grown in iodine-rich soil, onions, food colors and additives.

RDA: 150 mcg for adults
Optimal Level: From dietary sources
Maximum: 1,000 mcg
Signs of Toxicity: Goiter (swollen thyroid)

Iron

Iron—along with calcium—is one of the major dietary deficiencies in American women. Because of the blood lost during menstrual periods, in one month women lose almost twice as much iron as men. To metabolize iron in your body, you need copper, cobalt, manganese, and vitamin C. In turn, iron is required to metabolize the family of B vitamins. It promotes resistance to infection, forestalls fatigue, helps in growth, and can bounce back good skin tone. Iron is essential for the manufacture of myoglobin—the red pigment in muscles. It is also a component of the oxygen-carrying protein hemoglobin. Iron is crucial for your immune system in a number of ways. It enhances your overall resistance to infection, keeps your immune tissues healthy, and energizes your fighter white blood cells. Moreover, it vitalizes both white and red blood cells. Your white blood cells are the major immune-health guardians while your red blood cells carry essential oxygen to all of your body's tissues.

GOOD FOR THESE SYMPTOMS:

Depression, fatigue, pallor, weakness, headaches, heart palpitations, poor concentration.

SIGNS OF DEFICIENCY:

Anemia and fatigue, most common in infants and among women of reproductive age. Also frequent sickness or infections and chronic malaise. Iron-deficiency anemia reduces the ranks of your vital red blood cells. Deficiency may be common among infants and children. Consequences can be quite profound as deficiency can retard intellectual development of babies and preschool children. Can be cured with supplements. Teenage girls at high risk. One third of all young women have low iron stores. Low iron leaves women particularly vulnerable to Candida, the common vaginal yeast infection. In adult men and women, deficiency may be caused by internal bleeding through ulcers, intestinal polyps, or hemorrhoids. Taking too much aspirin or drinking too much alcohol can contribute to iron deficiency. Older Americans at risk for low iron.

SOURCES:

Liver, red meat, raisins, enriched and whole-grain cereals, especially farina, dried beans, peas, asparagus and leafy greens, raw clams and oysters, dried peaches, egg yolks, nuts, molasses, soybean flour, beans, poultry, and oatmeal.

RDA: 10 mg for men
18 mg for women
Optimal Level: 15 mg
Maximum: 25 mg
Signs of Toxicity: Liver toxicity, induced vitamin-C deficiency, metallic gray hue to skin or "bronzing" of skin.

Manganese

Manganese reduces nervous irritability, aids in muscle reflexes, improves memory, and helps combat tiredness. It's needed for normal bone building and is important in the production of thyrosin, the principal hormone of the thyroid gland. It is also essential for proper digestion and efficient use of food because it makes up enzymes that extract energy and metabolize proteins. It also helps the body properly use vitamin B_1, biotin, and vitamin C. Manganese is important for normal central-nervous-system functioning and reproduction.

OTHER BENEFITS:

- Plays essential role in blood clotting.
- For nursing mothers, important in the manufacture of milk.
- Can improve your memory.
- Helps people with debilitating weakness by stimulating the transmission of impulses between the nerves and muscles.
- Helps treat myasthenia gravis—failure of muscle coordination and loss of muscle strength.
- Plays role in the treatment of multiple sclerosis.

GOOD FOR THESE SYMPTOMS:

Weight loss, dermatitis, nausea, stomach problems.

SIGNS OF DEFICIENCY:

Growth retardation, reproductive difficulty, birth defects, and bone and joint abnormalities. Manganese deficiency is extremely rare.

SOURCES:

Nuts, unrefined grains, whole-grain cereals, vegetables, especially peas and beets, organ meats, bran, black tea, egg yolks, and fruits.

RDA: None
Optimal Level: From dietary sources
Maximum: 6 mg
Signs of Toxicity: Can reduce the body's use of iron.

Molybdenum

Molybdenum helps in the metabolism of both fats and carbohydrates. It is a vital part of the enzyme responsible for the use of iron in your body. It also helps prevent anemia and enhance general well-being.

OTHER BENEFITS:

- May protect against cancers of the esophagus and stomach.
- Can detoxify potentially harmful preservatives, sulfites.
- Reduces tooth decay.

GOOD FOR THESE SYMPTOMS:

Fatigue, general feeling of "poor health."

SIGNS OF DEFICIENCY:

Not known for humans. But lack may lead to premature aging and impotence in older men.

SOURCES:

Meats, whole grains, especially buckwheat, barley, and wheat germ, legumes, particularly lima beans, canned beans and lentils, sunflower seeds, and dark-green leafy vegetables.

RDA: None
Optimal Level: From dietary sources
Maximum: 400 mcg
Signs of Toxicity: Even modest intake of 10 to 15 mg a day may produce painful stiffness and swelling of the joints. Can also inhibit growth of bones.

Selenium

Men have a much greater need for this mineral than women. Almost half of a male's supply of selenium is in his testicles and portions of the seminal ducts right next to the prostate gland. Consequently, men need more, particularly if they are very sexually active, since this mineral is discharged in semen. It must be replaced for optimal sexual functioning. Selenium helps keep youthful elasticity in the tissues. In women, it alleviates menopausal symptoms, particularly hot flashes. In tandem with vitamin E, selenium works to slow down aging and toughening of the tissues that occurs through the breakdown process known as oxidation. There is evidence that selenium offers some protection against cancer. A lack of this trace mineral appears to slow down the immune system. It works in conjunction with vitamin E to give you more antibodies.

OTHER BENEFITS:

- Seems to protect against cancers of the prostate, pancreas, breast, ovary, skin, esophagus, pharynx, large intestine, kidneys, lungs, rectum, colon, and bladder and against leukemia.
- Protects against cardiovascular disease and stroke.
- Selenium plus E may help seniors by reducing anxiety and increasing alertness.

SIGNS OF DEFICIENCY:

Not known for humans.

SOURCES:

Seafood and meat, especially liver and kidney, brewers' yeast, radishes, cucumbers, garlic, eggs, mushrooms, wheat germ, bran, brown rice, whole-wheat bread, tomatoes, broccoli, onions, and tuna.

RDA: 2 mcg
Optimal Level: 150 mcg
Maximum: 300 mcg
Signs of Toxicity: Strange metallic taste in your mouth, dizziness, nausea with no apparent cause, lethargy, skin problems, progressive paralysis, fragile or black fingernails—even loss of nails as well as hair and teeth, or persistent garlic smell on your breath and skin. Acute poisoning causes fever, rapid breathing, gastrointestinal upset, inflammation of the spinal cord and bone marrow; can be fatal.

Sulfur

Sulfur helps assure the oxygen supply necessary for optimum brain functioning. It helps fight off bacterial infections, makes your hair more shiny, tones up your skin, and makes for healthy nails. You need sulfur to build the protein, collagen, that helps hold your body's parts together. It also helps your liver with bile secretion. Along with the B vitamins, sulfur works for basic body metabolism. Found in insulin, sulfur keeps your energy levels stable. It also works in heparin, a vital blood-thinning factor found in your liver and tissues. Sulfur also helps build the vital amino acids cysteine, cystine, taurine, and methionine.

OTHER BENEFITS:

May help alleviate arthritis.

GOOD FOR THESE SYMPTOMS:

Constipation, fatigue, sluggishness, psoriasis.

SIGNS OF DEFICIENCY:

Possibly sluggishness and fatigue. Strict vegetarians who eat no eggs at all are at risk for not getting enough sulfur.

SOURCES:

Best source is eggs, meat (especially lean beef), fish, garlic, onions, dried beans, cabbage, and asparagus.

RDA: None
Optimal Level: From dietary sources
Signs of Toxicity: Sluggishness and fatigue.

Zinc

Zinc is required for the synthesis of DNA. It also regulates muscle contractions and is essential for the synthesis of protein. Moreover, zinc helps in the formation of insulin. It is important for blood stability. Zinc directs the proper flow of body processes, the maintenance of enzyme systems and your cells. It has a normalizing effect on the prostate. Excessive sweating or overweight can aggravate zinc loss from the body. Zinc plays a key role throughout your immune system. It keeps crucial immune organs like the thymus and lymph nodes healthy and boosts the immune cells. Zinc is very important for pregnant women.

OTHER BENEFITS:

- May help protect against cancer of the esophagus and bronchial tubes and of the prostate.
- Helps postsurgical wounds heal faster.
- Alone, or in combination with vitamin A, helps treat acne if your acne is caused by a lack of zinc.
- Improves potency, sperm count, and testosterone levels if problems are caused by low zinc levels.
- May protect against herpes.
- Can help treat rheumatoid arthritis.
- May block the multiplication of cold viruses so you recover more quickly.
- Helps form insulin to keep your energy stable and strong.

- Helps synthesize protein in your body.
- Helps your muscles contract smoothly.
- Boosts every area of your immune health.
- Helps you absorb your vitamins, particularly the B Team.
- Crucial for the proper development of your reproductive organs.
- For men, it helps assure the normal functioning of the prostate.
- Helps build your cell membranes and even the genetic coding, DNA.

GOOD FOR THESE SYMPTOMS:

Slow or poor wound healing, hair loss, stress, frequent infections.

SIGNS OF DEFICIENCY:

Impaired cell growth and repair. Effects most profound on fetuses and children. In the womb, deficiency may slow the natural growth of the fetus and make the newborn baby grow more slowly. Other signs: poor wound healing, reduced sense of taste and smell, white spots on the fingernails, mental dullness and difficulty in concentration, hair loss, decrease in red and white blood cells, more susceptibility to infections. Zinc very likely to be lacking in teenagers' diets. Drinkers are at special risk because they absorb zinc at a reduced rate. Mild zinc deficiency can lead to low sperm count in men. A more severe lack can cause the male sex glands, the testes, to atrophy. Many older Americans don't get enough zinc.

SOURCES:

Meats like round steak, lamb chops, pork loin, liver; poultry, legumes, nuts, seeds, seafood, bran, whole-wheat flour, eggs, whole grains, pumpkin seeds, brewers' yeast, wheat germ, nonfat dry milk, and ground mustard. Animal sources have more readily available zinc.

RDA: 15 mg for men and women
Optimal Level: 75 mg

Maximum: 150 mg

Signs of Toxicity: Vomiting, diarrhea, drowsiness; induces copper- and/or iron-deficiency anemia, high cholesterol.

Drug Interactions: Oral contraceptives can decrease zinc.

Recommended Reading List

Brody, Jane. *Jane Brody's Nutrition Book*. New York: Bantam Books, 1982.

Hendler, Sheldon Saul, M.D., Ph.D. *The Complete Guide to Anti-Aging Nutrients*. New York: Fireside Books (S&S), 1984.

Hoffer, Abram, Ph.D., M.D., and Morton Walker, D.P.M. *Orthomolecular Nutrition*. New Canaan, Conn.: Keats Publishing, Inc., 1978.

Pauling, Linus. *Chemistry*. San Francisco: W. H. Freeman, 1975.

Pauling, Linus. *How to Live Longer and Feel Better*. San Francisco: W. H. Freeman, 1986.

Pauling, Linus. *Vitamin C, the Common Cold, and the Flu*. San Francisco: W. H. Freeman, 1976.

Pfeiffer, Carl C., Ph.D., M.D. *Mental and Elemental Nutrients*. New Canaan, Conn.: Keats Publishing, Inc., 1976.

Pfeiffer, Carl C., Ph.D., M.D. *Zinc and Other Micro-Nutrients*. New Canaan, Conn.: Keats Publishing, Inc., 1978.

Pritikin, Nathan. *Diet for Runners*. New York: Simon & Schuster, 1985.

Pritikin, Nathan. *The Pritikin Permanent Weight-Loss Manual*. New York: Grosset & Dunlap, 1981; Bantam, 1981.

Pritikin, Nathan. *The Pritikin Promise*. New York: Pocket Books, 1983.

Pritikin, Nathan, with Patrick M. McGrady, Jr. *The Pritikin Program for Diet and Exercise*. New York: Bantam, 1980.

Pritikin, Nathan, and Ilene Pritikin. *The Official Pritikin Guide to Dining Out*. New York: Bobbs-Merrill, 1984.

Randolph, Theron G., M.D., and Ralph W. Moss, Ph.D. *An Alterna-*

tive Approach to Allergies. New York: Harper & Row, 1980; Bantam, 1982.

Truss, C. Orian, M.D. *The Missing Diagnosis*. Birmingham, Ala.: C. Orian Press, 1982.

Index